The Which? Guide
Camping in the
South of France
and the Dordogne

The Which? Guide to Camping in the South of France and the Dordogne

Fizz Fieldgrass

Published by Consumers' Association and Hodder & Stoughton

The Which? Guide to Camping in the South of France and the Dordogne
was commissioned and researched by
The Association for Consumer Research and published by
Consumers' Association, 2 Marylebone Road, London N W 1 4D X
and Hodder & Stoughton, 47 Bedford Square, London W C 1 B 3D P

British Library Cataloguing in Publication Data
Fieldgrass, Fizz
  The Holiday Which? guide to camping in the South of France
    and the Dordogne.
  I. Title
914.404

ISBN 0 340 52818 4

Designed by Tim Higgins
Cover illustration by Martin Salisbury
Cartoons by John Holder

Photoset in Meridien series by
Tradespools Ltd, Frome, Somerset
Printed and bound in England by Richard Clay Limited,
Bungay, Suffolk

Contents

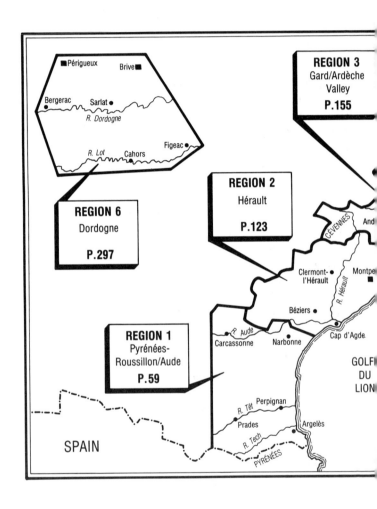

REGION 3
Gard/Ardèche
Valley
P.155

■Périgueux   Brive■

Bergerac
Sarlat ●
R. Dordogne

Figeac ●
R. Lot   Cahors ●

REGION 6
Dordogne

P.297

REGION 2
Hérault

P.123

And

CÉVENNES

Clermont-
l'Hérault
Montpe
R. Hérault

Béziers ●

REGION 1
Pyrénées-
Roussillon/Aude
P.59

R. Aude
Carcassonne   Narbonne ●

Cap d'Agde

GOLF
DU
LION

R. Têt Perpignan
Prades ●
R. Tech   Argelès

SPAIN

PYRÉNÉES

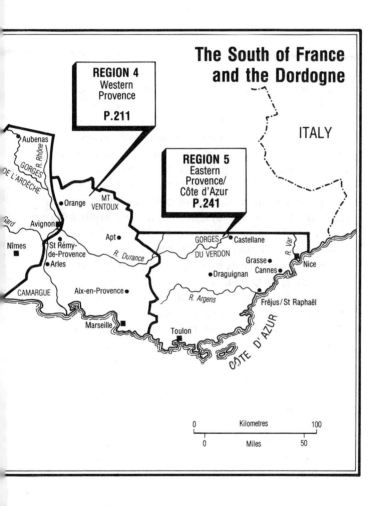

The South of France and the Dordogne

REGION 4
Western
Provence

P.211

REGION 5
Eastern
Provence/
Côte d'Azur
P.241

ITALY

Aubenas

GORGES
DE L'ARDÈCHE

R. Rhône

Gard

Orange

MT
VENTOUX

Avignon

Nîmes

St Rémy-
de-Provence

Arles

Apt

R. Durance

GORGES
DU VERDON

Castellane

R. Var

Grasse

Nice

CAMARGUE

Aix-en-Provence

Draguignan

Cannes

R. Argens

Fréjus / St Raphaël

Marseille

Toulon

CÔTE D'AZUR

0	Kilometres	100

| 0 | Miles | 50 |

Introduction

Camping? Even in this day and age of enlightened leisure-seeking the word still manages to trigger raised eyebrows. While many do not blink at the thought of hazarding the loos of Lima or of suffering snakes on safari, the idea of living in a tent for a fortnight, being forced to self-cater in primitive conditions – quite apart from having to put up with all those other people around you playing loud music and/or snoring at night – seems like purgatory. Nowadays, most of this is a myth, but one that has to be perpetually countered by holiday brochures containing question and answer sections about loos and insects in order to dispel any idea that it's all like *Carry on Camping*!

One of the problems in coming to terms with living in the open is that we in Britain have no tradition of 'continental camping', but rather tend to expect a throwback to the days of Baden-Powell. Our geographical and historical severance from Europe has not allowed us to do as the Dutch or the Germans when, at half-term, they load their families aboard the camper and take off for the Med. They aren't fussy if the camp isn't exactly a four-star fun palace. But for many British families such a holiday usually means just one glorious fortnight of the year when the kids are off school, Dad's just about had enough of the office and Mum is looking forward to turning Celebrity Brown. The reservations were made in the New Year, money has been spent, anticipation is high and it's a hell of a long way to go to get a bit of sun.

Of course, there's camping and camping. What may be one person's idea of holiday fun splashing about all day with his or her fellow countrymen may be another's idea of torture in a British ghetto. But the purist who prefers hectares of trees and a quiet stretch of river to yards of canvas and a busy swimming-pool isn't necessarily enjoying a superior experience. Parents of young children might consider it equal bliss to have the kids off their hands taking part in organised camp diversions, thus relieving them of the usual internecine tensions.

It all depends on your criteria – do you want to stay put for two weeks in a tent that's home from home, or would you prefer to travel around as the fancy takes you? You may have kids in tow or there may be just the two of you in the camper-van. You may even be by yourself with only a rucksack and a bike. Whatever your preferences, this Guide sets out to help you find your ideal site or sites. You will find the necessary factual information given in the form of symbols and details at the foot of each campsite entry, but it is with our written commentary that we hope to give you a view of what it is like to be there, and, through this, a sense of the site's character. In all, we have aimed to provide a unique Camper's Companion, not only in conveying the idea of camp life at a particular site, but also in suggesting a variety of rewarding places to visit in each region.

Camping in France

There are those who can escape the rigours of day-to-day life on a camping holiday and there are those, like it or not, who are bound to cart their little 'rigours' along with the rest of the luggage. But, for all, one thing remains gloriously constant. There's nothing which allows a more intimate experience with a foreign environment, its geography, its nature, its people – its very sights and sounds – than living and touring under canvas. And perhaps there's no better or more accessible a place, offering such variety in landscape, food and local colour, than the South of France.

There are over 11,000 officially approved campsites in France today, many of them coastal and/or in the south, where the climate is conducive to outdoor pursuits. These sites range from nothing more than a farmer's meadow to the nearest thing one could find to a hotel in the open air. Wherever they fall in the spectrum, certain basic amenities (especially those to do with sanitation and hygiene) are required before official approval is granted; there further exists a grading system whereby a site's star rating is determined by its fulfilment of particular requirements. All sites from one- to four-star are required by law to have a source of purified water, and are expected to have hot and cold running water (some one-stars don't necessarily have to offer hot water) and a daily refuse collection, be securely enclosed and have a public telephone. The main differences and improvements as you progress through the ratings relate to minimum size of pitch, ratio of space set aside for services to camp capacity, provision of food, electrical hook-up and general range of amenities.

Some campsite owners or managers impose certain restrictions which set the tone of the place. You may come across strict régimes of silence from an early hour, not uncommon in the majority of municipal sites, while in others the disco does not play beyond midnight. The time that a site's gates close at night varies according to its situation. Resort sites tend to stay open later than municipal sites, which are notorious for making sure that no-one turns into a pumpkin after 10 or 10.30pm (but all camps provide a parking space outside the gate for late returners).

Most campsites have at least a washing machine and an ironing board, and the larger sites more often than not are equipped with launderettes. Some discourage the tying of washing lines to trees by providing communal washing lines. As far as the washing of dishes is concerned, areas in the *sanitaires* are specifically set aside for the purpose.

Campsites are very safe places but of course it is always a wise precaution to sleep with your essential documents and money. Some sites provide safety deposit boxes at reception for anything particularly valuable.

If you find yourself in a very large 'holiday village' type of site with a sprawl of tents forming row upon row of similar-looking avenues, it might be a good idea to take your party on a tour of the camp so that they are familiar with its layout. That way you may be happier to give the children freedom to wander.

As the French have been perfecting *le camping* for thirty years, there are very few places in Europe that can match the quality of administrative efficiency and daily upkeep to be found in the majority of sites throughout the country. When deciding on a place to pitch the tent or park the camper-van, either for a fortnight's stay or a few days' stop-over, hardened campers suffer little angst these days over whether they will find clean toilets and a place to plug in the razor. This isn't to say that such fears are never fulfilled, but the more pressing question nowadays is one of compatibility.

For many the ideal could mean raving it up at an open-air disco under the star-filled sky of a warm Mediterranean night. In complete contrast, just to sit outside your tent with a portable lamp as your only source of illumination (and a rendezvous for every known species of insect in the South), with a glass of the local *vin de pays* in your hand, can be an acceptable substitute for Nirvana. Around you, against the shrill chirping of the cicadas in the background, you are aware of low, relaxed conversation in foreign tongues gliding across the scrub grass from the various spots of gentle, diffused, yellow light dotted low amongst the trees. You reach for your glass, sip the warming liquid fruit and stretch back, debating whether tomorrow you will bathe in some transparent stream that slips through a deep gorge or picnic upon a high ridge, feeling at one with all you see before you under a vast canopy of aerial blue. Now that's what we call Camping!

About this Guide

There are probably as many different sorts of campsite as there are types of people attracted to them. More and more sites and operators are offering 'statics' or mobile homes as an alternative to tents. This means paying more for a 'camping' holiday, which for some may defeat the object of living under canvas as a reasonably economic way of taking time off abroad – especially with a family. Caravanning or using camper vehicles are good compromises if you are going to make enough use of them to warrant the initial investment.

We set out to present a broad spectrum of sites that would suit most types of camper, from the retired couple, towing a trailer tent around quiet backwaters of the countryside, to a family intent on a fortnight's beach holiday with frame-tent stashed on the roofrack.

Our prime consideration was that a campsite should have an ambience which generates a feeling of well-being and relaxation. This is manifest in several features: the setting and attractiveness of the grounds; more than adequate sanitary arrangements; and a comfortable environment – privacy of pitches, shade, a sensitivity to the 'statics' factor (explained below) and a good managerial attitude.

A convenient location was also thought desirable, though we have not left out remote spots for many do have good road connections. But on the whole we have left out places that are reached only by tortuous routes, putting the site out of touch with interesting places to visit.

We felt that access to prepared food and a pool should always be a priority. Most of our sites fulfil these criteria or, at least, they are in the vicinity of a village with shops or a supermarket so that self-catering shouldn't present a problem. As for swimming, many municipal sites are near the town pool and coastal sites near a beach. Sometimes, a cooling stretch of river is on hand.

Before going into the field, we drew up a shortlist of likely contenders. Initially, those offering the most facilities warranted consideration. The Office de Tourisme star rating was an influence in that we felt a one-star site was usually too basic for most camping tastes, although we are proud to include the one we discovered in a superb setting, easy to reach and with a small pool (see Corsavy in the Pyrenees). Two-star sites were acceptable as long as they matched our criteria and many proved to be just as appealing, if not more so, than some carrying three stars.

Out of the 400 campsites visited over the six regions presented in this Guide, only half were thought fit to grace our pages.

The different types

Municipal sites run by local authorities have been included and inspected on the same principles as privately owned sites. Naturally, the former are not as luxurious but quite a few do maintain excellent standards and/or offer attractive environments. In the privately owned sector a lot of the 'fun' camps – more or less self-contained holiday villages – are generally three- or four-star sites.

High-rating sites are sometimes connected to a 'chain' for promotional purposes. Castel et Camping is a long-established chain originally based on a select number of locations associated with an historical building, such as a château. Paysage de France is a younger chain of 37 sites offering not much less in the way of amenities but tending to be smaller and more informal in prime countryside.

Naturist sites

To the French, the naturist holiday is much less of an outlandish option than it is for the British. We have included a few such sites as good examples: two in the Dordogne, one in Western Provence and one in the Pyrénées-Roussillon (see the ends of the relevant regional sections). They are very different from each another and, being just as much a family experience as any other camping holiday, they make interesting comparisons with conventional camping. Entry to naturist sites is rigorously controlled: you have to provide evidence of belonging to an organisation affiliated to the International Naturist Federation, such as the the Fédération Nationale de Naturisme (FFN) or the Central Council for British Naturism (CCBN) in Britain. (Jim Miller is the Council's French specialist.)

Addresses

Central Council for British Naturism	Jim Miller
Assurance House	8 Palmer Close
35-41 Hazelwood Road	Redhill
Northampton NN1 1LL	Surrey RH1 4BX
Tel (0604) 20361	Tel (0737) 761659

On the site

The sanitaire

One of the first questions to be voiced by a first-time camper in France is likely to be about sanitary arrangements. In fact, the majority of campsite proprietors with any business sense nowadays do invest in this area to provide clean, modern appointments. Some older sites do have the odd chipped tile instead of shining melamine but our main criterion was to check that hygiene was effectively maintained.

Most sites have at least one pedestal toilet among those *à la turque*. The hole-in-floor kind is usually confined to the men's side, though not always so. Where pedestal toilets are available, ironically, and more often than not, they actually have no attached seat, in order to make cleaning easier.

Where we have included a site which lacks seated toilets, mention is always made of the fact. Toilet paper is not such a rarity as you might believe; if it isn't provided in the cubicle itself, you will probably find a large, communal roll dispenser inside the main door of the block.

Where possible, we checked on facilities for disabled campers. These ranged from full suites of shower, toilet and washbasin to maybe just a loo with an extra wide door kept under lock and key. Again, we have detailed in our text examples worth mentioning. You would be wise to telephone in advance.

All the sites have some semblance of 'hot' water in their

showers. It's not easy to maintain a limitless supply of hot water. Depending on the time of day, we found the water to range from scorching to tepid, so if hot water is essential to you, take your shower at an unpopular time. Many sites run cold water only in washbasins, although some lay on both hot and cold, and use mixer taps.

Grounds

For many people, some degree of shade is a priority when it comes to being comfortable in a hot climate. In any case, an absence of greenery tends to make a site less attractive. However, where a very open camp has proved acceptable in other ways, we've included it while pointing out this drawback.

Since 1985, there has been an official ruling on the minimum size of pitch (*emplacement*) of campsites built after that year: two-star – 90m^2; three-star – 95m^2; four-star – 100m^2. Sites established before that date had *carte blanche* in the sizes of their pitches, regardless of their rating, so some of these today do have variable spaces on offer. We think it is important to have a certain amount of privacy; usually this is provided by a screen of hedging (perfected on the majority of municipal sites). On our travels we were not enamoured with sites that pack their pitches in without this form of territorial seclusion and we were disheartened by what we refer to as the 'grid system' – *emplacements* arranged in dead-straight rows off avenues at 90 degrees to them. This arrangement, found mostly on the larger sites, tends to give you the visually tedious environment of just another anonymous camping ground. Certain sites of this description have made their way into the pages of this Guide only because other aspects of the camp offset this factor.

Statics is the trade term for the permanent caravans and mobile homes kept on many campsites. In the more popular resort areas these are quite prolific and often are the site owner's bread and butter. We avoided camps with an over-abundance of these (some were no less than caravan parks), on the grounds that they do not constitute camping in its proper sense and, in any case, tend to be an eyesore. We have commented on them when relevant and mentioned if campsites sensibly group statics away from the main body of the grounds or perhaps keep them discreetly screened off.

All sites in the Guide have some sort of electrical supply laid on but for details on the amperage, we suggest that you ask the site for details as these can vary considerably.

Our top twenty campsites

Of the 200 campsites included in this Guide, the twenty that appear on these three pages turned out to be our favourites. They are indicated by our Starburst symbol ☼ at the head of each entry in the book. They are not necessarily the camps which provide every last luxury – indeed, some are graded as only two-star sites – but the impressive mix of an attractive and successful camping environment, a caring and efficient management and an individual approach lingered in our memory long after the visit.

Pyrénées-Roussillon

Le Brasilia **Canet-Plage** (page 94)

Large 'holiday village' site that successfully manages to disguise this usually negative attribute. Pleasant grounds in shady woodland, the beach on hand and plenty of family entertainment are alluring features.

Camping des Albères **Laroque-des-Albères** (page 101)

Very attractive rural two-star site whose management sustains a simple camping philosophy and yet supplies all the basics for an enjoyable family camping holiday.

La Haras **Palau-del-Vidre** (page 107)

Superbly landscaped, small, high-grade garden site on the edge of a sleepy village. Well-run, well-kept and offering a good communal atmosphere.

L'Eau Vive **Vernet-les-Bains** (page 118)

Tiny, exclusive site with excellent facilities and within easy reach of the town. The best family site in the lee of the Pyrenees.

Hérault

L'Oliveraie **Laurens** (page 139)

Delightfully secluded site, deep in the countryside, catering for both touring and family campers. Plenty of high-season activity laid on by the management who succeed in creating an informal party spirit in their small community.

Gard and Ardèche Valley

Domaine des Fumades **Allégre** (page 171)

An oasis of four-star French-style family camping in a very attractive and impeccably maintained environment. The unique little spa town comes alive with the weekend fête.

L'Arche **Anduze** (page 172)

Extremely shady and pretty two-star site with above-average facilities for the grade. The main draw is a scenic 'rockpool' on the River Gard.

Les Charmilles **Darbes** (page 182)

Excellent little high-grade family camp with outstanding views of the Ardèche. Children are looked after and adults warmly catered for by Madame la Patronne.

Domaine de Chaussy **Ruoms** (page 193)

A purpose-built four-star site that is compact enough to maintain a relaxed, informal atmosphere. High-quality amenities and a good situation within a light wood overlooking rolling countryside.

Le Val d'Arre **Le Vigan** (page 207)

Peaceful, understated, cool, good river site a couple of miles from a Cévenol town that is full of Mediterranean sparkle.

Western Provence

Domaine des Iscles **La Roque d'Anthéron** (page 233)

Well-designed, French-orientated, high-grade family camp that offers a relaxed atmosphere by day and a lively social life by night.

Eastern Provence and Côte d'Azur

Vallée du Paradis **Agay** (page 263)

Nearly paradise at this modest but very tidy and attractive landscaped site within easy reach of a beach at the prettiest resort on the Esterel coast.

Domaine des Naïades **Port Grimaud** (page 288)

Quiet sophistication in a four-star, well-organised environment, with a beautiful shady pine wood for grounds. Possibly the best restaurant terrace between Antibes and St Tropez.

Les Lauriers Roses **St Aygulf** (page 291)

The young, energetic, English-speaking management maintain an impeccable, small, high-grade site which attracts a regular British clientèle. Inland but handy for the coast.

Camping le Parc **St Paul-en-Forêt** (page 294)

Exquisite, silent and secluded site in pine woods in the Var hinterland. Ideal for getting away from it all without abandoning basic comforts.

Dordogne

Le Moulin de la Pique **Belvès** (page 313)

Elegant, serene camping grounds surrounding an imposing villa and small lake. Sophisticated amenities create a club atmosphere.

Le Paradis **St Léon-sur-Vézère** (page 336)

Possibly the top family site for the Dordogne, managing to avoid the 'holiday village' syndrome. Four-star, sensibly planned, well-landscaped site with excellent facilities – at a price.

Moulin du Périé **Sauveterre** (page 343)

Quiet, secluded and efficient site with a mill at its focus. Amicable Dutch management keep immaculate facilities and accommodate children's needs well.

Les Ormes **Villeréal** (page 349)

A country setting for family camping. The Dutch management strive to keep all ages happy with a range of amenities at their spacious site.

Soleil-Plage **Vitrac** (page 350)

Wonderful, easy-going atmosphere on this bustling site on a scenic stretch of the Dordogne, with two small beaches for river bathing. Pleasant *bonhomie* prevails at the evening terrace restaurant.

Organising your holiday

If you have children of school age, you are likely to take your annual summer holiday during July and August. Remember that France is on holiday at the same time and that the South is notorious for crowded roads and packed towns and beaches. This prime tourist time is of course also the most expensive.

If you are looking for an alternative and cheaper time to go, either side of the high season wouldn't be any less pleasant weatherwise. For some people, the slightly lower temperatures of spring, say, would be quite welcome. Conversely, summer sunshine, although on the cards, cannot always be guaranteed and it's not uncommon to have grey skies and rain in the middle of August in the Dordogne, for instance. As a broad guide, the average temperature in the south from Easter to June is 22°C (72°F), while in July and August it rises to 28°C (83°F).

Generally, holiday operators and campsites adjust their charges to 'seasons' which tend to be as follows: **low** from the time that sites open – normally Easter – until the end of June; a short **mid-season** in the first half of July; **high** from the middle of July until the third week of August; a **post-high** end season in which prices from the end of August fall sharply until the first few weeks of September, when most sites close for the year. Charges rise and fall accordingly. Very reasonable rates and discounts are offered for those seasons that fall outside the high season period. However, it's important to note that many camps are not fully up and running in the low season. This means that you should expect fewer organised events and maybe a limited use of facilities. After the high season many sites quickly run themselves down once the majority of the holiday population has left. It is advisable when booking in these periods to find out exactly what is or isn't available, either directly from the site or from your holiday operator. More and more of the larger camps which deal with a regular British clientele through package firms are beginning to appreciate that it is in their own interest to be fully operational earlier and some now make a point of mentioning this in their literature. Other types of cheaper holiday range from 'short breaks' to one-parent discounts.

Package versus D-I-Y

A great many families who regard themselves as camping holiday veterans, annually setting out with tent, kids, maps and a touring itinerary taking in the whole of Provence, originally gained courage under canvas by letting a camping package operator take care of their first few attempts. The main disadvantage of doing it this way is cost. As a basis for comparing 1990 prices, we took the model of a family of four comprising two adults and two children (one under ten, one under thirteen) taking a holiday in high season for fourteen nights, their destination being a campsite near Avignon. Included would be the essential booking arrangements – a channel crossing (in this example Dover-Boulogne), campsite accommodation and personal holiday insurance. Excluded would be minor fluctuations caused by site supplements and overnight stops where the difference in charges was found to be negligible. Overall, depending on site fees, one could save over *half* the outlay needed to book with either of the two main camping package operators (see below). (These calculations do not include initial outlay for the tent and other equipment.)

Another drawback – if you consider it a drawback – is the type and location of sites used by camping package operators. The Mediterranean coast is usually well catered for but as you go inland smaller companies tend to cover far less territory, leaving the big two, Canvas Holidays and Eurocamp, to operate in such regions. They also offer the largest selection in the Dordogne (although between them there are duplications). Another consideration which applies to these market leaders, as well as to some of their junior competitors who focus on the family holiday, is that you will find more of the 'fun-camp' type of establishment in their lists as opposed to those idyllic little out-of-the-way spots.

Of course, considerable advantages offset these drawbacks, the main ones being that all booking and insurance arrangements are taken care of by the operator. Nearly all package firms provide travel packs which include road atlases, regional maps, holiday planners and guides and GB car stickers. Some include children's travel packs.

They provide a fully equipped family tent on site (other than bedding) so you neither have to invest in all the camping gear nor transport it all down to the South of France. On site there are couriers for organised activities, and even babysitting. The campsites have been checked to make sure they meet the individual company's minimum standards. Most sites fall into the four-star category and others are never less than three-star.

A compromise between a full package and going it alone would be to use the services of a reservation agency. You are expected to be self-equipped but part of the service is similar to that of a package firm in that all booking is taken care of and you are supplied with travel-aid materials. Normally you do not have any on-site care by a company representative and sometimes you have to select a site from only those on the company's list. But a more diverse selection of campsites can be available, including the smaller, quieter site. It is much cheaper to holiday this way than to take the all-in package. You can expect costings to be pretty much on a par with your own and you may consider that any small difference is worth it in terms of savings in time and hassle alone. An advantage with Eurocamp Independent in this reservation-only type of package is that if your site happens to be one used in Eurocamp's main package programme you can share the benefits of its courier service. Another company, Select Sites Reservations, gives you an International Camping Carnet with its personal holiday insurance.

Certain package firms offer an 'independent travel' option. All this means is that while you use their tent accommodation, you go ahead and make your own travel arrangements. But because of the concessions they get from the ferry operators on your behalf, unless there is a good reason for doing it yourself, you do lose out.

The same applies if you are taking a Motorail option. The reduced rates that some operators are able to arrange with SNCF (French Railways) mean you're usually far better off accepting their prices than booking this part of the journey yourself, although you'd always be wise to do the sums first.

Self-drive holiday operators and reservation agencies

We include here a selection of (but not all) companies whose operations fall within the coverage of this guide. A full list of operators offering camping and mobile homes is obtainable from the French Tourist Office (see page 50). Along with each address we give a résumé of services and locations. All provide travel packs, and cater for children in terms of child care and/or entertainment.

Self-drive holiday operators

Canvas Holidays
Bull Plain
Hertford
Herts SG14 1DY
Tel (0992) 553535
● *All-in package* ● *Early booking discount* ● *Special low-season offers* ● *Independent travel option* ● *'Campfinder' independent service* ● *Motorail*
Mediterranean/Dordogne (well represented)/Ardèche/Languedoc-Roussillon

Carefree Camping
126 Hempstead Road
Kings Langley
Herts WD4 8AL
Tel (09277) 61311
● *All-in package* ● *'3 weeks for 2' low season offer* ● *Motorail*
Chiefly coastal, Mediterranean and Languedoc-Roussillon/Dordogne

Eurocamp
Edmundson House
Tatton Street
Knutsford
Cheshire WA16 6BG
Tel (0565) 3844
● *All-in package* ● *Early booking offers* ● *Low and mid-season 'Short Holiday' formula* ● *Low season 'Touring' formula* ● *Independent travel option* ● *Motorail*

Eurosites
Ainsworth House
Burnley Road
Rawtenstall
Rossendale
Lancs BB4 8EP
Tel (0706) 830739
● *All-in package* ● *Independent travel option*
Chiefly coastal, Languedoc-Roussillon/some eastern Provence/Dordogne

French Life
26 Church Road
Horsforth
Leeds
West Yorks LS18 5LG
Tel (0532) 390077
(or via ABTA agents)
● *All-in package* ● *Computerised personal over-route itinerary* ● *Motorail*
Mediterranean/Dordogne

Haven
W H Smith Travel Agencies
● *All-in package* ● *Early booking discount* ● *Low-season offers including discounts for single parents and senior citizens* ● *Independent travel option* ● *Motorail*

Côte d'Azur/Languedoc/
Dordogne

Keycamp Holidays
92-96 Lind Road
Sutton
Surrey SM1 4PL
Tel (081) 661 1836
● *All-in package* ● *Low-season*
'Bargain Breaks' and single-parent
discount ● *Group savings*
● *Motorail*
Mediterranean/Languedoc-
Roussillon/Côte d'Azur/
Dordogne

Sunsites
30 Princess Street
Knutsford
Cheshire WA16 6BN
Tel (0565) 755644
● *All-in package* ● *Motorail*
Côte d'Azur/Dordogne

Reservation agencies

Eurocamp Independent
30 Princess Street
Knutsford
Cheshire WA16 6BN
Tel (0565) 755399
● *Reservations from their list, or your*
independent choice (additional
charge) ● *Travel pack* ● *Use of*
courier service (where applicable)
● *Low/mid-season 'Go as you please'*
scheme ● *Motorail*
● *Camping carnet (provided only*
with personal holiday and car
breakdown insurance)
50 sites across our regions

Select Sites Reservations
Travel House
Pandy
Abergavenny
Gwent NP7 8DH
Tel (0873) 980770
● *Reservations from their list only*
● *Travel pack* ● *AA Route Planning*
(extra cost) ● *Low/mid-season 'Tour*
as you please' scheme ● *Camping*

Carnet provided with personal
holiday insurance
11 sites across our regions

Caravan and Camping Service
69 Westbourne Grove
London W2 4UJ
Tel 071-792 1944
● *Reservations from their list, or your*
independent choice (no charge)
● *Travel pack* ● *Group discounts* ●
Free stop-overs available on selected
sites and only for ferry-inclusive
holidays – see brochure
13 sites across our regions

The Caravan Club
East Grinstead House
East Grinstead
West Sussex RH19 1UA
Tel (0342) 326944
Membership of the Caravan Club
makes its reservation service
throughout Europe available to
caravan owners. It handles a
small selection of sites that come
within this Guide's territory. Club
members participate in a site
monitoring scheme. Along with
booking and special insurance
arrangements, the Caravan Club
provides detailed itineraries and a
'participation' list of other
members staying on your site.

The Camping and Caravanning Club (Pitch Abroad)
30 Princess Street
Knutsford
Cheshire WA16 6BN
Tel (0565) 650085
The Camping and Caravanning
Club handles a similar service for
ferry bookings and insurances but
does not maintain an individual
selected site list. It works in
conjunction with Eurocamp
Independent for inclusive holiday
bookings with certain discounts
for members.

Arranging things yourself

Booking a campsite

This is not as complicated as it might seem. Before you make bookings yourself, do some preliminary investigation, perhaps by referring to package operators' brochures, and certainly by sending off for the site's brochure, booking form and conditions.

Booking a pitch follows a standard procedure. Along with your completed form it is normal to forward a deposit, either by Eurocheque or a postal draft.

This is requested in a variety of combinations, sometimes a fixed sum for the first week plus a smaller amount for each ensuing week, or a similar sum for each week of your stay. In either case this is around £20-£30. In addition there is a booking fee, usually less than half this figure.The majority of campsites, certainly three- and four-star sites, accept reservations and a large percentage strongly recommend that people book in advance for the peak season. Sites that sometimes do not accept bookings at all are inclined to be two-star and below. Direct correspondence with a particular site will of course put you in the picture. It's useful to send with your letter an International Reply coupon bought from the Post Office. This in effect pays for return postage.

Some *départements* have set up their own reservation services, usually referred to as Loisirs-Accueil (see the ends of the individual regional introductions for addresses). They invariably charge no fee and have English-speaking personnel available.

Touring on spec

If you fancy being footloose, turning up at sites without any previous booking is a possibility, and is considerably easier if you are travelling in the low season and if your party is small. Biking can make for ideal touring and whether you are travelling on your own or as a couple, a small tent or two bringing in an unexpected few francs is a good enough reason for a site owner to squeeze you in somewhere. An advisable course of action would be to go for the more rural, less 'fun-camp' type of site as the latter are the ones which fill up quickly on long-stay bookings. Do have some idea of a route before you begin and make a note of likely sites on the way. Supplement this guide with the relevant departmental lists which give symbol profiles and phone numbers (from the French Tourist

Sample letter for booking at a campsite

Monsieur le Directeur
Camping _____

(address) _____

Date _____

Monsieur le Directeur,
Dear Sir

Je vous serais obligé de me communiquer rapidement vos conditions et tarifs
I should be grateful if you would let me know at your earliest convenience your rates and conditions

correspondant au séjour suivant:
for the following stay:

Arrivée le _____   *Départ le* _____
Arriving on (date)   Departing on (date)

Nous sommes ___ *adultes et* ___ *enfants âgés de* ___ *ans*
We are   adults and   children aged   years

Nous désirons réserver un emplacement pour une voiture* – tente*
We wish to book a pitch for a car* – tent*

caravane* caravane motorisée* louer une tente* caravane*
caravan*   motor caravan*   hire a tent*   caravan*

bungalow*
bungalow   (* delete where not applicable)

Veuillez me répondre directement à l'adresse ci-dessous:
Please reply to my address below:

Mr/Mrs/Ms _____ (block capitals)

(address) _____

avec mes remerciements,
Yours faithfully,

(signature) _____

Office or direct from the Office de Tourisme of the relevant region). It makes sense to ring your next intended site to check your chances of a pitch.

Even in the height of the season it is possible to be accommodated in this way, and it doesn't have to be just you and a rucksack. One couple with their three children with a boot full of camping gear spent a happy three weeks in mid-August taking in three sites from the Cévennes through to Vaucluse, and were turned away only once; the only advance booking expenses were coins deposited in payphones.

Booking the ferry

Your local travel agent should carry brochures for all the main ferry companies; they will make any bookings on your behalf or you can deal with the operators direct. Below you will find a breakdown of which ferry lines operate which routes. Tariffs fluctuate across seasons, peaking in July and August, but you can pick up cheaper rates for mid-week sailings. For caravans, some companies give special offers on their rates.

The quickest routes are Dover/Calais and Dover/Boulogne ($1^1/_2$ hours and $1^3/_4$ hours). These times are dramatically reduced if you go by Hoverspeed (35 and 40 minutes) but it's a little more expensive and subject to weather conditions. With the advent of the Channel Tunnel, ferry services are bound to become more competitive, offering more varied timetables and fares and innovations to cut sailing time. Already Hoverspeed are running a comparatively new Portsmouth/Cherbourg service using two giant wave-piercing catamarans. These make the Channel trip in 2 hours 40 minutes, cutting ferry times by roughly half. Hoverspeed plan to introduce similar services on the Dover-Calais and Dover-Boulogne routes from June 1991. Crossings should take about 40 to 50 minutes.

Port	Destination	Operators
Ramsgate	Dunkerque	Sally Line
Dover	Calais	P&O, Sealink, Hoverspeed
Dover	Boulogne	P&O, Hoverspeed
Folkestone	Boulogne	Sealink
Newhaven	Dieppe	Sealink
Portsmouth	Le Havre	P&O
Portsmouth	Caen	Brittany
Portsmouth	Cherbourg	P&O, Sealink, Hoverspeed
Portsmouth	St Malo	Brittany
Poole	Cherbourg	Truckline (Brittany)
Plymouth	Roscoff	Brittany

Brittany Ferries

Poole (0202) 672153   Cherbourg 33.22.38.98
Portsmouth (0705) 827701   Roscoff 98.29.28.29
Plymouth (0752) 221321   St Malo 99.82.41.41
                              Caen 31.96.80.80

Hoverspeed

Dover (0304) 240241   Boulogne 21.30.27.26
Portsmouth (0705) 755111   Calais 21.96.67.10
                              Cherbourg 33.20.43.38

P&O European Ferries

Dover (0304) 203388   Boulogne 21.31.78.00
Portsmouth (0705) 827677   Calais 21.97.21.21
                              Cherbourg 33.44.20.13
                              Le Havre 35.21.36.50

Sally Line

Ramsgate (0843) 595522   Dunkerque 28.21.43.44

Sealink

Dover (0304) 203203   Boulogne 21.30.25.11
Folkestone (0303) 220010   Calais 21.34.55.00
Newhaven (0273) 514131   Dieppe 35.82.24.87
Portsmouth (0705) 827744   Cherbourg 33.53.24.27

Documentation

You will need the following papers for yourself and your car.

Personal identification	Personal insurances	Car
Passport	£111 (health)	Vehicle registration document
International Camping Carnet (optional)	Personal holiday insurance	Certificate of insurance
		MOT certificate
Driving licence		'Green Card'
		Breakdown/recovery insurance (optional)

Personal identification

Passport

Check that all the party's passport(s) are valid for the period in which you travel. If any needs renewal give yourself plenty of time for the formalities. Two months is not an exaggeration in waiting time. A temporary alternative is the British Visitor's passport which can be obtained over the counter at any main Post Office (except Saturdays). With the completed form you should submit a couple of passport-sized photos and proof of identity. This will cost you £7.50. Children can be included on it if you wish.

International Camping Carnet

A Carnet is not necessary if you are holidaying via a package operator but is highly advisable if you're going independently. It has the dual role of identity card and confirmation of personal liability coverage: this can be anything up to £500,000 and can cover as many as 12 people in a party, depending on the insurance company your Carnet supplier is dealing with. It is also an acceptable substitute for your passport, which is usually retained by the management when you check in at the site. (You'll be needing that to hand, remember, when changing travellers' cheques or Eurocheques.) Carnets are issued to their members by the AA, RAC, the Caravan Club, the Camping and Caravanning Club and the Cyclists' Touring Club. If you are not eligible to obtain one through these bodies or your reservation agency doesn't offer them, you may obtain one for £7 through the GB Car Club, PO Box 11, Romsey, Hants SO51 8XX.

Driving licence

This must be a full licence. A provisional one is unacceptable. If you will be driving in France within a year of passing your test, you will be obliged by law to keep to a maximum speed limit of 90 kilometres per hour (56 mph), so you should stick a maximum speed sign on the back of the car.

Personal insurances

Form E111 – Emergency Medical Care

This certificate entitles you to receive treatment incurred through an accident or unexpected illness in EC countries and to claim against any costs. It is now a permanent form, not needing annual renewal. All family members may be included on one form. You can get the form from any DSS office or Post Office. Make sure you pick up with it an information booklet detailing refunding procedures.

Holiday insurance
Make sure you take out adequate insurance cover for your holiday. Aspects you should bear in mind are medical expenses, loss or theft of personal belongings and money, delayed departure or even cancellation of your holiday. Package companies may not offer as full a cover as you think, and if you want a full explanation of their policies over and above the summaries printed in the brochures, you are entitled to ask for one. You may find better deals through other sources. The February 1990 edition of *Which?* magazine carries a feature on this subject.

Car ID and insurances
You should always travel with your vehicle registration document, certificate of insurance and, if applicable, an MOT certificate. A **Green Card** from your insurance company will ensure that a fully comprehensive policy is maintained while you are abroad. Without it you will be covered only by minimum third party liability. **Breakdown and recovery insurances** are available through the holiday firm you book with or you can arrange this separately with an insurance agency, or with the AA or RAC.

Money

Eurocheque Unless you're going to spend your whole holiday with an attaché case full of readies handcuffed to your wrist, the most practical way of carrying money is in some form of cheque system. The most versatile is Eurocheque. It has the advantage of being a straight substitute for normal domestic cheque transactions. On request, your bank will – for a small charge – issue you with a cheque card with a guarantee limit of £100 and a cheque book enabling you to withdraw direct from your account. When abroad, you may then write out the amount of cash you require and exchange each cheque in any bank for local currency. You can also make purchases by Eurocheque where businesses display the EC sign.

Sterling travellers' cheques These are subject to the exchange rate at the time of converting into local currency. They should be accepted in any bank and quite a few campsites welcome them.

Currency travellers' cheques The advantage of these over sterling travellers' cheques is that the exchange rate is fixed at the time of purchase so you know exactly how much you have in spending power. The disadvantage is that you can use them only in conjunction with the particular French bank that your own cites as the recipient. However, **American Express** currency cheques are accepted by any bank. This type of cheque in any form is not acceptable on campsites.

PostCheques For those with a Post Office Girobank current account, PostCheques may be just as convenient as Eurocheques. You can buy a book of ten cheques for £6 and, with your cheque card, cash them at any French post office. Remember that any cheque system operates on the basis of commission and/or handling charges. A talk with your bank may determine your preference. Remember, too, that you will require proof of identity when cashing them, the most viable form being your passport.

Credit cards Credit cards can come in useful for getting hold of emergency cash through a bank, as well as paying for holiday purchases. The two most widely recognised in France are Visa (Carte Bleue) and Access (Eurocarte/Mastercard).

Cash Don't forget to convert some money into francs before you go for immediate needs and keep hold of some loose change in sterling for when you come back. You may want that odd few litres of petrol or a snack on the way home. Going out or coming in, try to avoid last-minute currency changes on the ferry as you'll lose on the deal because of low exchange rates.

What to take

Clothing

If you stick to the following guiding principles you shouldn't find yourself ending up with stuff lying in the bottom of your suitcase for two weeks:

- you will be staying on a campsite, not at the Savoy
- it will be hot, but **HOT**
- don't over-duplicate – you can wash it and wear it again.

Staple dress for all the family need only be T-shirts and shorts. Cotton is best for cool comfort. You will probably want to take just one reasonable dress or pair of trousers for an evening out on the town but unless you know you'll be keeping a roulette wheel company nightly, there's no need to overdo it. Daily wear can be kept to a minimum by the regular washing of a few items. If handwashing with travel tubes of liquid detergent seems a tedious task, remember that many campsites have washing-machines. Needless to say, clothes dry 'before your very eyes' in such a climate.

There are occasions when slightly warmer apparel will be needed. Nights can be quite cool, depending on the season and/or altitude, so a sweater or jumper can be a useful item and practical for cave or grotto visits. Track suits give the same benefit and can come in handy for a late-night trip to the loo. A cagoule or similar waterproof is not such a silly idea as you could get caught out by the odd storm, not uncommon in the Dordogne, for instance.

For children, in particular, protection from the sun is vital and some gear should be packed with this in mind. A couple of short-sleeved shirts (as opposed to T-shirts) will cover up neck and upper arms and you might even consider a long-sleeved sweatshirt. Sun hats are essential. Sandals or canvas shoes are all you require in the way of footwear. Some people like espadrilles (rope-soled canvas slip-ons). Trainers worn continuously tend to make feet sweaty so save them for the evenings, perhaps. A good idea for the beach or for paddling on pebbly river beds are plastic sandals. These are cheap and plentiful in French hypermarkets, so can be bought out there.

The car

It's advisable to give your car some form of service before venturing abroad. You may find that certain breakdown insurance policies insist upon it. It would be best to get this done a couple of weeks before the off in case any problems arise. Items you ought to be taking are a warning triangle (a legal requirement in France), a spare set of bulbs (not illegal to be without them but driving with a malfunctioning light is an offence), fire extinguisher, tow rope, tyre pressure gauge and a set of spare keys. Don't forget your GB sign for the back of the car. You may not want the weight and size of a full tool kit to take up space but at least include some pliers and a couple of screwdrivers and spanners; a small wrench can be useful. If you've never kitted yourself up with spares and aren't prepared to lay out for bits and pieces that you may never need, you can hire emergency packs and spares kits from your local dealer or motoring organisation. The AA provides these along with car alarms and roof racks.

When it comes to packing up the car those going on package holidays will have an easier time than an independent touring family lugging half a home with them. Tents are not that much of a problem: even small frame ones roll into quite a compact size. More awkward are things like boxes and cookers. As most camping furniture is designed to fold flat it makes sense for those articles to be the first in the boot. For savings on weight and space, clothes can be packed in rucksacks and hold-alls. Good rucksacks have 'spines' which prevent them, hence their contents, getting completely squashed. If you do use a rigid suitcase, one should be enough for the average family's wardrobe. Any more and you're overdoing it. Keep the tent by the boot lip if possible so that you can avoid having a load of gear cluttering your pitch before you get to erect the very thing to house it all. Don't forget to leave day/overnight travel bags for ferry or Motorail in an accessible place. Try to leave the inside of the car free of bulky items but if you've small children who don't need the leg room, rolled up sleeping bags can be tucked down behind the front seats. Pillows can serve as useful cushions should you be lucky enough for the kids to want to nap.

Sniggering neighbours shouldn't deter you from displaying all your paraphernalia outside your front door while you practise stuffing it in the car. If you find that you *must* use a roof rack, make sure that it carries the lighter goods. A roof rack is a temptation for loading more than perhaps is necessary and in doing so increases weight. This in turn will affect the car's handling. Wind resistance will make a difference in petrol consumption so try to keep things low. Above all, make sure eveything is protected from the elements and secure with cord or multi-expandable hooked lines (octopus straps). Remember to alter your tyre pressures for a laden vehicle in accordance with your manual's instructions.

Camping comforts

If you have yet to equip yourself for living under canvas, bear in mind that if you are satisfied with your sitting, eating and lying-down requirements, everything else should follow. It pays in the long run to invest in the more expensive camping furniture. Sturdier construction means a longer life-span for holidays to come.

Chairs and table

Don't just look at the chairs in the equipment shop, sit in them for a while. What of their stability? How well do they support the back? Do you get on with the arm rests? Will the children need them rather than just canvas stools? Will they double for both relaxing and eating at the table? Are they of a convenient height for the table you have chosen? The table itself: is it of sufficient area for the numbers who have to sit at it? Will it hold a complement of plates and bowls for meals? Some tables have independently adjustable legs which are very handy for setting up on uneven ground.

Cooking equipment

It isn't essential to duplicate your kitchen at home when camping. If you know you're not the adaptable type then you probably won't settle for less than a cooker with twin burners and grill: you can find ones that fold down to the size of two briefcases. But it is possible to set off from home with only the classic single gas burner and a portable barbecue and still allow your family to dine on adventurous cuisine. If your own barbecue is too impractical to take along, you could consider buying a small, compact type for holidaying. The latest innovation is the gas barbecue with reusable lava rock coals, which does away with cleaning out ash, let alone buying charcoal.

French supermarkets sell extremely good yet very cheap collapsible barbecues which can be one of your very first buys when you get out there if you wish to save on space on the outward journey. On the way back it could take the space of your consumables on the outward journey: a useful investment for the future. Existing off a barbecue becomes a way of life when eating *en plein air* and can be quite a tasty change from fry-ups. Read up a good barbecue cook book to see how versatile they can be. (A lot of campsites in the South – especially in wooded areas – won't allow you to use a barbecue on your pitch, for safety reasons. Instead, they provide communal ones in a 'safe' area, sometimes with seating to hand.) Your single burner is left primarily for boiling water for pasta and for cooking sauces (and the kids' beans!).

Beds

There are two alternatives when it comes to sleeping: air beds and camp beds. Air beds come in both double and single form; camp beds are single only. Air beds of course need pumping up – a laborious task if you've more than one – and you'll be surprised at their weight. Also, they are inevitably vulnerable to puncture. Camp beds are much lighter, can be assembled and dismantled in a minute and are surprisingly comfortable. A family compromise could be a double air bed for parents and camp beds for the children.

Shelter

Buying a tent is pretty much like buying a house: you want the most desirable and functional environment to suit your purposes at the best price. The nature of your holiday will determine the style of tent. The choice is wide and so are price ranges. Small ridge tents and igloo or dome tents are going to interest the hiker and biker more than the family, who will be comparing different kinds of frame tent. Another consideration is how often or how little you'll be on the move. If you are going to tour with your family, smaller, separate tents may be more efficient than a large family one which would be more suitable for a long stay in one spot. Camping and leisure centres usually sell off their display models in end-of-season sales and it's possible to pick up a good bargain if a tent hasn't been exposed to too much weathering: all the better if it has been erected indoors. You should always inspect a tent when it is up: in particular check if any of the poles are bent or dented or if the rubber rings that take the pegs are worn or broken. Also pay careful attention to the state of zips and seams.

Any tent, new or second-hand, should be seen erected so you can see exactly how much space there is and how the layout of the accommodation works. Find out what's involved in its assembly – how easy or complicated does it sound? The usual design is based on a frame of aluminium or steel poles which act as a dual support for a suspended inner tent, with integral groundsheet, and a draped outer tent. The whole is made taut by guy lines and pegs or stakes. You can have inner compartments that act as 'bedrooms' and flaps that zip open to make canopies. Check the various possible combinations of a particular model. If you know you are only going to use your tent abroad you may prefer it to be of cotton rather than nylon, which 'breathes' less easily. The advantages of nylon, though, are lightness in weight and easier handling all round. Concerning pegging down, you will need strong metal stakes for the hard, dry ground you'll encounter in the warm South and an iron mallet for knocking them in – not the limp rubber-coated type which is fit only for a soggy field in Wales.

Food

There is no need to take vast supplies of food with you. Just because people have cereal for breakfast every day does not mean they shouldn't alter their habits for the holiday. After all, a fresh baguette and croissants with honey is a more authentic way to start the day. Another reason to leave the cereal packets behind is that the long-life milk often sold on campsites has a taste that does not compel one to drink it in large quantities. If you are a milk drinker, you may find fresh, pasteurised milk (*lait frais*) more appealing.

You might like to take small quantities of salt, pepper, sugar (and marmalade if you can't do without it) as 'starter' packs to tide you over until you start some serious shopping abroad. Yes, you will need to stock up on that one British essential – teabags (and baked beans if you must). Any perishables should be restricted to consumption for the car journey (e.g. fruit). A reasonably sized plastic coolbox can act as larder and fridge on site, using either regularly re-frozen freezer packs or ice bought in. Either or both services are available for a fee on most sites. You could consider buying an electric or gas-operated portable fridge (if your vehicle has space to accommodate it). They usually open from the top and take the form of miniature chest-freezers. As they're reasonably economical to run (the gas type more so), one could pay its way in ice costs. A coolbox is also a very practical picnic hamper. You may wish to use two: a rigid type for the tent and a smaller, fabric zip-up type for outings.

There are wonderful things to choose for a southern French packed lunch: cantaloupe melons and peaches bought on the roadside, tins of tuna in tomato sauce, olives, pâté, garlic sausage and other cooked meats, cheeses, a baguette or two and a bottle of *bière léger* to wash it all down. Meanwhile, back at the tent, other foodstuffs should preferably be kept off the ground (in something called a 'hanging larder') or in sealed containers if kept on the floor. Remember, we are not the sole occupants of the Great Outdoors.

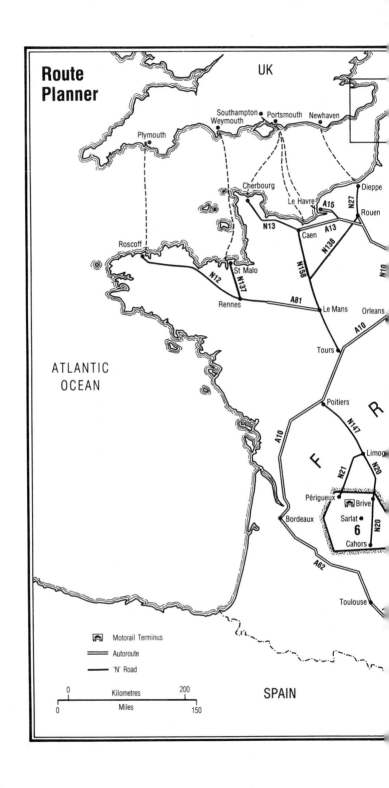

Route Planner

UK

Southampton • Portsmouth • Newhaven
Weymouth

Plymouth

Cherbourg

Le Havre **A15** **N27** Dieppe

N13 Caen **A13** Rouen

Roscoff **N138**

N158

St Malo **N10**

N12 **N137**

Rennes **A81** Le Mans Orleans

A10

Tours

ATLANTIC
OCEAN

Poitiers R

N147

A10 F Limog

N21 **N20**

Périgueux • 🚗 Brive

Bordeaux Sarlat •

6 **N20**

Cahors

A62

Toulouse

🚗   Motorail Terminus

═══   Autoroute

───   'N' Road

0   Kilometres   200

0   Miles   150

SPAIN

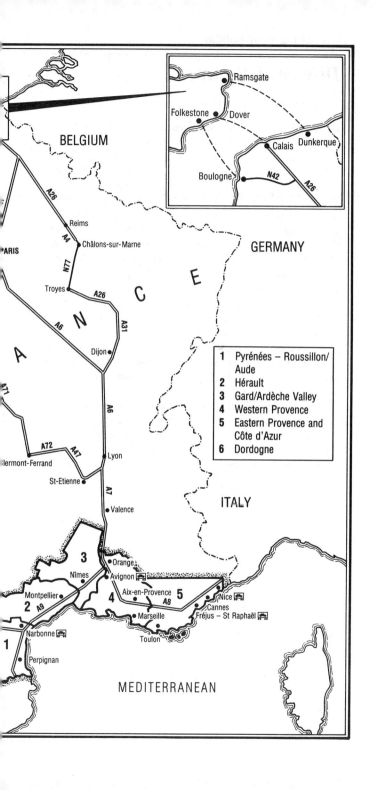

Driving all the way?

Autoroutes and alternatives

For speed, convenience and, surprisingly perhaps, safety, the
French motorway or autoroute system is worth the cost in tolls.
Nearly the whole of the autoroute system is toll-operated, other
than the peripheral routes round Paris, Lyon and Marseilles.
Distance and the type of vehicle determine the charge made.
You can expect to pay out roughly £60 in toll costs (return)
using autoroutes to reach the South. A Visa card and cash are
the two ways to pay (no cheques). Cash is essential where
there's an automatic 'bucket' collection for fixed price tolls over
short distances; otherwise, you collect a ticket at a toll booth on
entry and pay when you finally exit. Charges are higher if
you're towing a caravan, on average half as much again as a car
only. You can get a complete list of autoroute toll charges,
leaflet ER400, from the AA Overseas Routes Service, Fanum
House, Basingstoke, Hants RG21 2EA.

If you want to make the journey and stop-overs part of your
holiday you can take a cross-country route. There is a detour
scheme called 'Bison Futé' (the Smart Bison) which takes you
on lesser roads avoiding built-up or congested areas. These are
marked by green-backed signs displaying the words **Bis** or
Itinéraire Bis. Bison Futé maps can be picked up at service
stations or roadside information points. These tend to be more
concentrated in the South than the North of France.

Other useful pointers on the Bison Futé maps are petrol
station locations, a couple of hotel chains, useful for overnight
stops, and Courte-Paille Grill spots – French-style Happy Eaters.

Routes to the South

Autoroute itineraries come as variations on a theme, with the
AA, RAC and individual package firms all having their own
ideas. Below we give some suggestions for you to think about in
conjunction with a good road map.

Calais/Boulogne/Dunkerque The traditional route from
these ports has been via Paris (A26/A1/A6) but with recent
additions to the autoroute system it's now possible to take a
western or eastern route, avoiding the metropolis.

Calais A26 to Reims where you change on to A4. A4 exit for
Chalons-sur-Marne via N44. Then N77 to Troyes. Exit south on

N71 to join A26 which will merge with A31 north of Dijon. A31 by-passes Dijon and enters A6 at Beaune, eventually taking you to Lyon. A6 leads straight on to A7 for Orange, A9 Nîmes and west or A7/A8 Aix-en-Provence and east.

Le Havre/Caen/Cherbourg A15/A13 autoroutes towards Paris (Cherbourg-Caen N13), by-passing Rouen to the south. Cross over to N10 via A12 at Versailles. To Ablis and out south on N191 which intersects with A10. A10 to Orléans, changing to A71 to Clermont-Ferrand. Then A72 to St Etienne and N88/A47 link to the A7 at Givors, south of Lyon. Follow to Orange, then A9 for Languedoc or A7/A8 for the Côte d'Azur.

Dieppe N27 to Rouen (unavoidable). Over Seine to pick up D18 on eastern side of city. This puts you on A13. Then route as for Le Havre.

Routes to the Dordogne

The western half of France is nowhere as well provided with interchangeable motorways and it's impossible to go by autoroute all the way to the Périgord/Lot region.

Boulogne/Dunkerque A26/A1 to Paris. Take the Paris ring road. Exit on A6 to join A10 to Poitiers via Tours and Orléans. From then on it's N roads: N147 to Limoges and, depending on your destination, you go by the N21 to Périgueux or the N20 to Brive.

Cherbourg/Caen/Le Havre/Dieppe The individual routes from the French ports all converge on Le Mans as follows:

Cherbourg	N13 Caen; N158/N138 Le Mans
Caen	N158/N138 Le Mans
Le Havre	A15 to Pont de Tancarville (toll bridge); N182 Pont-Audemer; D130 Brionne; N138 Le Mans
Dieppe	N27/A15 Rouen; N138 Le Mans

Then N138 to Tours. Join A10 to Poitiers. Change to N147 towards Limoges and choose either the N21 for the western part of the Dordogne or the N20 for the eastern part.

Roscoff Take the D58 to join the N12 to Rennes. Then take the N157/A81 to Le Mans.

The AA Overseas Routes Service offers – for a charge of £10 and upwards – a precisely detailed personal itinerary in the form of a computer print-out which promises to be up-to-date as their database is being continually revised. Other than the necessary directions, you may request optional information such as descriptions of places of interest, roads, scenery and/or landmarks. Contact: The AA Overseas Routes, Fanum House, Basingstoke, Hants RG21 2EA.

The road system

France's road network is divided into:

A *Autoroutes*, which are equivalent to our motorways. The majority charge a toll according to the distance that you have covered. Emergency telephones are available every 2 kilometres, and stations, service or rest areas approximately every 20 kilometres.

N *Routes nationales*, which are similar to our A roads.

D *Routes départementales*: these are more rural routes.

Signs and symbols
Directions signs

Autoroute	white lettering on blue
N Roads	white lettering on green
D Roads	black lettering on white
Diversions	black lettering on yellow

Written signs

French	English
Allumez vos phares	Use your headlights
Centre ville	Town centre
Chantier	Roadworks
Chaussée deformée	Uneven surface
Déviation	Diversion
Gravillons	Loose chippings
Nids de poules	Potholes
Passage protégé	You have priority at intersection
Péage	Toll
Poids lourd	Alternative route for heavy lorries
Priorité à droite	Give way to the right
Ralentir	Slow down
Rappel	Remember (e.g. speed limit still operative)
Roulez lentement	Drive slowly
Route barrée	Road closed
Sens interdit	No entry

French	English
Serrez à droite	Keep well over to the right
Toutes directions	All routes
Travaux	Road works
Virages	Bends

Priorities

The indication sign for '*La Priorité*' is diamond-shaped with an inner white diamond on a yellow background. The same sign with a black diagonal through it denotes an end to the right of way. This is often found where a main route enters a town of any reasonable size. Unless there are signs to the contrary, you are obliged to give way to vehicles coming from your right.

As in Britain, right of way at the majority of roundabouts nowadays is given to vehicles already on the roundabout. If you do not see the usual red triangular warning sign carrying a notice reading '*Vous n'avez pas la priorité*', it is best to assume that that particular roundabout is still operating the old system of priority, where traffic already on the roundabout has to give way to traffic entering.

Speed limits

Dry roads	Kph	Mph
Autoroutes (tolled)	130	80
Dual carriageways/untolled roads	110	68
Urban roads	60/45	37/28
Other roads	90	56

Wet roads	Kph	Mph
Autoroutes (tolled)	110	68
Dual carriageways/untolled autoroutes	100	62
Urban roads	60/45	37/28
Other roads	80	50

A driver who has held a full licence for less than a year must restrict his/her speed to 90 kph (56 mph).

On a level autoroute in good daylight conditions there is a **minimum** speed of 80 kph (50 mph) for the fast lane.

Petrol

The different fuels in French service stations are as follows:

Super	Equivalent of 4-star	*Sans plomb*	Unleaded
Essence	Equivalent of 2/3-star	*Gasoil*	Diesel

The majority of petrol stations, especially in rural areas, are attendant-operated, whereas self-service stations (*'libre-service'*) are more frequently found on autoroutes and at hypermarkets. Do not assume that you will be able to pay for petrol with your credit cards.

Lead-free petrol is widely available.

Towing a caravan

When towing a caravan in France you should note that:

- The maximum permitted dimensions are 11 metres (length) and 2.5 metres (width).
- Speed limits for cars normally apply provided that the weight of the caravan doesn't exceed that of the towing vehicle.
- The appropriate speed limit discs must be displayed on the rear of the caravan. Some autoroutes impose an 80 kph limit for towing.
- The towing vehicle must be fitted with a right-hand-side wing mirror or at least an adequate rear-view mirror.
- No passengers may be carried in a moving caravan.
- A distance of 50 metres (160 feet) must be kept between the towing vehicle and the vehicle in front, outside built-up areas.
- Towing in the fast lane of a three-lane motorway is forbidden.
- On narrow roads you must slow down or pull in if you want to be overtaken.
- If a caravan is stationary on the road because of a breakdown or accident, a red warning triangle must be displayed 30 metres (about 100 feet) behind, whether the caravan is attached or detached.
- If you have borrowed or hired the caravan, you must carry written authorisation from the owner.

Overnight stops

Reserving overnight accommodation with your package holiday operator will mean one less thing to think about, but it is a more expensive option than booking direct. Finding somewhere to stay on spec is not so fraught with pitfalls as you might imagine. It could work out to be your cheapest bet. There's usually a hotel of some description in the smallest town, a well-known and commendable chain of over 4,000 being the

Logis de France. The famous Relais Routiers 'caffs' sometimes have basic accommodation as well as good square meals but you shouldn't expect motel-like facilities. Costs can be kept down by asking for a family room – the French system charges by the room rather than by the person. It's your prerogative to inspect any room offered and you don't have to accept the first one you're shown but, unless you're extremely fussy, you can be made reasonably comfortable for the night. You are not normally obliged to eat in a hotel's restaurant, although it might not go down too well if you don't. Collapsing into the hotel restaurant is certainly easier than walking around a town for half an hour comparing menus when you're tired and hungry. To give yourself a reasonable chance of finding somewhere to stay, don't leave looking till too late – ideally, you should aim to be booked in by six or so. In rural areas, especially, the hotel restaurant may not take orders after, say, 8.30p.m.

We give below some suggestions for arranging overnight stops as alternatives to camping en route. The hotel chains listed are also used by English camping package firms. A complete accommodation list can be obtained from the French Tourist Office (see the inside back cover of the Guide).

Chambre d'Hôte B&Bs in privately owned farm and village houses with set and graded standards.

French Country Welcome (Gîtes de France/Springfield) is an annual guide to these, containing some 6,000 addresses.

Logis de France An organisation of family-run low-grade hotels, inexpensive but adhering to strict standards. Mostly rural or in small towns.

Guide de Logis de France is available free (apart from 80p postage) from the French Tourist Office. Direct bookings only with the exception of a selection of Logis via **The Voyage Organisation**, 134a Uxbridge Road, London W12 8AA (081-743 5233)

Campanile hotel chain 200 small, modern two-star hotels across France. **Campanile**, Unit 8, Red Lion Road, Hounslow TW3 1JF (081-569 5757)

Ibis/Urbis hotel chain 240 two-star hotels across France; and **Novotel** 100 three-star hotels mainly on motorways and on the outskirts of cities.

Both these chains are represented in England by **Resinter**, c/o Novotel, Shortlands, Hammersmith, London W6 8DR (081-724 1000)

Other suggestions for places to stay can be found in:

- *Michelin Red Guide to France*: hotel and restaurant guide supplemented with town maps.
- *Hotels and Restaurants in France* (AA): directory of 2,500 hotels covering a broad spectrum of prices.
- *Routiers Guide to France*: lists 3,000 café-restaurants throughout France. A small percentage offer basic accommodation.

Kids en route

If even the school run can be a nightmare, you'll need some strategies for transporting children from one end of France to the other. Different age groups need entertaining in different ways and it is not our intention to go into details of travel games, story tapes and so on, but here are some basic pointers worth remembering.

Make your child or children as comfortable as possible to keep complaints and restlessness to a minimum. Pillows can double as cushions. Larger children may appreciate more leg room so bring the front passenger seat forward a notch if possible. And of course all children should be belted up at any time you are on the road.

Depending on their age, children need to have their journey broken at regular intervals if only to relieve the sheer boredom. Loo visits must dictate stops and just having the opportunity to stretch the legs or kick a ball around can make a refreshing change. Be prepared to stop on a regular basis and not to be in too much of a hurry to chivvy everyone back into the car because you want to get on. Think of your holiday as starting when you come off the ferry, not when you arrive at your campsite. With this in mind, if you can plan your stops in terms of timing and distance, so much the better. If you are going all the way by autoroute, service areas are your best bet with toilets, eating facilities and often play areas. Alternatives are designated rest areas, which also provide toilets, picnic tables and drinking water.

When considering what snacks or drinks to take on board,

two things to watch are chocolate – the 'melt' factor – and crisps – the 'crumb' factor (not to mention the empty packets). Apples and bananas are more practical as well as healthier. Bring drinks in cartons rather than cans (less packing space, more easily disposed of, generally safer).

Other indispensables: a roll of pedal binliners to tidy up as you go, a kitchen roll (more versatile than tissues) and disposable moist cloths in a dispensing pack. (And ear muffs for the driver...)

Times to travel

An early morning or overnight ferry will enable you to cover a lot of ground during the day. If you are motoring off the autoroutes, making use of the relatively quieter lunch hours between noon and 3 will help in negotiating towns. Be prepared for heavy traffic around the dates of 14 July and 15 August – the two most important public holidays in the French calendar.

Parking

Overnight parking in lay-bys is not legally permitted. Motorways have regular rest areas (*'Aires de Repos'*) for temporary breaks in long journeys but should not be looked upon as camping sites. (Toll tickets are valid for only 24 hours.) Some of these areas provide facilities for emptying chemical toilets and taking on fresh water.

Some towns prohibit the parking of caravans on the public highway and instead have selected places where you may stop for provisions.

Motorail

The easiest way to take a car-bound family to the South of France is by French Motorail. At the channel port (Boulogne, Calais or Dieppe), you take a short drive to the rail terminus. There you say goodbye to your car, having driven it on to a line of waiting transporter wagons, and cross the track to a separate train of couchettes. You'll find the others in the party already unwrapping the picnic supper bought earlier in the town. Then, if you are male, you take your glass of wine (you should always begin a holiday as you mean to go on) out into the corridor and, along with a row of other British males, rest elbows on a lowered window. You all lean out in the direction of the engine way up line. This ritual is, for some peculiar reason, thought to get the train away on time. It never does.

When you finally move, you take in your last breath of grey evening air, moist with salt and fish, and retire to your compartment. At bedtime, seats become bunks which you make up with the fresh linen and blankets provided. Through the night a minor miracle is performed by speed and time for at dawn, you will awake to a dramatically altered vista, saturated with a brilliant light. In the foreground regiments of huge sunflowers whizz past. Beyond, green fields of maize are cut in half by thin, dry roads with a solitary Citroën van journeying to low, distant, purple hills. You have come 600 miles and are only minutes away from an alternative lifestyle stuffed with garlic, cool rivers, deep gorges, and shuttered buildings in shadowed streets – all suffused with the dusty heat of a high Mediterranean sun. Easy!

As part of its wider European service, French Motorail runs nine overnight services from channel ports to termini in the regions we cover in this Guide. The most economical way for a family to travel is by couchette. A standard compartment comprises two tiers of three bunks which fold away for daylight travelling, the lower ones converting into normal bench seating. At the end of each carriage is not only a toilet but a little washroom. Couchettes are usually shared to make up a full complement and as there's no segregation of the sexes you aren't expected to change into nightwear.

Although many people eat a packed evening snack in their compartment, some trains have a self-service restaurant car: while the dishes are of a reasonable standard and generous in helping, they can be pricey.

If you are a couple or on your own and you want a little more luxury, a sleeper is the more comfortable alternative. These are divided into first-class single or double accommodation, and tourist class, consisting of two- or three-bed units. All contain their own washing facilities and have the extra service of a carriage attendant who can – at additional cost – supply you with drinks and light snacks. A continental breakfast with a choice of coffee or hot chocolate is inclusive in exchange for your breakfast ticket. While you check the map over croissants and jam your car is off-loaded for you and parked ready and waiting. Seasoned Motorail travellers know to be first off the train to avoid the queue, thus giving themselves an earlier start.

Holidaymakers who are touring by bike are also catered for on the Boulogne-Brive/Narbonne services. For an extra £16 a bicycle can be carried in the luggage van in its own protective cardboard cover. Other fare provisions are certain discounts on mid-week travel and reduced rates on some selected cross-channel services. You can book Motorail direct with SNCF, through some UK travel agents (not all) or with British Rail's Travel Centres. Detailed information from: French Railways (SNCF), 179 Piccadilly, London W1V 0BA (071-409 3518).

Motorail routes from French Channel Ports

Boulogne	Avignon, Brive, Fréjus/St-Raphaël, Narbonne, Toulouse
Calais	Narbonne, Nice
Dieppe	Avignon, Fréjus/St-Raphaël

Road versus rail?

Cost comparisons are never satisfactory as different people put a different value on factors such as saving time, comfort, convenience and price. Our back-of-envelope calculations show that a family of two adults and two children under eleven going to Avignon will pay about the same going Motorail or road, assuming that they spend two days travelling in each direction if they drive all the way (with tolls, petrol, overnight stops and meals). This does not take into account the unquantifiable factor of wear and tear on the car.

Maps

The two large-scale series below could be used in conjunction with each other for touring between and exploring individual localities.

Michelin 1:200,000 (2cm = 1km)

Unlike the old narrow strips of map that used annoyingly to cut across the area in which you were interested, the present revised format offers larger sheet sizes, thus fewer maps needed for a given region. Still in their distinctive yellow covers, they are ideal for touring and general navigational purposes. Maps 240 and 245 relate to coverage of this guide.

IGN Green Series 1:100,000 (1cm = 1km)
The IGN (Institut Géographique National) is France's
equivalent to the British Ordnance Survey. While these maps
are more expensive than *Michelin*, the scale is very practical – as
well as being very readable – for local cross-country exploration
by car. You may need more than one for the specific area that
interests you. Relevant to this guide are:

Dordogne (northern part, including the River Dordogne):
Nos. 47 and 48.
Dordogne (southern part, including the River Lot):
Nos. 56 and 57.
Aude/Pyrénées: No. 72
Hérault: No. 65
Gard: Nos. 59 and 66
Ardèche: No. 59
West and Central Provence: Nos. 60, 66 and 67
Alpes-Maritimes: No. 61
Var and Côte d'Azur: No. 68
IGN Special Touring Maps
Camargue (1:100,000): No. 303
Cévennes (1:100,000): No. 354
Dordogne (1:125,000) (covers the Dordogne *département* only).

For general navigation and north/south route-planning
Michelin Road Atlas of France 1:200,000
Michelin France 1:100,000 (European Red series No. 989)
Michelin France Motorway Atlas (No. 914) – a useful pocket-sized
booklet giving coverage of the national autoroute system
broken down into sections with an enlarged Paris area map.
Information on entries, exits, distances, toll charges, petrol
stations, service areas and so on.

Additional reading

The Holiday Which? Guide to France is now firmly established as a
leading guide to the country as a whole and its relevant sections
include much in the way of supplementary detail for our
regions. Priced at £10.95, it is available from bookshops,
including the Which? Shop at 359-361 Euston Road, London
NW1 3AL (071-486 5544), or by post from Consumers'
Association, Castlemead, Gascoyne Way, Hertford X, SG14 1LH
(postage and packaging free).

The *Michelin Green Guides* contain a wealth of information from the geography and geology of a region to its history, architecture and cuisine, followed by a concise gazetteer. English titles corresponding to our areas are *The Dordogne*, *The French Riviera* (including the Côte d'Azur), and *Provence*, which also takes in the Ardèche Valley and some of the Gard. In French only are *Pyrénées-Roussillon* and *Gorges du Tarn* (for the Cévennes and Languedoc).

A roof rack is a temptation for loading more than perhaps is necessary

French facts

French Government Tourist Office
178 Piccadilly
London W1V 0A1
Tel 071-491 7622

Business hours

Banks
Open Weekdays 9 to 12, 2 to 4 or 4.30.
Closed Sunday, and Saturday or Monday, depending on local variation. (Times are usually displayed on the building.)

Post offices
Open Weekdays 8 to 12, 2 to 7.
Closed Saturday afternoon and Sunday.

Shops
Open (in general) weekdays 9 to 12, 2 to 7.
Closed Sunday and Monday (or Monday morning).
Food shops usually open an hour earlier and some may operate on a Sunday morning (especially bakers). Hypermarkets tend to stay open much later than town shops, sometimes beyond 9 pm.

Museums, galleries, cathedrals and churches
There are no hard and fast rules about **museum and gallery** closing times other than they are not open on any of the public holidays and always close for lunch from 12 to 2. Otherwise, they generally shut for one day, usually at the beginning of the week and more probably Tuesday than Monday. Sunday openings/closings seem to be arbitrary. You should check such times with the local Syndicat d'Initiative; sometimes a well-informed camp reception may help.

Churches and cathedrals are usually closed to tourists during lunch hours and frown on sightseers during services. Those that are on the 'tourist beat' may well have hours of opening posted on the door.

Telephoning

To call France from the UK, dial **010-33** followed by the eight-digit number.

To call the UK from France, dial 19 (wait for the tone change), then 44, then the STD code minus the 0, followed by the number.

Example: to dial the London number 071-486 5544, you would dial 19-44-71-486-5544.

Paris variations From the UK dial **010-33-1** followed by the eight-digit number; from within France (outside Paris) dial **16-1**, then the number.

Phone cards Phone booths taking cards now seem to outnumber coin-operated ones. The *'Télécarte'* (with either 50 or 120 units) can be bought from post offices and newsagents.

Public holidays

These are the public holidays most likely to affect your holiday. Businesses are usually closed for the day.

March/ April	Easter Monday (but not Good Friday)
May	1 (Labour Day), 8 (VE Day), Ascension Day (about 5 weeks after Easter)
June	Whit Monday (2nd Monday after Ascension)
July	14 (Bastille Day)
August	15 (Assumption Day)

How to use the Guide

The Guide is divided into six regional sections across southern France:

1 Pyrénées-Roussillon and Aude
2 Hérault
3 Gard and Ardèche Valley
4 Western Provence
5 Eastern Provence and Côte d'Azur
6 Dordogne

A general map on pages 6 and 7 shows these regional divisions. Each regional section begins with its own enlarged map with towns and campsite locations marked by a triangle. There follows a regional introduction, plus a rundown on the towns and tourist attractions worth seeking out. The campsite entries for that region are arranged alphabetically after that, with any naturist sites at the end.

The site entry

Information on each campsite comes in six parts:

- **Site identification**—name, address and phone number (sometimes with an out-of-season number if known)

- **Verdict**—a brief summing-up of the site's main attributes

- **The entry**—a description of the nature of the site (note that special activities and/or entertainments referred to are usually organised for the high season only)

- **Symbols**—a visual résumé of facilities

- **Directions**—how to locate the site

- **The details**—additional information including details of prices.

The symbols

The 'recommended' starburst

The fact that sites have been selected for inclusion in the Guide
is of course a recommendation in itself (and see Caveats below).
We felt, however, that some camps stood out above the rest and
deserved to be recognised as such. See page 16 for our roll-call
of these sites.

The 'caveat' entry ⑦

We have included some sites that in the main offer a perfectly
respectable camping environment, depending on your holiday
priorities; however, we felt that some aspect might mar your
stay. We didn't want to exclude such sites outright, but at the
same time it did not seem fair to put them on an equal footing
with the others. The potential drawbacks are explained in the
entry.

Shade ○ ◑ ◕ ●

The degree of shade given for each site indicates to what extent
shade covers the site as a whole. Thus a site may have an
extremely shady corner which by itself would warrant our
maximum full black disc, but this may be only part of a camping
ground that is predominantly exposed. We would then print
the second symbol of the four. We try to elaborate on the type
of shade in the entry.

Size ⑤ Ⓜ Ⓛ

This signifies the pitch capacity:

Small   up to 200 *emplacements*
Medium 200 to 400 *emplacements*
Large 400 *emplacements* or more.

Atmosphere

This is intended as a rough indication of how active the site is in
its daily life, ranging from quiet through busy to lively. The
'busy' category does not necessarily mean noisy or disturbing,
just that there is an animated feel to the place. 'Lively' refers to
the night more than day and centres on the level of
entertainment. Even in large sites remember that sound –

especially music – travels. You may from time to time come across our description of a site being 'very French'. Some camps attempt to project the image of some sort of international playground, whereas 'French-style' campsites are usually quieter, more informal and relaxed, but often without the frills.

Children

When this symbol is used, it is not so much to indicate the availability of distractions and entertainment for them but that the site in general is one where they would warm to and where they wouldn't be at a loss for something to do. Nearly all campsites, whatever their grade, provide basic playground equipment. Absence of the teddy-bear doesn't necessarily mean the site is unsuitable. See the details at the end of the entry for more information, including the extremely few instances of campsites that we feel are unsuitable for children.

Swimming

The first symbol represents at least one swimming-pool (check the entry for details about a separate children's pool). The second symbol denotes that you can swim in a river or lake next to the site. The swimming fish means that the site is on the beach.

Food

In turn, these mean that on site there is: a shop for basic groceries; a restaurant; a bar; and that you can fetch cooked food for taking away to your *emplacement*.

Some site restaurants offer a full menu while others just provide a *plat cuisiné*. This is a set dish of the day which you can take back to your tent or eat at tables provided on the bar terrace, for instance.

Like any establishment catering for large numbers, bigger sites tend to offer less exotic menus. Pizzerias are becoming more common as a matter of managerial expediency. Some smaller, family-run sites make a point of offering a regional speciality.

Campsite meal prices are not always more expensive than outside. Generally, an attempt is made to match those of equivalent average restaurants in the area, and prices may even be cheaper at smaller sites.

No matter how sophisticated the site you will always find

frites. Don't think for one minute that French chips are anything like our soggy, oily, English variety. Nine times out of ten, they are crisp, golden and dry. Pack a large saucepan (with lid) for carrying them back with the rest of your take-away: campers are usually expected to provide their own containers.

As for specific dishes, when you see *steak haché* chalked up on the board, expect a cross between a beefburger and frying steak – it is in fact a shaped 'cut' of minced meat. Like French meat in general it will be undercooked by British standards, so you might want to ask for it *'bien cuit'* (well cooked).

Truite (trout) is a favourite dish of many sites, especially those in hilly regions with access to streams. Sometimes, such as in the Dordogne, you can buy trout from a local trout farm for barbecuing back at the tent. You're in luck if the camp cooks fresh *au feu du bois*. A wood-fire, kiln-like oven is used, producing a wonderful charred flavour and smell. Other victuals commonly on offer are *brochettes*, which we recognise as kebabs, and *merguez*, spicy, coarse-cut sausages.

Ablutions

The shower symbol denotes the existence of some semblance of hot water. We have discussed the problem of guaranteed hot showers (see Introduction); more details are given in the entry if need be. The washbasin representing individual cubicles means that *some* are to be found on site. It may be the case that not all of a campsite's *sanitaires* provide them. The washing-machine symbol needs no explanation, while the peg symbol means that the site provides washing-lines which the management prefers you to use, rather than decorating your pitch with the family laundry.

Play

This indicates that some choice of sports exists, ranging from ball games only to a whole gamut of recreational pursuits. These are itemised in the details. Although some sites have hardly anything in the way of such amenities, just about all manage a table-tennis table.

Disco

This can mean anything from taped music in the bar once a week to something akin to a permanent nightclub in full swing every night – more likely to be found in the big Mediterranean sites in high season. See the text for fuller details.

A note on the details

Directions

We try to give full details on how to get to the campsites, many
of which are in relatively remote spots. We urge you to use
them as a *complement* to large-scale maps (see page 47) rather
than on their own.

Ground

This is an indication of the general ground conditions for
pitching a tent. They can, of course, vary considerably
depending on the effects of weather.

Children

We list as fully as possible the various amenities available for
children. The entry itself usually expands on this. Some
amenities may be available only in the peak season.

Wheelchair

Any site that on our visit did not have special sanitary
arrangements for a disabled person in a wheelchair we have
described as 'not suitable'. We have described as 'tricky' those
sites which did have such facilities but where the terrain and
amenities were not widely accessible to someone in a
wheelchair. Further details are given in the entry where
appropriate. Some site owners keep the disabled toilet locked
and issue keys to wheelchair users for their sole use.

Food-cooling

Access to a means of keeping food and drink fresh and/or cold is
vital in this climate. With coolpacks, campsites either hire out
their own or will refreeze yours for a charge. (NB: the
Préfecture of the Alpes-Maritimes *département* in Eastern
Provence has declared it illegal for campsites to freeze campers'
coolpacks for reasons of hygiene.)

Sport

Here you will find a list of the sports and games available on the
site itself. Other activities may be easily accessible from the
camp, such as horse-riding and golf.

Season

Most campsites are open from Easter to September or October. We give as full details as possible.

Reservation

Most campsites advise that you should book in advance for the high season, but it is still possible to chance it. (See Organising your holiday.)

Charge

Campsites operate a tariff system whereby they charge separately for the pitch, and each person using the pitch (reduced rates for children), and sometimes for the vehicle, or a minimum charge for a pitch including a minimum number of people (e.g. 2 people, pitch and car 60 francs). An additional charge is then made per person above that number. If small children are given a discount, that information appears next, followed by an average cost of electrical hook-up. Even though we don't always give prices for electrical hook-up, all sites in the Guide have some electrical source. Different amperages carry different charges: you may want to contact the site in advance to find out what amperage is available and at what charge.

NB: All tariffs quoted are for the *high season*. Good reductions are usually made for the low to mid seasons. Prices quoted are also only representative in being the *basic* charge – usually for tent users – and are exclusive of any further supplements that may be incurred. Invariably, caravans and camper vehicles carry a higher charge, the differential fluctuating from site to site.

Remember, too, the *taxe de séjour*, which does not form part of our calculations. This is an obligatory local government tax at a fixed rate per person per day (generally 1 franc or 1.50 francs).

Campsite key words

Accueil	Reception (reservations)
Alimentation	Shop
Bac de linge/laverie/lavage	Laundry (handwash)
Bac de vaisselle/vaisselle/ eviers pour vaisselle	Washing-up sinks
Baignade non surveillée	Non-supervised bathing (usually in a river)
Charcuterie	Delicatessen
Chaud(e)	Hot
Chimique	Chemical toilet waste
Dépôt de pain	Bread counter (sometimes on sites not running a shop)
Douches	Showers
Eau non potable	Not drinking water
Emplacement	Pitch
Entrée interdite	Entry forbidden
Epicerie	Grocery
Froid(e)	Cold
Glace à rafraîchir	Ice blocks (for cooling food)
Lavabos	Washbasins
Location des vélos	Bike hire
Machine à laver	Washing-machine
Pataugeoire	Paddling-pool
Piscine	Swimming-pool
Pissoirs/urinoirs	Urinals
Plage	Beach
Plats à emporter	Take-away meals
Plats cuisinés	Ready-cooked meals (eaten in situ or taken away)
Salle de réunion	Public lounge
Toilette/WC	Toilet

Pyrénées-Roussillon
and Aude

Pyrénées-Roussillon

Pyrénées-Roussillon is a label conferred by the French tourist industry on what is really the area covered by *Département* 66, the Pyrénées-Orientales. There is certainly a diversity of scenery and atmosphere in this holiday area at the western end of the French Mediterranean – you can either bask on the beaches or take to the hills. The geography hardly gives you any middle ground except for the plain of the Roussillon proper, south of Perpignan.

The possibilities for camping reflect this differing landscape: for walking holidays or investigating the Catalan culture you can choose modest little sites in the hills or valleys, while there are plenty of coastal sites for beach holidays. In the more commercial parts of the seaside, there isn't an over-abundance of high-quality camping, but generally, whether inland or on the coast, you should at least be comfortable.

Along a near straight north-south run of sand from Le Barcarès almost to the Spanish border, the coastline possesses arguably the finest beaches of southern France or, at the very least, matching the best that the eastern Mediterranean can offer. Just south of that, a certain symmetry seems to exist between the western and eastern seaboards. As with the Corniche d'Or of the Esterel, Roussillon's craggy Côte Vermeille is punctured by pretty inlets. Canet-Plage and Argelès-sur-Mer are Riviera-style resorts, but toned down and a little more civilised. There's even a link in art history: modern masters such as Picasso and Matisse were associated both

Pyrénées – Roussillon and Aude

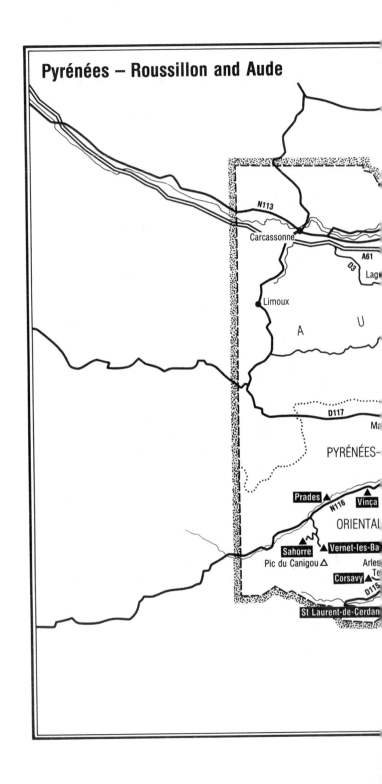

N113

Carcassonne

A61

D3

Lag

Limoux

A   U

D117

Ma

PYRÉNÉES-

Prades

N116

Vinça

ORIENTAL

Sahorre

Vernet-les-Ba

Pic du Canigou △

Arles

Corsavy

Te

D115

St Laurent-de-Cerdan

Amended charges

The high season charges at *Le Paradis*, St-Léon-Sur-Vézère in the Dordogne are as follows and not as indicated on page 336:

pitch 41.30 (francs); person 26.10; child (under 4) free, (over 4) adult price; electricity 13.50.

May 1991

a/s 204

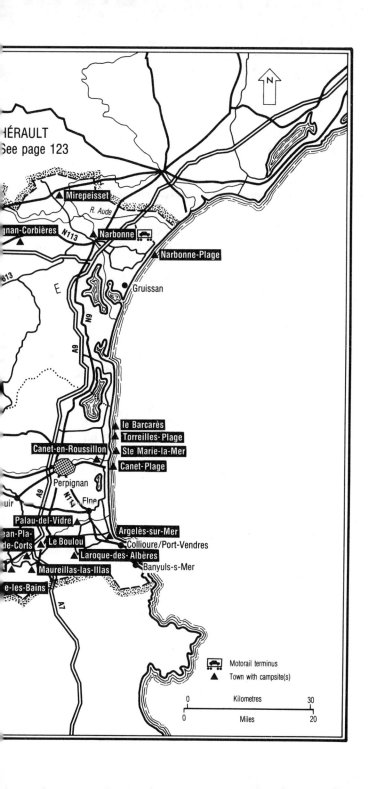

HÉRAULT
See page 123

▲ Mirepeisset

R. Aude

nan-Corbières
▲

N113

▲ Narbonne �car

Narbonne-Plage

● Gruissan

E

613

N9

A9

le Barcarès ▲
Torreilles-Plage ▲
Ste Marie-la-Mer ▲

Canet-en-Roussillon ▲

Canet-Plage ▲

A9

NT4

Perpignan

Elne

uir

Palau-del-Vidre ▲

ean-Pla-
de-Corts

Le Boulou ▲

Argelès-sur-Mer ▲
● Collioure/Port-Vendres

Laroque-des-Albères ▲
● Banyuls-s-Mer

▲▲
Maureillas-las-Illas ▲

e-les-Bains

A7

�car Motorail terminus

▲ Town with campsite(s)

0   Kilometres   30
0   Miles   20

with Vence, inland from Nice, and Céret and Collioure, inland from Argelès.

West of 'La Catalane', the A9, which hugs the N9 as it heads towards Spain, are three broad ranges of hills broken by the two valleys of the rivers Têt and Tech. In the north, bordering Aude, are the Fenouillèdes, the wine-producing territory of the Côtes du Roussillon. You can travel through it on the D117 passing through towns such as Estagel and Maury. Maury's *caves* make a fortified sweet wine and Rivesaltes in the low country north of Perpignan is the home of a respected Muscat.

The northern of the two valleys is that of the Têt whose river plain cuts a rough V into an area known as Conflent. Deep in its heart is the health spa, Vernet-les-Bains, squatting under the majesty of the Pic du Canigou, the last of the Pyrenean heights before they descend to the Mediterranean. The valley here is also the source of a unique marble, the 'Meuble Rose', used to enhance many a Romanesque church in these parts. Here, too, is Prades, a thriving town born of the prolific fruit industry of the Têt and Roussillon plains, which are covered with orchards of peach, apricot and apple.

The Têt and its southerly sister the Tech sandwich the next range, the Vallespir. This is a desolate but beautiful district concealing slithers of clear running streams and barely driveable roads appearing as unravelled yarn on the map. The Tech begins life somewhere below the Pic de Costabone south-west of Canigou and, sharing its valley floor with the D115, links the little towns of Arles-sur-Tech, Amélie-les-Bains, Céret, St Jean-Pla-de-Corts and Le Boulou. South of these lie the Chaîne des Albères, giving many vantage points for excellent coastal views. Along the length of its spinal ridge France finally becomes Spain.

This international border is but an insignificant division as far as culture and custom are concerned, for here you are in the Catalonia of old. You are reminded by the ubiquitous red and yellow stripes of the Catalan flag that the ancient Franco-Spanish mix of races still survives as a kingdom, albeit spiritually rather than politically. It has its own language and its own folklore, the latter coming to life in the summer festivals throughout the region.

These feast days, or 'Festa Major', are the social extension of the particular religious celebration of a town's patron saint and can last for up to a week with whole communities participating. There are sports competitions, funfairs, agricultural fairs and open theatre. The last usually goes hand in hand with street banquets when you may be lucky enough to be offered Catalan cuisine in the form of *sardinades* (grilled sardines), or a *bouillinade* (fish stew) or even *cargolades* (snails).

Perhaps the most renowned tradition of these festivities is the unique folk dance of the Catalans, La Sardane – whole days are sometimes devoted to it. This ritual of a dance can be seen in the summer celebrations in almost every town and village in Roussillon. Consisting of ever-increasing concentric circles of dancers, expanding as others add themselves to link hands, La Sardane is both a communal and a religious statement. The human rings ebb and flow accompanied by singing like a Gregorian chant in its unified delivery. The dance becomes more than a joining of hands: it is a timeless bond with an ancient past that for a moment re-creates itself in present and indeed, future generations. That's why it is sometimes referred to as the *danse éternelle*.

This, then, is the land of folklore, coupled with the romance of the Med: a high sun in a scorching blue sky; the brilliant green of vineyard hills and the cobalt sea; the natural harbours of Collioure and Vendres sheltering traditional high-prowed wooden fishing boats; crowded, shuttered houses reflecting white light and casting black shadow; churches of which the architecture is not quite French, not quite Spanish; and the heat of the air around you, hinting at the proximity of exotic lands across the water.

Argelès-sur-Mer

'The Pyrénées have got a beach!' exclaim the French Tourist Board brochures in slightly less than elegant English, but in a funny way this PR blurb does sum up what Argelès is about. Its environs take in the extreme southern stretch of Mediterranean coastal plain, ending where the Pyrenees fall into the sea. This backdrop of verdant hills contrasting with the flat, white band of sand leading to them must rank as the finest beachscape of the French coast. Three areas make up Argelès-sur-Mer, all linked by a network of narrow roads traversing hectares of pine wood and interspersed with farms. A couple of kilometres inland is Argelès village which is no competition for its 'alter-ego', **Argelès-Plage**. Here, at the central beach, is a smart collection of hotels and apartments bordering on a clean-cut boulevard of palms, pines and gardens. A grid of small avenues makes up the commercial heart of Argelès: a complex of pedestrian precincts lined with bars, restaurants and *glaceries*, fastfood counters and shops selling tourist goods. At weekends a craft market in one of the centre's car parks touts its wares late into the evening. To the north of these two conurbations lie woods and fields divided into 'zones' where most of the camping sites lie. Argelès-sur-Mer possesses more sites than any other resort in France, which may have something to do with the fact that it also experiences the most sunshine hours in the French Mediterranean. Above all, it's ideally positioned for enjoying the benefits of a seaside holiday coupled with sightseeing trips inland.

Arles-sur-Tech

Arles is an old town of narrow streets, with a thirteenth-century abbey. An interesting phenomenon here is the 'Sainte Tombe' a fourth-century sarcophagus which is permanently filled with water from an unknown source. West from here off the D115 is **Gorges de la Fou**, a very narrow gorge that you can walk through: the two cliff faces are sometimes no more than a metre apart.

Banyuls-sur-Mer

A small crescent of white-yellow sand meets the eye as the road turns and descends into this *petite*, refined resort that sits on the southern part of the Côte Vermeille. From Collioure to Cerbère, just before the Spanish border, this stretch of coast is to the western Mediterranean what the Côte d'Azur is to the east – delightful coves between roughly etched cliffs, only here they're not red but granite brown. The promenade following the arc of the beach has a row of canopied terraces that belong to the restaurants across the road. This is briskly crossed in the lunch-hour by a steady stream of tray-carrying waiters. It's not cheap to eat out but good cuisine is served, seafood being the obvious choice. If you prefer a cheap snack, there's always the likes of the Crêperie St Pierre tucked down one of the side streets. Turning inland, the hills of vineyards behind Banyuls are the source of the well-known *vin doux naturel*.

Le Barcarès

This is the most northerly of the Pyrénées-Roussillon beach resorts. Reached from the main routes of the A9/N9 via the D83 or the D627 coast road, both north of Perpignan, Le Barcarès is the holiday village that grew up by the sands. Most of the campsites are to be found in the wooded area to the south. **Port-Barcarès** to the north on the link road is the larger residential area with modern holiday apartments around the marina. It may not be as attractive as Canet-Plage, perhaps (see below), but offers similar distractions with a Marineland, nightclubs and restaurants. An amusing example of the last is the Lydia, a tub of a tramp steamer looking quite surreal sitting high and dry on lawn and tarmac, now a disco-restaurant. One for the family is the Waterpark, an open-air aquapark with huge, snaking waterchutes.

Le Canigou

At precisely 2,784 metres in height, the Pic du Canigou dominates the extreme eastern end of the Pyrenees. The most accessible point is only 600 metres from the summit at the Chalet Hôtel des Cortalets; you can walk to it via the two Grandes Randonnées footpaths (GR10/GR36) or cheat and take one of the jeeps of the regular service from Vernet-les-Bains.

Between this resort and the mountain you'll come across the Abbaye St Martin du Canigou, splendidly perched on its isolated peak. Canigou is impressive and seems to watch every move you make as you tour the small valleys at its base. Like a Monet painting series it changes colour through the day, ending in a soft pink glow as it reflects a setting sun. This is Canigou at its best. At its worst – especially in low season – it can cast a grey, damp spell over the area, deciding to tease with alternating dull electric storms and sudden clearances of cloud. On the night of 23 June, the day of St Jean, fires are lit on its heights and in the villages around, in celebration of Canigou as giver of peace and love to the Catalans.

Canet-Plage

Beach-life by day, night-life by night. Not too far from Perpignan on the D617, Canet-Plage has similarities with Argelès in that it is coupled with an inland town (Canet-en-Roussillon), and has a modern marina, an Olympic-sized pool and fine beaches. Where it differs is in its sophistication and night-life. From the sea Canet appears as one long string of hotels and apartment blocks lining the beach, which is about correct in terms of what the place has to offer. But this architecture is mercifully quite conventional compared to other so-called 'harmonies' of concrete and water as with, for instance, La Grande-Motte (see Hérault). At night in season, the Promenade de la Côte Vermeille comes to life as the seamless stretch of restaurant and bar terraces offers a spectrum of live musical entertainment into the evening. If you've still the energy by midnight, you can dance into the following morning in any one of the town's discos. On the other hand you may attempt to improve on your holiday pocket money playing the tables at the casino. A different sort of enjoyment can be had at the three museums (Toy, Car and Maritime) or the tropical Aquarium. As a diversion from the resort, on the D11 via St Hippolyte to the north-west, is the Château Fort de Salses, a menacing fifteenth-century fortress.

Céret

Céret is associated with the great innovators of twentieth-century art. The Museum of Modern Art houses, among others, works by Picasso, Chagall and Matisse, whose drawings were executed at Collioure (see below). Today Céret still attracts painters and ceramists and the town has a few galleries and shops representing their works. Tucked away off the main D115, it's a picturesque town of squares with huge plane trees cooling the air beneath, little restaurants and chic boutiques. In July bullfights take place in the Corrida, where seats in the shaded part fetch a premium ticket price. At other times the ring acts as a venue for festivities such as Les Sardanes. Back on the main road you'll probably pass three bridges that span the Tech. The oldest dates from the fourteenth century. Also known as Le Pont du Diable, it has a legend similar to the bridge at Cahors in the Dordogne. The engineer who was having trouble completing its span was approached by the devil, who offered to finish the job on the condition that he would be able to have the soul of the first person to cross it at cock crow the following morning. In desperation the man made this deal and that night the devil set to work. In the morning the engineer, full of remorse, persuaded a black cat onto the bridge, and the devil, surprised by this trick, dropped the last brick. A cock crowed in the distance and the cat made off, with the devil giving chase. Where that brick was meant to have gone, no other could be cemented in its place thereafter.

Collioure

No painter – not even Matisse, who is associated with this beautiful harbour – could have composed a more fitting picture representative of this Catalan coast. The cliff ride of the N114 dips down to sea-level, where a small bay has provided shelter for a fishing harbour since time immemorial. The harbour's entrance lies at the foot of a man-made peninsula of stone in the shape of a medieval high-walled fort. It complements Collioure's other building of historical note further round the shore, a no less austere-looking church. This edifice, projecting into a vivid blue sea, terminates in a magical stone tower, once a lighthouse. Its crowning, faded pink cupola suggests a strong Moorish influence. The best view of the whole, other than from the stony town beach in its lee, is the N114's descent to the town from the south. The main problem visiting Collioure (and it's certainly worth the visit) is that if you didn't give up on the dense traffic getting there, you will find parking all but impossible. Like neighbouring Banyuls, Collioure is the home of a local wine, this time a rich and individual red.

Elne

Between Perpignan and Argelès-sur-Mer on the N114 is the small town of Elne, the old religious centre of Roussillon. Its eleventh-century cathedral is a classic example of a Romanesque building, though the cloisters are of a slightly later period. In the first week of September Elne hosts the Catalogna Music Festival.

Grotte les Grandes Canalettes

This *grotte* (discovered in 1951) is south from Villefranche-de-Conflent on the D116 in the direction of Vernet-les-Bains. It contains six chambers, including a lake with 'atolls' formed by limestone deposits, the Sagrada Familia crenellations – so named because of their resemblance to Gaudí's church in Barcelona – and the Balcony of Darkness above the Fathomless Gulf. It's very warm inside and very damp (humidity 90%).

Perpignan

Perpignan is the historical capital of Roussillon, and dates from the time when this part of the world was a Roman province. The city is the embodiment of the region's history, revolving around the constant political friction between the royal houses of France and Spain with the Catalan people caught in the middle. In the thirteenth century James I of Aragon became the first of the three so-called Kings of Majorca, a kingdom which included the Balearic Islands, Roussillon itself and the lands to Montpellier. His spectacular palace stands today as a memorial to his short-lived dynasty. Other historical buildings worth a visit are the Gothic cathedral of St Jean and the Castillet, a fourteenth-century red-brick fort that's now a museum of Catalan culture. In the heart of the city is the Place de la Loge, its cafés full of people taking time out to see and be seen. Near the Loge, the Hôtel de Ville has the distinction of housing a torso by the sculptor Aristide Maillol. Take time to wander in the numerous fascinating old streets, some with façades going back to the fourteenth and fifteenth centuries. The Rues de l'Ange, de la Cloche and d'Or form pedestrian precincts with smart shops.

Port-Vendres

Port-Vendres is a natural deep-water port between Collioure and Banyuls on the N114. In fact, it's three ports in one, with a commercial dock for import and export (fruit from the hinterland further north), a busy fishing port and a small marina for pleasure craft. There are a couple of restaurants on the quay opposite the dock and a beach nearby.

Serrabone Priory

From the N116, take the D618 south of Bouleternère, then the D84. You will have some fine views from this anonymous-looking building, of which the interior is a vivid contrast in 'Meuble Rose', including carvings of angels and mythical animals. (The D618 appears as a tapeworm on the map and is the only complete north-south route midway between the Têt and Tech valleys. The hour you will take to negotiate it will seem like an eternity. Because its southerly stretch between St Marsal and Amélie-les-Bains rigorously follows the repeated contours of hills, you sense constant déjà-vu as you approach what seems to be the same bend leading to the same bridge over the same stream. Good panoramas on its high points, otherwise an 'interesting' driving experience.)

Thuir

South-west of Perpignan on the D612, Thuir is home of the Cusenier company (a subsidiary of the Pernod-Ricard group), which produces aperitifs such as Dubonnet and Cinzano. In the cellars of the Caves Byrrh, amidst 800 vats and casks, is reputed to be the largest oak vat in the world. There are free guided tours around the *caves* with a tasting session at the end. The town itself is an agricultural centre and a walk through its old streets is another pleasant diversion. West from here on the D48 is **Castelnou**, a fortified village on the edge of the hills of Les Aspres, with an eleventh-century château and thirteenth-century ramparts.

Aude

An immediate association with Aude along with its northern neighbour, Hérault, is that of wine. The Languedoc region is a rich source of *vin de pays* and between them these two *départements* produce the majority of it.

The greater part of Aude's hinterland is covered by sometimes rugged, high ranges of hills but never truly mountainous, sometimes *garrigue*, and often vineyard. You can travel through its splendid isolation with a wantonness verging on a 'lost-wish' (like a death-wish, but set on abandoning any hope of finding a main road again). This is serious countryside in the business of making a living off the land. It's for touring, rather than finding a place to stay put. A dearth of camping opportunities in any case puts paid to that.

Places of historical interest, either ruined or intact, seem to grow out of the scenery. Carcassonne is the largest and the finest walled city in Europe. It is approximately 60 kilometres due west of Aude's other city, Narbonne. Joining them are the through routes of the A61 and the N113 but instead of speeding along one of these, we recommend an early start in order to take a lazy tour that tastes a little of the Corbières countryside to the south.

From Narbonne, the D613 leaves the N113 west of the city and the D3 via Lagrasse takes you back on at Trèbes outside Carcassonne. You will pass the ruins of Les Castillets on a hill before your first stop, the **Abbaye de Fontfroide**, an eleventh-century Cistercian abbey (now owned privately but open to the public). Behind the high bell-tower and the abbey walls lie beautifully preserved cloisters of marble-pillared arches, the columns' capitals carrying carvings of real and imaginary beasts.

One of the pleasures of following this route is that it stays on the valley floor so there is little in the way of climbs, though the latter part does have its twists and turns. The halfway point, **Lagrasse**, is a pretty medieval *bourg* sitting by the River Orbieu – both hardly given space by the steep hills on either side – with a Benedictine abbey founded by Charlemagne. Even if you ventured no further than this, you would have had a taste of what the Corbières region hides away in its domain. After that the D3 enters the small gorge of Alsou (Le Sou) and follows this river some of the way before turning north where the land opens out into vineyards, then on through Pradelles and Monze lying below the Alarics, which are the last of the heights before you emerge at Trèbes.

South-west of Carcassonne, where the River Aude emerges from the Corbières heartland, is **Limoux**. This town has given its name to Blanquette de Limoux, a sparkling wine made by the *méthode champenoise* that is older even than champagne. To the north are the *caves* and châteaux of the Minervois which spills over into Hérault. The fort-like village of **Minerve** is perched on a craggy outcrop, separated from the adjacent hills. It can be reached from Mirepeisset on the D10 via the D607/907 (see the introduction to Hérault). Between here and Lézignan-Corbières on the N113, you will find the great Canal du Midi continuing its journey from Toulouse to Agde and the Mediterranean. **Lézignan** is the wine centre of the region. Its modern environs encircle the hub of its old quarter whose church projects a tower above the roofs of the town, much in the same way that a flagpole indicates the centre of a maze.

To the other side of Narbonne towards the coast is an unexpected alien landscape known as **La Clape**. This *'mini-massif'* of rocky promontories, interspersed with wild scrubland, is the product of glacial erosion, and evidence has been found of Neolithic dwellings in the small caves there. Its 'capital' is the village of Armissan, originally the focus of a Roman settlement, the Villa

Artimicianum. The whole is ringed by the vineyards of the La Clape wine, a local contribution to the range of Coteaux de Languedoc. You will probably cross this area on your way to Narbonne-Plage on the D168. This is a fairly unappealing small resort with one main avenue of nothing but eating establishments. The beach is not bad, though, and there's a little funfair further along the promenade road. It's also the Saturday morning venue for the market.

Further south down the coast **Gruissan** and **Gruissan-Plage** are linked by a road crossing the saltlake. The latter may be an uninteresting purpose-built holiday village but Gruissan itself is an attractive fishing village sitting below a pine wood on the stone-walled banks of Etang de Gruissan. Behind its houses on an outcrop of rock stands the round, stone landmark of the old Barberousse Tower, adding a visual piquancy to the scene. Gruissan also produces its own château-bottled Corbières.

A final foray south along the coast will take you to **Leucate** and the wine region of Fitou, a royal red that has graced the court of many a French king.

Carcassonne

Nowhere else in France, or Europe for that matter, can match the spectacle of this immense fortress town. If ever there were a Camelot it surely would have looked like this: a huge edifice of towers, turrets and ramparts composed in a mass of grey stone, watching the surrounding plain from high on a solitary hill. The nineteenth-century novelist Henry James described it as if it were an enormous model placed on a big green table.

The Cité of Carcassonne looks down on Carcassonne Ville Basse, the town that grew up on the opposite bank of the River Aude which divides the two. The arched bridge of the Pont Vieux leads you to the Porte d'Aude, one of two gateways to the citadel (the other, eastern entrance being the Porte Narbonnaise). You'll find that the battlements are made up of an outer and inner wall separated by open grass slopes. The streets inside are crawling with tourists in season but enough atmosphere prevails to give you a sense of the dramatic history that began with the Romans.

The site was a natural point of defence against anyone coming from the west along the only practical route through this juncture of the Massif Central and the Pyrenees. The Visigoths took over at the beginning of the fifth century and were responsible for erecting the inner wall. Carcassonne then enjoyed a prolonged era of peace until 1209 when the Papal crusade against the Albigensians put French against French in the name of God. Simon de Montfort laid siege to the city which fell in a fortnight. Its defences were strengthened in the thirteenth century by Louis XI and later in the Hundred Years War stood up to the Black Prince, Edward, who took out his frustration on the lower town.

What we see of Carcassonne today is the culmination of extensive restoration begun in the 1800s after historians made representations to the national government concerning the then deteriorating state of the place. Viollet-le-Duc was given the task of rebuilding Carcassonne's splendour. And even Henry James, who on the matter of preservation claimed his preference for the ruined to the reconstructed ('the one is history, the other fiction'), was duly impressed with the results.

Narbonne

Narbonne somehow sounds like a grand city but it is much smaller than you might think. It sits on top of (literally) what was once the capital of one of the four Roman provinces of Gaul which covered the whole of the South of France in Augustus Caesar's day. Nothing remains besides the Horreum in the old quarter. This is a section of what was once a vast subterranean storehouse, possibly the basement of a market that stood in the city's trading centre.

You can still appreciate some of Narbonne's historical background in the keep-like Archbishop's Palace and St Just's Cathedral, the latter a fine example of Gothic architecture. Placed together as they are (actually joined by a passage), they sit on the city skyline as one attractive multi-turreted building.

Flowing past them and slicing the town in half is the Canal de la Robine, not the Canal du Midi for which it is sometimes mistaken. That lies to the north, and the Robine is but an offshoot. The wide waterway takes on the guise of a pretty river with the tree-lined Promenade des Barques. The gardens on the opposite bank provide colour and a pleasant place to sit and watch canal boats drift by or moor up. Behind, the narrow streets have been pedestrianised to accommodate pricey little shops, but Narbonne hasn't really got its tourist act together commercially. Much more rewarding is to shop at the large indoor market of Les Halles de Narbonne on the corner of the Boulevard du Dr Ferroul, where all the region's natural produce seems to have been amassed under one roof.

Tourist offices

Comité Départemental du
  Tourisme des Pyrénées-
  Roussillon
Palais Consulaire
Quai de Lattre de Tassigny
66005 Perpignan
Tel 68.34.29.94

Comité Départemental du
  Tourisme de l'Aude
39 boulevard Barbès
11000 Carcassonne
Tel 68.71.30.09

▰▰ Amélie-les-Bains ▰▰▰▰

Hollywood Camping

La Forge-de-Reynès, BP No.3, 66110   tel 68.39.08.61
Amélie-les-Bains

Pretty, tiny site with good facilities for its size

Hollywood is a two-star site whose pleasant aspect high on a hill gives you a panorama of the Chaîne des Albères south of the road. For its size and grade the site comes with a good, modern *sanitaire* which has a combined suite of toilet, washbasin and shower for the wheelchair-bound. There is even a small, shallow pool for a refreshing dip and by the time you read this, it's likely that the owners will have carried out their intention of installing a larger, deeper one. The camp has squared-off *emplacements* with a few trees, but generally it's an open site and, with only 50 pitches, a place where you'll soon get to know your neighbours over a bottle of wine. At the edge of the camp is a large farmhouse where the management run a restaurant as a separate concern. For a fair price you can get good, domestic cuisine. Hollywood is handy for Amélie-les-Bains or for trips into the Tech valley. If you do drive down the D115 towards Arles-sur-Tech, you'll probably pass the two other campsites in this locality and wonder as to their merits. Although both are three-star, they didn't match our expectations. With Hollywood's competitive tariff, we thought you'd enjoy setting up the tent or unhitching the 'van here as the 'high spot' of your tour!

◑ ⑤ ⚲ ⇌ ⧰ ✕ ⵟ ⛵ ⻗ ⊒ ▣

Directions: Amélie-les-Bains is on the D115 west of the arterial north-south A9. As you approach from the east, you will pass under a bridge. Just past this on your left is a filling station and opposite, a large direction sign for the camp. This indicates you take a left by filling station at a wide junction. This made-up road goes uphill, forking to the left and the camp **Ground:** Hard **Children:** Not suitable
Wheelchair: Suitable **Food-cooling:** Ice sold, coolpacks frozen
Sport: Ping pong **Season:** 15 March to 15 Nov
Reservation: Advisable peak season
Charge: 2 people and car 50.50 fr

Argelès-sur-Mer

Sites summary There are 75 officially recognised sites in this 'daddy' of the western Mediterranean resorts, and for such an established holiday centre we found the campsites generally disappointing. An indication of the status quo is that only four sites out of the above number are four-star. For inspection purposes we arrived at a shortlist by picking the sites that had the most to offer in facilities (40 per cent of the total). The majority of better sites lie to the north of the town. Sites in the centre are mostly two-star and as a whole unappealing. But amongst these we did find two that were satisfactory. We also concluded that no campsite really deserved special recommendation. The single inescapable factor that influenced this decision was the presence (albeit not too obvious) of a large number of mobile homes. Because the environs of Argelès cover a large area you should obtain a location map from the local Office de Tourisme, Place de l'Europe, 66700 Argelès-sur-Mer.

L'Arbre Blanc

BP5, 66700 Argelès-sur-Mer	tel 68.81.26.49

Good food at this quiet site, useful for a comfortable touring stop

L'Arbre Blanc is the smallest and quietest of the few four-star sites in Argelès. Neither 'holiday' camp nor mere camping ground, it falls somewhere between the two. As would be expected from an all-year site, it's very well maintained, with plenty of floral decoration and neatly hedged *emplacements* laid to lawn. The small number of well-proportioned pitches follow a roughly circular roadway and are suitable for caravans. Shade is not too easy to find at l'Arbre Blanc and there are one or two other shortcomings. For instance, although not as visually disturbing as at some sites, a few mobile homes are dotted around. The sanitary arrangements could have done with some redecoration at the time of our visit and – for whom it matters – there was not one seated toilet. It is not even a site for the sporty, but its pool is quite inviting. What saved this camp from being dismissed out of hand, apart from its peaceful character and well-kept grounds, was the very good and reasonably priced food from the kitchen. It also provides the same fare for taking away.

🕐 Ⓢ 🏊 ⛴ ✕ ⚲ 👆 🏠 📺

Directions: The N114 south-east of Perpignan leads to Argelès. After passing through Elne, a straight run of road leads to crossroads. Take the central filter to turn left for Taxo (one of many 'zones' comprising Argelès). Further down you will come across a discreet entrance just off the road on your left **Ground:** Giving **Children:** Playground **Wheelchair:** Not suitable **Food-cooling:** Ice sold **Sport:** Volleyball **Season:** All year **Reservation:** Advisable peak season **Charge:** 2 people, pitch and car 75 fr

Camping de Pujol

Route de la Plage Nord,   tel 68.81.00.25
66700 Argelès-sur-Mer

Small, friendly site that is ideal for water-lovers

Situated in the rural zone of Pujol, the camping ground is in a natural wood and contains good-sized pitches laid to grass. Those towards the front are very well shaded, and the mobile homes are partially obscured by trees. As the homes are managed by an English operator there may be other British campers present. Perhaps the main attraction at this site is the small but unique pool complex behind the little bar and *crêperie*. Surrounded by a manicured lawn, with strategically placed palms, is a stepped series of three rectangular pools. Each pool is of a different depth and the highest is constantly overflowing into one of the lower ones, to form a thin sheet of a waterfall. The managerial approach is a personal one and although soirées are organised the general stamp of Pujol is one of a quiet time. Finally, you have the advantage of a reasonably short drive to the beaches and town centre.

🌓 Ⓢ 🧍 ⛴ 🛒 ✕ ⚲ 👆 🐾 🏠 📺 🔑

Directions: As for Les Piscines but continue further down the road to roundabout where you will find exit. The entrance is on this road, on your right **Ground:** Giving **Children:** Playground, swimming, organised events **Wheelchair:** Suitable **Food-cooling:** Ice sold

Sport: Volleyball, ping pong **Season:** 1 June to Sept
Reservation: Advisable peak season **Charge:** 2 people, pitch, car 72 fr

La Chapelle

Avenue du Tech, 66702 Argelès-sur-Mer   tel 68.81.28.14

Peace and cool shade, though not much else on this pleasant enough town-centre site

This is one of our two sites right in the heart of town (see Les Ombrages). Like its counterpart, it's set far enough from the main road to diminish any traffic noise. It's a fairly basic camping ground in terms of amenities, but of course its central location, with access to a supermarket and the main beach, makes any such provision redundant. There's also a pizza van and a *dépôt de pain* for your breakfast needs. The site has an extremely shady plot and high hedges screen off well-proportioned pitches on level ground. It's visually attractive and the atmosphere is typically French – very relaxed. If you wish to make a comparison with Les Ombrages, here are one or two considerations. La Chapelle is more tranquil and its *sanitaires* do have individual *lavabos* (but no pedestal toilets). It's also more expensive but this is the premium you pay for more shade and a little more seclusion. Les Ombrages may be more suited to younger campers.

Directions: Entering Argelès from the north, on the main road, there is a 'chicane' arrangement to regulate traffic speed. At the end of this you will see a block of flats, away from the road, on your right. Just after this, as the road bends to the left, you will see the camp entrance clearly signed (set back off the road, on your right) **Ground:** Giving **Children:** Playground **Wheelchair:** Not suitable **Food-cooling:** Ice sold, coolpacks frozen **Sport:** Volleyball, ping pong **Season:** 15 June to Sept **Reservation:** Advisable peak season **Charge:** 2 people, pitch and car 74 fr

A unique sand filtering process is used at Argelès-sur-Mer to keep beaches clean. The local health department also takes weekly samples of sea-water to check its purity. This vigilance has in the past won Argelès the European Community's award for clean beaches.

Les Criques de Porteils

Route de Collioure,   tel 68.81.12.73
66701 Argelès-sur-Mer

A refreshing change from resort plages. There are spectacular views from this cliffhanger site. A useful base for exploring the rugged coastline

Set on top of the rugged cliffs between Argelès and Collioure, Les Criques has a very enviable location for a campsite. With the Pyrenees behind you and the Mediterranean sea in front, these heights give you a stupendous panorama of Argelès and its broad bar of yellow-white sand stretching northwards to the horizon. The driveway from the entrance takes you past a little general store selling beach goods and groceries, and a simple café/restaurant where the meals are of the fastfood variety with a few *plats cuisinés*. This area overlooks terraces of pitches gently stepping down to the cliff edge. Not all of Les Criques is coastal-facing. A back part of the camp looks out towards the road and the vineyards of the Albères. A little shade can be picked up in these grassy 'compounds' of half-a-dozen pitches, each in an area of taller trees, more than can be said of the front area. Moreover, you don't have the feeling of being on top of your neighbour here. The little coves strongly resemble a Cornish scene with their dark, scattered rocks and pebble beaches. Criques de Porteils provides few diversions. Access to the beaches is by way of steep, stone staircases that almost enter the water and for this reason parents of very young children may not find the site 'user-friendly'.

🌓 Ⓜ ⚓ ⚮ 🐟 ✕ ♀ 🍴 ⛺ 🍳 📷

Directions: The N114 heads towards the coast south-east of Argelès-sur-Mer on the way to Collioure. Where the road draws level with the railway track (overhead wires just visible behind bank), you will see a road sign for camping directing you to turn right. This takes you past the Hôtel du Golfe around and back under main road and rail, then up to the cliff-top and camp (tall flags can be seen before you reach the site) **Ground:** Giving **Children:** Playground, not suitable for toddlers **Wheelchair:** Suitable **Food-cooling:** Fridge hire **Sport:** None **Season:** Easter to Sept **Reservation:** Advisable peak season **Charge:** Pitch 25 fr; person 22 fr; child (under 7) half-price; electricity 15 fr

L'Étoile d'Or

Route de Taxo-d'Avall, 66701 Argelès-sur-Mer	tel 68.81.04.34

Functional, typically French camp with shade, quiet and a pleasant pool area

A provincial French atmosphere characterises l'Etoile's entrance where, outside the reception building with its wrought-iron balcony holding an array of potted plants, a row of tables and parasols give the impression of a village café. Adjacent is the camp's self-service shop, offering a selection of fresh meat and groceries as well as a choice of local wines and fruit. There may be some British campers here enjoying what is predominantly a French family site, with its splendid long, rectangular pool and kiddies' pool providing enough room for splashing around. Or perhaps you'd prefer to sunbathe on the surrounding paved terrace of coloured brick. A few palms add more greenery to the mass of hedging and treetops of the camping ground behind. Various paths lead into a very shady glade of conifers and pines, affording seclusion to the marked *emplacements* beneath. On the whole l'Étoile is an example of the relaxed, casual French approach to camping, steering clear of the frenetic 'go-go' type holiday scene. A word about why the rubric says 'tricky' for handicapped people: at the entrance to the *sanitaire*, an awkward-looking ramp leading to an implausibly narrow doorway has a tight ascending curve and a high lip at ground level.

Directions: Take the N114 south-east of Perpignan towards Argelès. After passing through Elne, a straight run of road leads to a crossroads where you take the central filter to turn left for Taxo (one of the many 'zones' comprising Argelès). Follow the road down to the first right turn and the camp is just after you turn off **Ground:** Giving
Children: Playground, swimming **Wheelchair:** Tricky
Food-cooling: Ice sold **Sport:** Tennis, volleyball, ping pong, football, mini-golf **Season:** All year **Reservation:** Advisable peak season
Charge: Pitch 25 fr; person 23 fr

*Nowadays service is included in most restaurant prices (*service compris*) or sometimes quoted as a percentage on menus, so unless you're feeling particularly generous, a tip is unnecessary.*

Front de Mer

Route de Racou, 66701 Argelès-sur-Mer   tel 68.81.08.70

Immaculate facilities are just one of the attractions at this cool and shady two-star site that is close to the action

Just west of the town centre but close enough for the beach and shops, Front de Mer has many advantages over its rivals of a similar grade, the complete modernisation of its *sanitaires* being the most notable. Row upon row of tall trees almost completely arch the avenues leading into the camping ground, making this one of the best sites for cool and shady pitches in the town. The pitches are not too generous in size and as there's little in the way of screening between them, you do get a picture of tents and 'vans filling the place. Back at the entrance a collection of little hut-like buildings comprises a bar/*crêperie*, decked out in check tablecloths, a grocery shop and a beach bazaar. Added to this, a doctor visits the site six mornings a week.

● Ⓛ 🧍 🐾 ✕ ♀ 🤿 𝄔 ⛺ ▣

Directions: From the roundabout in the heart of the commercial centre in Argelès (between two car parks), go south towards the port and you will come across a second roundabout. Go straight across and immediately after is a right-hand turn. This takes you over a little bridge and the camp is on your right **Ground:** Hard to giving
Children: Playground **Wheelchair:** Not suitable **Food-cooling:** Ice sold **Sport:** Ping pong **Season:** Easter to end-Sept
Reservation: Advisable peak season **Charge:** 2 people, pitch and car 61.40 fr; extra adult 14.70 fr; electricity 14.70 fr

Le Neptune

Plage Nord, Argelès-sur-Mer   tel 68.81.02.98

Tastefully-designed buildings and a manicured appearance at this refined three-star site, but no swimming-pool

One would expect that the blatant maritime reference in the camp's name must mean that Le Neptune is right on the beach, but in fact this quiet, unassuming camp is set apart from the sea and the town. It has a very tidy, attractive setting. Generously proportioned grass *emplacements* and rows of tall, clipped hedges resemble those of a good municipal site. Neptune's ground plan is circular, with concentric rings of roads and sweeping arcs of hedges. Trees are planted in the style of a small park, but they cast little shadow, making the camp exposed to the sun. Good amenities include the pleasant *sanitaires* that continue the circular theme in their layout, and are decorated with mosaics of a sea god. There is a full *à la carte* restaurant but no shop, although the commercial centre is a few minutes' drive away. The only drawback to this site is the lack of a swimming-pool, only a wonderful, twisting water-chute. This omission may not encourage parents with children, but there were some families present when the site was inspected.

Directions: Assuming you are heading south on the D81 towards Argelès, you will see a built-up area ahead. After passing a small funfair on right, turn right at the road junction with traffic lights. Follow to the camp entrance, which is on your right **Ground:** Giving
Children: Playground **Wheelchair:** Not suitable **Food-cooling:** Ice sold **Sport:** None **Season:** Easter to end-Sept
Reservation: Advisable peak season **Charge:** 2 people, pitch and car 83 fr; extra adult 22 fr; child (under 2) 12 fr; electricity 16 fr

Les Ombrages

Centre-Plage, 66700 Argelès-sur-Mer	Out-of-season tel 68.81.13.55
	tel 68.81.29.83

Reasonably priced if rather basic site, but ideal central position for the beach, restaurants and shops

The second of our sites in the heart of town, three-star Les Ombrages is peculiarly placed as, in order to gain access, you have to cross another site that sits between it and the main road. One advantage of this position is that you have a 'buffer' as far as traffic noise is concerned. As the camp name suggests, a fair amount of soothing shade is in evidence. Resident rabbits lope about in the rear section of the camping ground: surprising for such a built-up area. They seem not to mind people, and campers equally ignore them. At least they keep the grass down in the camp's adequate, uniform pitches. The kiddies' area, also grass-based, has decent play equipment under the shade of tall trees and is completely fenced off from the site roadway.

Sanitaires are all in good order, although there are no individual *lavabos*. Take-away food and drink only is available, simply because shops, a supermarket and a multitude of eating places are just a short walk down the road. Les Ombrages is not really a 'holiday camp', but being reasonably priced is ideal if you want to be next door to the central beach and its accompanying commerce.

● Ⓜ 𝝣 🦺 🥾 🦮 🏠 ▣ ⚲

Directions: In the centre of Argelès is a roundabout between the two main car parks. This is in effect an exaggerated T-junction. Turn off the north-south road in the direction of Argelès village. Just before a bridge over a river is a right-hand turn where there is the camp's sign. Drive through the first site you enter to reach Les Ombrages
Ground: Giving **Children:** Playground **Wheelchair:** Suitable
Food-cooling: Fridge hire **Sport:** Tennis, volleyball, ping pong, mini-golf **Season:** 1 June to Sept **Reservation:** Advisable peak season
Charge: 2 people, pitch and car 62 fr; extra adult 17 fr; electricity 13 fr

Les Piscines

Route de Taxo, 66702 Argelès-sur-Mer   tel 68.81.06.38

A relaxed French atmosphere characterises this peaceful, rural retreat

When you arrive at the modest reception of this camp, you could be excused for thinking you were booking into a small, Gallic hotel. A varnished counter stands before an old-fashioned, winding staircase, and the bar next door smacks of provincial austerity. But walk through its patio door and a pleasant surprise awaits you. Right outside is a terrace of palms bordering the curved edge of a swimming-pool, set like a miniature lake in a woodland clearing. Les Piscines is situated in Argelès' northernmost 'zone' called Taxo, a quiet, rural mix of pines and farmland. This is reflected in Les Piscines' own environment of a peaceful, cool wood next to a vineyard. The large *emplacements*, although looking rather worn, are set in a grid of avenues running through the trees and separated by hedges. A few pitches, right at the back of the site, have an open aspect towards the Pyrenees. Not a lot goes on here, though the bar takes on the air of an animated social club in the evenings. Les Piscines is primarily a simple sanctuary to roll back to and kick off your espadrilles after a long day out.

● Ⓜ 🏄 🏊 🛒 ✕ 🍽 ☕ 🚿 🛒 🧺 💻 🖊

Directions: Take the N114 south-east of Perpignan to Argelès-sur-Mer. After passing through Elne, a straight run of road leads to a crossroads where you take the central filter to turn off for Taxo. Turn first right for Plage Nord and Pujol and eventually along this road you will come across the site entrance on your right **Ground:** Giving **Children:** Playground, swimming **Wheelchair:** Not suitable **Food-cooling:** Ice sold, coolpacks frozen **Sport:** Tennis, volleyball, ping pong, pool-table **Season:** Easter to Sept **Reservation:** Advisable peak season **Charge:** 2 people, pitch and car 70 fr; extra adult 18 fr; electricity 12 to 16 fr

Le Roussillonais

Boulevard de la Mer, 66702 Argelès-sur-Mer

tel 68.81.10.42

Compact and busy, but the above average amenities are well organised at this attractive beach site

This roughly square site sits by part of the fine stretch of sands found at this resort of resorts. The outlying pitches are quite exposed so the pine glade that surrounds the camp's epicentre may be preferable, although you shouldn't expect to be anything other than packed-in, cheek-by-jowl, as is usual for a site of this nature. At the end of the afternoon a calm descends as the cooking smells rise from burners and barbecues. The general impression is that no one is really disturbing anyone else. You can take your 'van or camper right down to the dunes where there is no respite from the hot sun, but in just three steps you can spread your towel on the sand or run into the sea – the north beach is populated mainly with the camp's sun-worshippers. A well-thought-out central complex comprises a triangle of three single-storey buildings with a cultivated patio in the middle. You can shop for fresh meat and fish, shaded by a canopy of extended roofs. Next door, a well-stocked supermarket and a grocer sell local produce. Also in the complex are a launderette, snack-bar, beach shop and a bar with pool-table. Sanitary arrangements are adequate, with a few seated toilets, though individual *lavabos* are not in all blocks. For its size – 700 *emplacements* – Le Roussillonnais' efficient square ground plan doesn't impose lengthy walks from one end, so you don't actually feel you are on a large site. As a bonus, the beach police, based next door in season, teach campers aged between 13 and 21 water-skiing, windsurfing and even horse-riding.

🌙 ⓛ 🧍 🛍 🛒 ✗ ♀ ☕ 🐾 ⛺ 🍴 🖨 ℘ 🎵

Directions: Approaching Argelès from the north on the D81, you will arrive at a roundabout just as the area begins to be built-up. Take the third exit. There's a camp direction sign here. At the bottom turn left at the T-junction (another direction sign). This road is a cul-de-sac that leads directly to the site **Ground:** Giving and sandy
Children: Playground **Wheelchair:** Suitable **Food-cooling:** Ice sold **Sport:** Volleyball, ping pong, wind-surfing, water-skiing
Season: Easter to 15 Oct **Reservation:** Advisable peak season
Charge: Pitch 24.80 fr; person 20 fr; child (under 3) 9.80 fr; electricity 13 fr

⑦ *La Sirène*

Route de Taxo, 66702 Argelès-sur-Mer   tel 68.81.04.61

Self-contained entertainment for all the family at this large four-star site

Two buxom mermaids on a huge entrance billboard entice you into La Sirène, which is nothing less than a self-contained holiday village. At the front you come across the busy commercial centre with an array of shops, from a supermarket to a newsagent. Here, too, is an open terrace with a *glacerie, crêperie* and large restaurant. Outside the bar is a sunken, circular area by a purpose-built stage with spotlights for the night's entertainments. The whole impression is that you're already at the seaside and all you need is the candy floss. In fact, with all these amenities, you needn't go into Argelès itself. You might even wish not to see the beach for two weeks, what with the attractive complex of two pools plus smaller paddling pools surrounded by grass for sunbathing. Walking into the camping grounds past the car port for washing your car, you'll find hedged *emplacements* arranged on an orderly grid system of small roads. It's not too packed down these avenues but a lot of pitches are reserved for the various package operators that favour the site. La Sirène offers nearly everything that a family on holiday would expect of a four-star establishment. The only drawback is its sheer size. You have a sprawl of a holiday village containing nearly 800 pitches, a lot of them given over to static mobile homes. Also, you could be in for long walks if you happen to be based at the opposite end to the amenities.

● ⓛ 🛉 ⛵ 🧺 ✕ ♟ 🌭 🐟 ⛺ 🗄 📼 ⚙ ♫

Directions: Take the N114 south-east of Perpignan to Argelès-sur-Mer. After passing through Elne, a straight run of road leads to a crossroads where you will take the central filter to turn left for Taxo. Follow this road all the way, past a crossroads with 'Magic Park' Recreations on your right and the entrance is ahead on your right **Ground:** Giving **Children:** Playground, swimming, organised events **Wheelchair:** Suitable **Food-cooling:** Ice sold **Sport:** Tennis, volleyball, mini-golf, windsurfing, archery, BMX track **Season:** Easter to Sept **Reservation:** Advisable peak season **Charge:** 3 people, pitch and car 140 fr

⑦ *Le Soleil*

Plage Nord, 66702 Argelès-sur-Mer   tel 68.81.14.48

Large, rambling site with private beach catering for all the family

Le Soleil is a reasonable four-star site with its own private beach the main attraction. A quick tour of the camp will start at the shady entrance with a little shop and general store by the reception. Further into the camping ground the *emplacements* seem to be a bit on top of one another – more random in their distribution beachside, more regimented the further into the trees you go. Generally, Le Soleil is not a neat-looking site, but the light woodland provides a fair amount of shade. The nearer the beach you are, the busier the atmosphere with pitches straining to contain cars, tents and even trailers with sea-going inflatables. The beach has areas for volleyball and mini-golf and there are nightly beach parties at the bar-discothèque. But, as with La Sirène, you will also find that the large spread of ground means a trek from the beach to the near-forlorn pitches stuck out at the back. The one compensation about being in this part of the site is the proximity to the new pool complex by the children's wooden fort and playground. All members of the family are catered for by a management that, for the size of the business, does try to maintain a visible profile in customer relations. Some sites of similar size provide a better, more practical environment: compare with Le Roussillonnais.

● Ⓛ 𝑡 ⌂ ⚓ ⚑ ✗ ♀ ☞ ☀ 🎋 ♨ ▣ 𝒫 ♫

Directions: Approaching Argelès on the D81 from the north, take the left-hand turn just after the town's name-board. When you turn you will see a direction sign for the camp. Follow the road all the way round the bend, where Le Soleil sits by the sea **Ground:** Giving
Children: Playground, swimming **Wheelchair:** Suitable
Food-cooling: Ice sold, coolpacks frozen **Sport:** Tennis, volleyball, ping pong, football **Season:** 15 May to 30 Sept
Reservation: Advisable peak season **Charge:** Pitch 45 fr; person 27 fr; electricity 15 fr

Taxo-les-Pins

Route Taxo d'Avail, 66702 Argelès-sur-Mer   tel 68.81.06.05

Relaxed and shady out-of-town camp with basic facilities. Good for a reasonably priced short stay

This is the most northerly of our Argelès sites, a short drive away from the town centre but not too distant from the Plage Nord. Because of its size and location, Taxo is a less hectic place than larger camps or those nearer town. Set by an open field with the Pyrenees in the background, the site maintains a busy but relaxed air. The centre of attention is the pleasant swimming-pool bordered by trees and potted plants. Opposite is the little restaurant with a gravel terrace under some shady pines. A cool, natural wood surrounds the inevitable mobile homes, *emplacements* of varying sizes and *sanitaires* with quite modern fittings. All in all, Taxo les Pins offers you basic comforts at a reasonable price, out of town. Perhaps suited for the short stay rather than a prolonged holiday but some may find it worth lingering a while.

● Ⓢ 𝑡 ⌂ ⚑ ✗ ♀ ☞ 🎋 ▣ ✀ 𝒫

Directions: Take the N114 south-east of Perpignan to Argelès. After passing through Elne, a straight run of road leads to a crossroads where you take the central filter to turn left for Taxo (one of the many 'zones' comprising Argelès). Pass camp direction sign on right further down. Follow road round slight bend and site entrance will appear on left

Ground: Giving **Children:** Playground **Wheelchair:** Not suitable
Food-cooling: Ice sold **Sport:** Tennis, volleyball, ping pong, football,
bike-hire **Season:** 15 Feb to 15 Nov **Reservation:** Advisable peak
season **Charge:** Pitch 32 fr; person 22 fr; child (under 4) 11 fr; pitch
with electricity 50 fr

■■■■ Le Barcarès ■■■■■■■■■■■■■■■■■

Directions for sites Le Barcarès is a resort stretched out
along a road parallel to the shore and comprises Port
Barcarès and Le Village. Assuming you have turned off
the D83, you will first go south through the port to arrive
at a roundabout. Go straight across and continue down
the long avenue with globe street-lamps lining its right-
hand side. This is Route de St Laurent, along which the
majority of the resort's camps are located. Below we list
our choice of five out of the ten in this area. The
directions for each site pick up from the avenue described
above. All site entrances are easily identifiable by large
name-signs.

Sites summary All but one site chosen are three-star
and, all things considered, we felt that no camp stood out
from the rest. *Floride* and *Paris* are typically 'French' sites,
with less stylish buildings, though sanitary arrangements
are quite acceptable and they do have some shade. The
best pool/restaurant setting must be at *Pré Catalan*. The
Oasis is a good runner-up to the other sites, and is the
cheapest. The *California* has a good atmosphere and
swimming-pool, but lacks shade and a full restaurant.

La California

Route de St Laurent, 66420 Le Barcarès   tel 68.86.16.08

*Well-organised but relaxed site, with lively evening
atmosphere. Good appointments all round*

Le California is an attractive place and has a regular British
clientele. A water-slide is positioned near the entrance, along
with a wine shop and pizza stall, all to the fore of the reception.
As you pass the main gate, through the row of conifers, you can

glimpse a very blue, large rectangular pool set by a terrace that has straw umbrellas befitting a Pacific atoll. Next to the pool, a low, red-tiled building houses the self-service snack-bar. This whole area takes on a completely different character at night, with the spotlit pool reflecting campers enjoying food and drink under a vast, star-clustered sky. As for the camping ground itself, there are good-sized grass *emplacements* secluded by tall hedging but there's not much shade. The decorative *sanitaires*, with modern appointments, are well-maintained and what there are in the way of mobile homes are kept right at the back.

☾ Ⓢ 🧍 🛶 🛒 ♀ 👍 ⚡ 🏔 🎣 📖 🎾 ♫

Directions: Follow the main avenue as described for campsites in Le Barcarès. After the right-hand bend, the site will eventually appear on your right **Ground:** Giving **Children:** Playground, swimming, organised events **Wheelchair:** Suitable **Food-cooling:** Ice sold **Sport:** Tennis, volleyball, ping pong, bike-hire, archery **Season:** Easter to Sept **Reservation:** Advisable peak season **Charge:** 2 people, pitch and car 79 fr; extra adult 22 fr; child (under 7) 12 fr; electricity 13 fr

Le Floride/L'Embouchure

66423 Le Barcarès   tel 68.86.11.75

A shady, wooded environment helps hide the fact that this is a busy beach resort camp. A good three-star, typically French site

These two campsites either side of the main road are under the same management. Le Floride holds the reception and amenities and l'Embouchure is no more than an annexe with access to the beaches. Le Floride's wide, tree-lined entrance terminates at a large house with clay tiles and shutters, the ground floor of which is taken up with the reception and bar. Across the way is the camp's self-service shop and directly opposite, screened by trees, is a long, narrow pool that has a big waterchute at one end. The paved, poolside terrace is decorated with small palms and shrubs. Further into the site very high conifer hedges shelter generous, if worn, *emplacements*. These are reached by shady paths that lead off the main gravel road. The density of the trees here masks the presence of other tents and caravans to a great extent. In the clearings within the wood are the 'tropical' *sanitaires*, so called because the low, white buildings with arched entrances are fronted with a bed of large, ornamental palms. To continue the horticultural theme, each has been given the name of a plant. Inside, they are tiled and generally in good shape. Over the road, l'Embouchure is a duplicate environment. Looking even more worn in appearance, its mature, rambling hedges and stringy conifers at least give a feeling of camping in a natural wood rather than a resort site. It is indeed very quiet on this side and has the additional option of *emplacements* with individual *sanitaires*.

● Ⓜ ⚲ ⩰ ⚶ ⚑ ♀ ⛟ �ₐ ⊟ ▣

Directions: This is the first camp on the avenue described in the general directions for Le Barcarès. Turn right for Le Floride which houses the main reception **Ground:** Giving **Children:** Organised events **Wheelchair:** Not suitable **Food-cooling:** Ice sold **Sport:** Volleyball, ping pong, bike-hire **Season:** Easter to Sept **Reservation:** Advisable peak season **Charge:** 2 people, pitch and car 80 fr; extra adult 20 fr; electricity 14 to 18 fr

L'Oasis

66423 Le Barcarès   tel 68.86.12.43

Reasonably priced, adequately maintained site, exposed to the sun. Friendly management organise plenty in the evenings

Appropriately for a place of this name, the main feature of the Oasis is the comparatively new pool complex comprising a main pool, a water-slide and a separate kiddies' pool. But also like its namesake, the site is almost completely exposed to the burning sun, as the few trees around don't provide any umbrella of shade. A gravel drive takes you through the small camping ground with its marked *emplacements* of various sizes, some hedged with dwarf conifers. Sanitary arrangements (which don't include seated toilets, by the way) are basic but satisfactory. There's lots of evening entertainment at the poolside self-service restaurant and bar with terrace. The approachable and informal management arrange anything from puppet shows to visiting cabaret. The Oasis is a friendly little spot that, while not perhaps as sophisticated as some its colleagues, is quite suitable for a short stay which doesn't find you digging deep in your pockets.

○ Ⓢ ⚲ ⟿ ⚊ ⚑ Ⓨ ⚐ ⋔ ⚘ ♫

Directions: The avenue bends to the right and then straightens. You will see the camp entrance on the right **Ground:** Giving **Children:** Swimming **Wheelchair:** Suitable **Food-cooling:** Ice sold **Sport:** Tennis, volleyball, ping pong **Season:** Easter to 1 Oct **Reservation:** Advisable peak season **Charge:** 2 people, pitch and car 69 fr; extra adult 17 fr; child (under 4) 10 fr; electricity 11 fr

Le Paris

66420 Le Barcarès   tel 68.86.15.50

A small and homely four-star site offering an attractive environment and good facilities

The large mock-up of the Arc de Triomphe that greets you at this campsite's entrance is more an attempt at humour rather than any pretentious connection with the capital city, for this Paris is a homely place, small, but full of *bonhomie* encouraged

you can even hire a jeep for the day

by the friendly owner and his mother, a cheery old lady. In the main, it is a tidy, orderly site providing hedge-lined *emplacements* either side of shady avenues. These adequately-sized pitches are less secluded than at Le Floride but just as cool and the general impression is of a more open and attractive site, with its clipped and shaped conifers. The pleasant *sanitaires* are in very good decorative order throughout, and include large individual shower cubicles combined with washbasins. By the arch are the pool, bar/restaurant and grocery shop. Disco evenings are organised along with the usual entertainment for a mixed clientele of young couples and families. You can even hire a jeep or motor-trike for the day, if you feel so inclined.

● ⑤ ⚲ ⚱ ✕ ⚲ ☛ ⚱ ▣ ⚘ ♫

Directions: Further along the avenue, as described in the general directions for sites at Le Barcarès, the camp is on the left where the road bends **Ground:** Giving **Children:** Swimming, organised events **Wheelchair:** Not suitable **Food-cooling:** Ice sold **Sport:** Tennis, volleyball, horse-riding **Season:** Easter to Sept **Reservation:** Advisable peak season **Charge:** 2 people, pitch and car 120 fr; extra adult 20 fr; electricity 15 fr

Le Pré Catalan

66420 Le Barcarès   tel 68.86.12.60

Attractive, animated site with good facilities

The accent here is very much on family entertainment as there's plenty of organised activity and facilities are good. Situated a 15-minute walk from the beach, Le Pré Catalan is a smart-looking place and the main attraction of the site has to be the wonderful setting of the pool. This is alongside a large, modern, villa-style building that wouldn't look out of place on the Côte d'Azur. Outside steps take you on to the balcony terrace by the restaurant. Leaning over the 'lattice' clay-tile wall, you can gaze down at the pool or the delightful surrounding garden planted out with palms and shrubbery. The camping ground is no less attractive, with flowering shrubs along the gravel road that takes you round *emplacements* laid to grass. These are marked by conifer trees and it has to be said that there isn't a lot of shade about in general. *Sanitaires* are in good order and pleasantly cool, with individual curtained *lavabos.* A large percentage of the site houses discreetly positioned mobile homes and caravans. This means that space is at a premium for the independent camper and the obvious advice is to book very early. An alternative is to reserve one of their own 'package' tents which come with all camping facilities.

● Ⓜ 🧍 🛌 🧺 ✕ ⚑ 🍴 🌿 🏠 🚽 🔲 🔧 🎵

Directions: After the right-hand bend in the avenue described, take the first right. You will see a sign directing you: the entrance is visible ahead as you proceed down the road **Ground:** Hard to giving **Children:** Playground, swimming, organised events **Wheelchair:** Suitable **Food-cooling:** Ice sold **Sport:** Tennis, ping pong, bike-hire **Season:** Easter to Sept **Reservation:** Advisable peak season **Charge:** 2 people, pitch and car 89 fr

▬▬ Le Boulou ▬▬▬▬▬▬▬▬

Val Roma Park

Les Thermes du Boulou, 66400 Maureillas   tel 68.83.19.72

Well-placed for exploring the region, this small site has an air of civilised relaxation

Run by a young French couple, this small, four-star site is basically a clearing in a wood. Despite its position to one side of the main road any noise is somewhat diminished by the trees. A floral entrance drive will take you to a shady little bar with a grass terrace. The bar is also the entrance to a small grill/restaurant, minimal in decoration but sublime in its interior of quarry-tiled floor under a beamed ceiling. Next door is the walled swimming-pool. Spacious grass pitches are screened by high hedges and are quite suitable for a 'van or camper. The one large, very well cared-for *sanitaire* has arched portals leading into an open grass courtyard, with covered appointments. We were told by a British couple about the little old lady who, in full song at six every morning, cleaned the loos. This is about as much disturbance as you'll get at Val Roma because, although soirées are held a couple of evenings a week in season, it is not a brash campsite. You're aware of people at play either at tennis or in the pool, but all with an air of calm and relaxation. The camp is well placed for exploring the Tech valley and the hills of

Haut Vallespir, or perhaps a day trip to the seaside at Argelès-sur-Mer. Considering you're only 7 kilometres from the border, even a visit to Spain is a possibility. The nearby town of Le Boulou is adequate for shopping but there are few eating places.

🌓 ⓢ 🕴 🚣 ⛴ ✕ ⚍ 👞 ✿ 🎪 ⌐ 🔲 ⚲

Directions: The N9 heads south out of Le Boulou, signposted in the direction of Barcelona. After going through traffic lights you will pass a casino on your left (the real thing, not a supermarket). A little further on Val Roma's entrance will be seen on your right, with tall flag poles visible **Ground:** Giving **Children:** Playground, swimming **Wheelchair:** Suitable **Food-cooling:** Ice sold **Sport:** Tennis, volleyball, ping pong **Season:** 15 May to 15 Oct **Reservation:** Advisable peak season **Charge:** Pitch 32 fr; person 23 fr; child (under 7) half-price; electricity 11.50 fr

▰▰ Canet-Plage ▰▰▰

✣ *Le Brasilia*

66141 Canet-Plage   tel 68.80.23.82

Large, popular site with a private beach and plenty of family entertainment. A good mix of fun with decorum

'Viva Brasilia' and 'Viva Holiday Time' exclaims the brochure at a campsite that has all the trappings of a holiday village. Past the reception and off the roadway, is a wide precinct in a neat, landscaped corner containing a *boucherie*, *boulangerie*, grocery and *tabac*. Adjoining is the restaurant of the bar and cafeteria: light, spacious and with contemporary décor in cool, neutral tones. Its floor space doubles as a disco in the evenings. Round the corner is a huge pool in the shape of a keyhole, with plenty of terrace space for sunbathing on the loungers provided. Le Brasilia's main attractions are that it has a private strip of silver sands and, unlike many other beach sites, it possesses a generous piece of shady woodland. In the centre, you will find the larger, more formal *emplacements* made attractive by their lawn bases and hedges giving some seclusion. In contrast, the pitches on the seaward side are smaller and more exposed. Although a big, popular site, Le Brasilia proves that such places can be pleasant, too. It somehow manages to appear smaller than its actual size, and thus more comfortable. One reason for this might be the ground plan. Pitch areas are either side of the main avenue leading from the entrance, which means that amenities and activities are accessible from all parts of the site. The attractive grounds are divided into different pitch areas which help to avoid the visual monotony sometimes experienced on larger sites. There are plenty of night-time distractions, of course, and if you keep the kids in pocket you probably won't see them for the best part of the evening: they'll be occupied with the games-room, which is nothing less than an amusement arcade that would do any seaside resort proud!

● ① 𝍌 ⛵ ⚓ 🛒 ✗ ♀ ☞ ☘ ♒ ⊟ ✂ ♫

Directions: The D617 leads from Perpignan (and the A9) to Canet-Plage. After the flyover at the large roundabout east of Canet-en-Roussillon get in left-hand lane at next roundabout to take second exit where you remain in left-hand lane to turn left at a statue. Stay in left-hand lane and at T-junction turn left off main road. Along this narrow road turn first right at bus-shelter. Camp directions signs are here. Go straight on at the next roundabout and continue to the site
Ground: Giving **Children:** Playground, swimming, amusement arcade **Wheelchair:** Suitable **Food-cooling:** Ice sold, coolpacks frozen, fridge hire **Sport:** Tennis, volleyball, ping pong, football, bike and sailboard-hire **Season:** 1 April to 31 Oct **Reservation:** Advisable peak season **Charge:** 2 people, pitch and car 80 fr; child (over 3) or extra adult 20 fr; electricity 13 fr

Les Peupliers

66141 Canet-en-Roussillon   tel 68.80.35.87

Basic and modest, this site is quiet and cool

If you want to stay around Canet and prefer a more subdued environment than is offered at Le Brasilia, then this site is the best alternative. Like Le Brasilia, this is also classed as a three-star site but here you have a modest, walled swimming-pool and in the centre of the tidy camping ground, a small shop and simple restaurant. The *sanitaires* are adequate in function and maintenance but the *lavabos* are communal only. The main asset of the site is that it is extremely shady and cool, being set in wood. Peaceful, secluded *emplacements* are bounded by tall hedges. It's a good 'second place' when compared with Canet's two other sites. They are both situated in the town on the port side amidst blocks of flats.

● ⓢ 🏊 ⛴ 🛒 🍴 🍷 👜 🏠 📮 🎣

Directions: As for Brasilia, and the camp entrance is found on your left along the last stretch of road beyond the last roundabout
Ground: Giving **Children:** Playground **Wheelchair:** Suitable
Food-cooling: Ice sold **Sport:** Tennis, ping pong, mini-golf
Season: 1 June to 30 Sept **Reservation:** Advisable peak season
Charge: Pitch 30 fr; person 20 fr; child (under 3) 10 fr; electricity 13 fr

▰▰▰ Canet-en-Roussillon ▰▰▰
Ma Prairie

66140 Canet-en-Roussillon   tel 68.80.24.70

Convivial, family campsite in quiet rural surroundings

There is more or less everything here to fulfil your holiday needs. Monsieur le Patron appreciates the value of personal contact, and gives the impression that he certainly enjoys his role. What makes him popular with his annual British clients is his ability to converse readily in English. It's what we could describe as a 'best-of-both-worlds' stay at Canet. At the end of a hot day on the sands of Canet-Plage, a five-minute drive will take you back to your shady pitch in the countryside and a refreshing splash in the pool. This, along with a plush bar lounge (the disco at night), lies on one side of the road to the camp while on the other is the main camping ground. The slight inconvenience in having to cross over to these amenities is outweighed by the fact that all the family-orientated entertainment, such as a masked ball or jazz soirée, is segregated from the peaceful, woodland setting of the pitches. On this side is to be found a small shop and the restaurant which also provides take-aways. Prices are reasonable for a four-star site. The *sanitaires* on our visit were a bit overdue for redecoration but otherwise they functioned satisfactorily. To conclude – and this must be a plus in any camp's books – the management pledge that *all* amenities are up and running from the first day of opening in May, not just for the high season.

● Ⓜ 🏊 ⛴ 🛒 🍴 🍷 👜 🐟 🏠 📮 📻 🎣 🎵

While tariffs for one-star and two-star sites are fixed by the département, *three-star and four-star sites are individually priced according to their owners' discretion, so discrepancies naturally arise between them in any given area.*

Directions: The D617 leads to Canet from Perpignan (and the A9). On a stretch of dual-carriageway, exit left down a slope signposted for Canet Village at a main interchange. At bottom turn right at T-junction under the flyover. Then first right round a bend and the entrance is visible on your right. Alternatively, if coming south down the D81, take the second exit at the roundabout on to the D617 heading west. Then come off again at the next interchange and left at T-junction under flyover **Ground:** Giving **Children:** Swimming, organised events **Wheelchair:** Suitable **Food-cooling:** Ice sold, coolpacks frozen **Sport:** Tennis, volleyball, ping pong, pooltable, sauna and Jacuzzi **Season:** 1 May to 30 Sept **Reservation:** Advisable peak season **Charge:** 2 people, pitch and car 98 fr; extra adult 26 fr; child (under 7) 14 fr; electricity 16 to 20 fr

▬ Céret ▬

Les Bruyères

Route de Céret, 66400 Maureillas   tel 68.83.20.62

Peaceful site with basic facilities and some pleasant hill-top views

Les Bruyères is a hill site that looks north across the Tech valley near the main Céret-Maureillas road. The driveway from the reception and bar leads up a gentle gradient to the rows of *emplacements* either side, nestling amongst small trees. Although the pitches (180 in all) are exposed to the sun you do have pleasant views, for the site covers a wide area of hill-top and the drive, illuminated at night, takes you across the top and around the side before you eventually return to the entrance. It's here that you're most likely to meet, as we did, Madame swinging in her string hammock cradling her portable phone – a favourite but functional toy of campsite management. Not quite Mme Defarge with her knitting, she does inspect you, not in judging whether you're Royalist or Revolutionary but if you're suitable material for her camp. Everything in this tranquil environment is a simple statement of taking time off. The minimal bar which also serves your *plats cuisinés* has some outside seating in case you prefer not to take food away. The swimming-pool is no more than a square of water set in level ground and the majority of *emplacements* are basic areas of ground that haven't undergone any fastidious planting-out. The reception hut stocks a small supply of bread, wine, fresh fruit and vegetables delivered from the farm. The site's thoroughly modern *sanitaires* are in good condition. Les Bruyères is a peaceful stay, perhaps more of a touring stop, but some may consider it pricey for what's on offer. The village of Maureillas is a bit of a backwater with a couple of shops and a bank. Céret will be your venue for purchases and eating out.

🕐 Ⓢ 🛵 🏊 🐟 🍷 🍖 🎋 ♿ 🔲

Directions: Leave Céret on the D618 to Maureillas. You will come across a big green sign on your right, warning you of the camp's proximity. Further on, just after the second green sign, the site entrance is on your right **Ground:** Hard **Children:** Playground **Wheelchair:** Suitable **Food-cooling:** Ice sold, coolpacks frozen **Sport:** Ping pong **Season:** Easter to 15 Oct **Reservation:** Advisable peak season **Charge:** Pitch 29.50 fr; person 19.50 fr; child (under 7) 14 fr; electricity 15 to 21 fr

Swinging in her string hammock cradling her portable phone

Les Cerisiers

Mas de la Toure, 66400 Céret   tel 68.87.00.08

Peaceful seclusion on this small, pretty, fruit farm. No catering facilities but not too far from shops and restaurants

Les Cerisiers is nothing more than a small, serene camping ground set in an orchard grove. One main track leads through a grass area with open *emplacements* in rows under the low trees. The site is part of a working fruit farm with the management residing in the large traditional *mas* (or farmhouse) by the camp. The wide gravel drive by the house is lined with colourful flowers, shrubs and an old cart stuffed full of potted plants. The little *sanitaire* to one side is pleasantly tiled and well kept. The nature of Les Cerisiers is manifest in the notice which reminds campers that the site is closed between 10 pm and 7 am, in emphatically large letters: 'SILENCE S.V.P.'. Naturally, the farm produce is for sale here (tasty peaches), along with local honey and wine. The joy of the place is that its utter seclusion is pleasingly deceptive as Céret is only three minutes' drive away, with shops, restaurants and a big Intermarché.

Directions: Leave Céret on the D168 east to Maureillas, passing the municipal site on your right. Go straight across at small roundabout. Beyond you will see, set back from the road, a big yellow sign with flags telling you to turn here for camp (a tight left-hand fork doubling back). This road winds its way to a fork where another big yellow sign advises you to turn left. This road bends to the right by a little track on your left and takes you down a straight lane, with conifers to the left, and camp on the right. Follow straight down to the farmhouse for the entrance
Ground: Giving   **Children:** Playground   **Wheelchair:** Not suitable
Food-cooling: Ice sold, coolpacks frozen   **Sport:** Ping pong
Season: All year   **Reservation:** Advisable peak season   **Charge:** Pitch 18 fr; person 9.80 fr; child (3-7) 5 fr; electricity 6.50 fr

A good alternative to a rigid plastic container for keeping a water supply at the pitch is a pliable 'sac'. This is a plastic bag of heavy-duty material finished at either end with a wooden rod to help keep its shape and with a stop-cock at the bottom of one side. It can be strung up from the nearest branch and, when travelling, has the advantage of packing flat.

Corsavy

Bellavista

Route de Batère, 66150 Corsavy   tel 68.39.17.55

The only one-star site in the book, this is a camp for the adventurous and is in magnificent mountain scenery

After the drive up into the glorious desolation of the hills hereabouts, you might be wondering what to expect at Bellavista. The site is nothing but a tiny, grass plateau in the centre of the mountain ridges that tail off from the mighty Pic du Canigou. You have virtually a 360-degree panorama of this splendid Pyrenean scene. You can easily imagine that you're cut off from mankind, while remembering that there's a proper made-up road giving you an easy, short drive back to the nearest town. This is a one-star location and expectations should be adjusted accordingly. Even so, Bellavista offers a small pool for a swim, and hot water in the showers. The one *sanitaire*, well looked after, also houses a couple of seated toilets and half-a-dozen washbasins. The grassy camping ground has a raised hillock in the middle with a few grey boulders as suitable geographical props and the whole is made attractive by small, planted conifers. In the centre of the site is a small building housing a tiny bar and kitchen. This last is a facility for campers wishing to prepare their own meals and might be especially useful for organised parties. Corsavy, the nearby village, has a restaurant, an *auberge*, post office, *boulangerie* and *épicerie*, and Arles-sur-Tech is in the valley below. So, if you fancy something outside the mainstream selection of sites, pack your walking boots and head for the hills!

Directions: Corsavy lies west of Arles-sur-Tech. To reach it, leave Arles on the D115 west towards Prats-de-Mollo. After going over red and white striped 'sleeping policemen', there is a fork to the right for Corsavy. This is the D43. Follow right through the village to where it turns sharp right at junction with the D44. There you will see a green sign on the left warning you the camp is 300 metres. Site entrance will then be seen on right **Ground:** Giving **Children:** Not suitable **Wheelchair:** Suitable **Food-cooling:** Ice sold **Sport:** None **Season:** 1 May to Oct **Reservation:** Advisable peak season **Charge:** Pitch 15 fr; person 15 fr

▰▰▰ Laroque-des-Albères ▰▰▰

Sites summary *Des Albères* (two-star) has a good family atmosphere and is the only site with a restaurant (for snacks) and a bar. The camp is reasonably shady with an attractive flowers. *Les Micocouliers* (three-star) is the most typically French of the three camps, and also offers the most shade and privacy in its large pitches. A shop and take-away are the only provisions in the catering line. *Les Planes* (two-star) is the smallest of the three sites and the least shady. There's a communal atmosphere in the open pitches but no regular supply of food or drink. You may enjoy its secluded position and good views.

❁ *Camping des Albères*

66740 Laroque-des-Albères	tel 68.89.23.64

Enjoy the quiet life at this very attractive two-star camp. A caring management makes you welcome

From your arrival at Camping des Albères you can see that it is an attractive place. As you follow the gentle ascent of a made-up road, you pass an upper terrace in the trees where the hill steepens. This is but part of a variety of surroundings that Albères can offer – across the way is a flatter, more open area with a wide vista of the Chaîne des Albères. This is a pleasing backdrop for the grass *emplacements* decorated with flowers. Further on, a dense copse accommodates small, secluded pitches for tents. Ever present is a proliferation of plant forms, from colourful flowers to giant succulents. These even adorn a *sanitaire*, the tiled interior of which is kept in very good condition. In the centre of the site, two glorious circular pools, one for children – set in a wide, paved terrace – gleam under the sun against a background of verdant foothills. Opposite the pools is the bar/restaurant with its cool, tiled interior. The management here is concerned to preserve what they feel is the essential character of the place – tranquillity as a natural complement to the beauty of the surrounding countryside. At the same time the regime is relaxed enough to allow a family atmosphere to flourish. It isn't an easy balance to achieve but by their personal attention and their effort to maintain a regular

101

clientele, Albères does persuade you that the pleasures of
simple camping are not to be dismissed.

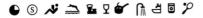

Directions: Laroque lies just south-west of Sorède on the D11. As you
leave Sorède you will pass village car park on your left. Immediately
after take the first left. Further along this road you will see a camp
direction sign at the first right. You will eventually find camp entrance
on this road on your left **Ground:** Hard **Children:** Playground,
swimming **Wheelchair:** Not suitable **Food-cooling:** Ice sold,
coolpacks frozen **Sport:** Tennis, volleyball, ping pong **Season:** 1 April
to 30 Sept **Reservation:** Advisable peak season **Charge:** Pitch 14 fr;
person 13 fr; vehicle 5 fr; child (under 3) 5 fr; electricity 11 fr

Les Micocouliers

66690 Sorède   tel 68.89.20.27

A cool, shady retreat, ideal for a peaceful stop-over

The shady glade with a few tents and a ramshackle sort of
reception that greet you when you arrive at Les Micocouliers
give a false impression of the actual size of the site. A formal
row of large *emplacements* divided by thick hedges line one side
of the drive that leads further into the quiet, dark, wood. Right
at the back, rows of *emplacements* sit snugly under the tree
cover. This is the sort of place where you can shut yourself off at
the end of the day's driving exploring the Tech valley and
experience nothing but an evening silence broken by birdsong
or the low conversation of other campers: Les Micocouliers is a
tourer's retreat. Basic comforts include a swimming-pool, a
little shop for breakfast fare, camping gas etc., and *sanitaires*
with individual cubicles of combined *douche* and *lavabos*. The
village of Sorède possesses a couple of bars and cafés, a
boulangerie, pharmacy and doctor. In the centre of the village is
the fourteenth-century Catalan château known as the Castrum
de Sureda.

Directions: The D11 runs south off the D618 between Argelès-sur-
Mer and Le Boulou. As you approach Sorède village the road forks,
with the D11 going left. Just after bearing left here, you will see the
camp entrance on your left **Ground:** Giving **Children:** Playground,
swimming **Wheelchair:** Not suitable **Food-cooling:** Ice sold,

coolpacks frozen **Sport:** Ping pong **Season:** 15 June to Sept
Reservation: Advisable peak season **Charge:** Pitch 37 fr; person 15 fr;
child (under 5) 10 fr; electricity 11 fr

Les Planes

Route de Villelongue-dels-Monts, 66740   tel 68.89.21.36
Laroque-des-Albères

Splendid isolation at this basic but characterful site

Beyond the card-operated, automatic barrier at the entrance to
Les Planes you will find the meaning of the word 'seclusion'.
This small plot of land rests peacefully amidst the meadows of
the southernmost part of the plain before the Pyrenees. In the
light shade of oak and mimosa, shallow stepped terraces of
dried grass and stone are the platforms for level *emplacements* of
a size that will accommodate a caravan. The pool, set in its tiled
sunbathing terrace, is the focal point of what becomes in season
a small commune of campers sharing an experience of – dare
we say it – spiritual calm. Sharing one another's company is
encouraged by your congenial host, a man who's as placid as
Les Planes itself. He will on occasion take those interested for a
day out walking in the foothills, and at times lay on the odd *plat
cuisiné*. With such arresting scenery in an island of calm, the
well-maintained *sanitaires* and the personal attention of the
management, Les Planes is an illustration of an exceptional
two-star environment. Self-catering is essential here, but there
are shops and a restaurant at Laroque and at nearby St Génis-
de-Fontaines.

Directions: The D11 heads west out of Laroque towards Villelongue-
dels-Monts. Along the way, you will round a right-hand bend to see a
400-metre warning sign for the camp. The next sign on your right
indicates the left-hand turn for the camp entrance **Ground:** Hard
Children: Not suitable **Wheelchair:** Not suitable **Food-cooling:** Ice
sold, coolpacks frozen **Sport:** Volleyball, ping pong **Season:** 15 June
to 31 Aug **Reservation:** Advisable peak season **Charge:** Pitch 20 fr;
person 16 fr; vehicle 10 fr; electricity 10 fr

*Make a beeline for the Syndicat d'Initiative in your nearest town. This will
supply you with all your sightseeing information as well as the latest on
exhibitions, festivals, etc. Many Syndicats recruit English-speaking staff.*

▰▰▰ Lézignan-Corbières ▰▰▰
Municipal La Pinède

RN113, 11200 Lézignan-Corbières   tel 68.27.05.08

Neat and tidy halt to break up a journey

La Pinède is a useful site for a break in a touring journey. As with most French municipal campsites attached to a large town, you will find the upkeep of the grounds to be of an above-average standard. However, this particular example is not as pretty as some, but gains high marks for effort. La Pinède occupies a low hill by the N113 and from the top you look over busy Lézignan. Gravel-surfaced roadways take you up here to little cul-de-sacs of level pitches. Throughout the camping ground these are hard-standing and are marked in the familiar municipal fashion with hedging. Sanitary arrangements are not de luxe by any means but are adequate. For a quieter stay you might prefer to establish camp a short climb up the hill. This will put some distance between you and the amenities just outside the camp entrance, which consist of the popular town pool, a disco and restaurant.

◑ ⑤ 🏃 🛶 🐖 ♀ 🏠 🍴

Directions: The N113 Carcassonne-Narbonne road skirts the town to the north. Here the entrance to the site lies by the main road (access to municipal pool). There are tall flag-poles here. For camp, turn left after passing pool and car park **Ground:** Hard **Children:** Not suitable **Wheelchair:** Not suitable **Food-cooling:** Ice sold **Sport:** Tennis **Season:** 1 April to 15 Oct **Reservation:** Advisable peak season **Charge:** Pitch 13 fr; person 13 fr; child (under 7) 8 fr; electricity 11.50 fr

▰▰▰ Mirepeisset ▰▰▰
Val de Cesse

Mirepeisset, 11120 Ginestas   tel 68.46.14.94

Peaceful river location. A useful stop-over on the Carcassonne to Béziers route

An island of lavender greets you at this very peaceful, well-maintained site which we took to be the local municipal. The site is a useful little place to know about if you're touring and is a comparatively cheap stay. A small gravel drive leads through an attractive, quite open camp with pitches marked off by hedges and landscaped with a few trees and flowerbeds. There is a general feeling of seclusion here as you are off the road and at the edge of the village. It is a fairly basic camping ground with a couple of small *sanitaires* with only three wash-basins apiece. Along one side, behind a raised bank and wire fence, is the River Cesse. This river reveals itself in the little adjacent park (with kiddies' playground) and makes a pleasant waterside setting for a small restaurant and terrace. There are a couple of shops and another restaurant in tiny Mirepeisset, but not too far away you can visit Sallèses-d'Aude, an appealing village on the Canal de la Robine. A terrace of pastel-painted, period houses by the waterway give a peculiar Dutch feel to the scene.

Directions: Mirepeisset lies to the south of the D5 due west of Capestang. Approaching from the east, take a left turn signposted for the village. Follow to T-junction and turn left. Road takes you over the road and round the back of the village. At a point where the road bears left, you will take a right which will lead to the camp. There are clear direction signs on this route. Alternatively, if coming from the west, turn right on the D607 (St Marcel-sur-Aude) then left for Mirepeisset on the D326, where you will pick up the last junction mentioned above. **Ground:** Giving **Children:** Playground **Wheelchair:** Not suitable **Food-cooling:** Ice sold, coolpacks frozen **Sport:** None **Season:** All year **Reservation:** Advisable peak season **Charge:** Pitch 11.50 fr; person 10 fr; child (2-7) 5.50 fr; electricity 9.50 to 16 fr

Narbonne

Le Languedoc

Chemin de Creissel, Avenue de la Mer,   tel 68.65.24.65
11100 Narbonne

Not a place for holiday revelries but a convenient three-star site for nearby town or beaches

Le Languedoc's position outside Narbonne, close to an autoroute toll point, not too far from the beach and next door to a hypermarket, makes it an ideal halt if touring. The owner, who converses in slightly broken English, keeps things tidy and efficient. There's a strict regime: gates close at 10 pm so the camp is quiet internally, but remember you are near the main road, so expect noise from that vicinity. An exposed area of gravelly *emplacements* with wild flowers and some conifer hedging forms the camping ground. The one large *sanitaire* is utilitarian yet clean, and off-season one half is sealed and heated. Back at the entrance is a bar and snack-bar for crêpes and take-aways. Its extended gantry roof gives ample shade to the open-air seating. Also there is the benefit of a small, shallow pool, enough for you to wade in and perhaps refresh yourself after a day on Narbonne-Plage, some 12 kilometres from here. As this site gets booked up quickly from mid-season onwards, it might be best to book ahead. Otherwise, there's always the chance of an overnight stay 'on spec', but phone ahead.

Directions: Take the Narbonne-East exit from the A9. There you will approach a T-junction where you can turn left for Narbonne centre. Cross over roundabout with pseudo-Greek column. On dual-carriageway, you will see on left a piece of modern architecture with more columns, called Le Parc des Expositions. Using filter, turn left here and then proceed down left-hand side of Montfleur hypermarket. The camp entrance is to be found a little further down this road
Ground: Hard **Children:** Not suitable **Wheelchair:** Suitable
Food-cooling: Ice sold, coolpacks frozen **Sport:** None **Season:** All year **Reservation:** Advisable peak season **Charge:** Pitch 26 fr; person 15 fr; child (under 7) 8 fr; electricity 12 fr

▬▬ Narbonne-Plage ▬▬▬▬▬▬

Municipal La Falaise

11100 Narbonne-Plage   tel 68.49.80.77

Spacious site – the best in the area if you want to stay near the beaches

A good example of a four-star municipal, this fairly large site (as far as municipals go) covers a ground area in the shape of a distorted circle. The main avenues take you round uniform, hard-standing *emplacements* squared off by hedges. These pitches give enough space for your 'van and for putting out the table and chairs. There is a feeling of space here and with its greenery La Falaise is not at all unattractive. An abundance of low trees breaks up the scene so you are not that aware of a mass of campers surrounding you. *Sanitaire* blocks are not modern but nevertheless are solid buildings in sound order. In the centre of the camp are the playground and snack bar/restaurant for take-aways. The general impression of La Falaise is one of a quiet canvas village in an amiable setting. A disappointing oversight for a four-star site is the absence of facilities for the handicapped.

🌙 Ⓜ 🏄 🏋 ✕ ♀ 🍴 🏮 ♻ 📷

Directions: The D168 leads to Narbonne-Plage from Narbonne. Just after a right-hand bend before the road enters the main part of town, you will see the camp on your left (with tall flagpoles) **Ground:** Hard **Children:** Not suitable **Wheelchair:** Not suitable **Food-cooling:** Ice sold, coolpacks frozen **Sport:** None **Season:** 1 April to Sept **Reservation:** Advisable peak season **Charge:** 2 people, pitch and car 52 fr; pitch with electricity 70 fr; extra adult 18 fr; child (under 7) 8 fr

▰▰▰ Palau-del-Vidre ▰▰▰▰▰▰

☀ *Le Haras*

66690 Palau-del-Vidre   tel 68.22.14.50

Serene retreat at this idyllic little camp, not too far from the coast

This small camp seems to be the original gardens of the fetching house, standing discreetly by the short driveway to the grounds. It's also the residence of the management who run Le Haras as a permanent site. It is superbly landscaped with large areas of lawn where the *emplacements* are arranged. A plus here is that the garden's nooks and enclaves prevent an arrangement of rows of tents and caravans. You are kept comfortably cool by the willows, conifers and pines that provide local patches of shade: a welcome relief in the overpowering heat of the afternoon sun. The *sanitaires* are worth a mention not so much for their good condition as their architecture. They are constructed on angled cantilever beams, which support a tiled roof hung over the whole of the block, and this contemporary design seems to work so well with its natural setting. Past the house and behind a hedge you'll find a modest pool bordered by ornamental shrubs and cacti. Adjacent is a small, open bar where in the evening, you might be entertained by a folk singer while eating a pizza cooked *au feu du bois*. The camp is not far from the main resort of Argelès-sur-Mer, and what better when returning from a day on a crowded beach to be greeted by the fresh greenery, attractive pool and the tranquillity of this small haven.

Directions: The D11 turns west from the N114 north of Argelès-sur-Mer, near where that road crosses the River Tech. This is the route to Palau-del-Vidre and Le Haras is situated on the very edge of the village as you approach, with its entrance on your left **Ground:** Giving **Children:** Organised events **Wheelchair:** Suitable **Food-cooling:** Ice sold **Sport:** Volleyball, ping pong, horse-riding **Season:** All year **Reservation:** Advisable peak season **Charge:** Pitch 31.20 fr; person 16.30 fr; child (under 7) 11 fr; electricity 12 to 19 fr

Prades

Camping Bellevue

Plateau de Sirach, 66500 Ria Out-of-season tel 68.96.10.62
tel 68.96.48.96

Pleasant hill-side two-star offering plenty of shade and good views. Awkward road for towing

Bellevue is high on a hill looking down on the Tet Valley and from some of the perimeter *emplacements* you get a 120-degree panorama of Prades in the distance, the river and road running along the valley floor, and the village of Ria lying under the steep sides of the Pla de Balençou. It's very peaceful and very shady up here with nearly every pitch having some protection from the sun. Bellevue wraps itself round this hillside, its steeply descending terraces following the contours. Access for those using wheelchairs could be tricky, although there is the provision of a sanitary suite of shower, washbasin and toilet. Most of the terrain isn't level, save for near the entrance where pitches are marked with small hedges. There aren't really any amenities to hand at Bellevue. In the reception building there's a little white-walled 'lounge' decorated with farm implements hanging under a beamed ceiling. It is furnished with old upholstered seating around quaint tables made from split tree trunks. Although there are no take-aways on site, Madame La Patronne will be pleased to phone your order through to one of the local take-aways back down on the main road, and once a week the paella lady visits in her van. Alternatively, there is a supermarket between here and Prades. But the view and the calm are the reasons for being here at all. And if it is of any influence on your decision, Bellevue has received its eighth 'Prix National' for floral campsites.

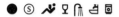

Directions: Going west from Prades on the N116 towards the commune of Ria and Sirach, you will find a left-hand turn by an Elf petrol station, which is the D26A to Sirach. Cross over automatic rail-crossing, and road begins to snake uphill (camp direction sign here). Go straight through village, taking right at top (another sign). Take right-hand fork at next junction (another sign) for camp **Ground:** Hard to giving **Children:** Not suitable **Wheelchair:** Tricky **Food-cooling:** Ice sold **Sport:** Ping pong **Season:** 1 April to 15 Oct **Reservation:** Advisable peak season **Charge:** Pitch 15 fr; person 13.50 fr; child (under 7) 8 fr; electricity 11 fr

Sahorre

Le Rotja

66820 Fuilla tel 68.96.52.75

A near-perfect setting for this smart, very quiet two-star site set deep in the countryside

Le Rotja is named after a trout-filled stream that courses through a green and sunny valley, where the scattering of homes here is known as the Commune de Fuilla. If you come at the right time of year, you could pluck an apple or two off one of the trees on this site which are a spillover from the orchard next door – for you are in the middle of fruit-growing territory. Such things reinforce the idea of a country garden in the middle of lush greenery set against the horizon of Canigou's hills. A gravel track leads round lawned *emplacements*, hedged for seclusion. Everywhere is spick and span. The clean little *sanitaire* contains three washbasins and toilets. The only other building is the bungalow housing a reception, where a few tables and chairs are set outside. There is no bar as such but you may have the occasion to sit and chat to the charming elderly

Patron over a glass of wine. The village of Sahorre has a café, a couple of restaurants, a butcher's and baker's and a small shop. To hand, by the car park where you turn off for this site, is a general store with a snack-bar/café and there's always the fortress town of Villefranche on the N116 for major provisions.

Directions: Just west of Villefranche-de-Conflent, on the N116, is a left turn before a river-bridge. This is the D6 to Sahorre. But before reaching the village, you travel through scattered buildings of the Commune de Fuilla. You will come across a small parking area on your left with a callbox and pink-walled church ahead on the opposite side. Between these is the right-hand turn for the camp **Ground:** Hard **Children:** Not suitable **Wheelchair:** Suitable **Food-cooling:** Ice sold **Sport:** None **Season:** 1 June to end-Sept **Reservation:** Advisable peak season **Charge:** Pitch 12 fr; person 10.50 fr; child (under 7) 7 fr; electricity 9.50 fr

▬▬ St Jean-Pla-de-Corts ▬▬

Les Casteillets

66400 St Jean-Pla-de-Corts   tel 68.83.26.83

Good, reasonably-priced facilities are on offer at this green, open camp

The situation of Les Casteillets couldn't be better for you take in the Canigou *massif* and the verdant expanse of the Albères. These two sweeping mountain ranges lie at the edge of the plain that holds a final cluster of French villages before the border. This site has been specifically designed in a 'dartboard' pattern – a circular ground with concentric roads and *emplacements* in the spaces between, radiating outwards. Some of the pitches are divided by hedges but in the main it's an open, flat ground with little shade. However, this very openness does give you a feeling of space. Les Casteillets maintains a rural calm and yet is not short of amenities. Its two-star grading belies the fact that you are offered a swimming-pool with a children's pool, a grocery store, tennis courts and a snack restaurant with bar. The *sanitaires* are modern, comprising the standard modular fittings. Because the camp is open all the year, there is a higher than average degree of site maintenance and for the price you would be hard pressed to find as suitable an equivalent in the immediate vicinity.

❶ ⑤ 〽 ➷ ⚑ ✕ ♀ ☛ 🎋 ⊟ ▣ 🔑 ♫

Directions: Heading east on the D115, there is an open stretch of road which then contains a short dual carriageway with a central filter for turning right, before St Jean-Pla-de-Corts. Take this and go across small intersecting roads (you will see a camp direction sign). Road begins to descend into woodland and just after you come out of dip, the site will be on your right **Ground:** Hard to giving **Children:** Playground, swimming **Wheelchair:** Suitable **Food-cooling:** Ice sold **Sport:** Tennis, volleyball, ping pong, giant chess **Season:** All year **Reservation:** Advisable peak season **Charge:** 2 people, pitch and car 59 fr; child 9.50 fr; electricity 12.50 fr

Les Deux Rivières

66400 St-Jean-Pla-de-Corts   tel 68.83.23.20

Sedate riverside site in natural woodland

One of two rivers here, the Tech, flows to one side of this camp, and its wild bank and wide, fast-flowing waters over smooth boulders set the scene for this location. The uncultivated woodland pitches are laid out among the trees with only the vaguest delineation. As it is light woodland as opposed to dense thicket, you don't get as much shade about as you might imagine. There is a certain 'scrubbiness' to this environment but this is part and parcel of its undisturbed setting. Sanitary arrangements are good: showers are in a satisfactory state of decoration, and the semi-individual *lavabos* are partitioned and have curtains rather than doors. Back through the wood, near the entrance, is a stretch of open ground with the camp's swimming-pool. At the house, just up the gravel road from it, is the reception: nothing else, mind you – not even a bar! But you can be served a *plat cuisiné* by one of the two old dears who keep things going here (a cheerful double-act) and who run a *dépôt de pain* in the mornings. You can also get them to drum up a cup of coffee now and then. Local wines, fruit and fresh vegetables, ice-cream and gas cylinders are available too. For stocking-up, St Jean has a *boucherie*, a chemist and a garage. On the main D115 heading towards Céret is a large supermarket and, of course, there's Céret itself. We would venture to suggest that this sedate site (there are no soirées or *animations*) would make a pleasant touring stop rather than a prolonged holiday stay, but you may think that Deux Rivières has as much to offer in its own individual way as the made-for-camping Casteillets above.

Directions: St Jean-Pla-de-Corts lies just south of the D115 on the D13, between Le Boulou and Céret. Turn off the D115 opposite the railway sidings, by a pharmacy. As you skirt houses, you will see a blue and white sign directing you to the camp. After crossing a long bridge over the river, the site entrance is immediately to your left (set back from the road), identifiable by a yellow and red signboard
Ground: Giving **Children:** Playground, swimming
Wheelchair: Suitable **Food-cooling:** Ice sold, coolpacks frozen
Sport: Volleyball, ping pong, football, mini-golf **Season:** 1 June to Sept **Reservation:** Advisable peak season **Charge:** Pitch 18fr; person 22fr; child (under 7) 11 fr; electricity 12 fr

St Laurent-de-Cerdans

Municipal Verte Rive

66260 St Laurent-de-Cerdans	Out-of-season tel 69.39.50.06 tel 68.39.54.64

Pleasantly green, basic municipal site in the heart of the Pyrenean foothills. Off the beaten track, this is a good spot for walkers

A long and winding road eventually leads to St Laurent-de-Cerdans, in the middle of some marvellous mountain scenery. St Laurent's municipal site is a small camp in a grassy clearing near the local stadium. Verte Rive has an uninspiring entrance by a couple of shed-like buildings, but once behind these you find a different story. The attractive roofs and church tower of the village, just visible over high treetops, vie for attention with the rugged cliffs of the Albères. A lot of the pitches are arranged in groups of four. Other individual pitches are found among the trees in the miniature parkland. Facilities include a small snack-bar and *dépôt de pain* and a single *sanitaire*. This is a basic blockhouse affair but it does possess some seated toilets and is in reasonable condition. Although the site is rather basic, the area is definitely one in which to spend some time. In the summer, this small community high in the beautiful Pyrenean landscape generates a whole tourist industry. There are enough events (many free) to occupy a week's stay at least: folk evenings, a craft centre, Catalan theatre and a selection of guided walks are just a few events on offer. For more information, contact the Bureau Municipal, Animation and Tourism, Rue Joseph Nivet, 66260 St Laurent-de-Cerdans.

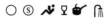

Directions: The D3 winds its way south of the main D115, turning off west of Arles-sur-Tech. Just before you come to the village proper, there is a small fork to the right (camp direction sign here). This dips down to some buildings which you pass and turn round the corner at their end, to find the site entrance **Ground:** Giving
Children: Playground **Wheelchair:** Not suitable **Food-cooling:** Ice sold, coolpacks frozen **Sport:** None **Season:** 1 July to 15 Sept
Reservation: Advisable peak season **Charge:** Pitch 9 fr; person 9 fr; per vehicle 3.80 fr; child (under 7) 5.50 fr; electricity 11.60 fr

▬▬▬ Ste Marie-la-Mer ▬▬▬▬

Le Lamparo

66740 Ste Marie-la-Mer   tel 68.80.64.77

Attractive, open site is a greener and quieter alternative to staying near the beaches

A wide, gravelled courtyard entrance leads you into a refreshingly green site, which is especially welcome if you're just returning from a day on one of the nearby beaches. The whole camping ground is one level area of grass traversed by the main driveway. Inside the camp gate is the reception and bar, the terrace of which looks on to the tennis court. Across the courtyard is a shop and on the white wall of the same building, a large spoon and fork sign signals that round the corner is Le Grilleton, the camp's restaurant, where pine tables are laid out under the roof's canopy. The open aspect of trees and lawn is not too diminished when full of caravans and tents, but there is no seclusion as the *emplacements* are separated simply by rubber ropes strung between the strategically placed trees. The proximity of one's neighbours doesn't seem to detract from the quiet and relaxed atmosphere, though, and if there is a minus here it's possibly noise from the road to one side. The site is close to a good north-south route, has the space for 'vans or campers and is near Ste Marie for the sea. Le Lamparo is ideal for a touring stop but we shouldn't wonder if the friendly management might persuade you to tarry longer.

○ ⑤ 🏊 🛒 ✕ ♀ 🏠 ▣ 🌙

Directions: Come off west side of large intersection on D81, east of Ste-Marie. Go straight across roundabout, heading into village. Then first left just after the village name sign. Camp entrance is on your right, just as road bends left **Ground:** Giving **Children:** Playground **Wheelchair:** Suitable **Food-cooling:** Ice sold, coolpacks frozen **Sport:** Tennis **Season:** 1 June to Sept **Reservation:** Advisable peak season **Charge:** Pitch 35 fr; person 15 fr; child (under 7) 7.50 fr; electricity 10 fr

Le Palais de la Mer

66470 Ste Marie-La-Mer Plage   tel 68.73.07.94

Modest, unpretentious site that offers a little more than most three-star surroundings

The neat shop with its cool, white interior at the understated entrance to Le Palais, is a hint that this may be a little bit more than your average three-star site. What you discover round the corner of the reception confirms this opinion for here is the focal point of the camp in the form of an elliptical pool screened by a wall of latticed open tile-work. This pleasing terrace is bounded on three sides by the single-storey red-roofed buildings of the restaurant and bar. The whole takes on a clubhouse scene by day, with bathers and barflies, and in the evening, becomes an inviting setting for a meal with friends. Le Palais is a small campsite covering a rough triangle of ground near Ste Marie's beaches. It has large pitches marked off with shrubs and trees dotted around but there is a sparsity of foliage which means little shade. Sanitary fittings and fixtures are sound. The family who run Le Palais take pride in their establishment and try to cater for all ages. Behind the bar is a discothèque for those whose energy hasn't been dissipated by a day at the beach. There is direct access to the beach via a path at the back of the camp which follows the curve of the canal, but it's a lengthy walk under a merciless sun. The alternative is to drive round to the sands at the end of the main road.

�
● ⑤ 🧍 🚣 🛶 🛒 ✕ ♀ 🍴 🦞 🏠 ▣ ♫

Directions: The D12 north-east of Perpignan is the route to Ste Marie-Plage. After a small roundabout, continue down road towards the beach. A little way down is a left-hand turn with camp direction signs for site. Le Palais is at end of the road, almost opposite the municipal site **Ground:** Hard to giving **Children:** Swimming
Wheelchair: Suitable **Food-cooling:** Ice sold, coolpacks frozen
Sport: Tennis, ping pong **Season:** 1 June to Sept
Reservation: Advisable peak season **Charge:** 2 people, pitch and car 74 fr; extra adult 19 fr; child (under 7) 12 fr; electricity 12 fr

▬▬▬ Torreilles-Plage ▬▬▬▬▬

La Palmeraie

66440 Torreilles-Plage   tel 68.28.20.64

Beautiful buildings modelled on Islamic architecture make this an unusually attractive camp, with first-rate facilities

The floral island at the entrance, with an old fishing boat in the middle, sets the style of this unusual campsite. When you've passed under the arch at La Palmeraie's entrance, you are confronted with a domed reception building resembling a miniature mosque. The architecture of the whole camp is modelled on this Middle-Eastern influence which must make it unique for these parts. Beyond the reception, the theme is continued in the classic simplicity of the bar and restaurant, sheltering from the relentless sun under wide arches. Inside everything is cool white, with Islamic-shaped mirrors and wooden screens. Even the menu-board echoes their design. Outside, tall palms adorn the terrace and the glorious pool which completes this oriental complex. As for the camping ground, a wide gravel avenue leads through to *emplacements* of reasonable proportions, hedged with shrubs and trees that offer some seclusion. However, the intermittent willows, conifers and pines do little to create significant amounts of shade. Further into the ground, pitches are grouped in fours or sixes. Even the *sanitaires* repeat the Arabian theme. Each is built around an open, planted patio. All facilities are ultra-modern and well maintained. The avenue at the back of the site becomes a path to the beach. A roped-off play area for children is set aside from the tents and roadway, and there's a useful patch of grass for them to kick a ball around. Evening entertainments are sophisticated affairs with *soirées dansantes*, cabarets and *repas-à-thème* partaken to the strains of a chamber quartet. Everything here is thoughtfully arranged and maintained, making it by far the best camp in the resort.

🌙 ⓢ ♨ 🚃 🎒 ✕ ♀ 🐞 🏠 ⊟ ▣ 🥄 🎵

Directions: From the D81 running parallel to the coast down to Canet, take the D11 to Torreilles-Plage. The D11 takes you towards the beach and La Palmeraie is on the right, with an easily identifiable entrance of a double arch **Ground:** Giving **Children:** Playground, swimming, organised events **Wheelchair:** Suitable **Food-cooling:** Ice sold, coolpacks frozen, fridge hire **Sport:** Volleyball, ping pong **Season:** 1 June to 1 Sept **Reservation:** Advisable peak season **Charge:** 2 people, pitch and car 78 fr; extra adult 20 fr; electricity 15 fr fr

▬▬ Vernet-les-Bains ▬▬▬▬

Sites summary The camping provision at Vernet seems inadequate, considering that it is the main resort in the southernmost part of the Pyrénées-Roussillon region. As Vernet is a spa town, the emphasis here is firmly on hotels and apartments and a selection of good sites is distinctly lacking. Of the three sites listed for the town, *L'Eau Vive* is the best if you're looking for a good family site. The other two camps are adequate touring sites and have comparable tariffs.

⑦ *Le Cady*

Vernet-les-Bains, Casteil 66820   tel 68.05.56.12

Small, pretty camp close to the mountains. Basic, good-value facilities but could do with some redecoration

Le Cady is a small, very scenic, shady site in a grassy clearing dominated by looming mountains which seem ready to tip themselves into it. Opposite a large roadside restaurant (run as a separate concern by the same management) is a row of *emplacements* lying in the shadow of mature trees. The rest of the camping area comprises two small, open 'campuses' either side of a river crossed by a short bridge. The constant roar of the waterfall may not help those who sleep lightly! The area of lawn on the roadside has trimmed hedges at the rear, accentuating the site's tidy appearance. The smaller 'campus' across the river meets a huge, craggy rockface and it's from here that you gain an excellent view of the towering mountains with their serrated edges cutting across the skyline. Although the site is graded as two-star and is acceptably priced for what it provides, at the time of inspection the showers and toilets were in need of some decoration, with chipped tiles and cracked paintwork. Please let us know about any improvements.

● Ⓢ ⵟ ⵉ ✕ ⵞ ⛏ ⫟ ⵲ ⧈

Directions: Turn off the N116 from Perpignan at Villefranche-de-Conflent, on the D116 that heads south. Follow the road, through Vernet-les-Bains, towards Casteil. As you go round a left-hand bend, you will see the camp on the right **Ground:** Giving **Children:** Not suitable **Wheelchair:** Not suitable **Food-cooling:** Ice sold **Sport:** None **Season:** Easter to Oct **Reservation:** Advisable peak season **Charge:** Pitch 19 fr; person 16 fr

Camping del Bosc

66820 Vernet-les-Bains   tel 68.05.54.54

Above-average facilities make for a pleasant stay at this unpretentious two-star site in a natural setting

Del Bosc is the most accessible of the Vernet camps simply because it's the first one you arrive at when taking the main route to the town. What strikes you first is the randomness of the place, for Del Bosc lies in some roadside woodland that has been allowed to retain its natural character. This means that its undulating, earthy ground at the front end, visually heightened by outcrops of rock, should not be thought of as neglect. In complete contrast is the modern design of the single amenities building. Its clean lines incorporate the reception, a well-stocked shop (with *dépôt de pain*) and a snack-bar. Also modern and very well fitted out are the three *sanitaires* of circular construction. Two out of three have facilities for handicapped people but we decided on a 'tricky' warning in the details below because of the rough terrain. More level ground can be found if one ventures towards the back of the camp. Away from the road things are much quieter and indeed take on a rural aspect as the clearing looks out over woodland to the Pyrenean peaks.

Unlike the front section of the camp, *emplacements* here are more formally arranged and laid to grass. Del Bosc is a mixed bag of a campsite but a reasonable base for expeditions into the region.

Directions: Turn off the N116 from Perpignan at Villefranche-de-Conflent, on the D116 that heads south. Before coming to Vernet-les-Bains you will see a camp sign on your right (on a right-hand bend) warning of camp entrance just further on, on your left **Ground:** Hard to giving **Children:** Not suitable **Wheelchair:** Tricky **Food-cooling:** Ice sold **Sport:** Ping pong **Season:** April to 30 Sept **Reservation:** Advisable peak season **Charge:** Pitch 17 fr; person 15 fr; child (under 8) 8.50 fr; electricity 9.50 fr

❁ *L'Eau Vive*

Chemin St Saturnin, 66820 Vernet-les-Bains   tel 68.05.54.14

Luxury family camping at this small, sunny site

L'Eau Vive reminded us very much of a tiny version of the high quality campsites to be found in the Dordogne. It has the similar good fortune to be set in some imposing scenery, and combines thoughtful provision for all members of the family with an exceptional standard in washing facilities. It is an immaculate camp, occupying a clearing in the fields that border the residential suburbs of Vernet. The Pic du Canigou in all its glory watches over this site, while in the foreground, where woods creep up to the edge of the site, the star attraction is a natural pool with its own patch of sand. The water is kept constantly fresh by a pump which draws supplies from the nearby river. A section is cordoned off to keep toddlers in the shallows. Somehow a swimming-pool, no matter how appealing in design, just would not have had the same impact. At the house, on this all-year site, the French family who are your cordial hosts will serve you a *plat du jour*. Two pristine, modern *sanitaires* complete the first-class facilities. The pitches consist of a single row of lawned *emplacements* either side of a gravel path. This area is exposed to the sun with no arborial umbrella, but the site itself is very secluded – ideal for getting away from everyone else without sacrificing your comfort. With only 57 available pitches it's essential to reserve as early as possible. An alternative would be to take advantage of the camp's canvas 'bungalows' – rigid tents, complete except for sheets.

Directions: As you enter the environs of Vernet (see del Bosc for location directions) proceed along the hedge-lined road before getting to the town centre proper. Halfway along is a right-hand turn over a river bridge, signposted Sahorre. Take this and drive to the end of a small parade of shops under an apartment block. At the end of the block, turn right. This is Ave de Saturnin. Along this road, take the left fork and after leaving houses and entering scrubland, you will eventually arrive at the camp (clear direction signs en route)
Ground: Giving **Children:** Swimming **Wheelchair:** Suitable
Food-cooling: Ice sold **Sport:** Ping pong **Season:** All year
Reservation: Advisable peak season **Charge:** 4 people, pitch and car 84 fr; extra adult 9 fr

Vinça

Le Canigou

Espira-de-Conflent, 66320 Vinça   tel 68.05.85.40

Basic but pretty two-star site, ideal if you've packed the walking boots. Suits caravans as well as tents

Named after Canigou because it lies in sight of this one dominating peak, this small, secluded two-star campsite is secreted away in the valley woodland, yet is quite accessible. It has an aura of clean, healthy outdoor living that urges you to put on your backpack. Sunlight through the spread of trees dapples the ground in the front part of this camp, where grassy pitches are arranged at random. The sound of running water here emanates from a brook that courses the length of the site. If you follow this stream you will be taken into the vale, passing more pitches on a low, stone-walled terrace. Further along, the path splits and bridges the stream to take you to yet another section, this time a long, narrow field of pitches in parallel rows divided by hedges. This back end of the camp is more open to the sun. A barrage across the brook has created a wider pool of water for bathing. The couple of *sanitaires* are pretty basic: one seated toilet among four, the same number of showers and communal *lavabos*. There's a nice, secure feeling in Le Canigou, a certain camaraderie, perhaps. Houses in the minuscule village of Espira-de-Conflent literally butt on to the church. From its vantage point you have a superb panorama of Canigou. At the next village of Finestret, you can pick up a section of the long distance footpath which will take you into the Canigou range.

Directions: Going west from Vinça on the N116, there's an open stretch of road with a lake on your right. You will see an orange sign warning you to turn left, followed by a yellow sign for the camp. Take the left-hand turn just after this which is the D25. Go right at the next fork onto the D55 (another direction sign here). At a little bridge over the river there's a turning to the left with a big yellow sign on some green railings. This is the camp entrance **Ground:** Giving
Children: Not suitable **Wheelchair:** Not suitable **Food-cooling:** Ice sold **Sport:** Ping pong **Season:** 1 April to 15 Oct
Reservation: Advisable peak season **Charge:** Pitch 18 fr; person 15 fr; child (under 7) 8 fr; electricity 14 fr

Municipal du Lac des Escoumes

66320 Vinça   tel 68.05.84.78

A lakeside setting, in serene surroundings, is the attraction at this simple site. A good stop-over en route *to Andorra or Spain*

For a municipal site, and a two-star one at that, Des Escoumes seems to be on the pricey side but the environment more than makes up for this. It must rank as one of the prettiest municipal campsites in the south of France. Descending into the camp, you discover at the bottom a mirror-smooth lake reflecting houses on the far shore, in the lee of low, rocky hills. The scene epitomises the tranquillity to be found in this green and shady parkland. Giant willows drape themselves at the water's edge where you too can drape yourself in one of the *emplacements*. On the other side of the drive, following the shoreline, are terraces of grass pitches. The rest of the camp meanders back into the seclusion of the trees covering the rear sections of the grounds. At convenient intervals are situated small stone-built *sanitaires* of a neat octagonal construction with tile roofs. Along with the usual facilities, each has a couple of showers and pedestal toilets with that rarity for campsites, attached seats!

Towards the far end of the lake you will find a couple of small, sandy inlets from which you can bathe. The lake bed drops quickly, so it's not suitable for youngsters. Des Escoumes provides no amenities, not even a *dépôt de pain*, so a trip to Vinça is essential for supplies. On hand, too, is a garage, post office and chemist.

Directions: Vinça is situated east of Prades and just off the N116. The turn-off (signposted) for the village is opposite a large lake and crosses over the railway. You arrive at a roundabout by a petrol station, where you take the first exit. Drive past a housing estate and this road bends left to take you to the camp (clear signs all the way) **Ground:** Giving **Children:** Not suitable **Wheelchair:** Suitable **Food-cooling:** Ice sold **Sport:** None **Season:** 1 June to Sept **Reservation:** Advisable peak season **Charge:** 2 people, pitch and car 37.50 fr; pitch with electricity 49 fr; extra adult 11 fr

For the naturist

Because naturists' sites tend to keep to the more secluded spots, they are invariably situated in some of the prettiest reaches of countryside that would be the envy of many a textile camp-owner. ('Textile' camping is naturist-speak for conventional campsites.) At La Clapère, hidden away in a lush valley at the foot of the Albères range, the Quenot family have created a campsite that blends in with the original landscape. The estate covers a large area of woodland comprising a variety of flora from bamboo to oak. You can roughly divide this terrain into valley and hillside. Through the former, flowing and tumbling over rock and boulder into transparent pools, is what must be the quintessential vision of a mountain stream. On higher ground, wide, level, grassy terraces face the scene of densely wooded hills with the Albères completing the panorama. On a more practical point, the *sanitaires* are worth a mention because of their unusual design. A pitched roof from ground to top ridge is angled to double as cover, as well as a sloping screen for solar panels. At the beginning of the camp, the reception

121

building has a small restaurant with a simple yet crisp interior. This is next to a sunny gravel terrace where you can sit and enjoy an ice-cold drink as you watch your friends enjoying a swim in the pool. Thinking how to summarise La Clapère, the word 'heavenly' arose. If ever there is for campers a Great Campsite in the sky, we would like to think that La Clapère is a very close version.

Domaine La Clapère
Route de Las Illas, 66400 Maureillas
Tel: 68.83.36.04

Hérault

By a quirk of geological evolution, Hérault is a strange mix of verdant valleys, gorges, startling geological phenomena and impoverished *garrigue* country (scrub). It's where the tail-end of the Massif Central finally peters out before the coastal plain of the Mediterranean. Without prejudice to other worthy areas, there might be a case for saying that the most intriguing of Hérault's sights lie roughly in its north-eastern quarter. This strange hotch-potch of countryside, the butt of the Causse du Larzac, demonstrates the peculiar erosion of its predominantly limestone composition through the natural bridging of rivers, impressive *grottes* and *dolomites*, alien outcrops of rock taking the uncanny form of a ruined piece of architecture of some lost civilisation. Here, too, are *cirques*, curved escarpments hollowed out of the hills as if some supernatural force had used a giant ice-cream scoop. Complementing this landscape, a scattering of dolmens (funereal standing stones) were erected in Neolithic times around the prehistoric village of Cambous. Strangely, in this area, they seem more the work of nature than of man.

One of the main features in these parts is the River Hérault itself, flowing out from the Cévennes foothills in the north to tumble through valley and gorge on its way to Agde and the sea. Both it and the Orb, the other prominent river of the *département*, offer stimulating conditions for canoeing. The town of Roquebrun on the latter is a national kayak centre.

To the south towards the coast is Montpellier, the region's capital, with a population of well over 300,000.

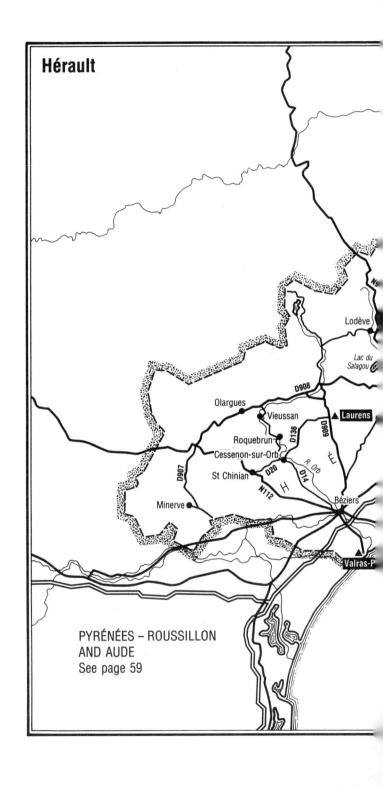

Hérault

Lodève

Lac du Salagou

D908

Olargues

Vieussan

Laurens

D136

D909

Roquebrun

Cessenon-sur-Orb

R. Orb

L'Y.

D20

St Chinian

D14

D907

N112

H

Béziers

Minerve

Valras-P

PYRÉNÉES – ROUSSILLON
AND AUDE
See page 59

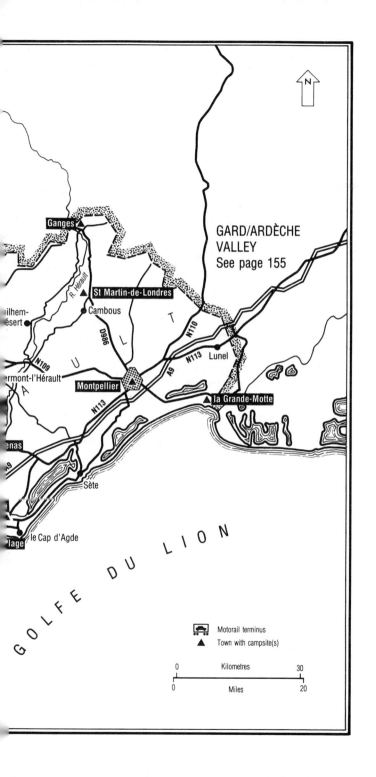

N

Ganges ▲

GARD/ARDÈCHE
VALLEY
See page 155

R. Hérault

▲ St Martin-de-Londres

Cambous ●

ilhem-
ésert ●

D986

T

L

N110

N109

U

A

Lunel ●

N113

rmont-l'Hérault

Montpellier

A9

N113

▲ la Grande-Motte

enas

9

Sète ●

lage ● le Cap d'Agde

G O L F E   D U   L I O N

Motorail terminus
▲ Town with campsite(s)

0   Kilometres   30

0   Miles   20

Visiting it is like eating a soft-centred chocolate: modern brittleness on the outside, a delightful taste of history discovered within. The university is part of that history, with the oldest school of medicine in Europe. Nostradamus gained his doctorate there in 1525.

Béziers, to the west, is the gateway into the wine country based on St Chinian and Minerve. In fact, all of Hérault's lowlands could be seen as one huge vineyard, but undoubtedly the best products stem from these two regions (see the Orb Valley below). Its valley heading north into the rugged Haute Languedoc contains the prettiest, if not the finest, of Hérault's scenery.

Camping is most prolific on the coast, especially on a string of beaches west of Cap d'Agde. Here you tend to have to gird up your sun-lotioned loins to face the rigours of packed places with all the discretion of a funfair. As the coastal resorts remain very popular with British holidaymakers we have concentrated on these, as good alternatives are hard to come by in the greater part of the interior. However, we have managed to find a few very pleasant sites there with great appeal.

Agde and Cap d'Agde

Agde's main claim to fame is that it was founded by the Phoenicians two and a half thousand years ago. It's a small community but full of life in season, with local fêtes providing colour for the visitor. Central to its social life is the one main street whose raised pavement is a convenient platform for a row of a half-a-dozen restaurants. Their terraces form a continuous wide strip of tables and chairs where evenings are a celebration of townsfolk and tourists alike enjoying good, inexpensive food (especially seafood), flowing wine and noisy conversation. Worth visiting is the twelfth-century cathedral of St Etienne which must be unique in its construction of black volcanic stone, which gives it the appearance more of a fort than of a church. If you follow the riverside D32 you will come to the town's fishing port, Le Grau d'Agde. From here you can take a boat trip to Fort Brescou, built in the 1600s as a prison on a rock of an island just off the cape.

Cap d'Agde, a natural, sheltered inlet, has been developed into a European centre for sport and leisure but unlike La Grande-Motte (and Le Grau-du-Roi – see Gard and Ardèche Valley) it has been executed with a sense of scale. Concrete blocks of holiday apartments abound but they don't impose themselves on the picturesque modern marina with its landscaped quay and square full of little shops. In the summer open-air exhibitions such as food fairs are held here: there's something very satisfying about walking among the stalls of wine and cheese, having a free nibble here and there, while the sun begins to set over masts and flying bridges, softening the harsh white of multi-dollar hulls with a pink hue. Other than the beaches, the one place for an essential family visit is Aqualand, reputed to be the largest (four hectares) waterpark in Europe. Plenty of safe shallow bathing is laid on for the tots while the older and more adventurous can experience artificial rapids, the Anaconda waterchute, a wet assault course, and a marine equivalent of free-fall in the shape of the towering Niagara slide. Go early in order to grab a picnic table for your packed lunch. Otherwise, there's a restaurant on site if you're not on a budget.

Béziers

The wine capital of the *département*, overlooking the Orb, with its cathedral of St Nazaire as a high point, stands out of the plain where once Hannibal came by with history's first intercontinental circus parade. Wine festivals are the main events of the year, of course (July: Côte Languedocienne; August: 'Fountain of Wine'; September: 'Harvest'; October: 'New Vintage'), but it has another side to it. Béziers is also known as the French Seville, for the first half of August sees the spectacle of the bullfight, which is somehow incongruous in this location, unlike Camargue-associated Arles or near-Spanish Céret.

Cambous

Four kilometres south of St Martin-de-Londres on the D986 Montpellier road, then left on to the D113, you'll find the well-preserved site of a prehistoric village dating from 2,500 BC. There were once twenty-odd such villages between here and Montpellier, suggesting that it was an important settlement. A reconstruction of the typical longhouse, resembling a marquee with low stone walls, supporting a roof of reeds and twigs, is open from halfway through June to the end of August.

Clermont-l'Hérault

This medieval town sits more or less in the centre of the *département* on the crossroads of north-south, east-west communications. Though its origins can be traced back to the time of Gaul, it grew as a fortified city in the Middle Ages, guarded by the Château des Guilhem. This is one of the better kept châteaux, in the Languedoc, with a dungeon, towers, ramparts, castle gate and underground vaults. The town has other medieval buildings, notably the church of St Paul.

Ganges

Southern gateway to the Cévennes, Ganges was the centre of the Cévenol silk industry in the eighteenth century. North of the town you can see the five- or six-storey buildings by the roadside which housed the silk farms. Ganges is also the birthplace of one Emile Planchon who was the chemist who saved Hérault's vines when they were threatened by a plague of the rampant vine-killing phylloxera louse.

Ganges is a good centre for two geological treats: **La Grotte des Demoiselles** and the **Cirque des Navacelles**. The surprise of the first series of caves (south of the town) is the chamber called 'La Cathédrale'. You don't know the meaning of the word 'cavern' until you've experienced the enormity of this one. Numerous pillar concretions lend themselves to the idea of Gothic architecture – organ pipes, even – hence the name. At Christmas a midnight mass is held in its depths.

The Cirque de Navacelles can be reached by the D130 via the D25 from Ganges which travels through the Gorges de la Vis. Navacelles sits in what can clearly be seen from higher ground to be the ghost of a meander once belonging to the Vis. The Cirque is the finest example of this phenomenon and tends to be on everyone's itinerary.

La Grande-Motte

'Risen from the desolate salt-lakes of the Aigues-Mortes gulf, this concrete Phoenix, a homage to sea and sun...' and so on. To some, this artificially created resort is an exciting illustration of contemporary European architecture, to others, the worst of Mediterranean coastal development. In a way it's more architecturally over-the-top than at Le Grau-du-Roi's expansive development. La Grande-Motte has been designed as an all-singing, all-dancing leisure resort with a golf course of international standard, tennis courts galore, nightclubs, casinos and watersports. Central to all this is the square of water that is its marina, which is all but encompassed by buildings whose structure can best be compared to metal cheese-graters of the four-sided tapering kind, right down to the rows of the pierced curves of windows. Squatting among them is the horizontal oval of the Palais des Congrés, its architect obviously inspired by the aesthetic form of a World War I tank. The town can be rather windswept at times and its impersonal blind façades are not conducive to relaxation. But then, you'll be at the beach most of the day and using the town's amenities and entertainment only at night when the place comes into its own.

Lodève

This old town of ancient streets and bridges is like the centre of a maple leaf with valleys as 'veins' radiating out from it. The geography has helped to create a Mediterranean climate of warm, sunny winters, so the area maintains a long season. It is a pot-pourri of scenery from the forests and rivers to barer high places, and vineyards and olive groves erupting from the scrub of the *garrigue*. **Les Plans**, **Campestre**, **Lauroux**, **Soubès** and **Fozières** are all tiny villages hidden away in the hills, each as delightfully unspoilt as the next. A few kilometres south on the D148 you'll find the large **Lac du Salagou** – very scenic, ideal for picnics, bathing and boating.

Immediately south of Lac du Salagou, the village of **Mourèze** in the base of this irregular bowl is surrounded by typical dolomitic formations of surreal rock forms like fantastic animals.

Lunel

Lunel is at the extreme eastern border of Hérault where the Camargue begins. The town is associated with bullfighting and has a medieval centre of little streets. Lunel's consistently temperate climate throughout the year benefits the Muscat grape used to produce a local sweet wine.

Minerve

At the far west of Hérault, Minerve seems pinned against the rising contours of this wild territory. Once a Cathar stronghold, all that remains today are the ruins of the castle from the period. There is a museum of archaeology and palaeontology and some little craft shops. Many of the local wine *caves* have outlets here. The River Cesse passes this way and is fascinating not only for its subterranean comings and goings but for an amazing series of natural bridges, a phenomenon that occurs elsewhere in the region.

A couple of detours south-west of the town on the D168 (via D10) are **Siran** and **La Livinière**. Going north out of Siran, you can climb the hills to the twelfth-century chapel of Notre-Dame de Centeilles from which there are wonderful views. La Livinière further on is a picturesque village of sloping streets and a covered market place. As with Minerve the area's *caves* are also represented here.

Montpellier

If you persevere with the horrendous road system that surrounds this city, you may be lucky enough to arrive not too exhausted to relish the sights of the medieval town that lies within the suburban morass. The focal point is the Place de la Comédie – a large square where the world and his wife arrange to meet – watched over by the Opera. Ascend the Rue Foch to the wide terrace of the Promenade du Peyrou looking out over the city and arrive at Montpellier's answer to the Arc de Triomphe, which was erected in the name of Louis XIV. You can also see heading out from this point an impressive aqueduct (modelled on the Pont du Gard – see Gard and Ardèche Valley) which was built in the 1700s to carry water from the hills in the north. One other worthwhile sight is the cathedral of St Pierre next to the School of Medicine.

The Orb Valley

Exploring the villages here in some very pretty scenery would be a satisfying day out. The Orb rises in the **Causse du Larzac** and snakes down south, then west, then turns south-east to make for Béziers. The upper half of that final stretch holds the most interest for the tourist. If you are based at the campsite in Laurens (see below) you can cut cross-country via the D136 – an outing in itself. Starting with **Cessenon-sur-Orb**, one of the oldest towns of the Languedoc, you can stop off to see the remains of the ancient Castrum.

If you take the D14, which follows the river north into much hillier country, the next visit is **Roquebrun**. This little village sits snugly between two wooded cliffs on the river's bend. As well as being a key canoe post, it also has a reputation for a very temperate climate, perfect for the cultivation of citrus fruits and eucalyptus.

Heading on, you might like to leave the road, more scenic now, to take a look at **Vieussan** before arriving at the junction with the D908. This is near where the Rivers Orb and Jaur meet. The last stop of this tour is not strictly in the Orb Valley but is worth seeing. Perched on a rock where the Jaur meanders past, **Olargues** is a medieval village of twisting streets and ruins of what were once its fortifications. Like Roquebrun, its climate is suitable for orchards to thrive, and it is also known for its chestnuts.

Pézenas

North of Agde and the A9, Pézenas has close associations with Molière but is also renowned for paved streets full of superb period architecture – stone buildings such as in the Rue Triperie Vieille, little squares and stone steps all hinting at the prosperity it knew in the fourteenth and fifteenth centuries. It has long been a centre for arts and crafts.

St Chinian

A diversion west from the Orb Valley tour (above) takes you on the D20 from Cessenon to St Chinian, whose wines from the Syrah and Grenache grapes carry an *appellation contrôlée*. This area, too, possesses an exceptional micro-climate. This is brought about by the presence of the Espinouse range to the north, which forms a protective weather barrier. In the town are the ruins of the St Laurent Benedictine abbey. An excursion north-west on the N112 will take you through the **Défilé** (Gorge) **de l'Ilouvre** and put you in touch with **Cauduro** and **La Louvière**, both offering splendid panoramas.

St Guilhem-le-Désert

In the Hérault valley north of Gignac is a solitary cluster of stone houses nudging a beautiful little Romanesque church by the village square with its one huge plane tree and a fountain. This diminutive community is dominated by a backdrop of craggy, wooded escarpments, a perfect grey and green foil for the yellow stone walls and dull red roofs beneath them.

Grotte de Clamouse is a little south of St Guilhem-le-Désert. From the outside you get good views; inside a variety of concretions abound; pillars, saucers, needlepoints and so on. The party-piece is a large, pure white form known as the Medusa because it resembles a cloaked figure with a head of snakes.

Tourist office

Comité Départemental de Tourisme
1 place Marcel-Godechot
34000 Montpellier
Tel 65.54.20.66

Agde

Domaine des Champs Blancs

Route de Rochelongue-Plage, 34300 Agde   tel 67.94.23.42

Tight on space perhaps, but good facilities for families and an atmosphere of fun

A wide, tarmac drive lined with trees and shrubs leads to the reception at this very French, family campsite. The area outside the reception resembles a diminutive ornamental garden, with a patio displaying stone cherubim, a profusion of pink flowers spilling out of troughs, and even a baroque-style stone table and chairs. Across the way is a sandy compound with a range of climbing frames and other play equipment; bench seating is provided for watching parents. There's even a special toddlers' *sanitaire*, tiled with a nursery frieze, complete with tiny pedestal toilets and a knee-high wash-basin. Nearby is the main *sanitaire*, also tiled, in a cool marine blue and white; a separate section of four baby bathrooms, each containing a small bath at waist height and a basin is next door. A launderette and hairdresser complete the good, well-kept facilities. The popular L-shaped pool, with diving-boards and slide, is set in a terrace of chequered paving by the low building that houses the *crêperie*, *rôtisserie*, shop and a bar-discothèque. In the evenings this becomes a rendezvous for the sub-teens as well as for older brothers and sisters. The camping ground is an area criss-crossed by gravel paths, running through blocks of tightly-spaced *emplacements*. The lack of space in which to stretch out is a drawback, but the pitches are reasonably shaded by thin trees, and the surrounding hedges provide some territorial privacy. If you are not unduly worried by such matters, then Champs Blancs has much to offer, especially if you are young at heart. It's well positioned for eating out in Agde, or for a day at Le Cap d'Agde. If you continue down the D32E, you will arrive at Rochelongue which has a quiet, pretty beach of rockpools and fine sand that doesn't become too populated.

● Ⓜ 🕽 ⩫ 🕮 ♀ 🖐 ★ ⋔ ⊐ ▣ ⅌ ♫

Directions: Go east out of Agde on the D912, which further on becomes the N112 to Sète. At the second set of traffic lights turn right (red camp direction sign here). Then at a mini-roundabout take the

third exit and just after is a right-hand turn (red camp signs at both points). You will then come to a T-junction. Turn left which will take you on a bridge over the N112. The camp will then be on your right
Ground: Hard **Children:** Playground, swimming, baby facilities
Wheelchair: Not suitable **Food-cooling:** Ice sold, coolpacks frozen
Sport: Tennis, volleyball, ping pong, mini-golf **Season:** 1 Apr to 30 Sept **Reservation:** Advisable peak season **Charge:** 4 people, pitch and electricity (6 amp) 155 fr

La Pinède

Route d'Agde, 34309 Cap d'Agde   tel 67.21.25.00

A well-organised, tranquil camp in a good location near the coast

La Pinède is a small, quiet campsite on the slopes of Mont St Loup, with uninterrupted views over the lowland from the town of Agde to the Cap. The car park and little shop just inside the camp gate give no hint of the pleasing grounds that become apparent as you begin to follow the gentle descent of the driveway. As the site name suggests, pine trees are present, dotted around the attractive grounds, with scattered almond trees and shrubs in flower. The trees are not dense, so while there is some shade, the open aspect allows a cooling on-shore breeze to penetrate the grounds. The level, gritty, red-earth pitches are of varying size, and those on high ground behind the pool area are terraced. As there are no distinct divisions between the *emplacements*, you can't fail to notice your neighbours. You may glimpse the Patron himself serving behind the restaurant bar beside the pool. In this neat building you can eat from a set menu or *à la carte*, order a take-away, or, if feeling lazy first thing in the morning, come here to be served a breakfast of coffee and croissants. The kidney-shaped pools, set in a terrace with palms, are in a prime position, beneath the wide blue sky. There is a sense of orderliness about La Pinède, indicated by the high-profile fire points and the many wooden-slatted bin-holders. It's a more sedate alternative to Champs Blancs and is convenient for the town of Agde and Cap d'Agde.

Directions: The D32E leaves a big roundabout on the D912 Agde to Sète (Intermarché here). Carry on up the D32E and you will see a large camp sign indicating entrance on your left. This drive will take you uphill to the site. (Please note that there are three separate D32E roads that head towards the coast. You should consult a map of the area if in doubt) **Ground:** Hard to giving **Children:** Playground, swimming, organised events **Wheelchair:** Suitable **Food-cooling:** Ice sold **Sport:** Volleyball, ping pong **Season:** 1 June to 15 Sept **Reservation:** Advisable peak season **Charge:** 2 people, pitch and car 84 fr; child (under 7) 11 fr; electricity 15 fr

Ganges

Le Val d'Hérault

34190 Brissac   tel 67.73.72.29

A tranquil, cosy atmosphere prevails at this camp, set in marvellous countryside, but not too far from town

The upper valley of the River Hérault is close to a landscape of gorges, *cirques* and *grottes*; the scenery surrounding this campsite raises expectations of a peaceful spot in the middle of green hills. Your hopes are rewarded by the sight of the steep slopes of the Séranne ridge, visible across the road. The reception building, which is also home to your host family, houses a snack-bar and veranda, set out with tables and chairs under a sloping, clay-tiled roof. A small *épicerie* sells fruit, dairy products and fresh bread in the mornings. The camp is divided into two sections, the main part forming a cool glade of small, gnarled trees. The track circles round to pitches marked out by rows of stones on the hard, gravelly ground. The other section of the site is a more undefined area of natural wood and copse, better suited to small tents. The clear water of the River Hérault flows by horizontal slabs of white-grey rock, perfect for sunbathing after a swim. Quiet and relaxed are the key words to describe this site; the atmosphere is that of a small community enjoying the secluded position and general comforts – just the sort of camp to look forward to after a day's sightseeing.

Directions: Join the D4 by crossing the river-bridge just south of Ganges centre, on the D999. At the T-junction after the bridge, turn left for Brissac. After a long, straight run, go through the village on the D4 towards Causse-de-la-Selle. Eventually you will come to the site entrance on your left, indicated by a big brown signboard

Ground: Hard **Children:** Playground **Wheelchair:** Tricky
Food-cooling: Ice sold, coolpacks frozen, fridge hire
Sport: Volleyball, ping pong **Season:** 15 Mar to 15 Nov
Reservation: Advisable peak season **Charge:** 2 people, pitch and car
50 fr; child (3-7) 5.75 fr; electricity 11.50 fr

■■■■ La Grande-Motte ■■■■■■■■■

Sites summary There are eight campsites in La Grande-Motte, all on the same road, in a quiet area behind the heart of the resort, but still handy for the beaches and shopping centre. The three selected for this guide were the ones which impressed us the most, although it must be said that in general, facilities for entertainment and eating out are limited on the sites as such a wide choice is available in the resort. Price-wise, the sites are comparable, with *Le Garden* possibly the best value. For a superb environment (though hardly anything else) the prize must go to the *Municipal Lou Gardian*.

Directions for sites To reach the camps, approach La Grande-Motte from the interchange on the main D62 north of the resort. This puts you on a broad avenue, where you filter right following the Centre Ville signs. At a major crossroads with traffic-lights, turn right on to a dual carriageway taking you to the commercial centre. This is the Avenue de Carnon. After passing under a footbridge take the next right, Avenue de la Petite Motte. This is the road where the camps are; the first two sites on your right will be *Le Garden* and *Lous Pibols*. The municipal site is further down on your left, just the other side of a college.

Le Garden

34280 La Grande-Motte	tel 67.56.50.09

Quiet, genteel site with standard facilities but little in the way of entertainment

Set back off the road and sharing the same drive with Lous Pibols (see below), Le Garden has the air of a cool, restful camp and gives the impression of having been long established. As you stroll through the grounds, the mature trees and the worn pitches and architecture all point to age. The *emplacements*, arranged in a grid system of avenues, are given shade and privacy by the tall trees and high hedges. The *sanitaires* are traditional, solid buildings, decorated with a blue and white marine design and comprise various small rooms for your ablutions, washing-machines and laundry. It's a more comfortable environment than most modern constructions and along with seated pedestal toilets there's even a wall dispenser which issues disposable paper rings for the seats. By the roadside, accessible to the general public, are a newsagent, grocery and a couple of boutiques. There is no swimming-pool, as the beaches are so close, and the variety of places in which to wine and dine in this holiday playground of a resort means that sites generally don't do much in the catering line either. Le Garden is no exception and the bar/cafeteria, with tables outside under a blue awning, serves basic fare: *plats du jour* and steak *haché*; not very sophisticated, in spite of the atmosphere created by the cane furniture.

● Ⓜ ⚡ 🐛 ✕ ⚲ 🐟 🎣 ⚒ ▣ ∥

Directions: See Directions for sites at beginning of La Grande Motte
Ground: Hard **Children:** Playground **Wheelchair:** Suitable
Food-cooling: Ice sold, coolpacks frozen **Sport:** Ping pong
Season: 1 Mar to Oct **Reservation:** Advisable peak season
Charge: 2 people, pitch and car 99.50 fr

Lous Pibols

34280 La Grande-Motte   tel 67.56.50.08

Similar in many ways to Le Garden next door, but visually more attractive, this basic camp is best suited to self-caterers

Lous Pibols is the immediate neighbour of Le Garden and could be mistaken for an extension of the latter, with its similar, tall poplars at the entrance. It presents a marginally more attractive environment, with an abundance of flowering shrubbery, a more open and therefore sunnier aspect created by the scattered trees, and a less rigid arrangement of pitches leading from avenues that curve through the grounds. The worn, hard-baked *emplacements* are surrounded by tall hedging and the sanitary facilities have more modern fixtures and fittings than at Le Garden. A solitary shop and a snack-bar are the only catering facilities on the site.

Directions: See Directions for sites at beginning of La Grande-Motte
Ground: Hard **Children:** Playground **Wheelchair:** Not suitable
Food-cooling: Ice sold **Sport:** None **Season:** Mar to Sept
Reservation: Advisable peak season **Charge:** 3 people, pitch, car and electricity 132 fr

Municipal Lou Gardian

BP 16, 34280 La Grande-Motte

Out-of-season tel 67.56.00.77
tel 67.56.14.14

Prim and pretty municipal site offering an excellent camping environment, with shady pitches

If it weren't for the tents and caravans, you might think that you had wandered into the municipal pleasure gardens, instead of the municipal campsite, such is the profusion of colourful flowers. Rarely have we seen such a beautifully cultivated ground, and it's not just its landscaping that's praiseworthy – the whole upkeep of the site is to be complimented, from the properly kerbed, asphalted roadways to the svelte, level lawns. The grassy enclaves of pitches are satisfyingly dark and cool under an abundance of tree coverage. Most are bound by hedges or rows of small shrubs. As you may imagine, on a site of this nature, everywhere is calm and peaceful. The spick-and-span *sanitaires* are modern, but, Gentlemen note, 'standing room' only unless you sneak into the handicapped toilet. There are no facilities for eating on the site, but at the *dépôt de pain* you are assured fresh baguettes (baked on the spot) for breakfast.

Directions: See Directions for sites at the beginning of La Grande-Motte **Ground:** Hard to giving **Children:** Not suitable
Wheelchair: Suitable **Food-cooling:** Ice sold, coolpacks frozen
Sport: None **Season:** 31 Mar to 13 Oct **Reservation:** Advisable peak season **Charge:** 3 people, pitch and car 108 fr; child (under 7) 14 fr

Laurens

✸ L'Oliveraie

34480 Laurens   tel 67.90.24.36

Delightfully secluded, rural campsite that caters for all the family

L'Oliveraie is close to the geographical centre of the *département* of Hérault, at a point where the sparse landscape of craggy outcrops, characteristic of the southern Massif Central, meets the rolling vineyards of the more fertile lowland plains. The camp's entrance, with gateway pillars supporting cartwheels either side, sets the tone of the site; a gravel avenue divided by a flowerbed leads you further into the beautifully still camping ground, bounded by the sweeping horizon of densely wooded hills. Towards the centre of this small site, passing the rustic touch of an old wine cart, you will come across the shadier gravel pitches of varying size. The *sanitaires* are well appointed, especially the one in the lower, newly-developed section of the camp. This all-year camp gives the impression of being a well-tended site and paths of crazy paving between pitch areas and scattered shrubbery make it an attractive environment. To the right of the camping ground, a small gate separates the accommodation area from that of entertainment. On one side of a tree-lined thoroughfare is the snack-bar veranda decked out with parasols and bedding plants. You can sit eating your grill or pizza, cooked *au feu du bois* in the open, while watching other campers enjoying themselves in the swimming-pool edged with fruit trees, and a strip of lawn on which to dry and sunbathe. Although this is an isolated location, there are enough events organised in the high season to ensure that no member of the family is left out – folk soirées, fancy dress competitions, games, pony and trap rides, as well as horse-riding and organised rambles in the countryside. The Patron and his wife are a hard-working couple who take pride in their camp and are enthusiastic in their concern that your stay should be an enjoyable one. It's always a bonus to know that such people have your pleasure as well as your pocket at heart.

Directions: Laurens is just east of the D909, north of Béziers.
Approximately 2 kms further north of Laurens a line of pylons appears
on the right-hand side of the road. At the end of this row, before the
power-lines cross to the other side, there is a right-hand turn (camp
sign here but obscured). The site is a little way down on the left
Ground: Hard **Children:** Playground, swimming, organised events,
baby facilities **Wheelchair:** Suitable **Food-cooling:** Ice sold,
coolpacks frozen **Sport:** Tennis, volleyball, ping pong, archery,
cycling, horse-riding, walking **Season:** All year
Reservation: Advisable peak season
Charge: 2 people, pitch and car 65 fr

▄▄▄▄ Montpellier ▄▄▄▄▄▄▄▄▄▄▄▄▄▄▄

Le Plein Air des Chênes

Route de Castelnau, 34830 Clapiers,   tel 67.59.10.98
Montpellier

*A family holiday treat, with French style, at this luxury
site with good pool complex*

Le Plein Air des Chênes has all the trappings of a country club,
set in a long strip of woodland between the town of Clapiers
and open fields that touch Montpellier's suburbs. We were
surprised to find this type of site in this region simply because
you couldn't describe the area as being in any way resort-
orientated. Its average size, plentiful shade provided by a mixed
conifer and deciduous wood, and good range of amenities make
this campsite devoted to all-round entertainment a popular
choice with French families. It also manages to avoid the tacky,
'holiday village' atmosphere that often accompanies the larger
family camp. The level *emplacements* are arranged formally
under the trees in the shady woodland towards the back of the
site. *Sanitaires* are six-sided blocks, in reasonable order, but with
no toilets of the seated variety. An option might be to ask for
one of the pitches with an individual *sanitaire*. For a few pounds
a day more, you are provided with your own shower, seated
toilet, wash-basin and sink for washing-up. These de luxe
pitches are outside the wood and are therefore more exposed.
The lack of seated toilets is a drawback, but an oblique plus is
that the lack of such a facility puts the British package operators
off using such a place, which means you could find yourselves

being the only Brits on a site of this calibre for a change! The three large swimming-pools of differing shapes and depths are set in a delightful area that could be described as a garden lido, with firs and willows bordering the paved pool-side terraces, bounded by an ample area of lawn on which to sunbathe. Eating facilities consist of a cafeteria serving ice-creams and a salad, perhaps, and a restaurant in the form of a raised, hexagonal building skirted by a balcony-style veranda that overlooks the tennis courts and adventure playground. In the evening you might like to dine in the restaurant's cool green interior, furnished predominantly in pine. Entertainment is the raison d'être of this camp and daytime activities such as water-polo matches, a gym club by the pool and treasure hunts, give way to night-time diversions such as a soirée, bingo, Trivial Pursuit, and maybe a casino night. Every Wednesday evening something a little different is arranged, perhaps an outdoor buffet evening with cabaret. You certainly won't have a lot of time to sit and twiddle your thumbs at this site.

the lack of seated toilets is a drawback

Directions: Clapiers is a town all but swallowed by the northern suburbs of Montpellier. Approaching from the east on the D65 (northern perimeter road of Montpellier), take the D112 to Clapiers. Before the town you will come across a right-hand fork by a triangular island next to open land. A camp direction sign is here. Turn and proceed down the road towards the wood. The camp is on your right **Ground:** Hard to giving **Children:** Playground, swimming **Wheelchair:** Suitable **Food-cooling:** Ice sold, coolpacks frozen, fridge hire **Sport:** Tennis, volleyball, ping pong, football, water-polo **Season:** All year **Wheelchair:** Not suitable **Charge:** 4 people, pitch and car 115 fr

Pézenas

Domaine de Montrose

34120 Pézenas	tel 67.98.52.10

A simple site, with rustic buildings in the middle of vineyards, makes an ideal touring halt

Domaine de Montrose is an interesting little campsite, if only for the speculation it engenders as to whether it was, or indeed still is, associated with the surrounding vineyards. There is no escaping the authentic farming character of its cluster of rural buildings with buff, cracked walls, white, stone lintels and various levels of sloping rooftops. The fairly open camping ground has enough trees to give the earth-based pitches sufficient shade. For a site of a plain but not unattractive appearance, the sanitary arrangements have good, modern fittings. Don't be fooled by the rustic exterior of the buildings: beyond the bar, a bare wooden staircase will take you up to the split-level floor, where discos are held under multi-coloured spotlights. There's a modest swimming-pool decorated with a few shrubs and flowers and in the evenings soirées are laid on, as well as trips to the local *cave* for wine tasters. Domaine de Montrose is a useful touring stop if you're travelling on the A9 (a little south of here) or driving down from the Tarn *département* via the N9 to Roussillon. As the site caters for itinerant visitors it might be worth stopping by on spec.

It's normal for your stay on a campsite to be charged from midday on the day of arrival to midday on the day of departure.

Directions: 4 kms south-west of Pézenas, on the N9 to Béziers, there is a small right-hand turn where the main road is long and straight. Turn right at the T-junction immediately after this turn. Further along, take a left-hand turn (camp sign is here) and a drive through a vineyard will take you to the site **Ground:** Hard to giving **Children:** Playground **Wheelchair:** Suitable **Food-cooling:** Ice sold **Sport:** Volleyball, ping pong **Season:** 1 June to 15 Sept **Reservation:** Advisable peak season **Charge:** 2 people, pitch and car 55 fr; child (under 7) 5 fr; electricity 11 fr

■■■■ St Martin-de-Londres ■■■■■

Pic St Loup

34380 St Martin-de-Londres   tel 67.55.00.53

Small, pleasant country campsite, but lack of foliage means it's rather exposed to the sun

Named after a prominent peak to the east of this region, the campsite of Pic St Loup is on high ground behind the tiny village of St Martin-de-Londres. It enjoys a pleasant, open aspect and a sweeping view of the plain of vineyards, interspersed with woodland. A small road runs through the first sections of grass *emplacements*, bounded by low, stone walling. Further on, the road leads onto a small field with more grass pitches. All this ground is completely exposed to the sun, so don't expect to keep your tent or caravan cool. The lower terrace on this side of the camp holds the rectangular swimming-pool, with an area to sit and watch the bathers where there is some shade provided by the few trees. The two *sanitaires* are in good order, with surprisingly roomy shower-cubicles, and also a special section for children. The young, energetic owner arranges family soirées and an occasional junior disco, but 'nothing too lively', he tells us. A good position (with easy access) that is close to regional sights, a reasonable tariff and general *bonhomie* are the factors that make this a pleasant place to stay, but only if you like it hot!

Directions: St Martin-de-Londres is approximately halfway between Ganges and Montpellier on the D986. There is a small turn-off on the main road, directly opposite the small village square. This is the D122

and you will see a camp direction sign here. Some way along here, take the first left up a track where you will see the tall flagpoles of the entrance ahead **Ground:** Hard **Children:** Playground **Wheelchair:** Suitable **Food-cooling:** Ice sold, coolpacks frozen **Sport:** Volleyball, ping pong, football, mini-golf **Season:** Easter to Sept **Reservation:** Advisable peak season **Charge:** 2 people, pitch and car 45 fr; child (under 7) 6 fr; electricity 9 fr

▬▬▬ Valras-Plage ▬▬▬

Sites summary For convenience we have lumped the three beach resorts of Valras-Plage, Sérignan-Plage and Portiragnes-Plage (also known as Redoute-Plage) under one heading as they are close to each other along the coastline, stretching out eastwards towards Vias-Plage. There are two dozen listed three- and four-star sites between them. Valras is a rather characterless, small, modern town with a grid of streets comprising apartments, tacky beach shops and a scattering of eating places. The majority of campsites in the area are similarly exposed to the elements, being large, anonymous grounds, littered with statics. Of the three sites we've chosen, except for the three-star *Lou Village*, the remaining two follow the mould of big, four-star 'holiday camp' sites. They both have tightly-packed pitches sprawling over a large area of ground, with a large number of mobile homes, but good entertainment facilities.

Directions for sites *Valras-Plage* can be reached from Béziers via Sérignan on the D19. On approaching the town, follow the road as it bears right. You will arrive at traffic-lights where there is an array of green camp direction signs. Turn right and this leads to the shore. At the bottom T-junction turn right and take the shore road. For *Lou Village* take the first left after the road has turned inland and for *La Yole*, continue straight up until you see the camp on your left. Alternatively, if coming from the A9, take the Béziers Ouest exit and then the D37E south, which will lead to *La Yole* directly. *Lou Village* will then be first right after that. As *Les Sablons* is actually at Portiragnes, directions are in the entry.

Domaine de la Yole

34350 Valras-Plage   tel 67.37.33.87

Large, self-contained campsite with good entertainment facilities, but sanitary blocks could do with an upgrade

La Domaine de la Yole is a 'holiday village' type of camp with roughly 1,000 *emplacements* and is blessed with a moderately attractive and shady situation, courtesy of the light woodland that pervades the grounds. The camp differs from many sites of the same size in that its recreational and commercial facilities are more or less in a central position. The small street of shops comprises a supermarket with fresh meat and delicatessen counters, a general shop selling items such as batteries and newspapers, a launderette and a hairdresser, as well as a *boulangerie* and *pâtisserie*. Close by is an impressive array of food outlets: a pizzeria, cafeteria, *friterie* for take-away chips and a café and bar. A large, raised sun terrace surrounds two big swimming-pools and there's even a special section near the pool complex for the supervised Club des Jeunes, with its own inflatable and a soft drinks counter. The greater part of the camping ground is equidistant from these amenities, but the site extends further westwards (away from the main road), so if you are allocated a pitch number starting with a 7 or an 8, expect to be a little way from the pools. Made-up roads take you past a lot of static caravans to the reasonably-sized but rather tightly-packed grass pitches. There's no real privacy here – just the tall trees marking out the corners. Pitches are grouped into sections of approximately 100 *emplacements*, with each group around a *sanitaire*. All these are of the old-fashioned blockhouse type, which seem to be revamped annually with a new coat of paint. Some blocks have more modern interiors than others, but there are usually no more than a couple of seated toilets for men. On our visit a small irrigation channel near the children's play area had silted up and was producing an offensive smell. Although this is a large site that attracts a lot of package operators, the splitting of the camp into defined areas with avenues that round corners relieves the visual monotony of a grid system.

Directions: See Directions to sites at the beginning of Valras-Plage
Ground: Hard **Children:** Playground, swimming, organised events
Wheelchair: Not suitable **Food-cooling:** Ice sold **Sport:** Tennis,
volleyball, ping pong, mini-golf, bike-hire **Season:** May to Sept
Reservation: Advisable peak season **Charge:** 2 people, pitch, car and
electricity 110 fr

Lou Village

BP 30, 34350 Valras-Plage	Out-of-season tel 93.87.40.63
	tel 67.37.33.79

Packed beach site, but not too large and plenty of shade to keep you cool

This camp is virtually next door to Domaine de la Yole, but is a
more comfortable size, with only half the number of pitches.
The ambience is different, too; entertainment is on offer, but
the approach is less ostentatious. Round the corner from the
entrance the roadway leads to the bar and restaurant by a small
supermarket. There is a shady, gravel terrace where you can
relax with a drink. The restaurant serves slightly more basic fare
than at Domaine de la Yole, such as steak *haché* or omelettes,
but is also much cheaper. Opposite this area is the purpose-built
stage for live groups or other evening entertainment. Tall trees
screen off sections of *emplacements* to create an illusion of space,
as well as camouflaging the closeness of tents, caravans and
mobile homes. Foliage is denser here, providing some welcome
shade. *Emplacements* become more open as you approach the
beach, with only small, sparse conifers among the pitches.
Sanitaires are in good condition and have seated toilets. Before
you reach the sea, a couple of natural pools are supervised for
bathing and watersports. As Lou Village is one of the cheaper
places to stay at this resort, it is perhaps the better bet for those
on a budget or with children who do not need entertaining
every minute of the day.

● ⓛ 大 ♨ ✕ ♀ ☛ 🏛 ⎄ 🔲 ⚲ ♫

Directions: See Directions for sites at the beginning of Valras-Plage
Ground: Hard **Children:** Playground, organised events
Wheelchair: Not suitable **Food-cooling:** Ice sold, coolpacks frozen
Sport: Tennis, volleyball, ping pong, football, bike-hire, windsurfing
Season: 24 May to 10 Sept **Reservation:** Advisable peak season
Charge: 2 people, pitch and car 75 fr; electricity 13 fr

⑦ *Les Sablons*

34420 Portiragnes-Plage   tel 67.90.90.55

Good entertainment and facilities at this large, self-contained site, but lack of privacy may be a drawback

This site is along the coast at Portiragnes-Plage, a little further east from Valras-Plage. The entrance to Les Sablons holds a lot of promise: tall trees cast shadows across the drive, bridged by a double portico of square pillars supporting a narrow, tiled roof. To one side is the reception and small commercial centre with self-service restaurant, *pâtisserie*, *boulangerie* and a small open vegetable market. More activity is centred on the contemporary building on the left which houses a pizzeria, restaurant, and bar with video games. A large, open, paved terrace surrounds the swimming-pools full of happy families cooling off in the water, or burning up in the sun, or alternating between the two! *Animateurs* are employed to amuse the kids at the special children's corner. Enthusiasm may begin to wane once you enter the camping ground beyond. Earth-based tracks lead off the main avenues into row upon row of pitches with no natural boundaries: there is nothing in the way of seclusion or privacy, the only compensation being the shade given by the light woodland. This cover decreases towards the periphery of the grounds, resulting in exposed alleys of seemingly continuous canvas. Away from the older area of the camp, which centres around the amenities and enjoys direct access to the sands, the site has developed in sections of regimented rows of *emplacements*, so you could be in for a long trek to the centre of activities. However, if you manage to reserve an *emplacement* prefixed with the letters B, C or O (standing for Bosquet, Carignan and Oustalet sections), you'll be in a shadier position and better placed for facilities. Sanitary arrangements are good, and the fittings are more modern than at Domaine de la Yole. Facilities for the handicapped include a suite of *lavabos*, shower and toilet, but these are situated at the back end of the camp, far away from the main areas of activity.

☉ ⓛ 🧍 ⌲ 🏊 🛒 ✕ ♀ 🥾 🐾 ⛺ 📶 🎵

Although you are not obliged to return to your camp before it closes for the night, you are expected on such occasions to park in the overnight space outside the gate and walk to your tent.

147

Directions: Portiragnes is south-east of Béziers on the D37, off the N12. Continue through the town following the D37 towards the beach (travelling with the Canal du Midi on your right). At the roundabout take the second exit, signed Plage-Est. Go down a tree-lined dual carriageway to the site **Ground:** Hard **Children:** Playground, swimming, organised events **Wheelchair:** Tricky **Food-cooling:** Ice sold, coolpacks frozen, fridge hire **Sport:** Tennis, volleyball, ping pong **Season:** 1 Apr to Sept **Reservation:** Advisable peak season **Charge:** 2 people, pitch, car and electricity 110 fr

Vias-Plage

Sites summary Farinette-Plage, to give Vias-Plage its correct title, is the beach resort for the town of Vias, a couple of kilometres inland. The heart of the resort is right at the end of the D137 from Vias and is nothing but a row of rather tacky commercial enterprises: eating places for ice-cream and fastfood; shops selling clothes, beach goods, cheap jewellery and souvenir pottery; bars – one even advertises pints served in the 'happy hour' – and the Santa Maria discothèque. There are three quite separate camping areas – Plages Ouest, Sud and Est. Half the listed sites for all these areas are three- and four-star. From the fourteen sites, we took a look at the seven offering the most facilities. Our five finalists below are all in a central position. The far-flung ones in isolated fields near the western beach were found to be characterless camping grounds. *Le Bourricot* has the edge as an attractive, quietish place to stay at a reasonable cost. It is the only one without a pool, but the beach is only a matter of yards away. Young families may prefer nearby *Le Napoléon*: it's slightly more expensive but includes some extras. *Camping-Club Farret* lacks shade but has plenty of entertainment for families. The two 'big boys' as we've called them – *Carabasse* and *Salisses* – are your mighty and less mighty holiday camps respectively: frenetic family fun but then that could just be what you're looking for. These are situated away from the beach at the top end of the resort.

Le Bourricot

34450 Vias   tel 67.21.64.27

Get away from the hustle and bustle of the beach at this shady retreat

About 150 metres from the beach is the pleasant, small campsite of Le Bourricot, a very shady spot, which is unusual for a site so close to the shore. Unpretentious buildings roofed with red clay-tiles form a forecourt near the entrance to the camp. They house a small shop and a snack-bar/restaurant with seating outside under the few tall trees in the clearing. Nearby is a sandy enclosure containing a children's playground with basic equipment. Le Bourricot's large, sandy *emplacements* are screened by conifer hedges and the arrangement of the pitches in small compounds that are fenced off and lined with trees creates the feeling of several miniature sites. The whole camp is covered by dense foliage, except for the central open portion which gives you the option of a sunny pitch. The *sanitaires*, while a bit old-fashioned (with wooden doors) are quite adequate and contain seated toilets. The general atmosphere is quiet here: it's not the place to come for discos. Soirées are gentle affairs with perhaps a communal dinner with a singer/guitarist. It was a relief to find a camp such as Le Bourricot down among the tourist trap of shops at Plage-Sud, and once you've passed through its plain white gates you could almost think yourself in the country.

● ⑤ ♨ 🏪 ✗ ⚥ 🏛 ⛶ ▣

Directions: Take the D137 over a canal, heading straight for Plage-Sud. Just before the beach is a right-hand turn where a blue camp sign indicates the site is just up this road. The entrance is on the right
Ground: Giving and sandy **Children:** Playground **Wheelchair:** Not suitable **Food-cooling:** Ice sold, coolpacks frozen, fridge hire
Sport: None **Season:** 20 May to 20 Sept **Reservation:** Advisable peak season **Charge:** 2 people, pitch and car 80 fr; electricity 13 fr

Campsites usually operate an order system for take-aways and dépôts de pain. The take-away orders should be placed well in advance; times are usually listed at the counter. You would normally give your name and order for bread and croissants at the site's shop, if there is one, or possibly at the bar.

Camping-Club Farret

34450 Vias-Plage   tel 67.21.64.45

A busy site, by day and night, and rather exposed to the elements, but a good choice in this resort

A tarmac thoroughfare, bordered with ornamental palms, leads past the reception and into the camp's grounds. The first noticeable feature at the site is the lack of trees to give any cover to the mass of packed-in *emplacements*. Nevertheless, the flowers and hedges by the wide, made-up roads at the top end of the grounds look quite decorative. Caravans and camper-vans in this part fill the suitably-sized *emplacements*, while towards the rear of the camp, nearer the beach, the smaller pitches are taken up by numerous tents. This is a less sheltered area that can be exposed to the wind as well as the sun. A diversion for the kiddies here is a log structure in the form of a galleon (which is in addition to the site's playground). Not too far from the site entrance, the commercial centre by the pools comprises the shops and bar with cafeteria. The latter is large enough to become the venue for indoor entertainment in the evenings, having a purpose-built stage covered in speakers and lights, with a banner across the top of the curtains bearing the legend 'Holiday Folies'! Camping-Club Farret is a busy beach site but with a little more appeal than some in the same mould, and if you're young and carefree, you could enjoy all the entertainment that it has to offer.

Directions: Take the D137 to Plage-Sud after going over the canal from Vias. As you enter the commercial area of the resort, take the first left by the *gendarmerie*, where you will see a sign for the camp
Ground: Some pitches hard, some sandy **Children:** Playground, swimming, organised events **Wheelchair:** Not suitable
Food-cooling: Ice sold, coolpacks frozen, fridge hire **Sport:** Tennis, volleyball, ping pong, golf-practice, windsurfing, bike-hire
Season: May to Sept **Reservation:** Advisable peak season
Charge: 2 people, pitch and car 85 fr; extra adult 25 fr; electricity 10 fr

---

Never tip waste water, such as from washing-up bowls, on to the ground at a campsite, but always do so in the sinks provided at the sanitaire. *There too you will find special provision for disposing of any chemical toilet waste.*

La Carabasse

Farinette-Plage, 34450 Vias   tel 67.21.64.01

Big, busy four-star site, literally 'awash' with good family entertainment, but rather noisy

A roundabout of flowers and trees greets you as you roll up outside the entrance to this busy, family camp. As you would expect at a site of this size, there's a commercial centre consisting of the usual self-service, grocery and bazaar. Behind this parade of shops that fronts onto the road, and around the back of the mini-golf, you'll find a take-away counter opposite an old swimming-pool. The older building nearby houses the restaurant, with an extended terrace outside with tables arranged between hedges; as it is right by the roadside it's not really an interesting place to sit and eat. But the main attraction is further into the camp. If you follow the avenue from the entrance, you pass the few pitches that have a satisfactory amount of shade, then suddenly the grounds open out to reveal a vast paved clearing which appears to be filled with water. This is what the camp brochure describes as a 'Californian-style pool'; we'd call it a miniature S-shaped lake. Of varying depth and supervised by attendants, it is likely to bring the water-lovers running. The whole area is a concrete lido, on a raised platform of paving, completely exposed to the sun. As for the rest of the camp, it's the same old story of tightly packed pitches, little seclusion from your neighbour, if any at all, and nightly entertainment in the form of the disco pounding away – in short this camp is big and busy!

Directions: Go through Vias town towards the beach (you will cross the Canal du Midi) and just after the bridge on your right is a funfair. La Carabasse is immediately after, on your left **Ground:** Hard
Children: Playground, swimming, organised events
Wheelchair: Tricky **Food-cooling:** Ice sold, coolpacks frozen, fridge hire **Sport:** Tennis, ping pong, bike-hire, mini-golf, horse-riding
Season: Mid-May to Mid-Oct **Reservation:** Advisable peak season
Charge: 2 people, pitch and car 107 fr; child (under 2) free; extra person 17 fr; electricity 16 fr

Children should be discouraged from playing around shower blocks.

Le Napoléon

Farinette-Plage, 34450 Vias   tel 67.21.64.37

Small, pleasant, family-run four-star site that caters well for children; close to the beach

Like Le Bourricot, this camp is situated behind the parade of shops at the beach end of Vias-Plage. Le Napoléon is a relatively small, four-star site, reasonably shady but not as shady as Le Bourricot where the trees are smaller and broader. A small roadway takes you through to a shop selling local produce and a bar/restaurant with a *feu du bois* chimney in an attractive clearing. The restaurant has a covered courtyard with matting on the ground, where rows of tables have been placed outside around the edge. The addition of a well-equipped playground and swimming-pools creates a good, central area of activity. In the evenings, while the children are playing table tennis, or are on the swings, mum and dad can sit down to a meal at a good price, from a reasonably varied menu of basic dishes. The main part of the camping ground is made up of *emplacements* with mobile homes dotted about in between. Sanitary arrangements are good, with the provision of a baby bath. We met one satisfied GB couple with young children on the last day of their holiday who happened to book up through an operator more or less on spec. Le Napoléon is not too dissimilar to its neighbour Le Bourricot, which is a three-star site; Le Napoléon is slightly more expensive, but then you do have little extras such as the pool and individual water and electricity points.

● ⓢ 🜨 🝤 ✕ ♀ ☞ ✸ 🝪 ⊟ ▣ ℘

Directions: Take the D137 from Vias over the canal and straight through to Plage-Sud. In the parade of shops, you will see on your right a large camp sign indicating the entrance **Ground:** Sandy **Children:** Playground, swimming **Wheelchair:** Not suitable **Food-cooling:** Ice sold, coolpacks frozen, fridge hire **Sport:** Tennis, ping pong **Season:** Easter to 1 Sept **Reservation:** Advisable peak season **Charge:** 2 people, pitch, car and electricity 106 fr; extra person 13 fr

If you don't want a full bottle of wine with your meal, ask for either a quart *(roughly four glasses) or* demi-quart *(two glasses) of house wine, usually a palatable* vin de pays, *which comes in a jug.*

Les Salisses

34450 Vias   tel 67.21.64.07

A good choice as a typically French, four-star family site

A very pleasing and busy entrance area awaits you at Les Salisses: a group of white buildings with sloping red-tiled roofs, set back from the main road, are decked out with hanging plants and surrounded by flower borders, lawns and shrubbery – all very pretty. Low arcades form two sides of the pool terrace, and round the corner, bathers have the option of a twisting waterchute. This hive of activity includes the reception, pizzeria and sauna and solarium suite with naturist pool. Across the car park is a snack-bar and another restaurant/*crêperie*. The short driveway into the camp becomes an avenue from which smaller paths lead off into a grid system of grass pitches, marked out by small trees and conifers. Les Salisses appears greener than some of the other sites in the area and the mixed foliage creates an attractive environment. *Sanitaires* are well appointed, and include a couple of baby baths. There's also the possibility of reserving *emplacements* with individual *sanitaires*. Towards the back of the camp the children's playground has wooden climbing frames and beyond this is mobile home territory. On a more critical note, we did notice that there were a couple of small play areas, both next to communal barbecues and bin collection points, and wondered at the wisdom of this arrangement. To sum up, Les Salisses is a popular site, but is a manageable size and a comparatively civilised place in which to camp.

🍺 Ⓜ 🧍 🏊 🛶 🗡 ♀ 🥾 🦌 🏚 🛝 📺 👜 🎵

Directions: Go through Vias town towards the beach (you will cross the Canal du Midi) and just after the bridge, on your right, is a funfair. The site is further on, on your right, opposite La Carabasse
Ground: Hard to giving **Children:** Playground, swimming, organised events **Wheelchair:** Suitable **Food-cooling:** Ice sold, coolpacks frozen **Sport:** Tennis **Season:** Apr to Sept **Reservation:** Advisable peak season **Charge:** 2 people, pitch, car and electricity 105 fr; extra adult 20 fr

If you want to maximise the little shade your pitch may be offering but are unable to determine the sun's direction, try the old stick-in-the-ground trick and watch the progression of its shadow before erecting your tent.

Gard and Ardèche Valley

Gard

The Gard region lies to the west of the arterial A9 heading south from Avignon, and deceptive cartography may fool you into thinking that there is nothing much in the way of excitement here. Looking at the map in a triangle roughly between Alès, Montpellier and Avignon, indeed there doesn't seem to be much promise. General Marcus Vispanius Agrippa may have thought the same when he came to carry out various civil engineering projects in the first century BC. But we bet that towards the end of the contract he wasn't in too much of a hurry to return home.

Of all the regions in the Guide where foreigners might go picking about to satisfy their tourist lust, the Gard is the most aloof, the most private. Unlike the Dordogne, whose river is only part of the package, the River Gard *is* the Gard. It grows from a collection of impetuous streams high in the Cévennes hills, turning into a noble river gliding through the plain and scrubby *garrigue* landscape.

If you were painting on canvas instead of with words, the Dordogne's visual appeal would be its obvious colouring, its orderly conception – the river, the château, the cliff . . . It would probably have been a favourite area for Constable if he had ventured this far. But in the Cévennes, its forest blanket straddling the Hérault/Gard border, the landscape is random, wilder, more sensual. We're talking Impressionists here – Seurat, Monet, the shimmer of heat haze in the steep verdant hills. Look out from the ramparts of the fort-like meteorological station on top of Mont Aigoual, in the southern end of the

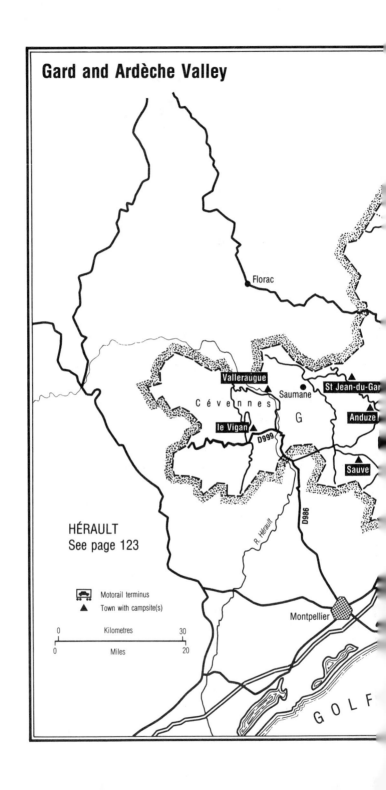

Gard and Ardèche Valley

Florac

Valleraugue

Saumane

St Jean-du-Gar

Cévennes

G

le Vigan

D999

Anduze

Sauve

HÉRAULT
See page 123

R. Hérault

D986

Montpellier

Motorail terminus

▲ Town with campsite(s)

| 0 | Kilometres | 30 |

| 0 | Miles | 20 |

GOLF

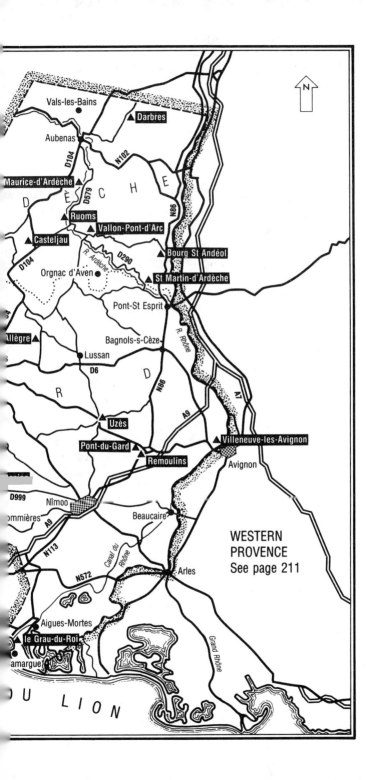

National Park, and you will see how to reproduce space and distance with colour and tone. Each receding range grows paler towards the open-blue horizon. Sombre greens eventually give way to faint mauves as you strain to follow the Park into Lozère.

Somewhere down below, a young River Gard (also called Gardon) trips over the polished brown stones of its river bed. You can admire the river's journey from the heights of the Corniche or explore it in the gorge where cool, glass-rod waterfalls dive into deep pools tucked into smooth white boulders. A secret place of such a description lies under the Pont des Abarines, a single span roadbridge vaulting the gorge with parabolic grace.

When you tire of the river, the Gard region has plenty more to offer. We list below some of the main towns and other sites that no visitor to the area would want to miss.

Aigues-Mortes

The name is as fascinating as the place. Aigues-Mortes means Dead Waters for it was once actually by the sea. Now it's about five kilometres in from the coast and while no longer surrounded by a moat, is still close enough to the salt-water lakes of the western end of the Camargue to retain something of its original character – no less so inside its walls. Second to Carcassonne it is probably the best preserved fortified town in the South and like that city can similarly impress from a distance in the middle of a flat, melancholy plain of salt marshes.

Aigues-Mortes was developed in the thirteenth century by Louis IX from a small fishing harbour into a port from which he could embark on his crusades to the Holy Land. The ramparts on which you can walk form a huge rectangle punctuated by turrets of the gates set in the walls. The largest, the Constance Tower, was the original keep that protected the harbour. Good views are to be had from here. Below, the grid plan of streets retains something of what it must have been like living here in the Middle Ages. Well worth the detour.

Anduze

Anduze is known as the Port des Cévennes. It sits between twin cliffs at the head of the gorge where the Gard exits and the traveller enters that terrain. Behind a façade of provincial trade lies the old quarter, oozing Mediterranean culture that has embedded itself in the ageing walls of narrow apartments, with terracotta pots and window-boxes exploding with colour at every storey. Slip through the arch and you're in a narrow street with the smell of bread and the rustic charm of hand-turned pottery. Turn the corner and suddenly you're in the covered marketplace which is stuffed with swollen, scarlet tomatoes, honey jar pyramids, sweet-smelling cantaloupe melons and witch-chinned old women offering produce to olive-dark younger women with rich-brown eyes. The light glares, the shade cools and the ancient circular fountain capped with a cone of peacock-coloured, rounded tiles and stained with generations of *marchés*, trickles water to provoke thirst.

The busy café-filled main street features the fourteenth-century Tour de l'Horloge, a small stone tower that displays not only a clock but a sundial, too. There is a Super-U supermarket close to the station and the open market day is a Thursday.

Avignon and Villeneuve-les-Avignon

Even though Avignon is on the eastern side of the Rhône (which forms the departmental boundary between Gard and Vaucluse), we've included it in this region because for many visitors to the Gard it's their introduction to the area, and certainly feels part of it in spirit. It acts as a marker where the Languedoc to the west becomes Provence to the east. An outer shell of residential sprawl all but envelopes the old walled city.

In 1308 Pope Clément V established an alternative Pontifical court away from Rome, where for the next 70 years his successors maintained the papacy from the magnificent fortress of white stone known as the Palais des Papes. In fact there are two palaces, the Old and the New, built in successive periods. These buildings stand in a commanding position on the Rocher des Doms, topped by the terraced gardens.

Between here and the palace square a motor 'train' operated by the tourist office runs up and down the zig-zig paths for those preferring to ride rather than walk up the hill. The square – a permanent focus for tourists – is a large paved open space with troughs of flowers and a traditional fairground roundabout in one corner. Artists tout their paintings and drawings by the stone staircase leading up to the main palace doors which are set in a façade of arches.

Back on the rock's terrace you can look down at St Bénézet bridge, the Pont d'Avignon of the song. It is now an incomplete span, time and flood having left their mark. Across the river is the silhouette of the St André Fort standing above Villeneuve-les-Avignon. In the fourteenth century Villeneuve became an overspill town for the cardinals of the court who built very select residences for themselves. The castle is open to the public and its siting on the small hill of St André gives correspondingly lovely views back across the river to the Popes' Palace and a pale Mont Ventoux in the distance.

Beaucaire and Tarascon

Beaucaire is in the Gard and Tarascon is in the Bouches-du-Rhône. Each has its castle, though they are in totally contrasting states of repair. Beaucaire's is a ghost of its former glory, having been pulled apart by Cardinal Richelieu in the seventeenth century. Tarascon's, on the other hand, is beautifully intact, its solid, square battlements rising majestically from a rocky bank of the river. The guided tour of its interior reveals some fine Gothic detail in its architecture as well as a panoramic view from the top. The town of Tarascon is associated with the legend of the Tarasque, an aquatic, lion-headed monster that lived in the Rhône occasionally to emerge and gorge itself on local women and children. It was finally defeated at the hands of St Martha, she of Stes Maries-de-la-Mer on the Camargue coast (see Western Provence). Behind the main thoroughfare you will find the old Rues des Halles where shops hide under a low, thick-pillared arcade which ends with the decorous façade of the seventeenth-century *mairie*. Round the corner in the Rue Proudhon is a little museum dedicated to Provençal life.

The Cévennes

At the southern tip of the Massif Central is a vast, wild, mountainous region cut into by gorges and rivers. Its heartland is designated a national park to protect its flora and fauna. Perhaps the most inspiring part is the heavily forested area around Mont Aigoual. The region is easily penetrated by following the Corniche des Cévennes (the D9) from Florac to near St Jean-du-Gard, but if you want a more adventurous drive taking in some stupendous scenery, try the route which takes you from Saumane, right over the top and down to Valleraugue. From the D907 north of Saumane, turn left on to the D20. At Les Plantiers pick up the D193: this takes you up to the Col du Pas (800 metres – the peak is a relatively easy climb if you are appropriately attired). From there, the D10 winds its way down to Valleraugue, centre of the local apple industry and a base for walkers.

Mont Aigoual at over 1500 metres is quite accessible by car and has on its granite summit a meteorological observatory that acts as a ski station in winter. Built in 1887 by the French equivalent of the Forestry Commission – the Cévennes having undergone an extensive programme of reafforestation since the turn of the century – its handsome building of fort-like appearance is an excellent viewpoint. On a clear day you can see Mont Blanc in the Alps.

If you are based in one of the Anduze campsites you will have positioned yourself very conveniently for some interesting things to see in this locality. From Anduze station you can take the *train à vapeur* to **St Jean-du-Gard**. The black slab of a steam engine hauls old wooden-seated rolling stock through a pretty scenic route that cannot be appreciated from the road. As this is a tourist train it stops now and then for photo opportunities. St Jean-du-Gard is a typical little Cévenol town where, while waiting for your return journey, you can visit the Museum of the Cévennes Valley, illustrating the lifestyle and natural history of the area.

The following are visits lying between the Anduze and St Jean-du-Gard:

- **Le Bambuseraie de Prafrance** – (just north of Anduze towards Générargues D129 from Anduze): exotic gardens containing a forest of bamboo and water gardens.

  Musée du Désert–(Le Mas Soubeyran, D50 from Anduze via Générargues): devoted to the history of the French Protestants of the region who suffered persecution in the seventeenth and eighteenth centuries.

- **Grotte de Trabuc**–(directions as for Musée du Desert): has a subterranean waterfall and a lake. Among its concretions is the '100,000 Soldiers', its numerous vertical structures looking like an army lining battlements.

- **Pont des Abarines**—(D50 from St Jean-du-Gard): pack a picnic and a parasol and spend all day in this gorge under the bridge in one of the most beautiful spots in the Languedoc for river-bathing. Park your car – you'll see others – on the eastern side of the bridge (*after* crossing the river if you're coming from St Jean-du-Gard). You will have to search a bit for a well-defined path that descends the steep, woody cliff. With care, but without danger, it can be done – children, hamper and all – in only a minute.

Les Fumades, Serre du Bouquet and Les Concluses

North-east of the industrial town of Alès, eight or so kilometres along the D16, is a place that to all intents and purposes exists only at weekends. **Les Fumades** is a spa, with just a casino, a hotel and a residential clinic, for the waters discovered here in Roman times are considered to have therapeutic properties for respiratory ailments. The place bursts into life on Sundays when families from miles around come to spend an afternoon picnicking on the green, playing *pétanque*, attending the tea-dance on the casino terrace or treating the children to pony rides.

Les Fumades sits on the western edge of the weird landscape of the **Serre du Bouquet**. By taking the D7 south from the spa and then the D607 at Brouzet-les-Alès, you will come to Mont Bouquet (630 metres), giving you wide vistas from the Cévennes to Vaucluse. Alternatively, you can drive along the scenic D37 going east from Fumades past the ruins of the Château d'Allègre and cross-country to Lussan, a walled town splendid on its small hill. Picking up the D143 then the D643 you can head for **Les Concluses**, a bare-rocked gorge carved out of the ground by the Aiguillon. The river dries up in the summer so it's possible to walk a length of its bed. There's one spectacular point (the Portail) where the opposite rock-faces touch almost above your head.

Le Grau-du-Roi and Port-Camargue

Ancient and modern lie side by side here. To take the ancient first, **Le Grau-du-Roi** is a charming fishing port of twin quays lining the sea exit of the Canal du Rhône coming from Aigues-Mortes. It is a major trawling base, netting around 6,000 tons of fish annually. 'Grau' is the word for a natural opening in the sandbars common to this part of the coast, that separate sea from salt-lakes. 'Roi' refers to its origins when Henry IV planned its development as a permanent harbour to prevent regular silting. It was only in the mid-nineteenth century that it became the town we see today.

Port-Camargue, lying east of Le Grau-du-Roi, is an example of how modern development can attain some sort of harmony with a natural – in this case, marine – environment: not like La Grande-Motte described in the previous region. Conceived some twenty or so years ago, Port-Camargue is an artificially created residential yacht harbour and with its 'islands' of low-rise flats and holiday homes is probably the 'modern' equivalent of Port Grimaud (see Eastern Provence). It's worth taking a drive around the lagoon to see what has been done here. Close by are the beaches and campsites.

Nîmes

Once a source of a certain textile ('de Nîmes'). Founded on the legend of the springwaters here belonging to the healing god Nemausus, Nîmes is the last of Languedoc's big cities before you arrive in Provence. Although similar in size to Montpellier it is easier to traverse and seems a more relaxing town to walk about in. The legacy of Rome co-exists comfortably with seventeenth-century streets and twentieth-century commerce and it is this glimpse of the once ruling Empire that brings visitors here.

The prime attraction is the Arena (Arènes). It is the best preserved example in Europe, far more intact that the amphitheatre of Arles, smaller, yet built earlier – about 50 AD. Sitting high in its top terraces, it is easy to imagine 20,000 spectators calling for the blood of gladiators – a little more difficult to do when the floor has been fitted out with seating and a speaker-choked stage for a rock concert! A more regular type of venue are the summer *ferias* where bulls instead of lions contest the hand of man.

Two other related sights are the Maison Carrée and the ruins of the Temple of Diana. Maison Carrée is not in fact square, but it strikes one immediately because of its adherence to an obvious Greek architectural formula, including columns topped with Corinthian capitals supporting a triangular entablature. Built in the first century as a temple, though no-one knows to whom, it is nowadays a museum for Roman remains. The second sight is also a temple, dedicated to the goddess Diana, and hardly complete at all. But its ruined state has quite a romantic appeal, all the more for being situated in the beautiful Jardin de la Fontaine which is at the end of the straight run of the water-split Avenue Jean Jaurès. Here it was, at the source of Nemausus's spring, that an army engineer, set about landscaping these grounds some time in the eighteenth century. Today, we are rewarded with delightful lake-filled terraces of lawn and greenery. Within them is the remnant of a strange octagonal tower – the Tour Mague – which could have been a part of the old city's fortifications.

Twelve kilometres or so out of Nîmes you can visit the **Perrier bottling plant** and the spring itself (guided tours on weekdays only). From Nîmes take the N113 going south-west to Lunel; turn left onto the D139 before Codognan.

Pont-du-Gard

Agrippa's Pont du Gard is surely the all-time great of Gallo-Roman antiquities. A length of yellow-gold arches, the remaining section of a mighty Roman aqueduct that once carried water from Uzès to Nîmes (a distance of some 30 kilometres), it still holds within its precision-laid stone blocks an aura of dignity, nobility and a sense of divine purpose. This huge symbol of an imperial past defies you not to feel humbled by its dominant stride, linking the cliffs either side of the river gorge. Ideally, it should be viewed from the side away from the adjoining road bridge, so that the three tiers of arches – the top far smaller than the lower two – can be seen to best advantage. Down here you can bathe in the shallow waters of the Gard and avoid the mass of clicking autofocuses. Through the top tier is a conduit that used to carry the water. You can walk with a stoop through this and, if bravery permits, climb through one of the occasional gaps in the roofing to stand on top. It is not quite as dangerous as it looks, the width there being over ten feet – like standing in the middle of an average size room but 130 feet up.

Sommières

Sommières is a small medieval town, its old quarter hidden behind gated walls. The bridge carrying the road (the N110) over the river to meet the town wall head-on is of Roman origins and can get jammed with traffic in the summer. The narrow cobbled streets are now given over to pedestrians who can enjoy the two market squares, the Marché-Bas, lined with shadowy arcades, and the Marché-Haut, the old corn market. Saturday is market day and you may catch the local brass band performing.

Uzès

The town dates from the eleventh century; the Ducal Palace with its handsome fourteenth-century Viscount Tower is still standing. The sensitively restored Place de la République, once the scene of the herb market in the Middle Ages, is sleepy during the week, but still evokes that era with its crowded Saturday market.

Around the corner from this bustle is the Fenestrelle Tower, a remarkable twelfth-century round, colonnaded tower: Pisa revisited but smaller and upright. It stands by the cathedral of St Théodorit and the grounds of these buildings open out onto a wide terrace, the Promenade Jean Racine (the playwright who spent some time as a youth in Uzès). From its balustrade you can look out across the undulating *garrigue* that surrounds these parts.

If you are planning to visit Uzès, make sure you know which exit of the one-way system you'll want afterwards – otherwise you'll be made to go round in circles if you miss it.

Ardèche Valley

The *département* of Ardèche lies on the western side of the Rhône covering a narrow area from near Lyon in the north to Orange in the south. The Ardèche valley with its famous gorge cuts through the bottom third – the Bas Vivarais – and it is in this popular area that we've concentrated our attention.

The valley is another region of limestone composition and therefore of underground rivers, gorges, caves and river erosion. There, too, you find the familiar landscapes of white-grey rock mottled with the deep green of dense foliage. Orchards and vineyards abound, benefiting from the Mediterranean climate.

The **River Ardèche**, in its mid-section between Aubenas and Vallon-Pont-d'Arc, travels through a wider, gentler terrain than the higher ground from where the rushing waters derive. By the time the river has reached here it has gained a calmer disposition.

The river descent by canoe can be done in a day or, if you prefer to prolong it, there are a couple of staging posts for pitching down overnight. These have washing facilities and fresh water. There's a plethora of choice for canoe rental agencies, the majority being along the D290 on the south side of Vallon. You must be able to swim but those who can't can be taken by professional canoeists in a six-man boat. The costs of hiring a two-seat canoe (single kayaks are available) is anything between £25 and £30 and includes life-jackets, watertight containers for your belongings and the return minibus fare back to Vallon. If you don't fancy the full-length trip, an alternative is to take the mini-descent of six kilometres. Novices may be reassured to learn that the Ardèche is at its most placid in the summer months.

Aubenas

Aubenas is less inspiring to be in than to view from a distance, standing alone on a solitary rise from the valley floor. It is the centre of the fruit-preserving industry in these parts. The town bristles with a sense of purpose but does not hold much attraction for the visitor other than being a reasonably pleasant watering-hole.

Going north-west on the D435 you'll come to **Vals-les-Bains** wedged between volcanic cliffs. They act as a channel for the Volane which flows into the Ardèche here. Vals is a long, narrow spa town squashed onto the banks of the river, and it produces its own mineral water from numerous local springs.

One of these is in the cedarwood grounds of the Casino park and sends out a natural fountain every six hours. The waters are meant to be good for digestive complaints.

The D579 follows the valley linking Aubenas and Vallon-Pont-d'Arc and can be a tedious drive in season. It wasn't built to take the amount of excessive traffic that uses it, yet efforts are constantly being made to up-grade particular stretches. A two-part detour avoiding two-thirds of this run is the D104/D4 from Aubenas. At Bellevue you turn on to the D4 for Ruoms. The road runs along the Ligne Gorge, offering a glimpse of the typical ruggedness of these parts.

Aven d'Orgnac

Orgnac-l'Aven, a town lying south-west of the Ardèche Gorge, has two underground attractions in its vicinity. The **Aven d'Orgnac** (*aven*: cave) is a vast cavern divided into two main chambers, the Chaos Chamber and the Red Chamber (so-called because of the colour of the rock). The Chaos Chamber is quite remarkable in its giant calcinate forms illuminated by a strange blue light emanating from somewhere above. You could easily believe that this was the landscape of another planet. The **Grotte de la Forestière** is a more conventional *grotte* some distance from the cave and has a variety of concretions. You might also like to visit the **Museum of Prehistory** in the town.

Another *aven*, the **Aven de Marzal**, is to be found north of the Gorge (turn north off the Corniche on to the D590 across the Plateau des Gras). Metal steps like a giant fire escape take you down 120 metres through various sections, ending in the Diamond Chamber of which the walls dazzle with a multitude of crystals. Back above ground is a prehistoric 'zoo' of repro dinosaurs.

Gorges de l'Ardèche

The Ardèche Gorge is possibly the more 'tourist-friendly' of all southern French gorges. The road, twisting and turning on high, keeps you spellbound by 30 kilometres of precipitous limestone cliffs, some more than 300 metres in height. One bend after another brings you out onto a vantage point giving an even dizzier view than the one before. At each stop, far, far below you will see the glass-green winding tape of the river transporting intermittent strings of canoes, looking no more than melon seeds in a gutter.

The D290 begins climbing from outside Vallon to follow the cliff edges. Using a large-scale map you can identify the viewing platforms (*belvédères*) at strategic bends. The most concentrated group that give out onto supremely dramatic panoramas are on the highest stretch (the Haute Corniche) beginning at the Cirque de la Madeleine. This natural amphitheatre of an immense cliff, carved precisely out of the land, is approximately the mid-way point of the drive. The road leaves the gorge for a while but then returns at the Grande Belvédère, which looks down on the last bend in the river.After zig-zagging chaotically round this curve in the cliffs the road drops quickly to the valley, and the drama of the gorge is no more. On the low rise of the opposite bank you will see the fortifications of ancient Aiguèze as you enter St Martin-d'Ardèche – nothing special but possessing a few well-patronised restaurants.

Pont d'Arc

Although any piece of the river, whether from above or below, could be regarded as a highlight of your visit, the most frequently photographed spot is the Pont d'Arc (just east of Vallon-Pont-d'Arc on the D579). This natural stone bridge (reached by foot) is the result of thousands of years of erosion by the river eating away at what was, it is assumed, a small fissure in the rock. Today the arch is 60 metres wide.

Ruoms

This is a depressing one-street town saved by its old walled and towered hub. There's a useful supermarket on its southern side by an automatic rail crossing. Campsites begin to proliferate at the foot of **Sampzon**, a village reached by a single lane bridge over the river from the D579 and up a succession of hairy hairpins. Sampzon sits on a high rock and can be readily identified by the TV mast on top. The village is minute but the views are good.

Vallon Pont d'Arc

This is the starting point of the descent into the Ardèche Gorge. Surprisingly, it's nothing special as a town but its narrow streets are packed with small, sometimes intimate, eating places.

Tourist offices

Comité Départemental de
  Tourisme
3 place des Arènes
BP 122, 30011 Nîmes
Tel 66.21.02.51

Office de Tourisme d'Alès et des
  Cévennes
Chambres de Commerce d'Alès
BP 49, 30101 Alès
Tel 66.78.49.00

Office de Tourisme des Gorges de
  l'Ardèche
Cité Administrative
07150 Vallon Pont d'Arc
Tel 75.88.04.01

Comité du Tourisme des Gorges
  de l'Ardèche
8 cours du Palais
BP 221, 07002 Privas
Tel 75.64.04.66

■■■ Allègre ■■■

⑦ *Château de Boisson*

Boisson-Les Fumades, 30500 St-Ambroix   tel 66.24.85.61

Castle-living, but the price is not the only drawback

For many people, the idea of staying in the grounds of a real château would seem the pinnacle of a camping holiday, so it's unfortunate that Château de Boisson is one of our 'caveat' entries. The Château sits on a hill in the village centre, but you don't get to enter in grand style through its arched gateway – a pity. The reception and car park are at the bottom of the hill, a narrow strip of ground with its own *sanitaire* serving the rather worn and cramped pitches at this end. The rest of the two-tier site is up within the actual grounds of the Château. You may not be that impressed by the two-minute climb up to all the facilities – lugging the laundry, for example – but once up there, you'll find a pretty, circular pool edged with a paved sunbathing terrace and potted plants. Here, too, is a small modern restaurant (prices are a little above average – and barbecuing is not allowed). Beyond is an attractive gravel courtyard terrace by the decorative main door to the Château's apartments. The pitches at this level are also tight on space. The *sanitaire* within the castle building is on the old side and, when we visited, could have done with a bit of redecoration. It would be perfectly possible to isolate yourself here and enjoy feeling like a lord for a few days but you'll certainly have to pay for it. In fact, camping here plays second fiddle to what is seen as the more prestigious side of the business, a residential summer painting school. You can also stay in self-contained flats within the Château.

● ⑤ 🏊 🛶 🏪 🍴 ♀ 👍 🏠 ♿ 🔲 🎾

Directions: The D16 runs north-east of Alès. A right-hand turn, the D37, takes you over the River Auzon. After crossing this take the first left at a crossroads. You will see Boisson village on a rise ahead. The site entrance is a turn-off on your right **Ground:** Hard
Children: Playground, swimming **Wheelchair:** Not suitable
Food-cooling: Ice sold **Sport:** Tennis, ping pong **Season:** 15 April to Sept **Reservation:** Advisable peak season **Charge:** Pitch 43 fr; person 22 fr; electricity 16 fr

✿ Domaine des Fumades

Les Fumades, 30500 Allègre   tel 66.24.80.78

Four-star French-style family camping – an oasis in this desolate region

The desolate region referred to in our verdict is the Bouquet Plateau (see the Introduction to this region). Fumades-les-Bains is a unique spa and the small site that takes its name is full of joie de vivre, in a very attractive environment. Everyone congregates at the lively end, the open-air bar by the road, particularly on Sundays when visitors to the spa's fête swell the mainly French company. This is a self-contained area separated from the main buildings by a wide lawn. Tables and chairs are set out under a huge, white umbrella. Further in down the drive, you'll find a tall, stone building housing the cool vault of the camp shop next to a traditional-looking restaurant, with a warm atmosphere typical of the site in general. Attractive flower beds, an ornamental pond spanned by a small wooden bridge, a fountain and a swimming-pool set in a sunken terrace – all tell of meticulous upkeep in verdant grounds. The camping area is behind all this, well away from the lively part of the site. Two parallel avenues lead you through groups of four *emplacements*, each screened by tall conifer hedges. Right at the back, the ground is less formally laid out among trees and is more suited to smaller tents. No need to worry about washing arrangements here – one spacious, modern block in the middle of the pitches is properly equipped and maintained: there are even wall-mounted, hand-held hair dryers like miniature vacuum cleaners. On top of all this, the entertainment you would expect from a high-grade site is regularly laid on by the hospitable owners, Monsieur and Madame Sauquet.

● ⑤ 🏃 ⌂ 🐄 ✕ ♀ ☙ 🏠 ⛩ 🗑 ☂ ♫

Directions: Take the D16 going north-east out of Alès until the crossroads with the D241. Turn right and follow road through to Les Vieilles Fumades, then straight on keeping the green of Les Bains on your left and the camp will be on your right **Ground:** Hard to giving **Children:** Playground, swimming, organised events **Wheelchair:** Not suitable **Food-cooling:** Ice sold, coolpacks frozen **Sport:** Tennis, ping pong, mini-golf **Season:** May to Sept **Reservation:** Advisable peak season **Charge:** 2 people, pitch and car 75 fr; extra adult 18 fr; child 10 fr; electricity 10 to 15 fr

▬▬▬ Anduze ▬▬▬

☼ *L'Arche*

30140 Anduze	tel 66.61.74.08

There's an abundance of shade at this very attractive site, which features a wonderful rockpool on the River Gard

Beyond the reception and automatic barrier at the site's entrance is probably the coolest as well as one of the most picturesque camping grounds in the area. Reasonably spacious pitches, rather regimented in rows, lie under an almost continuous canopy of dark foliage. Halfway along there's a break in the trees, revealing a vineyard and the gorge of cliffs of the River Gard. Then, down past more *emplacements* on wide decks of terraces, you eventually arrive at the snack-bar, which serves fastfood and *plats cuisinés*, and a large, well-stocked shop – unusual for a two-star site – notable for its meat and cheese counters. Other plus marks are good washing facilities for disabled campers, as well as a couple of baby baths with hand showers on the ladies' side. A secluded, flowery bar terrace is an intimate setting for lantern-lit after-dinner drinks. But the main draw of the site lies at the far end: as the trees thin out, you find yourself on a stone-walled promenade which gives on to a wonderful river scene. The Gard at this point has widened out to create a large 'rockpool' strewn with huge greyish-white boulders, their bright surfaces contrasting with the matt green of the densely covered hills either side of the gorge: a very pretty part of the river indeed. It is best to keep toddlers on the stony *plage*, away from the shallows and boulders, which are pitted with potholes. And the reason for the site's name? – the high arches of the railway bridge up river that carries the steam train from Anduze, its whistle echoing through the gorge.

● Ⓜ 🦮 🖼 🛒 ✕ ♀ 👞 🐾 ♒ 🗑 📮 🔧

Directions: Take the D907 north out of Anduze, following the left bank of the Gard, and soon after going under a railway bridge take the fork that drops to your right. The next fork – also to the right – will take you to the site entrance **Ground:** Giving **Children:** Playground **Wheelchair:** Suitable **Food-cooling:** Ice sold **Sport:** Volleyball, ping pong **Season:** April to Sept **Reservation:** Advisable peak season

Charge: 2 people, pitch and car 41.50 fr; extra adult 12.50 fr; child (under 7) 7 fr; electricity 12 to 14 fr

Castel Rose

30140 Anduze   tel 66.61.80.15

Pretty and peaceful riverbank setting for this relaxed, two-star site where you have space and shade. Wonderful value

Castel Rose is the laid-back neighbour of l'Arche (see above), but apart from the liberal amount of shade you couldn't find two more different sites offering such diverse and desirable camping. This site's broad triangular forecourt is at the foot of a large, sheltered, traditional stone *mas* (farmhouse). Two simple white buildings with clay-tile roofs introduce you to Castel Rose, one the reception, the other the café/bar with more tables outside than in. There's also a shop with basic commodities, but as ice-creams and a portion of *frites* are about all you can get here in the way of food, self-catering is a must (no problem, though, as the town is only a stone's throw away). A tennis court behind a tall hedge by the forecourt is a plus. The camping ground itself occupies a long stretch of cool, grassy bank along the River Gard, and would be a lovely spot for putting your feet up for a few days in the middle of a touring holiday. Space is not at a premium so there's no need for strictly defined *emplacements* – you pitch your tent along the bank or (on the higher level) where spaces between the trees allow. In season, the friendly English-speaking Dutch owners arrange for the river to be dammed, a practice not uncommon in these parts, in order to raise the water level for bathing.

● Ⓜ ♪ ▭ ♨ ♀ ⋒ ⎃ ▣ ⚲

Directions: Take the D907 north out of Anduze, following the left bank of the Gard. Soon after going under a railway bridge, take the fork that drops to the right (camp direction sign here). This will lead to the site entrance on the right **Ground:** Hard to giving
Children: Playground **Wheelchair:** Not suitable **Food-cooling:** Ice sold **Sport:** Tennis, volleyball, ping pong, fishing, canoeing, boules
Season: 15 Mar to Oct **Reservation:** Advisable peak season
Charge: Pitch 13 fr; person 13 fr; child (under 8) 8 fr

Children should be discouraged from playing around shower blocks.

⑦ *Cévennes-Provence*

Corbes-Thoiras, 30140 Anduze   tel 66.61.73.10

Dramatic setting, good general amenities, but only for the really adventurous at its upper levels

As soon as you enter this camp you are at once struck by its supreme location plumb in the middle of a small valley, encircled by the lush green hills. Unless you've a keen sense of adventure with energy reserves to match, you would be wise to pitch your tent here at ground level, where all the amenities are to be found: a shop with general goods as well as food, a bar and somewhere to sit and eat a dish from the *rôtisserie*. Nearby is a small parkland area with a mini-golf course, tennis court, playground and table-tennis tables, all landscaped into the grounds. This area accounts for only a small part of the site's 30 hectares. The rest is uncompromising terrain in the shape of steep, rugged hills covered in woodland. The rest of the pitches dotted around, and the nine small *sanitaires* serving them, are reached by a network of four kilometres of arduous winding roads. Some are in sandy clearings at the edges of hills, from where you get a good panorama looking down into the camp, with the Cévennes countryside as a backdrop. If you think the exercise would do you good, these plots might be acceptable but the ones at the cliff-tops are only for the extremely hardy and cool-headed – it would be easy to get lost up here. The isolated pitches perch just back from the near-precipitous cliffs and you would be well advised to keep a few days' supplies at the tent, in case you can't face the constant negotiation of the hairpins down to the camp centre and back again. Rock-climbers will be rewarded by fantastic views of the River Gard far below, as it wraps itself round the extremities of the whole property. The helpful *patron*, M Marais, is happy to show off his thirty-year scrapbook of press-cuttings.

Directions: Take the D907 from Anduze towards St Jean-du-Gard. After 4 km, you will see a camp direction sign pointing down a right-hand fork into the valley. This takes you across a narrow river-bridge (another camp sign here). You then pass under a railway bridge. Just after this a made-up road climbs round a couple of hairpins before you arrive at the camp itself (on your right) **Ground:** Hard

Children: Playground **Wheelchair:** Not suitable **Food-cooling:** Ice sold **Sport:** Tennis, volleyball, ping pong, fishing, pétanque, mini-golf **Season:** 1 Apr to 15 Oct **Reservation:** Advisable peak season **Charge:** 2 people, pitch and car 65 fr; extra adult 13 fr; child (2-7) 9 fr; electricity 12 fr

Domaine de Gaujac

Boisset-Gaujac, 30140
Anduze

Out-of-season tel 66.61.82.44
tel 66.61.80.65

Best all-round Anduze site for both touring and family stays. An indefinable sense of 'well-being' here

The directions may seem complicated but the effort is undoubtedly worthwhile. A final straight run of open road brings you towards the tall pines that help to give Gaujac its individual stamp. As you escape the heat and the glare in the welcoming shade of the entrance, you get the instant impression that here is a place where you could really enjoy doing very little. It is also, we were told, one of the few camp-

or commandeer the kid's rubber dinghy

sites at which you need hardly any time to feel completely settled in. Just inside the entrance is the chalet-style restaurant and bar. The gravel terrace outside comes alive at night with campers tucking into generous helpings chosen from a reasonable menu, while children find new friends around the table-tennis tables under the trees opposite. During the day, the main activity centres on the marvellous natural 'lido', created by the damming of the Gard which runs by the camp's grounds. A wide stretch of water bordered by a long, stony *plage* provides a suitable location for the kids to use the inflatable dinghy. At the end of the afternoon, when you return to the bar for a drink, they'll probably be expending their inexhaustible energy in the pool around the corner. As far as tents are concerned, there are three separate sections. The main one is also the shadiest and the most attractive. An elliptical road takes you through conifer and pine with good-sized, secluded pitches. To one side a path ascends to some small, pretty terraces of *emplacements* of similar size. You have to cross a narrow public road to reach the second and perhaps the quietest ground, this time a more open aspect with pitches marked in uniform rows. The third section lies by the camp entrance. The sports facilities are here, as well as the *sanitaire* with appointments for the handicapped. All Gaujac's *sanitaires*, while not modern, are kept meticulously clean. The camp is efficiently administered by the Family Bernabeu who treat it as their second home, as do many of their guests who return year after year.

Directions: At Anduze, cross over the Gard on the east side of town. Turn right at a T-junction. This is the D910 that climbs away from the town. When you get to a right-hand bend, take the sudden right-hand turn (camp direction sign here). This is the D106. Cross over the next crossroads and follow the road to a small roundabout. Continue straight over this and turn right at the next crossroads. You will see a camp direction sign here on the wall of a cream-coloured building at the corner. Follow the road, passing small villas on your left. Take the next left-hand fork which leads to the camp   **Ground:** Hard
Children: Playground, swimming   **Wheelchair:** Suitable
Food-cooling: Ice sold   **Sport:** Tennis, volleyball, ping pong, football, horse-riding, mini-golf   **Season:** 15 Apr to 20 Sept
Reservation: Advisable peak season   **Charge:** 2 people, pitch and car 69 fr; extra adult 13 fr; electricity 13 fr

Le Fief

Massillargues, Attuech, 30140 Anduze　　　　tel 66.61.81.71

A very neat little two-star site with an attractive small pool. Ideal for a short stay

Le Fief is up against considerable competition but would be ideal for a short stay if you were happy to pay a little more than at Castel Rose for extra amenities. What strikes you first is how well the grounds are kept, with tidy rosebeds, trees on a scale compatible with the camp's size and a grassy garden area. Two huts house the reception, shop and take-away counter. Some of the pitches are quite shady but many are rather exposed. The camp's most desirable feature is at the back, a very attractive oval pool set in a paved terrace, with trestle tables and parasols on one side by the grill/bar. A path leads from here down to the river but many people would be happy to rely on the pool.

Directions: Take the D907 heading south out of Anduze to Attuech. Fork left onto the D982. Straightaway you will see a camp-sign on the right warning of a left-hand turn for the site down a track through a vineyard **Ground:** Giving **Children:** Not suitable **Wheelchair:** Not suitable **Food-cooling:** Ice sold, coolpacks frozen **Sport:** Volleyball, fishing, boules **Season:** Easter, June to Sept **Reservation:** Advisable peak season **Charge:** 2 people, pitch and car 58 fr; extra adult 13 fr; child 6.50 fr; electricity 12 fr

La Pommeraie

Route de Lasalle, Thoiras,　　　Out-of-season tel 66.51.46.55
30140 Anduze　　　　　　　　　　　　tel 66.85.20.52

Family fun and four-star entertainment in attractive Cévennes countryside

The rural drive along winding roads into the Cévennes hills does not prepare you for the hurly-burly of La Pommeraie. The camping ground itself is basically a small, flat plain by the Salindrinque, a shallow stream and a pleasant place to paddle. This part of the site isn't so very attractive, but La Pommeraie's general atmosphere of *bonhomie* is compensation for the rows of regimented trees and close pitches. All the activity centres on

177

the front of the camp, with the prominent white main building, the large pool and tennis courts by a grove of tall trees. There's also an array of sports facilities here, from basketball to badminton. In the main building, you'll find a cool, crisp-looking bar/restaurant, brightly decorated with palm-trees, animals, flowers and fruits, under a translucent tent-like roof. Steps at the back take you down to a small terrace for drinks. The walls here are lined with painted cut-outs of trees and birds. Along the side of the camp, by the road, are more activities: a large covered area – the Boulodrome (for *pétanque*) painted wih murals of Cévenol scenery – doubles as an entertainment centre in the evenings. From the playground next door a children's train gives rides around the site. Camp life is augmented in season by two full-time *animateurs* to keep the kids happy, and on the other side of the grounds, away from the *emplacements*, is a separate building housing cinema and disco. Obviously, in summer, the Cévennes hills around here are alive with the sound of music!

Directions: On the D907 going north from Anduze to St Jean-du-Gard, filter left at a road junction onto the D57 towards Lasalle. After winding your way for a few kilometres, you will eventually see the site below and off the road to your left. There are huge camp nameboards that can't be missed **Ground:** Giving **Children:** Playground, swimming, organised events **Wheelchair:** Suitable
Food-cooling: Ice sold, coolpacks frozen, fridge hire **Sport:** Tennis, volleyball, ping pong, football, basketball, bike-hire, badminton
Season: May to Sept **Reservation:** Advisable peak season
Charge: 42 fr per pitch; extra adult 13 fr; child 10 fr; electricity 22 fr

■■■ Bourg St Andéol ■■■

Camping Le Lion

07700 Bourg St Andéol   tel 75.54.53.20

A pleasant journey-breaker, perhaps before the last leg to the coast. Adequate three-star facilities with a pool for each star!

Bourg St Andéol is a rather nondescript town between Montélimar and Orange, but being very near the N86 and not far from the A7 (Autoroute du Soleil), it might be just the point to break your journey south. Rosebeds and a stone lion presiding over a small bushy roundabout welcome you at the gravelled entrance. By the bar terrace and snack restaurant are three pools for adults, children and tinies, and beyond, gravelled drives take you through a small green park into the shade of large trees. As Le Lion is a small, contained site, children can wander to the pools or playground without parental worry. You don't get seclusion here – although the ground is spacious, there's no separation between *emplacements*, so you'll be seeing a lot of your neighbours. Adequate appointments are to be found in the three *sanitaires*. The fare at the snack-bar is modest, but the town is at hand for a few restaurants or for supplies to cook yourself.

● ⑤ ⫪ ⇌ ⪤ ✕ ⵙ ☞ ⋇ ⋒ ⊟ ▣ ℘

Directions: From the centre of town pick up the D86 signposted Viviers and Le Teil. You'll see a red and yellow camp sign on your right warning you to turn right. This turn takes you down and under a road bridge (N86). You will see the camp soon after this **Ground:** Giving **Children:** Playground, swimming, organised events **Wheelchair:** Not suitable **Food-cooling:** Ice sold, coolpacks frozen **Sport:** Volleyball, ping pong, football, mini-golf, boules **Season:** 1 Apr to 15 Sept **Reservation:** Advisable peak season **Charge:** 2 people, pitch and car 45 to 62 fr; extra adult 12 to 16 fr; child (under 7) 6 to 8 fr; electricity 13 fr

▄▄▄ Casteljau ▄▄▄▄▄▄

Mazet Plage

07460 Berrias-Casteljau   tel 75.39.32.56

You don't have to be a canoeist to appreciate this out-of-the-way river spot. Back to nature in an unusual pocket of scenery

First a word about the area. Le Bois de Païolive is a strange wooded territory cut through by the Chassezac, a tributary of the River Ardèche. Coming by road from the relatively familiar landscape of an open river plain, you enter a far more foreboding scene bereft of any real population. In a depression thick with oak and chestnut, ancient grey rock forms are exposed here and there. The Chassezac has carved a gorge here, the top of which can be reached by foot from Mazet-Plage. The campsite of the same name is right by the river in a very secluded spot below and away from the road. It is very cool, very green and has a quiet beauty about it with the flat, fresh river water reflecting the smooth indented grey cliff faces upstream, appearing as if modelled in clay. The *plage* is a stony strip stepped down from the tree-lined banks which edge the tiny camping ground, and from where canoes can be easily slid into the river's ambling flow. The site itself – a shady and tidily kept grass clearing just before the gorge – has open pitches either side of a made-up track. One simple building acts as reception, shop, bar and snack restaurant for basic *plats cuisinés*. The two *sanitaires* at the camp borders are basic but jolly in primary colours – and there is a seated loo in each. Mazet-Plage is one of those hidden places that makes you feel that only you have discovered it – a little pocket of exclusive solitude.

Directions: Casteljau lies to the west of the D104 (Aubenas-Alès road). Take the turn-off halfway between the River Chassezac to the north and where the main road forks with the D111 to the south. As you drive into Le Bois de Païolive you will pick up a big yellow sign for the camp at a crossroads. Go straight on until you reach a T-junction, where you turn left (another camp sign here). Then almost without warning, after a left-hand bend, there's a fork descending off the road to the right. This time there's a red and white nameboard announcing the camp entrance down this road **Ground:** Giving
Children: Playground **Wheelchair:** Not suitable **Food-cooling:** Ice sold, coolpacks frozen **Sport:** Tennis, ping pong, canoeing, fishing, boules **Season:** Easter to Sept **Reservation:** Advisable peak season
Charge: 2 people, pitch and car 56 fr; extra adult 13 fr; child (under 7) 9.50 fr; electricity 13.50 fr

▰▰▰▰ Crespian ▰▰▰▰▰▰▰▰

Mas de Reilhe

Crespian, 30260 Quissac   tel 66.77.82.12

Very attractive hillside setting for this peaceful site which, while short on amenities, is acceptable for a family stay

The Mas de Reilhe itself, a dominating 16th-century yellow stone building with a tall, central, square tower, is not immediately visible from the site entrance. What you do see are two levels, one a 'ground floor' grassy flat area (the obvious choice for caravans), the other a 'first floor' of pitches snug on pretty, pine-covered terraces. Both offer good shade. A made-up road curves round a gentle hill up to well-defined *emplacements* under the trees – from here you can survey the camp below and the sweeping countryside. No part of the camp feels claustrophic: there's a good balance between the two levels. At one end of the main building, the *mas*, is a tiny vault of a bar, all rustic charm with its white-painted stone interior and simple wooden furniture. You fetch your morning bread from here. Outside, one huge tree shelters a small gravel terrace where you can sit and sip a glass or two of wine in the evenings. People come here for the peace and quiet; there's not much activity apart from the pool (beautifully screened in a flowery setting), volleyball, ping-pong and a few evening entertainments (over by 10 o'clock); but children are not forgotten, with a full-time *animateur* in season, and a puppet theatre that calls by from time to time. While this is fine for little ones, teenagers might be rather bored. The *sanitaires* are good and modern, and the proximity to main road communications means that Mas de Reilhe is ideally situated for day-tripping.

Directions: There's a major crossroads between Nîmes and Quissac (east and west), and Alès and Sommières (north and south). These roads are the D999 and the N110 respectively. Take the N110 to Crespian a couple of kilometres to the north. As you approach the village and see its nameplate ahead, there's an immediate turn-off to the right. This road takes you down to the site entrance
Ground: Hard **Children:** Playground, organised events
Wheelchair: Not suitable **Food-cooling:** Ice sold **Sport:** Volleyball, ping pong **Season:** All year **Reservation:** Advisable peak season
Charge: 34 to 40 fr per pitch; 17 to 20 fr per person; child (under 7) 8.50 to 10 fr; electricity 15 fr

---

Pitching by a river or lake may seem an attractive idea but gnats and mosquitoes feel the same way. An easy remedy is to rub or spray repellent on your limbs at night or, if you prefer, use a slow-burning diffuser for the tent. You may also be thankful that you packed the ant-powder.

▬ Darbres ▬

☼ *Les Charmilles*

07170 Darbres, Villeneuve de Berg   tel 75.94.25.22

Excellent little family camp with outstanding views

Every aspect of this small family camp is exceptional. The view
first: Les Charmilles is exhilaratingly high on the southern edge
of the Coiron Plateau looking out over spectacular miles of
valleys and hills. You might easily be tempted to sit and stare all
day, only to leave your seat on the terrace now and then to cool
down in the pool. But that's not the only thing here to spoil
you. The attractive camping ground, mostly grass and mostly
level, is shaded by a small but spacious wood of oak and
chestnut. Good modern washing arrangements feature a
toddlers' toilet and a babies' bath. The simply furnished
restaurant overlooking the pool is an unpretentious tiled affair,
and offers good home cooking in the shape of a variety of *plats
cuisinés*. Other services to supplement your catering are the
morning *dépôt de pain* and a visiting butcher and pizza man. The
lady of the camp is keen that everyone should feel part of one
big happy family, something that is possible in a site with only
90 *emplacements*. She fosters this by her communal soirées; for
older children there's a junior disco. (Quietness reigns after
11pm, as it should on a site of this nature.) Younger children
are kept busy during the day by a full-time *animateur*, messing
about with paints or going on nature rambles.

● ⑤ ♨ ⇌ ⬱ ✕ ♀ 🐾 ⚓ 🏠 ⛏ ▣ ⚲

Directions: The easiest way to reach Darbres, lying east of Aubenas, is
from the D224 picked up at Lavilledieu on the N102 to the south. The
camp is well signposted on the approach to the village. As you leave
Darbres, a green sign at a fork in the road tells you to take the right. The
site entrance will eventually appear on your left **Ground:** Giving
Children: Playground, swimming, organised events
Wheelchair: Suitable **Food-cooling:** Ice sold, coolpacks frozen
Sport: Tennis, volleyball, ping pong **Season:** Easter to Oct
Reservation: Advisable peak season **Charge:** 2 people, pitch, car or
caravan 69 fr; extra adult 15 fr; child (over 5) 8 fr; electricity 11 fr

*Film can be affected by prolonged heat so if you have a coolbox you could tape
any spare rolls in their containers to the underside of the box's lid.*

Le Grau-du-Roi

Sites summary There are a dozen sites for what is really Port-Camargue, the modern marine development on the eastern side of Grau-du-Roi's bay. All are situated along a back road that skirts the port to the north. Half of the total are actually four-star but we found that this didn't count for much. For example, the *Elysée Résidence* turned out to be no more than a vast mobile home village like an industrial estate, concentrating on the provision of a range of sports plus training. A rule of thumb seems to be that the further along the road you go – and the further from the Port's centre and better beaches – the grades drop and the sites are more exposed. We have ended up with four camps, *La Marine* being the only three-star among the other higher grade group.

Directions for sites There are a few approaches to *Le Grau-du-Roi*; the D62/62a interchange north of the town; the D979 coming in from Aigues-Mortes; the D255 coast road from La Grande-Motte. The D979 runs due north from the harbour and D62b exits east of it at a roundabout. Follow this to the next large roundabout and take the third exit, the D255b, which is the road where all the campsites are to be found. Except for *l'Eden*, all the camps are along here with entrances on the right. For *l'Eden*, there's a right-hand fork at the top end of the road that doubles back. Just follow this around and down. All sites are clearly signed.

L'Abri de Camargue

| Route du Phare de l'Espiguette, | tel 66.51.54.83 |
| Port-Camargue, 30240 Le Grau-du-Roi | |

Reasonable run-of-the-mill four-star family site

A glossy brochure in four languages sets the seal on this streamlined camp. You come to l'Abri for its entertainments in a 'clubhouse' environment. The main focus of the camp is its pool surrounded by sun-loungers and the bar terrace the other side of some wrought-iron railings. There's an indoor pool (heated at the beginning and end of the season). Children may not have their own pool but are kept happy with club activities every morning. The rest of the family can go on excursions, for example to the Camargue, or join in the musical soirées or discos in the evenings. The small restaurant is nothing to write home about, and the camping ground is a rather dull grid system of straight, made-up avenues. *Emplacements* are of a reasonable size, though a bit on the worn side, and there are only a few hedged areas. Tall trees do give good shade, though. Mobile homes are in considerable evidence here, and can be rented. You may not be too bothered by the lack of atmosphere if you intend to spend your time at the lively top end of the camp or at the nearby beach.

● Ⓜ 🏃 ⛵ 🚣 🛒 ✕ ♀ 👍 🐟 ⛺ 🛁 📷 🎵

Directions: See Directions for sites at beginning of Le Grau-du-Roi
Ground: Hard to giving   **Children:** Playground, organised events
Wheelchair: Suitable   **Food-cooling:** Ice sold   **Sport:** Ping pong
Season: 1 Apr to 15 Oct   **Reservation:** Advisable peak season
Charge: 2 people, pitch, car and electricity 155 fr; 3 to 5 people, pitch, car and electricity 165 fr

L'Eden

Port-Camargue, 30240 Le Grau-du-Roi   tel 66.51.49.81

Colourful family site with good ambience as well as environment. A watchspring could unwind here

The low, white buildings either side of the main drive don't give a lot away when you first arrive, but once inside, you are greeted by a colourful scene of shrubs and flowers that continues throughout the camp. Despite the camp's size, people seem to treat l'Eden as home rather than as an hotel – here is a place for going about the serious business of unwinding. The camp's layout has a great influence on this. Take the pool area, for instance: lots of surrounding foliage but not enclosed, making for a good communal atmosphere. The main camp road is a floral boulevard setting for the site's supermarket and neat, simple restaurant. As you wander further into the grounds, the shrubbery is still very much in evidence, providing plenty of shade and coolness. Although the good-sized pitches are fairly regular in their plan, lots of hedging and trees help to give a sense of seclusion so that this popular site, while busy, doesn't make you feel like a sardine. Smart *sanitaires* offer some combined shower and wash-basin cubicles, and, again, there are plenty of plants to jolly up the exterior. The management lays on the usual evening fun, as befits a four-star resort site.

● ⓛ 🕇 🛶 🗲 ✕ 🍷 🥄 🦌 🏠 🛗 🗔 🎿 🎵

Directions: See Directions for sites at beginning of Le Grau-du-Roi
Ground: Hard to giving **Children:** Playground, swimming, organised events **Wheelchair:** Suitable **Food-cooling:** Ice sold, coolpacks frozen **Sport:** Ping pong, bike and windsurfer hire, mini-golf
Season: Apr to Sept **Reservation:** Advisable peak season
Charge: 2/3 people, pitch and electricity 160 fr; extra person 26 fr

Les Jardins de Tivoli

Chemin de l'Espiguette, Port-Camargue, tel 66.51.82.96
30240 Le Grau-du-Roi

The luxury of your own sanitaire *plus good recreational facilities may let you disregard a certain blandness in the camping ground*

Les Jardins de Tivoli come in three sections: the front is the main camping ground, the back is for mobile homes, and in between is the walled heart of the camp, where you'll find the pool and the tennis court. Here, the covered veranda of the poolside bar and restaurant provides the only shade. In the evenings the area is transformed into an open-air nightclub with the purpose-built stage put to good use for a variety of entertainments. Sensible planning is also the hallmark of the camping area. At first sight the ground plan seems formal and linear, but in fact the pitches in little avenues off a main broadway are grouped in threes, many shaded and all hedged and made private from each other. At the back of each group is a cluster of clay-tiled huts, which turn out to be individual *sanitaires* for each pitch. Each has two compartments: one a combined shower and toilet, the other with a wash-basin and kitchen sink. Hot water is provided by an electric boiler. Bearing in mind this sophistication, low-season prices are particularly good value (60 fr for one person, up to 120 fr for five people). (Note that five is the maximum number of people allowed per pitch.)

● ⓛ 🏊 ⛵ 🛒 ✕ 🍷 👆 🐾 🏚 ⊣ 🎣 🎵

Directions: See Directions for sites at beginning of Le Grau-du-Roi
Ground: Hard **Children:** Playground, organised events
Wheelchair: Not suitable **Food-cooling:** Ice sold, coolpacks frozen
Sport: Tennis, volleyball, ping pong, mini-golf, boules **Season:** 15
Mar to 15 Oct **Reservation:** Advisable peak season **Charge:** Up to 5
people, pitch, car and electricity 185 fr

La Marine

Route du Phare de   Out-of-season tel 66.51.53.45
l'Espuiguette,   tel 66.51.46.22
Port-Camargue,
30240 Le Grau-du-Roi

Quiet modern site notable for its pools. Complicated tariff

The fourth and last of our Grau-du-Roi sites is also the furthest
away from the centre of Port-Camargue, so you might wonder
if its name was really apt. But it does have some aquatic
connection in the shape of three pools. One is by a pleasant
terrace decked out with blue and white awnings. This relaxing
spot is a quieter alternative to the more recent roadside
showpiece complex of pools and grill-restaurant. This consists
of wide sunbathing terraces looking onto two pools – one for
children – of geometrical design. Despite such modernity, La
Marine comes over as a homely site and, according to some
British regulars we met there, is pleasantly quiet, not that
evening entertainment is completely absent. We found the
grounds rather open to the sun and a bit dry and dusty, but as
the amenities on offer include attractive *sanitaires* we thought
La Marine worth including. The tariff system is quite
complicated – the price given below is for a simple tent for two
people in high season. The pitch charge for four people with a
caravan rises to 158 fr, so be warned.

● Ⓜ 🏄 ⛵ 🛒 ✕ 🍷 👆 🐾 🔲 🎵

Directions: See Directions for sites at beginning of Le Grau-du-Roi
Ground: Hard **Children:** Swimming, organised events
Wheelchair: Suitable **Food-cooling:** Ice sold, fridge hire **Sport:** Ping
pong, bicycle hire **Season:** 1 Apr to 15 Oct **Reservation:** Advisable
peak season **Charge:** 2 people, pitch and car 60 fr

Pont-du-Gard

International Gorges du Gardon

30210 Pont-du-Gard   tel 66.37.00.02

An endearing transport caff of a camping site, right down to the plastic check tablecloths! Popular, very cheerful, and good for a stop-over

It's not often that you find a regular two-star site with plenty of character, but here is one. This is matched by the personality of the breezy, happy-go-lucky Madame who tirelessly runs the camp with her family. You will find here a small, shady halt on the River Gard. The majority of random pitches are sheltered under oaks and other trees, the foliage becoming denser towards the river. A separate, more open area behind the entrance has defined *emplacements* suitable for vans or campers. *Sanitaires* are basic but incorporate some seated loos. There's not a lot in the way of recreational pursuits – the playground is minimal – but children will be quite happy (and safe) roaming around the camp or paddling or bathing off the stony shore of the river at the bottom of the camp. The bar/restaurant is the focus of the International with homely, well-worn, plastic check tablecloths and curtains. Basic fare with chips is the order of the day and there's a little shop, too, that acts as a *dépôt de pain* first thing in the morning. A little rough on the ground this site may be, but the hospitality certainly makes up for any lack of refinements. It has a good reputation among British tourers, and deservedly so.

Directions: North of the Pont-du-Gard on the D981 to Uzès, there is a straight bit of open road bordered by a line of trees. As you round a bend after this, you will see a big stone building on your right. Take the left-hand turn just beyond it. In a field you will see a big orange disc signifying the camp's proximity. This road bears left, then right at a T-junction with a track. Go all the way down to the site entrance
Ground: Hard   **Children:** Playground   **Wheelchair:** Not suitable
Food-cooling: Ice sold, coolpacks frozen   **Sport:** None   **Season:** Apr to Oct   **Reservation:** Advisable peak season   **Charge:** 2 people, pitch and car 45 fr

---

It's normal for your stay on a campsite to be charged from midday on the day of arrival to midday on the day of departure.

Valive

30210 Pont-du-Gard   tel 66.22.81.52

Small, quiet two-star site with a pool, offering a retreat from the crowds that swarm around the beautiful Roman aqueduct

Valive is another two-star camp in the locality but unlike the International it is not the sort of place that one gets 'involved' in. It has less of a communal feel, so might appeal more to people who prefer keeping themselves to themselves. It is more sedate, larger in ground cover than the International and more organised in the placing of its pitches, which are fairly open in areas of grass beneath clusters of trees. The *sanitaires* with their western-style swing doors are well maintained and have seated loos; some are suitable for disabled people. You are not on the river here but there is a small swimming-pool and a paddling-pool by a snack-bar (the fare being less varied than at the International). Other differences are that Valive is open all year, and some entertainment is laid on in season. And of course you are more or less on top of the famous Pont-du-Gard aqueduct itself – eater of rolls of 35mm exposure – and if you like you can take a daily walk down the road to spend some time in or out of the water by the stony river *plages* at its foot.

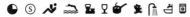

Directions: At the aqueduct itself, opposite the car park on the north bank (*rive gauche*), there is a small road where you will see a camp direction sign. Take this and you will eventually arrive at the site entrance on your left **Ground:** Giving **Children:** Playground, swimming **Wheelchair:** Suitable **Food-cooling:** Ice sold, coolpacks frozen **Sport:** Ping pong **Season:** All year **Reservation:** Advisable peak season **Charge:** 2 people, pitch and car 44 fr; extra adult 12 fr; electricity 9 to 12 fr

---

Some geological terms:

Abri *rock shelter*	Cirque *amphitheatre*
Aven *cave*	Gorges *gorge*
Belvédere *panoramic viewpoint*	Gouffre *chasm, gulf*
Causse *limestone plateau*	Grotte *grotto, cave*

Remoulins

La Soubeyranne

Route de Beaucaire, 30210 Remoulins   tel 66.37.03.21

Quiet, rather bland, four-star camping with high-standard facilities

La Soubeyranne has the elusive quality of being attractive without your being able to put your finger on what makes it so. True, it has four stars to its credit; true, it's very well kept; true, the swimming-pool is a desirable stretch of blue water set in a small, sunny terrace. There's also the delightful entrance where an island of exotic shrubs sets off two low white buildings with terracotta roofs. Climbers add yet more profusion of colour round the little arch that leads to the camping ground. If only the rest was as visually pleasing. Once through the arch you come upon hot, dry, level, fairly open ground, generally rather thin on cover, although some of the worn-looking *emplacements* away from the centre do catch better shade. It doesn't take much of a breeze (and it can get quite windy) to whip up the dusty surface, especially when cars pass on the main gravel drives – rather a drawback. Several package operators use La Soubeyranne so you'll come across quite a few British holidaymakers. They must be drawn by the good facilities the camp offers: clean, modern *sanitaires*, the neat restaurant with flowers on each table, the pool screened by hedges. The site couldn't really be called a family site because no specific entertainments are laid on and the emphasis is on peace and quiet. However, there's a kiddies' pool by the main one and a wooden adventure playground nearby.

🌙 Ⓢ 🏕 🛶 🧺 ✕ ♀ 👋 🏠 🛗 🔲 ⚕

Directions: Going west out of Remoulins, turn left at the T-junction after the bridge. Shortly after that turn left again onto the D986, to Beaucaire. There is a red camp direction sign here. Pass under a railway bridge and you will see the site entrance further down the road on the left **Ground:** Loose **Children:** Playground, swimming **Wheelchair:** Not suitable **Food-cooling:** Coolpacks frozen, fridge hire **Sport:** Tennis, volleyball, ping pong, boules **Season:** Apr to 15 Sept **Reservation:** Advisable peak season **Charge:** 2 people, pitch and car 71 fr; electricity 15 fr

Municipal La Sousta

Avenue du Pont du Gard,   tel 66.37.12.80
30210 Remoulins

An excellent choice for the Avignon area. This professionally run camp has much to offer for a long or short stay

Forget the 'Municipal' bit, for a start, as it's inaccurate in name and nature. La Sousta is actually leased from the council by a local conglomerate and is congenially and professionally run. The setting gives the site a head start – extensive, extremely shady and attractive pine and oak woodland that borders the Gard, not far from the aqueduct at Pont-du-Gard. Pitches are randomly placed among the trees and there are also some wider areas for caravans. Because of the spaciousness, even when the camp is busy your own little nook can remain peaceful. A walk through the wood will take you to the river for a swim, or you might prefer to participate in one of a range of sporting activities (golf, mini-golf, fishing, canoeing, badminton) or take advantage of La Sousta's multi-sided pool at the front of the camp. Also here is an exceedingly good play area with a sandpit and a wooden 'assault course'. Over the way is the low main building housing reception, a cool grocery and a small bar/ restaurant round a central, paved, covered terrace. This becomes the venue for evening entertainment, perhaps dancing or a cabaret. All in all, a good place for a stay of more than just a few days.

● ⑫ 🏄 ⛵ 🏊 🍴 🍷 ⛳ 🐟 🏛 🎱 📞 🎵

Directions: At Remoulins, take the main road heading out west over the river. At the T-junction on the other side of the bridge, turn right onto the D981. The camp is along this road on your right
Ground: Some hard, some sandy **Children:** Playground, swimming, organised events **Wheelchair:** Suitable **Food-cooling:** Ice sold, coolpacks frozen **Sport:** Volleyball, ping pong, mini-golf, small golfing green, badminton **Season:** 10 Mar to 18 Nov **Reservation:** Advisable peak season **Charge:** 2 people, pitch and car 64 fr; extra person 15 fr; electricity 13 fr

In the event of your losing your passport or having it stolen, immediately report this to the police who will issue an official form in lieu of your loss.

Ruoms

La Bastide

Sampzon, 07120 Ruoms   tel 75.39.64.72

Supremely maintained three-star site that stands out a mile over others in the vicinity. Pretty river location, too

For a site south of Ruoms, La Bastide is hard to beat. It is set in a triangular field of fresh, green lawn backing onto the River Ardèche. Abundant foliage borders two sides, with a clearing in the middle, giving you the choice of pitching your tent in sun or shade. The tidy appearance of the ground speaks of considerable care. *Emplacements* are marked and roomy, helping to give the impression that here one can breathe. Down at the wide water's edge the white stone *plage* stretches from the wood to the arches of the twin road and rail bridges that give an architectural focus to the scene. An excellent reason for stopping here is the state-of-the-art sanitary block, an investment that reflects the management's positive business attitude to provide the best within their means. In the enclosed interior one section is completely devoted to a row of facilities for disabled people, while another has a self-contained changing room fitted out with a babies' bath and toddlers' loo. As a bonus to your peaceful stay, if you wish for a change from the site's snack-bar/pizzeria, a small stone building above La Bastide's entrance, a hotel run by the camp as an independent venture will provide a good meal or two.

Directions: South of Ruoms on the D579 there's a sweeping left-hand bend; here, there is a right-hand fork where there are traffic islands. Turn here on the D111 and continue up the road. The site entrance is on your left a little after crossing the Ardèche over a bridge
Ground: Giving **Children:** Playground, organised events
Wheelchair: Suitable **Food-cooling:** Ice sold **Sport:** Tennis, volleyball, ping pong, football **Season:** 15 Mar to 15 Sept
Reservation: Advisable peak season **Charge:** 2 people, pitch and car 65 fr; extra person 14 fr; electricity 14 fr

Always pack a couple of table-tennis bats and balls, as nearly every campsite possesses a table or two. Some receptions also keep standard board games handy for loan.

La Digue

Chauzon, 07120 Ruoms	Out-of-season tel 75.39.63.80
	tel 75.39.63.57

This secluded spot by the river offers you a chance to get away from the tourist beat when touring

It's not as complicated to get here as the directions imply, and if you like the idea of spending some time in a cool retreat with access to a river, La Digue will appeal. It's a simple site – a natural wooded glade tucked away on one of the quieter reaches of the River Ardèche. You won't find made-up drives or manicured *emplacements* here but the site maintains a good balance between offering a pleasant camping ground and preserving the original habitat. Generously-sized pitches are spaced out evenly among the trees, enjoying protection from the sun. The washing block is quite adequate with one seated toilet. Although there's a little shop and snack-bar, you should count on self-catering here. Remember, you're not far from Ruoms which has a useful supermarket. Down by the river at the back of the site a pleasant sandy shore gives you a chance for a dip or a spot of fishing (undisturbed apart from canoeists). Perhaps a prettier location for a swim and a lie in the sun is the small waterpark you passed on your way to the camp. This faces a steep, grey cliff cut in the valley, making for a pleasing background to your afternoon's relaxation.

Directions: Chauzon lies on the D308, a turning off the D579 north of Ruoms. You cross the Ardèche over a high bridge, and the road swings right by a small waterpark (camp direction sign here). In the village, turn right at a T-junction, then first left, then first right (all signposted for camp). At the next T-junction, take the left turn which becomes a narrow track. Eventually you will see an orange nameboard on your right. Here the road swings off to the right for the site entrance
Ground: Giving **Children:** Playground **Wheelchair:** Not suitable
Food-cooling: Ice sold **Sport:** Tennis, volleyball, ping pong, canoeing, fishing **Season:** Easter to Sept **Reservation:** Advisable peak season **Charge:** 2 people, pitch and car 56 fr; extra person 13 fr; child (under 7) 8 fr; electricity 10 fr

It is always a wise precaution to sleep with your essential documents and money. Some sites provide safety deposit boxes at reception.

☀ *Domaine de Chaussy*

Lagorce, 07150 Ruoms   tel 75.93.99.66

Full marks to a small luxury site that provides a fine family base

For once, here is a four-star site worthy of its grading. Often in such a modern, purpose-built camp there is a feeling of 'Now we're here, we'd better enjoy it' but the pleasure at Chaussy is far more spontaneous. The situation helps, of course – high on a hill overlooking rolling countryside, where the freshness of the air hits you. The small size of the camp – fewer than 200 *emplacements* – contributes towards a sociable atmosphere, and the camping ground itself is in an attractive light wood, not without its shade. The size of the pitches is reasonable, and although they lack natural screening, the trees help to give privacy. The *sanitaires* are spick and span and include washing cubicles for disabled people as well as wide-door toilets. All very pleasant, but the main attraction of Chaussy is the cluster of modern airy buildings along a fine wide terrace containing two pools, and plenty of room for sun-worshipping or sitting at tables with parasols. The restaurant/bar is a modern, light and airy building looking out on to the terrace. All members of the family are well looked after in terms of entertainment. Domaine de Chaussy may seem pricier than other sites in the locality but is definitely the best value.

● ⑤ 🎿 🛶 🦪 ✗ ♀ 🦞 🏛 🛗 🔲 ⚲ ♫

Directions: Just outside Ruoms, on the D579, there's a turning east which is the D559 to Lagorce. You will see a camp direction sign here. After a short drive, you will round a left-hand bend and see ahead, on a rise, a pink building with balconies. Continue round this bend and the site entrance is a sharp right   **Ground:** Hard to giving
Children: Playground, organised events   **Wheelchair:** Suitable
Food-cooling: Ice sold   **Sport:** Tennis, volleyball, ping pong, cycling, boules, archery, billiards   **Season:** Easter to Sept
Reservation: Advisable peak season   **Charge:** 2 people, pitch and car 100 fr; extra person 23 fr; electricity 15 fr

Destination signs appear to point across the road rather than parallel to it and may take a little getting used to. The 'arrow' traffic light for road filters is far more common than in the UK and should be watched for at junctions and turn-offs.

Le Ternis

07120 Ruoms	Out-of-season tel 75.93.93.76
	tel 75.93.93.15

Modest, attractive French camp life in a pleasant natural wood overlooking the Ardèche countryside

Le Ternis is a neighbour of Domaine de Chaussy (see above) but of course being next door does not mean that it is at all similar. The two sites do share the same sweeping view of Ardèche countryside, but here you will find more of a French air and a wilder terrain. Sandy pathways track through a spacious wood thick with oak, and pitches are randomly spread around these grounds. The blend between camp and surrounding scenery is almost seamless, making the whole very green and attractive. Some aspects of the site – buildings, pool, play equipment – are of a modest character compared to those at Chaussy. It's the difference between a comfortable guest-house and a plush hotel: there's no reason not to be happy in either. The single low building with a long, sloping, tiled roof with an awning sits by the open, brick-paved pool terrace. At this rendezvous the informally arranged tables and chairs are hardly ever empty. The same goes for the plain but homely bar in the evenings. In season diversions are also laid on from poolside aerobics and a round of sports competitions to organised excursions and fancy dress dances. At a more modest cost than Chaussy, Le Ternis provides a gentle holiday environment in a very pleasant setting with more of a local flavour.

● ⓢ 朮 ᐃ ᒪ ✕ ♀ 👟 🐾 ⋒ ⊟ ▣ 𝒫 ♫

Directions: Outside Ruoms on the D579, the D559 heads off east to Lagorce. There's a camp direction sign at this junction. Along this road, after a left-hand bend ahead of you, you will see a low pink building with balconies. Take a right-hand fork at this point to the site entrance **Ground:** Giving **Children:** Playground, swimming, organised events **Wheelchair:** Suitable **Food-cooling:** Ice sold, coolpacks frozen **Sport:** Tennis, ping pong, canoeing **Season:** Easter to 20 Sept **Reservation:** Advisable peak season **Charge:** 2 people, pitch and car 73 fr; extra person 16 fr

If arriving at an unfamiliar site on spec, you should be allowed the privilege of inspecting its suitability before you commit yourself to booking in.

■■■ St Alban-Auriolles ■■■

Le Ranc Davaine

St Alban-Auriolles,   Out-of-season tel 75.37.16.88
07120 Ruoms   tel 75.39.60.55

Traditional camping with all mod cons in a pretty site in a quiet backwater, yet near the Ardèche Gorge

The idea of pitching down on yellow-dry grass under a scattering of oaks in a silent piece of open country may for some readers be an incentive to pack the tent and head this way. Some may think it sounds a little too '*au naturel*', lacking desirable comforts. Le Ranc Davaine manages a happy blend of both: providing the satisfaction of an authentic open-air holiday, and spoiling you with little luxuries. At the front of the site, there is a small aesthetically designed leisure area – nothing excessive and kept in scale. The main feature is an asymmetrical pool, landscaped with boulders and an amusing tall concrete sculpture in its centre. The terrace extends back to the modern, open-plan restaurant and bar (with disco at the back) built in traditional timber and tiling. You will be hard pressed to find such sophistication around this way, particularly in such rural surrounds. *Sanitaires* are modern, too, with toddlers' loos near the pool by the laundry room. One other attraction is the Chaussezac running below the edge of the grounds. A little river beach is reached by climbing down a steep path, so tiny ones should perhaps be given a helping hand. The general ambience of Le Ranc Davaine is a very relaxed one, casual even. This site is three-star going on four and it can also be only a matter of time before the package ops come sniffing around. Don't forget that we (and you?) were here first!

◑ ⑤ 𝑥 ⛴ ▭ ▧ ✕ ♀ 👆 ☘ � ⛍ 𝒫 ♫

Directions: South of Ruoms on the D579, there's a right-hand turn off a sweeping left-hand bend (the D111). Follow through till Les Tessiers, where you take a right turn over the railway past an old station. After going over the River Chassezac, turn left at the T-junction. Further down this road you will see the flags at the camp entrance
Ground: Hard   **Children:** Playground, swimming, organised events
Wheelchair: Suitable   **Food-cooling:** Ice sold, coolpacks frozen

Sport: Tennis, volleyball, ping pong, football, mini-golf, fishing
Season: Easter to 15 Sept **Reservation:** Advisable peak season
Charge: 2 people, pitch and car 76 fr; extra adult 15 fr; child (under 10) 11 fr; electricity 13 fr

St Jean-du-Gard
Château de l'Hom

30125 Saumane   Out-of-season tel 66.83.90.89
                                            tel 66.83.91.61

Tranquil site in a verdant setting, yet a sociable time can be had, too. An ideal base for exploring the Cévennes

You come to this miniature valley plain of a camp for the silence – and, of course, the wonderful presence of the lovely Cévennes hills, covered, as it were, in some deep-piled viridian carpet. After a drive through this region of forest slopes, the roads mimicking the twist of valley streams, you are greeted at the entrance of Château de l'Hom by a light cluster of possibly

even a Mr Muscle and Miss Campsite Contest

the tallest campsite trees in the region. The main camping area is exposed, and *emplacements* here could be described as a friendly distance from each other. If you seek seclusion (and don't mind a bit of a walk to the nearest *sanitaire*), go for a pitch on the series of terraces at the back of the grounds. Although no less exposed to the fierce summer sun, they have beautiful views. The campsite lies in the lee of a high hill dense with conifer with the green shallows of the St Jean – one of the many streams that flow into the Gard – at its base. You can sunbathe here on the flat, pebble banks or commandeer the kids' rubber dinghy for a while. Alternatively, over on the opposite side of the camp there's l'Hom's refreshing pool by the raised covered veranda of the bar/restaurant (take-away possible); for other food supplies there's a general shop and a *dépôt de pain*. You may think you're in the middle of nowhere, but the evenings bring regular entertainments in the shape of folk-singing soirées, bingo – even a Mr Muscle and Miss Camping contest. But your prime preoccupation here will be discovering this lovely region by car or on foot.

🌙 Ⓢ 🏊 🛶 🖥 🧺 ✕ ♀ 🍴 🏠 🗑 🔎

Directions: West of St-Jean-du-Gard on the D907 is a village called l'Estréchure. After going through the village, take the first left over a river across a stone bridge. On the other side is an immediate right-hand turn where you will see the camp entrance **Ground:** Hard to giving **Children:** Playground **Wheelchair:** Not suitable **Food-cooling:** Ice sold, coolpacks frozen **Sport:** Tennis, volleyball, ping pong, football, bike-hire, fishing **Season:** Easter to 15 Oct **Reservation:** Advisable peak season **Charge:** 2 people, pitch and car 52 fr; extra person 12 fr; electricity 12 fr

Les Sources

30270 St Jean-du-Gard   tel 66.85.38.03

Quite basic but bijou two-star site with a big pool in a shady Cévennes wood

This tiny, serene, two-star site squats in the beautiful shade of some pretty Cévenol woodland. As you enter the camp, to one side you'll see a single plain building which houses the reception and a bare bar/café. Outside in a garden area are a few tables to sit at and a couple of table-tennis tables. Not much to write home about so far, but then you clap eyes on a long rectangular pool that seems out of proportion with the rest of the camp. The ground rises gently away from the front clearing into a wood with secluded grass *emplacements*. By these is a quaint little sanitary block with the legends 'Adam' and 'Eve' above the two entrances. Inside, everything's painted a dazzling white and canary yellow, but there's only one seated loo (supposedly for disabled people, but the door is no wider than the others and there are no fixed handrails). Les Sources provides a peaceful halt for a touring holiday, and although food is limited to take-aways, you only have to go down the road to St Jean-du-Gard for buying in or eating out.

Directions: Leave St Jean-du-Gard to the north on the D983, crossing the main east-west D907. There's a camp direction sign here. At a fork go right onto the D50. After a couple of tight bends, you will see a high orange and green sign indicating the site entrance, which is a sudden fork to the right off the road **Ground:** Giving **Children:** Playground, swimming **Wheelchair:** Not suitable **Food-cooling:** Ice sold, coolpacks frozen **Sport:** None **Season:** 1 Apr to 15 Sept **Reservation:** Advisable peak season **Charge:** Pitch 11 fr; person 12 fr; per vehicle 5.00 fr

■■■ St Martin-d'Ardèche ■■■

Camping des Cigales

30760 St Julien-de-Peyrolas   tel 66.82.18.52

Tiny and tranquil jewel-in-the-crown site in Madame's back garden! Self-catering a must

Camping des Cigales is a really tiny site – only thirty-odd pitches – in the compact grounds of Madame Allarde's house, on a triangular plot of land just across the river from the village (St Julien-de-Peyrolas). It's an interesting alternative to the bigger camps at the other end of the Ardèche Gorge and perhaps would be suitable for a short stay if you wanted a temporary base to investigate the area. It would also be a good point for taking off to the Gard and the south. It is very, very quiet here, which is how Madame likes it – definitely no activities or entertainments. But it is a private sort of place with an exclusive quality which has much to do with being made to feel that you are Mme Allarde's guest. It's got a jewel-like setting too, a hedged patch of green mottled with a little shade cast by a cluster of trees, with arable fields all around. The one *sanitaire* is well kept, and for any laundry you have the use of Madame's washing-machine. No shop, but she runs a *dépôt de pain* in the mornings. There are restaurants back over the bridge in St Martin-d'Ardèche and for more major shopping the town of Pont d'Esprit on the Rhône is a short drive away on the N86 via the D901 (this last you pick up further along the road from Cigales – turn left at the T-junction).

◑ ⑤ ⚿ ⌂ ♿ ▣

Directions: Take the suspension bridge crossing the River Ardèche as you leave St Martin-d'Ardèche (the D141). After going round a right-hand bend, you will find the camp entrance on your right
Ground: Hard **Children:** Not suitable **Wheelchair:** Not suitable
Food-cooling: Ice sold **Sport:** None **Season:** All year
Reservation: Advisable peak season **Charge:** 2 people, pitch and car 42 fr

▰▰▰ St Maurice-d'Ardèche ▰▰▰

Domaine du Cros d'Auzon

St Maurice-d'Ardèche, 07200 Vogüé   tel 75.37.75.86

Exquisite hotel setting to spoil you – shame about the walk to it from your tent. Shelling out for activities may not bother you, seeing what's on offer here

Two businesses exist side by side here and it is thanks to the hotel half, a typical old stone *mas*, that campers have such a delightful setting in which to take a swim or sip a drink. The restaurant, traditional in farmhouse browns and reds, high-beamed ceiling, dark-stained furniture, tiled floor and white cloths, is a lovely place for a candlelit dinner. Outside, secluded from the pools by a hedge and flower-bed, is the smaller of two cool terraces offering the novelty of a skittle alley. The grounds are elegantly landscaped: a statue here, a touch of floral colour there. The camping ground is very peaceful and pretty, too. Gravel drives lead to grassed over *emplacements* of a reasonable size, and some are fairly shady. Nearby, a stable of ponies awaits eager children to ride them. Washing facilities are perfectly acceptable. So what's the bad news? We just wish it were possible that these two desirable elements – hotel and camping ground – were closer together. Perhaps we are too miserly in not wanting to dig into our pockets to pay for the supervised play area with the swingboats, the four-wheel bike-carts, the mini-golf, the tennis and the ponies (there is some free play equipment, though). And although no footwear of any description is allowed in the pool area (a normal requirement), on our visit the surface around the edge was of small pebbles set in chipped concrete tiles, cutting one little girl's feet. A pity, for this site, if expensive, has much to offer.

Directions: From St Maurice-d'Ardèche, take the D579 towards Aubenas (north). You will pass through a collection of houses at a main road T-junction known as Vogüé-Gare. You continue past this junction (on right) and a little further on is a left-hand turn where you will see a camp sign directing you. Follow the road straight to the site (not round left-hand bend, otherwise you will end up in a gravel depository) **Ground:** Giving **Children:** Playground, swimming **Wheelchair:** Not suitable **Food-cooling:** Ice sold **Sport:** Tennis, volleyball, ping pong, skittle alley, mini-golf, pony rides, bike-karts, canoeing, kayaking **Season:** 1 June to 15 Sept **Reservation:** Advisable peak season **Charge:** 2 people, pitch and car 70 fr; extra person 15 fr; child (1-7) 10 fr; electricity 10 fr

■■■ Sauve ■■■

Domaine de Bagard

30610 Sauve   tel 66.77.55.99

Small, easy-going four-star site with plenty of family atmosphere in a picturesque river setting

A narrow bridge over the mirrored surface of the Vidourle is your access to Domaine de Bagard's discreet location. This camp is a refreshingly casual four-star site on the south-eastern border of the Cévennes, sandwiched between the river and a cliff of forest and grey rock. In fact, it is more than a campsite: villa-style holiday apartments are grouped on stone-walled terracing at the cliff's base, giving the scene a pleasant visual feature. They complement the site's one building – also in stone

– which is the popular restaurant, fronted by a long, table-filled terrace leading up to its doorway under a striped blind. Inside the high-ceilinged barn of a room, the rafters exposed, a wooden bar takes up the length of one side. Cheerful serving staff typify the animated, easy-going nature of the camp. Across the way are the tennis courts and a playground set in a small cultivated lawn screened from the pool area by hedges. It's obvious that considerable effort has been made to make these grounds attractive. From here a single driveway bordered by a stone wall at the bottom of the cliff begins to take you into the camping ground proper. This is a shady strip of land following the calm Vidourle (good for a spot of canoeing). Gravelled avenues of tall, mature trees lead off this made-up road to grass *emplacements* of a good size, some hedging giving a certain amount of privacy as well as creating ornate surroundings. The *sanitaire* block here is in slightly less good shape than the one by the swimming-pool but both have modern appointments. Domaine de Bagard provides plenty of family fun in the evenings, plus organised daytime rambles or horse-rides into the glorious hills. The village of Sauve further along the main road is worth exploring – a medieval village on the river where a maze of steep, stone steps takes you up through narrow silent streets past aged houses wedged in a chaotic pile against the cliffside. One or two restaurants are possible candidates for an evening out from the camp. Domaine de Bagard has most of the attributes for a relaxing time – with or without the family – and is also ideally positioned for quite a few sightseeing journeys, lying as it does very near the Gard/Hérault border. You can quite easily reach some of the visits described in the Hérault section

Directions: Sauve is a village off the D999, due west of Nîmes on the way to Le Vigan. The camp is visible from the road just east of the village, on your right **Ground:** Hard to giving **Children:** Playground, swimming **Wheelchair:** Suitable **Food-cooling:** Ice sold **Sport:** Tennis, volleyball, ping pong, canoeing, bike-hire, horse-riding, organised rambles, fishing **Season:** 3 Apr to 30 Sept **Reservation:** Advisable peak season **Charge:** 2 people, pitch, car and electricity 100 fr; extra person 12 fr

Children should be discouraged from playing around shower blocks.

Uzès

Le Mas de Rey

Arpaillargues, 30700 Uzès	tel 66.22.18.27

Little haven of tranquillity, but not without some comforts

If your idea of perfect camping is to escape to solitude yet not be without too many creature comforts, Le Mas de Rey may be your answer. It's hidden away in the countryside outside Uzès amid pastureland and light woods, encircled by a ring of splendid oaks, which gives the peculiar impression that this is England at the height of summer. Sixty pitches small, and pretty with it, Le Mas de Rey greets you with a large open lawn at the front of its single squat building that houses reception and shop. Immediately behind are the camp's two lovely pools – one elliptical and one circular (and smaller) for children. Shade is at a premium in the camping ground itself, the grassland criss-crossed by rows of conifers, and some *emplacements* are marked with little shrubs, but peace comes in abundance. The two small *sanitaires* are on the old side but function efficiently and are well kept. The friendly Dutch family owners lay on snacks and take-aways but you'll mostly be catering for yourself with stocks bought in Uzès three miles back up the road.

Directions: Go west out of Uzès in the direction of Moussac on the D982. You will cross an automatic rail crossing followed by a bridge over a river. Then, after picking up a camp direction sign giving you a 100 metre warning, you will arrive at the site entrance on your left
Ground: Giving **Children:** Playground, swimming, organised events
Wheelchair: Suitable **Food-cooling:** Ice sold, coolpacks frozen
Sport: Volleyball, ping pong **Season:** Easter to 15 Oct
Reservation: Advisable peak season **Charge:** 2 people, pitch and car 58 fr; extra person 12 fr; children under 4 free; electricity 12 fr

---

No matter how bad your French you'll quickly gain respect by trying to use the language. A liberal sprinkling of 's'il vous plaît's and 'pardon's will stand you in good stead. A hearty volunteered 'Bonjour!' to your neighbour may also help dispel any prejudice about the 'cold English'!

Valleraugue

Le Pied d'Aigoual

30570 Valleraugue	Out-of-season tel 67.82.21.48
	tel 67.82.24.40

Very basic but restful and attractive site offering a useful touring stop away from crowds

Not exactly at the foot of that mountain (Aigoual) which lies at some distance behind the camp, Le Pied d'Aigoual is a basic, unassuming two-star site offering a useful stop-over on a touring holiday. It's a tidy pocket of land with intermittent shade for its 80 pitches provided by small, scrubby trees, and there's even the bonus of a pool in which to freshen up. Amenities consist of a fairly unsophisticated *sanitaire* (but with some seated loos), a simple bar in the hut of the building that is reception, and games in the shape of volleyball, table tennis and a 'boulodrome'. The village is at hand for a butcher, baker and *vin de pays*.

○ ⓢ ⚓ ⛴ ♀ ⋔

Directions: Go out of Valleraugue west on the D986. Cross the River Hérault and shortly after, opposite an orchard on your left, you will come across the camp around a bend. Watch out for an illuminated beer sign sticking out from a hedge on the right-hand side – this is the entrance **Ground:** Hard **Children:** Playground **Wheelchair:** Not suitable **Food-cooling:** Ice sold **Sport:** Volleyball, ping pong **Season:** June to Sept **Reservation:** Advisable peak season **Charge:** 2 people, pitch and car 38 fr; extra person 10 fr; child (under 7) 8 fr; electricity 9 to 12 fr

Vallon Pont d'Arc

Sites summary Other than Sampzon, with its poor selection of campsites on the Ardèche, Vallon is the main camping centre for this popular tourist area. Three of the four camps back on to the Ardèche where you can bathe (even better at the actual Pont d'Arc) and you can wander without hindrance onto any one of them via a riverbank path that links their rear boundaries.

Directions for sites Just south of the town the D290 heads east to the Gorge. All three camps lie on the right-hand side of the road after the bend past a series of canoe hire agencies.

Camping l'Ardéchois

07150 Vallon Pont d'Arc   tel 75.88.06.63

Four-star site with pukka amenities but chokka camping

L'Ardéchois is the only four-star camp in the area and it does offer the superior amenities and entertainments that those stars imply. A smart modern complex at the site entrance has luxury facilities such as a huge bar/restaurant and a pleasing two-level sunbathing terrace containing irregular-shaped pools. From the point of view of entertainments and other distractions, a good time can be had by all. But when it comes to the camping ground you might feel rather let down, for the pitches are packed in with little privacy, despite the cover from rows of trees. The *sanitaires* are well maintained (though shower pressure may not be perfect), but unless you're very outgoing and active and like to spend your days away from the tent, you won't like the 'tent village' syndrome.

● Ⓜ 🏃 ⌂ 🖴 🍖 ✕ 🍷 🥾 🏛 ♨ 🔲 🎣

Directions: See Directions for sites at beginning of Vallon Pont d'Arc
Ground: Giving **Children:** Playground, swimming, organised events, baby facilities **Wheelchair:** Suitable **Food-cooling:** Ice sold
Sport: Tennis, volleyball, ping pong, canoeing, kayaking **Season:** 15 Mar to Oct **Reservation:** Advisable peak season **Charge:** 2 people, pitch and car 99 fr; extra person 22 fr; electricity 14 fr

Mondial Camping

Route des Gorges,   tel 75.88.03.79
07150 Vallon Pont d'Arc

A very French camp with a good camping ground in deep shade. Basic life-style for an active holiday

Mondial seems to be one of the older camps in the area, if you go by the buildings and the more established vegetation. The facilities are by the roadside with a bar/restaurant serving snack meals such as spaghetti bolognese, plus a general shop and a pool (heated when necessary, as is the *sanitaire*). As you go into the grounds you are struck by how marvellously dark and cool everything is beneath the foliage – quite different from that of its neighbours. A good spread of large trees and small criss-crossing paths help to prevent any visual monotony. You also have the advantage here of hedged-off enclosures of half a dozen pitches each, making the place feel less like a scout camp! The camping population has a mix of families and young couples as well as small parties, but most seem enthusiastically involved with the main preoccupation of this location, the river-borne descent through some of the most inspiring scenery in this part of the world.

● Ⓜ 𝑖 ⌂ ▱ ☕ ✕ ♀ ☝ ⌂ ⊿ ▣

Directions: See Directions for sites at beginning of Vallon Pont d'Arc
Ground: Hard   **Children:** Playground, swimming
Wheelchair: Suitable   **Food-cooling:** Ice sold   **Sport:** Tennis, ping pong, canoeing   **Season:** 15 Apr to 15 Oct   **Reservation:** Advisable peak season   **Charge:** 2 people, pitch and car 85 fr; extra person 20 fr; child (under 7) 15 fr; electricity 13 fr

La Plage Fleurie

Les Mazes, 07150 Vallon Pont d'Arc   tel 75.88.01.15

Tranquil, leafy riverside camp away from the town. An ideal touring stop

Away from the hubbub of Vallon's tourist beat, yet within easy reach of the town, is this serene and exceedingly picturesque site on one of the quieter banks of the River Ardèche. An aviary of parakeets and other exotic birds greets you, a boisterous beginning to what is otherwise 'Camping bien calme', as the camp's motto has it. Although the site has over two hundred *emplacements*, these are divided between two distinct grounds in the shape of the letter T: the vertical a rectangular field (more suitable for caravans), and the horizontal a long, narrow strip along the river bank, sheltering in a cool, lush wood. The motto is a fitting one, you concur, as you get the Primus going for a coffee and a quiet read by the still, green waters that reflect the smooth grey cliff opposite. The site's small bar has a cosy pine interior, and snack meals and take-aways are the thing. Other amenities consist of a food shop, butcher's, bank, post office and doctor on the site. Very good *sanitaires* are equipped with a full range of facilities for disabled visitors. We learned from Madame, who keeps an ever-watchful eye on the camp, that she leaves up to 50 per cent of the pitches free for spontaneous tourers, great for anyone not wanting to plan the holiday down to the last detail.

Directions: Take the D579 going west out of Vallon. Along a straight stretch of road you will see a big red sign for 'Le Point Disco 2000'. After a second red sign, take the first left to Les Mazes. At a T-junction, turn left (camp direction sign here), then first right by a low, white building. Continue straight on to what seems like a track at the end of the road between some wire fences. Go down to find the camp at the bottom **Ground:** Giving **Children:** Playground **Wheelchair:** Suitable **Food-cooling:** Ice sold, coolpacks frozen **Sport:** Volleyball, ping pong, canoeing, pedalos, sailboards **Season:** Easter to Sept **Reservation:** Advisable peak season **Charge:** 2 people, pitch and car 59 fr; extra person 12 fr; child (under 7) 8 fr; electricity 11 fr

Le Provençal

Route des Gorges,   tel 75.88.00.48
07150 Vallon Pont d'Arc

Green and pleasant camping on an unpretentious site, yet still with good facilities

Unlike L'Ardéchois next door, Le Provençal doesn't shout about itself. Its main building is of more conventional design made colourful by striped blinds and awnings. On one side of the drive are the tables and chairs outside an unfussy restaurant; steps take you to a level above the reception to a small self-service shop stocked with fresh groceries. Opposite, a children's play area is laid out under a huge, beautiful willow tree, and on your way to the camping ground, you pass the swimming-pool (heated when necessary). It's fascinating to see how two sites sitting on top of one another can create such a different environment. Le Provençal somehow achieves a more spacious feel even though its pitches are hardly larger. Clipped conifers here and there help to mark the boundaries of the grassy *emplacements* off the two parallel main avenues. The trees are more mature and help to make the place shadier and look less of an open site. Although the various amenities of a three-star site are on offer (shop, restaurant, take-away counter as well as a disco), a quieter, relaxed atmosphere prevails: this is a site that seems to 'back off' and let you get on with shaping your own holiday. *Sanitaires*, by the way, are modern and clean.

Directions: See Directions for sites at beginning of Vallon Pont d'Arc
Ground: Hard **Children:** Playground, organised events
Wheelchair: Suitable **Food-cooling:** Ice sold **Sport:** Tennis, volleyball, ping pong, canoeing, kayaking, pétanque, fishing
Season: 15 Mar to 15 Oct **Reservation:** Advisable peak season
Charge: 2 people, pitch and car 83 fr; extra person 20 fr; electricity 15 fr

Le Vigan

☼ *Le Val d'Arre*

30120 Le Vigan   tel 67.81.02.77

Relaxing cool, green site well placed for exploring the southern Cévennes

On Saturdays, Le Vigan, a small market town at the southern edge of the Cévennes, bursts at the seams as people congregate in the tree-lined elongated central square. During the week, the cafés are a nightly rendezvous for a surprisingly young local population. Le Val d'Arre, just outside the town, is a three-star with plenty to offer the carefree camper for more than a day or two, although it would also be a good stop-over. Via an interesting-looking bridge by an aqueduct you arrive at a large, ivy-covered stone building (reception), before the main drive swings away into the grounds past the agreeable swimming-pool. Tables and chairs here are handy for eating pizzas from the twice-weekly pizza van as well as ice-cream or drinks from the camp shop. Eats the rest of the time will be from your own barbecue – no hardship, since the town is so close for supplies. You have a choice of pitch: either under the umbrella branches of uniform rows of small trees in a wide, shady glade, or along the more secluded narrow bank of the Arre. It's here near the playground by the water's edge that the river tumbles over a gentle waterfall to snake its way through white-grey boulders. Old villas on the opposite bank are mirrored in its reflection. In the evenings, most people gather round the camp's fulcrum – the central illuminated patch where *pétanque* is played in earnest.

● ⑤ ♨ ⌂ 🏊 ⛱ 🏔 ⬚ ▣

Directions: Head east out of Le Vigan on the D999. Where the road becomes straight with a line of trees on your right and a cliff on your left, watch out for a right-hand fork that suddenly drops away from the road. This will lead down to a small, high aqueduct with a road bridge over the river. Turn right to cross this, then road takes you to camp entrance **Ground:** Giving **Children:** Playground, swimming **Wheelchair:** Not suitable **Food-cooling:** Ice sold **Sport:** Volleyball, canoeing, pétanque, fishing **Season:** 1 Apr to 20 Sept **Reservation:** Advisable peak season **Charge:** 2 people, pitch and car 47 fr; electricity 14 fr

▬▬ Villeneuve-les-Avignon ▬▬

Municipal de la Laune

Chemin St-Honoré,   tel 90.25.76.06
30400 Villeneuve-les-Avignon

Immaculate, ornamental and silent camp below the castle

Laune should really be spelled 'lawn', for here you are camping in nothing less than ornamental gardens worthy of a ticket entry for Sunday visits! This is a great example of a well-shaded, library-silent, horticulturally excellent municipal site, very convenient to reach and of course ideal for Avignon and sightseeing in the vicinity (but no pool, though). A kerbed gravel roadway takes you round the camp, with well-defined grass *emplacements* leading off. Trees are a decorative mix of tall conifers and weeping willows, and there's an island rockery of lavender and alpines by the modern reception, snack counter and basic shop back at the entrance. The washing block is pristine and includes toilets and showers for the disabled. The tariff is not particularly low for a municipal site – but you do have to pay for an exclusive bit of peace and quiet, while having a prime base from which to discover the area.

● ⑤ ♨ ✕ ⚲ 🏔 ⬚

Directions: Outside Villeneuve-les-Avignon, where the D980 rounds the hill of St-André fort, there is a set of traffic lights at a crossroads. Assuming you may be coming from Avignon, turn right for the site (signposted) **Ground:** Giving **Children:** No special provision but not unsuitable **Wheelchair:** Suitable **Food-cooling:** Ice sold, coolpacks frozen **Sport:** None **Season:** Easter to Sept **Reservation:** Advisable peak season **Charge:** Pitch 12 fr; person 15 fr; vehicle 8 fr

Western Provence

Although many a Briton thinks of Provence vaguely in terms of anywhere in the South of France between the Rhône in the west and Nice in the east, its true Roman origins lie in the two *départements* that make up the region we cover in this section – Vaucluse and Bouches-du-Rhône. It was indeed at Aix (Aquae Sextiae) that Gaul first encountered Latin civilisation one hundred years before the Birth of Christ, and the might and influence of the Roman Empire can still be felt all over this compact area.

Scenically, Provençal imagery is as acute in Vaucluse as anywhere in Var or the Alpes-Maritimes to the east (see Eastern Provence); fields of chrome yellow as if Van Gogh's spirit had been around personally painting each sunflower; huge quilts of pulsating mauve-blue lavender fields, an optical vibration as smarting as those devised by Vasarély; perched villages of ochre and terracotta lifted from a Cézanne canvas. Wherever you go your eye is infused with a crisp, yellow light, while horizons beyond your field of vision tirelessly support the weight of blue above.

One of the smallest *départements* of France, Vaucluse has probably the densest concentration and variety of sights for the tourist, ranging from archaeological visits to natural phenomena. Vaucluse also happens to be France's greengrocer, producing the nation's largest output of fruit and vegetables, especially tomatoes which, along with onions, olive oil and garlic, form the basis of many a Provençal dish, of which ratatouille is but one. Truffles and asparagus come in plenty, and luscious

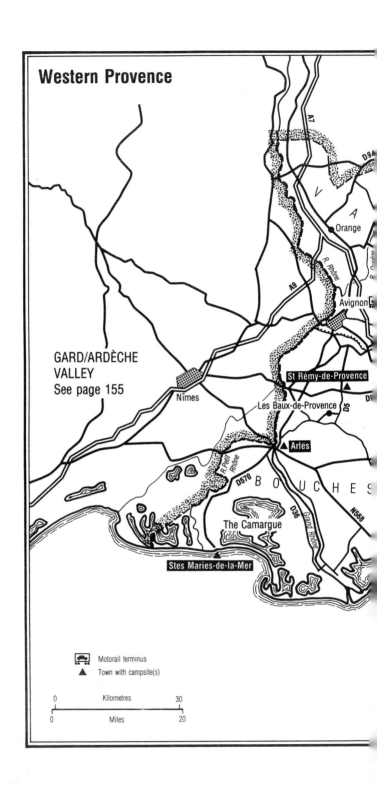

Western Provence

GARD/ARDÈCHE
VALLEY
See page 155

Orange

R. Rhône

Avignon

St Rémy-de-Provence

Nîmes

Les Baux-de-Provence

Arles

R. Petit
Rhône

D570

B O U C H E S

The Camargue

D36

Grand Rhône

N568

Stes Maries-de-la-Mer

A7

D94

V A

A9

D5

Motorail terminus
▲ Town with campsite(s)

0	Kilometres	30
0	Miles	20

N

Vaison-la-Romaine

D938

D974

△ Mont Ventoux

▲ Bédoin

Mazan

D942

Sault

▲ Villes-sur-Auzon

Carpentras

D4

Venasque

L

U

e-sur-la-Sorgue

Murs

S

Gordes ▲

Roussillon

N100

D2

Apt

D943

Cavaillon

Bonnieux-Lourmarin

D973

Ansouis

R. Durance

▲

▲ Pertuis

La Roque d'Anthéron

-de-Provence

N7

U

R

H

Ô

N

E

A8

EASTERN
PROVENCE/
CÔTE D'AZUR
See page 241

Aix-en-Provence

A7

A8

Étang de Berre

A52

Marseille

A50

soft fruits, large quantities supplying the crystallised confectionery industry centred on Apt, while Cavaillon has a reputation for succulent melon.

Charcuterie is a hallmark, too: as well as the familiar saucisson d'Arles, nearly every butcher in the villages of the hills manufactures his own sausage or pâté. In Lower Provence fish is more common on the menu; when you're tired of *bouillabaisse* ring the changes by trying a *brandade* of salted cod, pounded with olive oil, cream and garlic.

As ever, where there's good food there's good wine. Choose from the Côtes du Lubéron, Ventoux or Rhône, or a Coteaux d'Aix-en-Provence or Tricastin perhaps. Prince among the reds is the age-old Châteauneuf-du-Pape, while a more recent yet interesting upstart is the Coteaux des Baux. Also from this region comes the luscious sweet Muscat from Beaumes-de-Venise.

Turning from gastronomy to geography, this region is divided into distinct physical components. In the north is the most significant visual feature of the landscape for miles around – Mont Ventoux, the gentle giant of Provence. The curve from its south-western lee shelters the Vaucluse Plain, which is in effect the market garden of the nation, with Carpentras its focal point. To the south is the Vaucluse Plateau which eats into the heart of the *département*. It holds in its environs – especially the southern foothills – some of the area's prettiest villages, which certainly match up to anything that Var or the Alpes-Maritimes can muster. Places like Gordes, Murs, Venasque, Roussillon and St Saturnin-d'Apt all have their individual charm. At the western end of these foothills is the source of both the River Sorgue and the *département*'s name, the Fontaine de Vaucluse (from Vallis Clausa, the Closed Valley – see below).

The Coulon valley is the lowland continuing south, stretching from Cavaillon in the west to past Apt in the east. Beyond are the last highlands of the region in the form of the Lubéron range, made up of the Petit and Grand Lubéron. They form a near-continuous ridge, only

split by the Combe de Lourmarin, which carries the
D943, an area of haunting yet peaceful beauty, where
rock face and vegetation appear indiscriminately thrown
together. The drive is an interesting one with a blind
bend almost every minute of the journey. The road
continues to Apt and after the Combe, climbs to give you
glimpses over the Coulon valley. Other high places in the
range give you equally good panoramic views and little
clinging villages to visit. The whole area is protected by its
designation as a National Park.

The Lubéron's southern slopes drop to the valley of the
Durance, whose wavy blue line on the map also marks
the end of Vaucluse and the beginning of Bouches-du-
Rhône. Cartographically, this *département*'s seaward side
ressembles the frayed edge of a moth-eaten cloth, holed
with the salt-lakes of the Camargue in the west, the near
land-locked lagoon of the Etang de Berre and finally, in
the east, the bay of Marseilles. The city of the bay is the
second largest in France with a population of over a
million, its life and history revolving around its
importance as the country's number one port: it was
founded by the Phoeniceans as a harbour for their small
colony called Massala. Although today a certain amount
of colour and myth is attached to its recent, seamy past
and the daily life of the dockside, Marseilles' vast
industrial sprawl may deter the visitor from seeking out
its few attractions.

To the north of these watery places are the principal
towns of Arles, Salon-de-Provence and Aix. Also on your
itinerary should be St Rémy-de-Provence and the
mysterious Les Baux, a rocky citadel where now only
history's ghosts reside.

Aix-en-Provence

The spa town of Aix started as Aquae Sextiae, the founding
town of the first Roman province in Gaul, which took its name
from the warm spring waters of this site. The fifteenth century
saw it as a centre for intellectual excellence when the court of
Provence under King René became known as the most refined

in Renaissance Europe. René himself was an outstanding and erudite scholar. Over the centuries Aix developed into a town rich in cultural activity, reaching its zenith in the 1700s. This richness is still manifest in the delightful town-planning of the period: avenues of trees, noble tall town houses, and fountains upon fountains. If it isn't enough to taste history by walking around the old quarter that stretches south from the Cathédrale de St Sauveur – a patchwork of architectural styles in itself – there are quite a few museums to visit: one of old Aix, another of tapestries, and of fine art (the Granet), as well as Cézanne's studio set up as it was in his last days in Aix. For all your promenading, without a doubt you should finally stroll down the Cours Mirabeau, the supreme boulevard of southern French towns, where majestic plane trees arch the wide concourse, shading busy shops and cafés. The scene is visually heightened by three splendid fountains placed at intervals along its length. Before you leave Aix, don't forget to buy yourself a present of *calissons*, a marzipan speciality from the prime national source of almonds.

Ansouis

Ansouis is a pretty, peaceful hamlet east of Cadenet and north of the D973 and is worth the detour for its château (attractive gardens outside, interesting detail inside) and for its Musée Extraordinaire. The museum, a renovated stone Provençal house, is the culmination of one man's life interests (Georges Mazoyer) brought together as a disparate collection of artefacts, from antique Provençal furniture, to bounty from under the sea, to unique pieces of sculpture. You are led through a couple of rooms with examples of wooden furniture of a rural style, then, like Alice, you come across something completely different and unexpected. A stone vaulted cellar is half-museum, half-art gallery devoted to the submarine world. In glass cabinets are M Mazoyer's underwater treasures gleaned from numerous diving expeditions to Martinique – corroded cannon balls, coins, shells, coral and so on. Lining the walls are his impressive paintings of marine life and submerged wrecks as well as some superb wrought-iron sculptures of skeletal fish forms. The *pièce de résistance* is the final 'grotto', complete with running water and lit through a blue stained glass window.

Apt

Apt is a thriving town known for its manufacture of crystallised
fruit as well as being a distribution point for the truffles grown
in the region. It is not a particularly attractive place except
where tall trees border a river across from the brick-paved
square awash with bars and *glaceries*. There's a marked contrast
between the impoverished back streets and pedestrian precincts
that form a shop-filled maze leading from the twelfth-century
Cathedral of Ste Anne. On Saturdays, the place spills over:
traffic queues, market, crêpe and ice-cream stalls, cafés packed
with teens filling in time.

Arles

At the point where the Rhône meets the flatlands of the
Camargue lies Arles, a city with a glorious past that began with
the Greeks. Later under Rome it became a major
communications point and by the fifth century had established
itself not only as a trading capital of the Mediterranean, but also
as a political centre for Gaul under the Roman emperor
Constantine. In the Middle Ages it was known as the Kingdom
of Arles.

Today it thrives on tourism and the recent rice production of
the Camargue. Its most famous resident is Vincent Van Gogh
who, in the last couple of years of his life here, was at his most
prolific, creating his most famous works. Arles' history is
encapsulated in many of its museums but if you have neither
the time nor the enthusiasm for them all, you should not
neglect the Arena. Although the amphitheatre at Nîmes is more
intact, the one here is larger and more visually stimulating,
maybe due to the incomplete nature of its architecture. Its top
ring of open arches incorporates three towers left over from
medieval times, when the arena was converted into a fortified
town, complete with houses and a church. The amphitheatre is
the venue for bullfighting in the summer months. Close by are
the remains of a Roman theatre. If you want a place to sit for a
while and sip a *thé citron*, walk down the Rue des Arènes to the
broken columns of the Place du Forum to find a café in the
shade. If your appetite has been whetted, turn to the church of
St Trophime, also in the city centre, with its beautifully worked
west door and cloisters of equally ornate stone carving.

From the considerable list of museums, perhaps the best choice would be the Museon Arlaten – Provençal for Arles Museum. This was founded by Frédéric Mistral who won the Nobel Prize for literature in 1905, honouring his endeavour to keep the original Provençal language alive through his writings. He upheld the view that such a revival should go hand in hand with a general education on Provençal life, to which this museum is now dedicated. On the southern side of Arles is the Alyscamps, south of the junction of the Boulevard des Lices and the Avenue Victor Hugo. The Alyscamps is a whole avenue of a burial ground lined with defunct tombs and sarcophagi, the remains of a cemetery used for more than 800 years from the days of Roman rule.

Les Baux-de-Provence

North-east of Arles a range of hills, the Chaîne des Alpilles, provides a *scène sauvage* for the outstanding promontory of Les Baux. Half-built by the hand of Nature in the form of a mass of craggy limestone erupting from the landscape, half-built by Man in the form of an impregnable fortress town, the passage of time has somehow gelled these two endeavours into one. Les Baux's citadel, now in ruins, was once the home of a merry and rapacious dynasty of the Lords of Baux who ruled this roost and the lands around for nearly 300 years in the Middle Ages. Views from the top are no less than breathtaking. Best to avoid the high season, though, when this mirage becomes overrun with tourists.

Bonnieux and Lourmarin

Two perched villages either side of the Lubéron hills, linked by the Combe that cuts them, vie with each other for being the prettier. Only when you have climbed to the top of **Bonnieux**'s hill isolated in a sea of fields do you appreciate the commanding position. It is crowned by a plain twelfth-century church and from its pleasant walled terrace you can look over the litter of rust-coloured tiled roofs of houses tumbling down the slope, and take in lovely vistas of Provençal countryside across the sweep of the valley to the plateau region.

At first sight **Lourmarin** is similar to Bonnieux but it doesn't rise to the same height. Its main claim to fame is as the burial place of Albert Camus. Old winding streets between stone walls twist their way up to the small fifteenth-century château, from the turret of which you can see a good swathe of the Lubéron. Even if you don't get that far, a peek through the large, wooden, studded doors at the ivy-covered entrance will reward you with a delightful composition of an open courtyard surrounded by a first storey of a stone arcade surmounted by another floor with a continuous wooden-railed balcony.

The Camargue

The very name Camargue conjures up romantic pictures of French gauchos on horseback (*gardians*) watching the distant grazing of wild, black bulls across a flat plain of grasses broken by slivers of still water. This isn't too far from the truth, only to spot these or the equally famous flamingoes or wild horses is less likely on a chance drive through the region than if you join a guided tour. There are a number of choices. You can go on an organised bus tour with commentary (from Le Grau-du-Roi or Stes Maries-de-la-Mer) or take a jeep 'safari' (from Stes Maries). The pleasurable alternative is a waterborne trip on a French (and very junior) version of a Mississippi paddle steamer embarking from the mouth of the Petit Rhône just west of Stes Maries.

The wide delta of saltmarshes and *étangs* (lagoons) that lie between this offshoot of the Rhône and its big brother to the east is now the Camargue Natural Regional Park. The park's centre for information is north of Stes Maries on the D570 at Pont de Gau. Here, you will find exhibitions on the local environment, audio-visual presentations and a viewing room looking onto a typical landscape of the delta. Close by is a bird park devoted to species found in the Camargue. Aviaries recreate the natural environment of some birds that you wouldn't otherwise see easily, and there's an opportunity to observe other species in the wild along designated nature trails within the confines of the Park. The official Nature Reserve which takes in the Camargue's largest area of water – the Etang du Vaccarès – is off limits to the public, so for those of an ornithological bent the bird park's marshes are an ideal substitute. The Nature Reserve's own information centre (open to all) is at La Capellière, situated on the D36B bordering the eastern shore of the Etang. Two other more esoteric areas represented are the aquatic flora and fauna centre, La Palissade, at Salin-de-Giraud, and the Camargue Museum on the D570 south-west of Arles. This last is housed in a large converted sheep barn and enlightens the visitor on the life of the Camarguais, the inhabitants of the region.

Carpentras

Carpentras, south-west of Mont Ventoux, is an attractive town of 30,000 inhabitants. It is at the centre of what in the thirteenth century was the Comtat Venaissin, a parcel of land given to the Holy See when, on Philip III's invitation, Clément V decided to leave Italy and the petty insurgencies of the time. In this respect the Comtat could be seen as the first French Papal seat before Clément's successor moved to Avignon a quarter of a century later.

Tree-lined boulevards in the older part of town lead to the two dominant buildings of the law courts and St Siffrein Cathedral at its hub. Tucked behind the two is a Roman arch dating from the first century with two large standing figures in relief that have survived well since. For more about the Comtat's history, there's a museum off the Boulevard Albin-Durand on the west side of town. Just north-east of the cathedral is the oldest synagogue in France: originally built in the 1400s, it was the focal point of the ghetto that numbered 1,000 people before the Revolution.

Appropriate to the pivotal town of the fertile Vaucluse Plain, the main preoccupation here is food, evident from the profusion of fresh produce to be seen at the Friday market. One speciality is '*perle noire du Comtat*' a truffle embedded in a vol-au-vent. Another are the triangular boiled sweets, like striped pieces of amber, known as *berlingots*.

For an interesting excursion, south on the D938, **Pernes-les-Fontaine**, the Comtat's capital before Carpentras, has a fascinating and very photogenic collection of architecture from the Middle Ages huddled around the old bridge over the Nesque.

Cavaillon

Not only is Cavaillon the home of melon cultivation but France's second largest national market, handling a vast array of other fresh produce from the Coulon valley. From early spring the town is a daily warehouse for all manner of fruit and vegetables, sending trucks and trainloads to the rest of the country. To its western side the streets finish at the Mont St Jacques where, from a Roman arch at the Place François-Tourel, you can pick up a path that ascends this steep hill to a chapel on the top. This little trip offers yet another opportunity to have an uninterrupted and quite glorious view of the Vaucluse countryside.

Les Dentelles de Montmirail

The Dentelles are a range of limestone peaks due west of Mont Ventoux and due south of Vaison-la-Romaine. The remarkable alien landscape of their jagged silhouettes – thin, pointed, razor-sharp ridges that are naturally pierced, creating ruined window spaces in a forbidden city – would be perfect for another Star Wars epic. A good route through this range is the D90 from Malaucène (south of Vaison on the D938) to Beaumes-de-Venise.

Fontaine-de-Vaucluse

In a cliffside cave rain water drained from the plateau fills a pool. Suddenly and as if by magic the pool reaches overflowing to spill over like some sudden mountain rapid to replenish the Sorgue. This extraordinary place can be reached from just north of l'Isle-sur-la-Sorgue on the D25 or by picking up the D24 off the N100 to the south. The best time to visit is in the spring: not only will there be fewer visitors but also the gushing waters are more plentiful.

Gordes

You are in for a real treat if you approach Gordes from the south on the D2. If Mont Ventoux didn't exist as a visual symbol for Vaucluse then this spectacularly placed village would do nicely. A jutting spur of limestone rock thrown up from the valley floor supports the town, which climbs in tree-covered tiers to the summit, topped by church and château. The buildings, constructed of the same stone as the rock they sit upon, seem to grow out of this natural edifice. Coupled with this is a sweeping background panorama of fields below.

The château houses the Vaserély Museum, which covers all aspects of the artist's work, including figurative painting and sculpture as well as his renowned Op-Art screen prints. South near St Pantaléon is a Stained Glass Museum illustrating the history of the craft, plus an exhibition of contemporary work. Due north is the Abbaye de Senanque, secreted away in the narrow, isolated Senancole valley. It is one of the best preserved examples of an architecture employed by the Cistercian order of the twelfth century and looks stunning in this setting. The abbey buildings are now occupied by the Centre for Saharan Studies with permanent displays on desert life and survival.

To the south-west lies the Village des Bories. *Bories*, found scattered through the plateau and the Lubéron, are semi-pyramidic drystone huts narrowing to a point at the top. These crude dwellings were common to rural life of old. The 'village' is a restoration of such buildings enclosed by a low stone wall, and presented as an open-air museum. Gordes holds its annual wine festival in July, but is also good fun on Tuesday (market day).

Gorges de la Nesque

The D942 is the high Corniche road of the Gorges between Villes-sur-Auzon and Sault, which is worth a stop. The town, perched on the northern rim of the Vaucluse Plateau, is the centre of the Vaucluse lavender industry, and in the summer the surrounding lowlands between the plateau and Ventoux are transformed into a hill-to-hill carpet of violet-blue fields.

L'Isle-sur-la-Sorgue

The town is known as the 'Little Venice' of Vaucluse. The River Sorgue splits before the town to encircle it with two streams that rejoin as it continues its journey. Small waterways slip from these to entwine themselves with the web of Sorgue's streets. This is indeed a pretty place, full of reflections of inverted buildings, greenery and flowers. Generous shade-giving plane trees add grace to a scene wholly restful on the eye. If you walk away from the church square down the Rue Denfert Rochereau, and then turn left, you will find the Rue des Roues, where a street runs parallel to a canal with a series of waterwheels like some multiple sculpture in corroded iron. The Sorgue waters from old have always been harnessed for driving mills – the first probably for the town's domestic use in milling corn. Later they drove machinery for the silk and woollen industries. Now silent, the wheels have so merged with this green water scene that their presence could be mistaken as deliberate ornamentation if you didn't know any better.

Mont Ventoux

At 1909 metres high, this is the Giant of Provence, the low country from which it swells and rises making it look even more immense. Immense yet tame, for these are roads that make the summit accessible, the best choice probably being the D974 from Malaucène following the ascent of Ventoux's western ridge. From below, the mountain seems snow-covered in summer but, although winter months see skiers on the slopes, the snows vanish in spring, laying bare a white cap of stone and shingle. The viewing table on the summit will help with the game of spotting landmarks. Even on a less than clear day you should be able to make out without too much trouble the Camargue, the Cévennes, the whole of Vaucluse and the Rhône Valley. On a really clear day you might be lucky to see as far as Le Canigou, the old man of the Pyrénées-Orientales.

Murs and Venasque

Here you have two villages for the price of one sightseeing tour between Apt and Carpentras on the D4. This scenic route takes you right across the western end of the Vaucluse Plateau with a twisting drive through the Combe de Vaulongue before emerging from the hills. The village sits in a small, high plain in the middle of the plateau in one of the few places clear of forest. Little rectagular blocks of yellow ochre houses huddle around a plain medieval château and church standing proud on a rise above them.

Go north and you'll arrive at Venasque, which presents a different aspect altogether, for before it lies the Vaucluse Plain with the towering Ventoux rising behind. The village is far more squat than Murs and is important for two ancient religious connections with the seventh-century. The chapel of Notre Dame-de-Vie lying on the outskirts contains the tomb of a bishop of Carpentras named Bohetius, and back at the village is what is thought to be one of France's oldest ecclesiastical buildings, the Baptistery.

Orange

Orange, north of Avignon, lies just east of where the A9 autoroute splits with the A7. This busy, provincial town was once a major city in the days of the Roman Empire and Rome's legacy can be seen in probably the two best perserved antiquities in southern France. The theatre – considered to be the finest and most complete example of its type in all Europe – comprises a semi-circular auditorium built into a hillside and a magnificent near-intact stone façade over 100 feet in height and 300 feet long backing the stage area. The site lies just south of the town centre, but if you enter Orange from the north on the N7 you will come across a magnificent triple arch commemorating victories in battle and the colonisation of the town in 36 BC. Although a certain amount of restoration has been carried out, most of the carvings and reliefs are in their original state.

Roussillon

High on an isolated crop of hills rising from the Coulon valley north-west of Apt, Rousillon attracts its share of trippers, and deservedly so. Here is one of two areas unique for their ochre soil (the other is near Rustrel – the so-called Vaucluse 'Colorado' north-east of Apt). A magnificent view is to be had from the terrace of an eleventh-century fort-like church at the top of the village's steep streets. Climb the Rue de Casteau, narrow, cobbled and picturesque, past twee craft shops with expensive ceramics. Look back to see a Florentine scene painted on large wooden doors under an ornate stone lintel across the road. Once at the church you can gaze out on to the plateau, across to Mont Ventoux and over the Coulon towards the Lubéron. Then you can cut back for a spot of light lunch outside one of those restaurants/*crêperies* you passed on the way up. One last panorama to take in before you leave Roussillon can be seen from the drive to the town cemetery just off the main road. This is of the Chaussée des Géants, a range of rugged ochre cliffs, their luminous red-orange perfectly complemented by the dark green clusters of pine growing here.

Saintes Maries-de-la-Mer

The legend behind the name of the capital of the Camargue
describes the arrival of a boat that had been set adrift in
Palestine containing, along with some of Jesus's disciples, Mary
Salomé, mother of James and John the Apostles, Mary Jacobé,
sister of the holy Virgin, and their black servant Sara. The two
Marys who lived on and died at this spot had their remains
buried here, and over the centuries it became a place of
Christian pilgrimage. At the same time gypsy folk adopted Sara
as their patron saint. Today, while the two Marys are celebrated
on their respective saints days, so too is 'Saint' Sara. The gypsy
pilgrimage takes place annually on 24 and 25 May during
which religious ceremonies are contrasted with bullfights in the
arena, horse races and fairs.

Stes Maries is a strange place. After the long, barren drive
down the D570 you finally roll into what appears a provincial
seaside resort with a few cafés and shops. As the road
penetrates the town almost to the beach you can park on the
Avenue de la Plage and make your way to the promenade and
gaze out towards the low horizon of the Mediterranean. Here –
especially in late afternoon – is an eerie light indeed. This
magical air hovers over the little pedestrianised streets in the
western half of the town. Admittedly, these are put over to the
touting of food and souvenirs to the multitude of daytrippers
but the general atmosphere is saved by the church set apart by
three small squares. More a mythical fort than a place of
worship (actually fortified against the Saracens), it has no tower
as such but a keep like structure topped with an open belfry of
four arches supporting a central fifth: an austere sanctuary for a
desolate land of marsh and dune and mournful sky.

St Rémy-de-Provence

St Rémy, the birthplace of Nostradamus and the place where
Van Gogh was once committed temporarily for asylum, is a
pleasant enough town to be in but its importance rests in an
area to its south side as you exit on the D5 towards Les Baux.
Here are the twin historical sites of Les Antiques and Glanum.
The latter is a complex of archaeological excavations which
reveal a Roman settlement of a high degree of sophistication,
including forum, baths and temples. As the whole is nothing
more than a ground plan mapped out with the remains of

foundations, it's best to supply yourself with some explanatory literature. Even without such a guide, though, a little imagination can quite easily conjure up a long-gone lifestyle.

Vaison-la-Romaine

Buried in the northernmost reaches of Vaucluse beyond Mont Ventoux, Vaison sits comfortably by the River Ouvèze, its sunny streets always managing to contain the tourist throngs in the summer. Behind them, in the quarters of Puymin and Villase, the foundations of villas and a basilica tell of a great centre of wealth and culture for the first four centuries AD. The plans of courtyards and gardens are clear enough to evoke a good idea of daily Roman life. On top of a cliff on the opposite side of the river, the Haute Ville, remarkably preserved, came into being in the Middle Ages when the local population, harassed by bands of marauders, decided to move onto the hill where a castle already existed. The townsfolk turned to the Roman remains for building materials and some of this masonry can be seen incorporated in the houses. A pleasurable afternoon may be spent here wandering around the narrow streets opening onto little squares, eventually persuading you to ascend to the ruined castle itself to look down over the modern Vaison and across the Ouvèze valley. Tuesday is market day.

Tourist offices

Chambre Départementale de
   Tourisme de Vaucluse
La Balance
Place Campana
84008 Avignon
Tel 90.86.43.42

Parc Naturel Régional du Lubéron
1 place Jean-Jaurès
84400 Apt
Tel 90.74.08.55

Arles

Municipal Les Pins

13990 Fontvieille   tel 90.54.78.69

Peace and calm in the shade of beautiful pines at this tidy municipal site; self-catering is a must, though

A classic municipal site, Les Pins is in a secluded nook just outside the centre of the attractive little town of Fontvieille. At the camp, neatly laid out gravel paths lead off the main avenue to orderly grass *emplacements*, bounded by rows of light shrubs, and as well as the atmosphere of calm and tranquillity that often characterises a municipal site, pine trees provide an ample degree of shade. The *sanitaires* are in good order and there are a few seated toilets, too. There's only a basic playground to keep the children amused on this site, but a modest, attractive municipal pool is not too far from the camp, behind the Château de Montauben. As the camp is so close to the shops and general amenities, there are no eating facilities; in fact, little else is offered, other than a very civilised environment in which to spend a few days. An interesting visit on your doorstep is the Moulin de Daudet, the one-time house of the nineteenth-century writer, Alphonse Daudet; in the preserved windmill is a small museum devoted to the author's life.

Directions: Fontvieille is on the D17, off the N570 going north out of Arles. From the town go east on the D17. Start from the right hand side of the church to enter the one-way system. The road brings you out onto a main road out of town. Immediately after joining it, bear right to take a right-hand fork. (Green and yellow camp direction sign is here.) Follow this road to the next right turn (another camp sign here). The site is down here on your right **Ground:** Hard to giving
Children: Playground **Wheelchair:** Not suitable **Food-cooling:** None **Sport:** Ping pong **Season:** 1 Apr to 15 Oct
Reservation: Advisable peak season **Charge:** Pitch 20 fr; person 11 fr; child (under 7) 7 fr; electricity 14 fr

---

Spring weather in Lower Provence can still be dominated by the Mistral which blows hard most of the winter. This cold, dry wind blows down from the north through the Rhône Valley from the Massif Central.

▰▰▰ Bédoin ▰▰▰▰▰▰▰▰▰▰▰

Municipal de la Pinède

84410 Bédoin	tel 90.65.61.03

Shady, hillside municipal site; handy for the good local pool complex

The village of Bédoin is clustered around its old church, in the shadow of Mont Ventoux. The camp nestles in a pine wood on a steep hill and is quite a change from the 'ornamental garden' type of site so favoured in this region. Here, you can experience the more natural feeling of camping in an open wood, with a generous amount of shade, rather than being in pitches regimented together between hedges, as is often the case on municipal sites. Although small in terms of pitch numbers, the camp covers quite a lot of ground. A made-up road spirals to the top of the hillside, with level, hard-standing *emplacements* leading off. In spite of the steep ground, the site is suitable for those towing a caravan, too. Appointments are adequate, but the big plus must be the marvellous pool complex with three swimming-pools; special rates are offered to campers who want to make use of this additional municipal facility.

Directions: Approaching Bédoin from the south, on the D974 from Carpentras, you will see a large brown sign indicating camping, tennis and pool at 200m. Turn left here. The road swings left and leads to the site, opposite the municipal tennis courts **Ground:** Hard
Children: Swimming, organised events **Wheelchair:** Not suitable
Food-cooling: Ice sold **Sport:** Tennis, volleyball, football, mini-golf
Season: Easter to Sept **Reservation:** Not accepted
Charge: Pitch 11 fr; person 15 fr; vehicle 8 fr; child (under 10) 9 fr; electricity 11 fr

---

The olive, cultivated in abundance throughout Provence, was originally brought to the French Mediterranean by the Greeks around 2,500 years ago. Olive oil (as 'virgin' oil) comes from the first pressing after the harvest and 'fine' oil is that which is derived from adding water to the mashed olives when pressed for a second time. Until the 1800s the oil was used in Marseilles soap when it was replaced by other vegetable oils such as coconut.

Gordes

Camping des Sources

Route de Mars, 84220 Gordes   tel 90.72.12.48

Worth visiting for the stupendous views. Good pool makes this site ideal for a touring break

You may not be too impressed as you pull up by the hut-like office at the entrance to this site, but the thought of driving out again will be banished by the beautiful panorama of Provençal countryside that greets you, spread out beyond the camp. Just beyond the entrance is a recently built timber and concrete *sanitaire*, of a peculiar appearance. Handicapped toilets are provided in this new block, but bear in mind that if not pitched close by, you'll have some rough ground to cross to get there. *Sanitaires* are, in general, of an acceptable standard and the gravel pitches amongst stubby oaks nearer the entrance give way, lower down the site, to more attractive orchard-like terraces, with level *emplacements* towards the centre of the site. Here you will find the bar and restaurant, which is no more than a *crêperie*, although none the less desirable for that. From its bamboo-covered terrace, you can look out over the blue oasis of the swimming-pool, with its quota of recumbent bodies of various shades of brown. Then, taking your time over a cold beer, you can take in the glorious vista that these heights offer. Camping des Sources is a three-star site managed by a relaxed and genial family. For sightseers, precariously-situated Gordes has a château, and similarly spectacular views can be enjoyed from these heights, too.

Directions: Gordes lies to the north of the N100 (NE of Cavaillon), near a straight run of the D2. The first camp direction sign you will see is where the road sweeps round towards the village ahead of you. In the village centre, bear left (another camp direction sign is here). This is the D15. Eventually you will see the camp sign, with a large sun symbol, appear on your left. Turn here and the track leads to the camp
Ground: Hard **Children:** Playground **Wheelchair:** Tricky
Food-cooling: Ice sold **Sport:** Tennis, volleyball, ping pong, boules, horse-riding **Season:** All year **Reservation:** Advisable peak season
Charge: Pitch 8 fr; person 18 fr; vehicle 6 fr

▅▅▅ L'Isle-sur-la-Sorgue ▅▅▅

Municipal la Sorguette

Route d'Apt, 84800 L'Isle-sur-la-Sorgue	tel 90.38.05.71

A tidy, pleasant municipal site in an area with lots to see and do

This very attractive site is by an enchanting shallow stream, running through a cool wood. An encircling made-up road leads to large enclaves of approximately four grassy pitch areas, each group being sectioned off with tall, manicured hedges; lack of shade may be a problem here. The environment is similar to that of a small municipal gardens and has a grass children's playground with climbing equipment. That *bête noire* for British campers, the toilet facilities, comprise seated toilets only for the ladies and toddlers. You can barbecue at your *emplacement* or pick up a take-away from the small shop and bar complex at the end of the camp. The kids can canoe or paddle in the shallow stream while you take a quiet walk by the clear, running water in the welcome shade. After supper, you could stroll along the little canals at L'Isle-sur-la-Sorgue or settle down at the picturesque art nouveau Café de France opposite the church, and let the world 'go hang' for a while.

🌑 Ⓢ ⚞ ⚏ ⚲ 🐚 ⚵ ⋔ ⊒ ▣ ✦ ℘

Directions: From the town centre, take the N100 towards Apt. As you go out of the town, you will see a camp direction sign with a main route sign. Just before a traffic island on this main road is a big camp direction sign, directing you to turn left. This takes you into a service road, with a hotel to your left, and the camp entrance to your right **Ground:** Hard
Children: Playground, baby facilities **Wheelchair:** Not suitable
Food-cooling: Ice sold **Sport:** Tennis, volleyball, ping pong, boating
Season: 15 Mar to 31 Oct **Reservation:** Advisable peak season
Charge: Pitch 15 fr; person 14 fr

Provençal bullfighting differs from the Spanish version in that the contest is not to the death, although this is carried out in the corridas *of Arles and Nîmes (duels fought between bulls and men from Spain). The Course à la Cocarde, as it is known, requires the competitor (*le razeteur*) to snatch safely a rosette (*cocarde*) from the bull's horns. The bulls for these fights are bred in the Camargue.*

Mazan

Le Ventoux

Route de Bédoin, 84380 Mazan   tel 90.69.90.00

Basic site in an isolated spot provides an attractive, peaceful retreat in the lee of Mont Ventoux

Named after the mountain that dominates the landscape for miles around, Le Ventoux is a peaceful and secluded camp in a very quiet area. This site is strictly for tourers; all that's on offer is a single *sanitaire* (just one seated toilet) with showers that last, according to the notice, for six minutes, and a little shop where you can get your breakfast if you wish. Take-aways are also available and the village is not far away for other purchases. A welcome retreat from your travels is provided by a pleasant swimming-pool and shade from small, spindly oak trees. And if you prefer to stay on the side of the camp from which you can enjoy an uninterrupted view of the mountain, you'll find that the *emplacements* are each provided with a roofed porch on square columns, so that you can escape from the sun. This is a thoughtful addition from the owner whose villa sits in the site grounds.

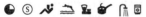

Directions: From Mazan (due east of Carpentras), take the D70 Caromb road, heading north. At the first left-turn you come across, you will see a camp direction sign. You will then drive through a vineyard until you approach the camp on your right **Ground:** Hard **Children:** Not suitable **Wheelchair:** Not suitable **Food-cooling:** Ice sold **Sport:** None **Season:** All year **Reservation:** Advisable peak season **Charge:** Pitch 7 fr; person 12 fr; vehicle 7 fr

If you want to maximise the little shade your pitch may be offering but are unable to determine the sun's direction, try the old stick-in-the-ground trick and watch the progression of its shadow before erecting your tent.

Be prepared to leave all types of footwear outside a camp's pool area. People usually leave shoes just by the pool entrance.

Pertuis

Municipal les Pinèdes

Avenue P Augier, 84120 Pertuis   tel 90.79.10.98

A good, if basic, place for a short stay; the site is near to a 'luxury' pools complex

As Municipal les Pinèdes is on the edge of an escarpment, you may be fortunate enough to bag one of the pitches overlooking the lush valley, with its patchwork of vineyards stretching into the distance. Near-immaculate maintenance is the hallmark of this small, basic site, just a five-minute walk from the town's lido-like swimming-pools. A shady central area of the camp, more suitable for tents, is bounded by a broad area leading to the larger, marked-out *emplacements* for caravans. *Sanitaires* have seated toilets for women but not for men – this is perhaps to be expected on a municipal site. There's a snack-bar, with take-away food available, and, for those marvellous municipal pools down the road, you can buy an entry card at a special camper's rate. Pertuis itself is a developing town, hauling itself upmarket with a pedestrianised area of shops and businesses. It is not touristy, so if you fancy pulling up for a few days near a typical local community, instead of staying in splendid isolation in the surrounding country, Les Pinèdes should do nicely.

Directions: Leave Pertuis on the D973 heading east towards Manosque. As soon as you leave the town, take a right-turn at the crossroads (pharmacy on your left). The camp is signposted here, along with a swimming-pool. Another sign at the next road-junction tells you to go straight on. Going up the hill, you will pass the pool complex on your right. Just after the brow of the hill, turn left (sign here) to the site entrance **Ground:** Hard to giving **Children:** Playground **Wheelchair:** Not suitable **Food-cooling:** Ice sold **Sport:** Tennis, basketball, bike-hire **Season:** 1 Mar to 31 Oct **Reservation:** Advisable peak season **Charge:** Pitch 7.20fr; person 10.20fr; vehicle 7.20fr; child (under 7) half-price; electricity 8 to 15.50 fr

While tariffs for one-star and two-star sites are fixed by the département, three-star and four-star sites are individually priced according to their owners' discretion, so discrepancies naturally arise between them in any given area.

▰▰▰ La Roque d'Anthéron ▰▰▰▰

☼ *Domaine des Iscles*

13640 La Roque d'Anthéron   tel 42.50.44.25

Good facilities and evening entertainment at this well-designed camp with something for everyone

It has been said that the area surrounding the short route from the town centre to this site does not hold much promise, but in the words of one satisfied camper, who turned up at the camp on spec, 'here is a place to unwind and maybe let your hair down a bit'. A spacious, flag-lined driveway leads to the cool, modern reception building, and the restaurant opposite looks inviting. Domaine des Iscles is a level site, mostly grassy, with *emplacements* that follow an informal ground plan; the shadier pitches are behind the circular pool. Along with the camp's layout, the multi-section design (under a rafter-supported roof) of the *sanitaires* (only one seated toilet per block) contributes to the feeling of spaciousness, surprising for a medium-sized site. In the high season, the camp comes to life every evening: the kids enjoy the games machines, while mum and dad can relax with a drink by the pool. The restaurant terrace, under a bamboo canopy, can be as busy as any in town – perhaps *brochettes* might be grilled on the communal barbecue for a couple of hungry families; others might queue for a giant take-away pizza. In fact, every day and night, the management lays on an event – children's ping-pong contests, rambles, bike trips, soirées, discos, film shows and beauty contests are just some of the events on offer at this three-star site with a four-star feeling.

◐ Ⓜ ⚡ ⌇ ⊟ ⚑ ✕ ♀ ☝ ☘ ⌂ ⊟ ☷ ∜ ⟋ ♫

Directions: From the old part of the town, round the corner from the church, opposite a stone-arched gateway, the D67 leads out with a line of tall trees along its right-hand side. (Blue camp direction sign at beginning of road.) At the bottom, you go under a road-bridge, immediately followed by a short tunnel taking you under the canal. Emerging, you bear right then take an immediate right (signposted). You are now running parallel to a canal dyke on your right. Further along will be the camp sign, signalling you to turn left. This will take you to the camp entrance **Ground:** Hard **Children:** Playground, swimming, organised events **Wheelchair:** Suitable
Food-cooling: Ice sold **Sport:** Tennis, volleyball, ping pong

233

Season: All year **Reservation:** Advisable peak season **Charge:** Pitch 24 fr; person 19 fr; child (under 7) 11 fr; electricity 16 to 20 fr

▰▰▰ Roussillon ▰▰▰▰▰▰▰▰▰▰

L'Arc en Ciel

Route de Goult, 84220 Roussillon   tel 90.05.67.17

Beautiful seclusion can be enjoyed at this bijou site with a small pool

The camp of L'Arc en Ciel and the neighbouring village of Roussillon are just the sort of places that a tourer 'off the beaten track' might relish. The shady tranquillity of this small site, tucked away in a light pine wood, clinging to a hill, is a major attraction. Pitches are arranged at random amongst the trees and the ground is rough with loose gravel forming the base. The old-fashioned but well-maintained *sanitaires* have separate washing cubicles and, surprisingly for such an out-of-the-way site, even the civilised inclusion of bidets. The swimming-pool is no more than a large circular bath, rather like a concrete Jacuzzi, but still a good means of cooling off for a spell. You'll have to rely on your own home-cooked *côte d'agneau* on the communal indoor grill and glass of *vin de pays* after a day exploring the exhilarating countryside, as this camp offers no food provisions. However, nearby Roussillon can provide you with a *charcuterie* and *boulangerie* as well as a garage and pharmacy.

Directions: Turn off the N100 (L'Isle-sur-la-Sorgue and Apt road) at the village of Lumières (north of the road). Go through the next village of Goult, on the D105, to turn right for Roussillon. After crossing the small level bridge, fork right on the D104. Eventually you will see a wind-pump in a field by the road on your right. The site is after the next bend, on your right **Ground:** Loose **Children:** Playground **Wheelchair:** Not suitable **Food-cooling:** Ice sold **Sport:** Ping pong **Season:** 15 Mar to 31 Oct **Reservation:** Advisable peak season **Charge:** Pitch 7 fr; person 10.50 fr; vehicle 7 fr

Although you are not obliged to return to your camp before it closes for the night, you are expected on such occasions to park in the overnight space outside the gate and walk to your tent.

St Rémy-de-Provence
Municipal Mas de Nicolas

Avenue Théodore-Aubanel,   tel 90.92.27.05
13210 St Rémy-de-Provence

Attractive, tranquil four-star municipal site, with a good pool

Set in immaculately-maintained landscaped grounds, Mas de Nicolas must rank as one of the best municipal sites for miles around. Its well-maintained appearance gives the impression of a pleasure garden rather than a campsite. A tarmac road lined with globe street-lamps leads to open lawns and *emplacements* hedged for privacy. You won't find a variety of recreational pursuits or organised evening entertainment at this site, but there is a large, curved swimming-pool at your disposal, beyond a wide lawn, near the entrance. The bar serves soft drinks only and lack of any eating facilities means having to fend for yourself at mealtimes. As a municipal site, there are some rules to be adhered to, for instance, washing lines are provided near the *sanitaire* so you won't be allowed to string up your 'smalls' between tent and tree. The camp gates shut promptly at 10pm, after which time you must leave your car outside and walk back to your pitch. The whole environment has been thoughtfully planned and even when busy, a sense of decorum seems to prevail at this comfortable site.

Directions: From the centre of the town, take the D571 north to Avignon. There is a right-hand turn with a camp direction sign, then take the first left turn. Just past a large building, set back from the road (on left), is the camp entrance (also on the left, before the road narrows) **Ground:** Hard to giving **Children:** Playground **Wheelchair:** Suitable **Food-cooling:** Ice sold, coolpacks frozen **Sport:** Ping pong **Season:** All year **Reservation:** Advisable peak season **Charge:** 2 people, pitch and car 53 fr; child (under 10) 8 fr; extra adult 15 fr; electricity 11 fr

No matter how bad your French you'll quickly gain respect by trying to use the language. A liberal sprinkling of 's'il vous plaît's and 'pardon's will stand you in good stead. A hearty volunteered 'Bonjour!' to your neighbour may also help dispel any prejudice about the 'cold English'!

Pégomas

13210 St Rémy-de-Provence   tel 90.92.01.21

Friendly ambience is a big plus at this site, popular with the French; it's in a good position in the middle of town

The two advantages of staying at Pégomas are its position right in the heart of the town and its good little swimming-pool. The camping ground is pleasant enough, with mostly grass *emplacements*, some of which are screened by hedges of giant rushes. Sanitary arrangements are passable, although one British visitor we spoke to thought that the water pressure in the showers needed sorting out. Eating facilities comprise a bar and take-away food. A friendly atmosphere prevails, in part generated by the *bonhomie* of the French population, and if you've read the entry for the other site at St Rémy, this may be the deciding factor. The more casual approach at Pégomas lends a certain character to the site, and set against the indifferent but efficient management at the municipal camp, here you'll find amiable hosts to put you at your ease.

Directions: Leaving town on the D99 towards Cavaillon, you will see a camp sign directing you to take the next left-hand fork. Further down this road is a big blue and yellow camp sign on the left **Ground:** Hard to giving **Children:** Playground, swimming **Wheelchair:** Not suitable **Food-cooling:** Ice sold, fridge hire **Sport:** Volleyball **Season:** Mar to Oct **Reservation:** Advisable peak season **Charge:** vehicle 10 fr; 2 people and pitch 57 fr; extra adult 19 fr; electricity 12 fr

■■■■ Stes Maries-de-la-Mer ■■■■
⑦ *Municipal Le Clos du Rhône*

13734 Stes Maries-de-la-Mer   tel 90.97.85.99

Four-star beach site, good for a short-break

For a short visit to take in the sights of the Camargue, you couldn't be more conveniently situated than at Clos du Rhône. Both the campsites at Stes Maries-de-la-Mer are municipally owned and share the characteristic of being rather exposed to the elements, although La Brise is definitely more windswept and sand-blown. The slightly higher charges at Clos du Rhône are reflected in the better kept grounds and generally more attractive environment. At its entrance is a 'sculptured' swimming pool complex in white-painted concrete, consisting of low, walls that surround three small free-form pools. The deep blue water contrasts sharply with the white terracing and you need sunglasses just to protect yourself from the reflective glare of this area. No shade is provided in this part of the camp, but there is some foliage to alleviate the wide, open aspect of the site. As is usual on beach sites, pitches are very much on top of one another and there is little privacy. One welcome addition to counteract the exposed nature of the grounds is the provision of *emplacements* with pergolas. These are log porches that offer shade from the merciless sun and can be used either as a car port or for a small tent; this luxury costs an extra pound per day, but well worth it if you can manage to get one. *Sanitaires* include handicapped toilets and a couple of other seated toilets, but, considering this is a four-star site, they are not marvellous. Although close to the beach, this isn't the sort of campsite to feel comfortable in for a prolonged stay. It is best as a seaside touring stop, but don't forget to pack the insect repellent in high season, to keep the gnats away!

○ ⓛ 𝍅 ⇋ ⚏ ⚓ 𝍔 ⇃ 🖻

Directions: Follow the main shore road heading west from the town centre (this is the D38). After about 2 km, a left-hand turn will lead to the site entrance **Ground:** Sandy **Children:** Swimming **Wheelchair:** Suitable **Food-cooling:** Ice sold, fridge hire **Sport:** Ping pong **Season:** 15 Apr to 31 Sept **Reservation:** Advisable peak season **Charge:** Pitch 23.80 fr; person 24.10 fr

▰▰▰ Vaison-la-Romaine ▰▰▰

Le Moulin de César

84110 Vaison-la-Romaine   tel 90.36.06.91

Pleasant, medium-sized, shady site, convenient for the ancient town and interesting locality

A welcome retreat from the burning sun and glare of the road awaits you at this pleasant, cool site, with its tall trees that provide an ample amount of shade in the central part of the camp. Such an environment makes an attractive setting for a campsite that hums quietly with activity. The reasonably spacious camping ground comprises marked-out, or more random pitches in level, wooded parkland. A relaxed atmosphere prevails and, although in season tournaments and children's activities are in operation, the ambience doesn't seem to be disrupted. The site backs onto the Ouvèze, a clear, inviting river that's shallow enough to let the children paddle in safety. The town of Vaison-la-Romaine is an interesting place, with its Roman history and medieval old town (the Haute Ville) perched on the cliff. On the other side of town is a supermarket, handy for those self-caterers who don't want to take advantage of the camp's own catering facilities.

● Ⓜ 🏃 🦺 ✕ ♀ 🦌 ♿ 🛏 🔲

Directions: The D151 is on the south side of the town. It is the turning just before the stone bridge that takes you out on the D938. This is directly opposite the cliff on which the château sits. You will see a camp direction sign here. Follow the D151 and after a left-hand bend, you will see the camp on the right (the road has a sleeping policeman)
Ground: Hard to giving **Children:** Playground, organised events
Wheelchair: Suitable **Food-cooling:** Ice sold, coolpacks frozen
Sport: Volleyball, ping pong **Season:** Mar to 31 Oct
Reservation: Advisable peak season **Charge:** Pitch 13 fr; person 16.50 fr; child 7.80 fr; electricity 9 to 16 fr

■■■■ Villes-sur-Auzon ■■■■■

Les Verguettes

84570 Villes-sur-Auzon   tel 90.61.88.18.

Immaculate little site, with a tempting pool; an attractive village is nearby

A prim and proper place is Les Verguettes (be sure to park your car between and not across the parking lines)! But this bijou, strictly-run site is an attractive proposition, featuring a tidy, rose-decorated paved terrace by a small rectangular pool, with a couple of trees giving shade. The setting makes it look more like a large ornamental pond at a country home. Nearby is a small bar/grill with a white, rustic interior. The owner of Les Verguettes pays attention to details, such as the plants adorning the first-class *sanitaire*. Although the facilities are well appointed, the marked grass *emplacements* off the main avenue may prove a disappointment, depending on your priorities. Although there are some tall cypresses along the way, generally, the camping ground is devoid of any mature growth and this lack of foliage makes it a very hot place indeed. But perhaps you won't be on-site for much of the day: the nearby Gorges de la Nesque is worth a visit and within easy walking distance is the village, with its few shops for stocking up and several bars in which to relax.

○ ⓢ 🏄 🏊 ✕ ⛾ ♨ ♻ ▣ ⚡

Directions: The D492 leaves Villes-sur-Auzon due west to Carpentras. If you approach from this direction, you will see large camp signs. (There are none to speak of as you leave Villes-sur-Auzon down a tree-lined avenue.) Halfway down this road, on your left, is a wide entrance with iron railings to one side. This is Les Verguettes **Ground:** Hard **Children:** Playground **Wheelchair:** Not suitable
Food-cooling: Fridge hire **Sport:** Ping pong **Season:** 1 June to 30 Sept **Reservation:** Advisable peak season **Charge:** Pitch 10 fr; person 20 fr; vehicle 16 fr; electricity 11 fr

Be sure to park your car between and not across the lines

239

For the naturist

On rare occasions you find a campsite that is literally a self-contained world devoted to the pursuit of health, relaxation, recreation and culture: *Domaine de Belezy* is just such a place. For those who have already discovered the pleasures of such a camping lifestyle, this entry will probably be preaching to the converted. First and foremost, what makes the whole place swing is the atmosphere of *bonhomie* that prevails at the camp. It's almost as if you recognised a masonic handshake, or found yourself to be among others of your own ethnic minority in a strange land. Children are given a lot of time and attention, and their mutual friendships seem to endorse the essence of naturist philosophy. They are considered to be just as important clientele as their parents and entertainment ranges from the 'baby-club' nursery to the daily events organised by the camp's *animateurs*. Belezy is also trying to establish a summer school - it's claimed to be the first of its kind. As for the adults, every facility is here: beautiful, secluded pitches in shady woods; a wonderful pool complex with bar and restaurant, sauna and acupuncture; music rooms; a separate dormitory for those who are packed up the night before an early start; countless sporting activities including archery; crafts such as pottery, even a clothes boutique called 'London Underground', run by an enterprising Englishman: the list is endless. If you've not sampled the delights of a naturist holiday, perhaps the thought of how little packing you'll need to do is an added incentive.

Domaine de Belezy:
BP3, 84410 Bédoin Tel. 90.65.60.18

Eastern Provence and the Côte d'Azur

The Côte d'Azur represents the South of France in all its glory: villages perched on hilltops, mimosa and pine, olive groves, palm promenades under a luminous sky by an amethyst sea, home to the pioneers of modern art. From travel pages to holiday brochures and from guidebooks to photographic essays destined for the coffee-table, all have done their bit to instil in our minds the archetypal imagery that will flash on cue like so many snapshots whenever we hear 'Côte d'Azur' or 'Riviera'. The problem with visiting this region, though, for so long the British idea of a civilised Continental holiday, is matching the media promotion with the reality.

Regrettably, the Med's oldest tourist trap is showing considerable strain and if you didn't make the effort to seek out the authentic *vie provençale* of this south-eastern corner of France, disillusionment would soon set in.

Two factors prevail: the visiting population and development. The coast in the height of season has to contend with the locust swarms of bodies on the beaches and in the towns, and the dawdling bumper-to-bumper ant marches of the cars on the roads. The trick of avoiding the summer months by going in mid-season has already lost its effect: June is becoming just as crowded. If you insist on being a beach animal, go early or late. Fortunately, the temperate climate provides very warm, sunny days in both spring and autumn and although you may well catch a shower or two, you will also catch the countryside in full colour. The flora here reacts to the

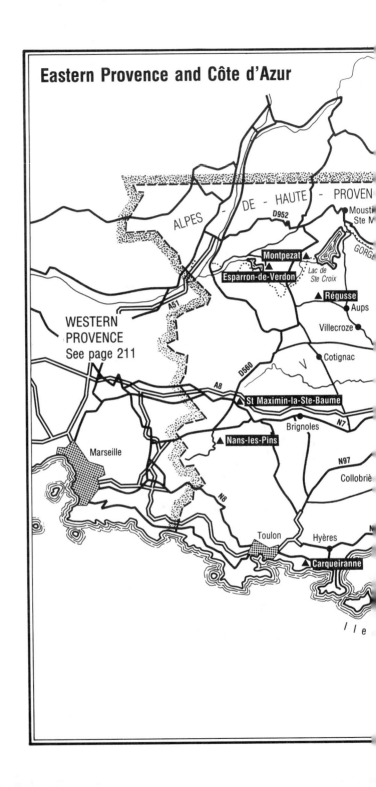

Eastern Provence and Côte d'Azur

ALPES - DE - HAUTE - PROVEN

D952

Mousti
Ste M

GORGE

Montpezat

Lac de
Ste Croix

Esparron-de-Verdon

Régusse

Aups

Villecroze

WESTERN
PROVENCE
See page 211

Cotignac

D560

A8

St Maximin-la-Ste-Baume

N7

Brignoles

A51

Nans-les-Pins

N97

Collobriè

Marseille

N8

Toulon

Hyères

Carqueiranne

I l e

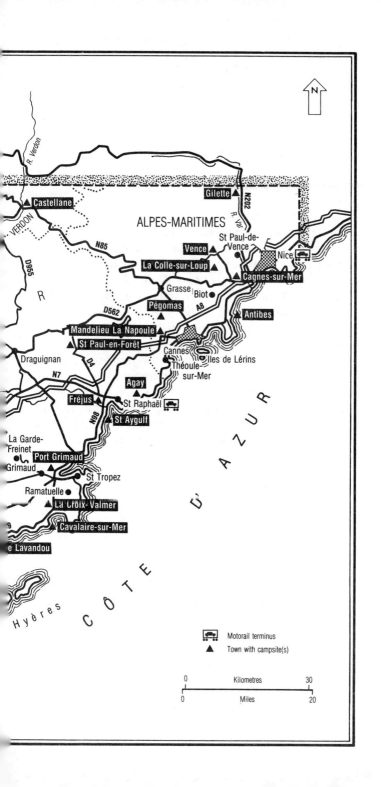

N

R. Verdon

Castellane

VERDON

ALPES-MARITIMES

Gilette

N202

R. Var

N85

Vence

St Paul-de-Vence

Nice

D955

La Colle-sur-Loup

Cagnes-sur-Mer

R

D562

Grasse

Biot

Pégomas

A8

Mandelieu La Napoule

Antibes

St Paul-en-Forêt

Draguignan

Cannes

Iles de Lérins

D4

Théoule-sur-Mer

N7

Agay

Fréjus

St Raphaël

N98

St Aygulf

C O T E

La Garde-Freinet

Port Grimaud

D' A Z U R

Grimaud

St Tropez

Ramatuelle

La Croix-Valmer

Cavalaire-sur-Mer

e Lavandou

Hyères

C O T E

Motorail terminus

▲ Town with campsite(s)

0   Kilometres   30

0   Miles   20

particular climatic conditions by coming into flower twice in the year in those very seasons.

So where can you find 'Provence'? The answer is to take to the hills. These are a-plenty – enough to absorb any number of sightseers. But you have to get right into them and not linger in the foothills on the edge of town, for it's here that you notice the second harbinger of the fate of the tourist industry – Planners' Blight. Where there is need, there is often greed too. While people coming to the region demand the benefit of golf courses of international standard, country-club-style hotels and time-share holiday homes, the initial exploitation of this boom now continues unchecked: at the moment developers seem to have *carte blanche*. Anywhere between Antibes and Grasse and Cagnes and Vence the hills are alive with the sound of construction. The crane is a new species competing with the pine. If the Impressionists were around now, setting up their easels, their palettes would contain an awkward hue of salmon pink in great quantity, ready for numerous brushstrokes to dot landscapes with little squares representing new buildings. Mercifully, the geography and demography further west into Var is such that it doesn't allow for the same opportunistic development as in this niche of Alpes-Maritimes.

It isn't all gloom and doom. On the coast, things get better away from Cannes on the *corniche* road to St Tropez, with a slight reversal around Fréjus and St Raphaël. This is where the Argens valley splits the two ranges of the Maures and Esterel Massifs. The rugged Esterel hills covered in cork oak and pine – that is, where the scourge of forest fires hasn't left its mark – oblige the main routes to follow the lowland break along the edge of the Provençal tableland in the north and, in the south, to hug the coastline. Between, a vastly reduced population is represented by a scattering of tiny, isolated communities.

The Maures is the greater range rising to the east of Hyères. To the south, the area is a mass of connecting arterial roads such as the A57, N97 and N98, and the area is dominated by the urban mass of Toulon, home of the French navy. Those with a penchant for ships and naval history may fight their way through the seasonal traffic to get there but most would prefer to view at a distance from Mont Faron which at 500 metres lies behind it. Near the summit is a building housing a memorial to the Allied liberation of south-east France in 1944.

The N98 taking you away from Toulon, via Hyères, will later on meet the D559. This becomes the Corniche des Maures and links some of most pleasant resorts of the Côte d'Azur: Le Lavandou, Cavalière and Cavalaire-sur-Mer are the main ones, while little havens include St Clair, Aiguebelle and Le Rayol. Large or small, all have beaches of fine sand sheltered by the heights of Les Pradels, the coastal chain of the Maures. One chunk of the Massif pushes out into the Mediterranean, pinched by the Baie de Cavalaire to its south and the Golfe de St Tropez to its north. Three capes protrude from this – Lardier, Camarat and St Tropez. Between the latter two runs the Plage de Pampelonne, over four kilometres of glorious sands. Things get busier on the second leg of the coastal road from Port Grimaud to St Raphaël, with Ste Maxime, Les Issambres and St Aygulf in between, although good beaches are still to be found.

Inland, you can find Collobrières (on the D41 north of Bormes-les-Mimosas) hidden in the forests of the surrounding hills. The hairpin road goes through the Babaou Pass which gives lovely views seawards. From the village of Grimaud (over to the east along the D14), with its ruined castle and streets dating from the Middle Ages, the D558 will lead you up into the hills to La Garde-Freinet. Set back on the heights behind the village are the remains of a Saracen fort with origins going back a thousand years. One industry local to La Garde-Freinet is the manufacture of corks for wine bottles from the plentiful source of cork oak in the vicinity.

Once on the tableland behind, the perimeter cutting a rough diagonal right through the lower section of Var, you really are on your way to leaving the crowds behind. In the west is Brignoles, a historic market town that has become the centre for the wines of the Côtes de Provence. This is Coteaux Varois territory, home of a young, fruity rosé. In its northern environs you'll find pretty little villages with castles and fountains like Correns, Montfort and Carcès near a secluded lake of the same name.

Beyond here you are heading for Haut-Var. Cotignac and Villecroze have grown up on wine and olive oil coming from adjacent pockets of lowland in the surrounding wooded hills. Both are linked to caves in this limestone region, especially Villecroze where in the 1500s some caves were adapted for housing, including built-in windows. To the village's north-east is Tourtour, set on a hill giving extensive views. Tourtour has not one but two ruined châteaux.

Aups is the main town of this area of woods and forests. Going on towards the northernmost border of Var you will reach the Verdon with the Lac de Ste Croix and the famous Gorges du Verdon (see below in the detailed sightseeing section).

A similar journey northwards from coast to countryside, this time with the Massif de l'Esterel as a starting point, presents a different picture. What the Esterel lacks in square kilometres it certainly makes up for in wonderful scenery. The geology here differs dramatically from that of the Maures. Its volcanic composition has produced rock in distinct colours such as turquoise, green, blue and, the most common, an earthy red. You can pick up speckled stones in the same matt colours if you walk along Agay's beach. Instead of the sheltered bays of flat beaches that the Maures coast offers, Esterel's ragged, ruddy peaks cascade into the sea to form tiny bays or creeks, sometimes revealing submerged reefs just under the water's transparent surface: the headland of Cap du Dramont and the small Pointe du Cap Roux are classic examples. Other beauty spots include Le Trayas and Miramar which sit at either end of the small Figueirette Bay. After rounding the Pointe de l'Aiguille, before you get to the trendy resort of La Napoule, Théoule-sur-Mer has some pleasant beaches.

Access to the mountainous heart of the Esterel is difficult with very rough, narrow roads but for a little taste you could go north out of Agay following the river's valley, then turn right round the back of the peak of Rastel d'Agay where, forking right once more, you will come to a ford. Continue if you are feeling really adventurous but otherwise you can experience some of the domain more comfortably by travelling on part of the Aurelian Way. This is the N7 which will take you past the Esterel's highest peak, Mont Vinaigre. The Aurelian Way once joined the Roman Empire's first City to Arles in the Rhône delta, linking Nice, Fréjus and Aix-en-Provence.

The D4 from Fréjus helps you penetrate the hinterland, taking you to sleepy places such as Bagnols-en-Forêt and St Paul-en-Forêt, their names indicating what to expect in terms of vegetation. Further north you'll come across a whole string of magical Provençal villages with little squares and fountains, ruins and ramparts. Bargemon, Seillans, Fayence, Tourrettes are all worth a visit, as are Callian and Montauroux to their east and Cézaire-sur-Siagne to their north-east. This cliff-edge village boasts a small driveable gorge and a *grotte*.

We found camping in this region somewhat of a surprise in that there was not a marvellous selection of sites. It was a particularly marked case of sorting out the wheat from the chaff. For instance, out of our shortlist of 30 camps within a concentrated triangle between the points of Nice, Grasse and Cannes – coping with probably the densest holiday population in season – we found that only a third appealed to us. A common off-putting factor was the proliferation of 'statics', permanently sited caravans and mobile homes which make sound business sense for site owners but which are disappointing intrusions for the ardent camper. Quite a few of these sites turned out to be no more than caravan parks. Once into Var you can find some useful family sites, usually in the coastal resorts, and some enjoyable out-of-the-way spots for the enthusiastic tourer. But, in the main, unless you strive to lose them, you are never far from the crowds and unless you go to the extremes of the *département* – either on the Esterel coast or in the Verdon wilds – you may feel hemmed in by roads, autoroutes and the rest of the visiting masses. The Provence of Vaucluse and Bouches-du-Rhône to the west (see Western Provence) seems to offer a freshness not as yet made stale by prolonged commercial exploitation, though tourism there plays perhaps a subordinate role to that of the region's major industries, agriculture and market gardening.

Agay

Agay has been christened the Ruby of the Côte d'Azur and with good reason. Where the Massif d'Esterel makes the coastline bulge between St Raphaël and Cannes, its golden red volcanic rock meets the Mediterranean in a torn edge of craggy inlets, the vivid colour adding to a palette of turquoise of the shallows and viridian of the pines. Agay is further like a jewel in that its bay is set in the contour of the bulge, like a stone set in a ring. This near-circular bite into the coast makes an excellent anchorage for the large motor yachts of the cruising classes. A scimitar of sand is sheltered between the points of Cap du Dramont and the lesser Pointe de Baumette. With the added protection of the beautiful Esterel hills behind, this position provides a year-round temperate climate. The little town centre consists of a promenade of a few shops, cafés and eating places, and there's a small Wednesday market outside the Post Office. The beach is very popular in season but is perhaps at its best before the summer really starts.

Antibes

Like many places along the eastern seaboard of Mediterranean France, Antibes was founded by the Greeks. Antipolis, as it was then, grew up where a small peninsula juts into the sea between Cannes and Nice. The tip of the peninsula is Cap d'Antibes and today has on its western side Juan-les-Pins, international resort and jazz festival centre. Antibes lies on the opposite coastline facing east towards Nice. Once you've negotiated the sometimes appalling summer traffic to get to it, the old town amply rewards you with stepped and narrow picture-postcard streets that lie behind the road following the sea wall. Just south of the harbour in this quarter, next to the Romanesque church, is Grimaldi Castle. This château was host for a while to Picasso after the war and is now a museum housing some of his prolific work of the time, which includes ceramics and sculpture as well as paintings. Continuing south, you can begin to explore the Cap proper. You might think this was the most likely place for a lighthouse. Not so, for the most prominent position is a high point inland called the Plateau de la Garoupe a little to the north: from here one of the most powerful beams on this coast shines out for almost fifty miles.

Biot

To the north of Antibes and close to the area's campsites on the D4 is the pretty little village of Biot. It has a long tradition of pottery crafts, its history dating from the time of the Phoenicians. The industry grew out of the availability of a suitable clay soil. A much more recent craft established here (in the past 30 years) is that of glass-blowing: the technique can be seen demonstrated in the glassworks a little way out of the village. Biot was once the home of the artist Ferdinand Léger; a museum nearby celebrates his work.

Cannes

Cannes is the entertainment industry's equivalent of Mecca. Our immediate association with the playground of the Côte d'Azur is the annual International Film Festival held each May. This has spawned other such gatherings for the television and music businesses: quite a reputation for what was once a quiet fishing village at the beginning of the 1800s. An Englishman by the name of Lord Brougham discovered the resort when an outbreak of cholera prevented him from continuing to Nice, his original destination. You can either treat the town as a place to be seen in, or play a lower tourist profile in preferring to explore some of the place. The former, of course, means the beaches by day, lying below the elegant and rich Boulevard de

la Croisette, and the clubs or casino by night. But there are
rewarding visits to be made without much travelling involved.
Le Suquet, the old quarter on the western edge of Cannes'
centre, nestles in the lee of the small Mont Chevalier
surmounted by a square twelfth-century watchtower. From up
here you look down to the rest of Cannes and out to the **Lérins
Islands** offshore (another possible excursion). On the larger of
the two islands is Fort Royal, once the prison of the legendary
Man in the Iron Mask. Controversy still exists as to his identity.
Many theories have been proffered, from bastard brother of
Louis XIV to a black page of Queen Maria Theresa who became
her lover. Way over on the eastern side of town is another
much higher peak at Super-Cannes. On this summit is an
observatory giving excellent views across the Riviera to Nice
and inland to the mountains of the Italian border.

If you want a change from gazing at scenery, try **Vallauris**
on the north-east outskirts. It is a renowned centre for
ceramics, put on the map by Picasso after the war. Today,
amidst a whole variety of pottery crafts, other artisans turn out
hand-made furniture, wooden sculpture and toys.

Draguignan

This is the capital of the Var *département*. Its name stems from an
ancient legend of a dragon that apparently lived in the
marshlands that once existed in the region. Like all such beasts
it met its end at the hands of a saint, in this case St Hermentaire.
The town lies in an isolated plain to the north of the Argens
valley and La Provençale, the A8 autoroute. The old streets in
its northern half, dating from the thirteenth century, are
gathered round the town's higher point, the Tour de l'Horloge.
Round the corner from the nearby St Michel chapel you'll find
the pretty and shady Place du Marché, a pleasant spot to sit and
rest. On the eastern fringe of Draguignan is the American
Military Cemetery, the resting place of 800 servicemen who fell
in the southern Allied advance of 1944. Out of town to the
north the D955 will give you a scenic ride through the **Gorge
de Châteaudouble**.

Fréjus/St Raphaël

Roughly midway between Cannes and St Tropez are these two
linked towns. Fréjus can be split four ways – the town, the port,

the beach and the past. The town centre is summed up by the Rue Jean-Jaurès, lovely in the morning sun as it curves gently through chic little shops, the odd art gallery or two and tempting windows of the *boulangeries* towards the few palms of the Place de la Liberté. If you cut back into the side streets you will emerge into another small square, the Place Formige, where stands the plain early Gothic cathedral. In the dark and cool interior behind tall wooden doors and opposite the nave entrance is an ancient baptistery. It reputedly dates from the fifth century and for a moment the misty half-light filling the tall, narrow octagonal vault of sombre stone and black columns switches you back to such a time.

Back to the present and very much up-to-date is Port Fréjus, best reached from the town centre via the tree-lined Boulevard de la Mer leading south to its western side. Here, as everywhere on this coast, is a marina development, every day looking like the International Boat Show with rows of gleaming yachts moored by its arcaded waterfronts. On both sides of the marina's outlet to the sea are beaches, the main, wide Fréjus-Plage lying on its eastern side.

Finally, the roots of Fréjus are to be found on the northern edge of the town – the Roman remains: relics of the arena, theatre and aqueduct are no more than ruined shadows of their former glory. Once, Forum Julii, founded by Julius Caesar, was a thriving city and major naval base within the protection of its encircling walls. A canal gave its inland harbour, now non-existent, access to the open sea.

St Raphaël, linked by the N98 coast road with Fréjus-Plage, also began life in the days of Rome but this time as a holiday resort, a purpose it has maintained. It, too, has a beach, though the place comes into its own at night. Its little square port provides an attractive marine setting for an evening out, for either taking cocktails in the bars and *glaceries* of the Cours Jean Bart or dining in the open in the predominantly restaurant-filled Quai Albert Premier, both these avenues forming one corner of the port's perimeter. The quay is popular for dog-walking residents or families on holiday taking the night air under a line of dark plane trees, their leaves given an iridescent glow by the soft illumination of street lamps.

Gorges du Verdon

The daddy of the gorges of France: of its many sections the deepest, known as the Grand Canyon, makes the Gorges d'Ardèche seem a mere ditch. The River Verdon is not a grand river in the Dordogne or Rhône league, just a tributary of the lengthier Durance. But this in no way detracts from the uniqueness of the canyon's awesome depths coupled with its savage beauty. Ironically, figures alone can defeat the intention of giving some idea of scale but, for the record, cliffs here sometimes rise to 700 metres – that's over twice the height of those of the Ardèche – and can narrow at the bottom to no more than six metres.

There are two routes that allow you to take in this giant rip in the landscape. To the south is the D71, the Corniche Sublime, which runs most of the Canyon's course; on the north side – probably the handier road to reach – is the D952, a road of intestinal twists and turns all the way from Castellane to Moustiers-Ste Marie due west. **Castellane** can be considered the resort town of the region, snug beneath the Verdon's lesser cliffs east of the Canyon and watched over by the church of Notre-Dame-du-Roc on top of a precipitous limestone outcrop. The town is a pleasant, relaxed place with streets of tall stone apartment buildings, a medieval gateway topped with a belfry, the Romanesque Eglise St Victor, an open square and the ancient Lion Fountain. If you follow the Verdon's progress westwards it goes through a couple of metamorphoses, first as the huge **Lac de Ste Croix**, then suddenly back into a winding river of varying widths, snaking on through the Basses Gorges du Verdon – a mere scratch in the earth's surface compared to the Canyon – and opening out once again, though more modestly, into the serene **Lac d'Esparron**, with its flat chrome strip of water presenting precisely inverted images of everything within its shoreline.

Grasse

Sitting on the edge of the Provençal Plateau and about 15 kilometres inland from Cannes is this pleasant town famous for creating base scents for the perfume industry – pleasant, that is, once you are out of the frequent through-traffic on the N85 (the Route Napoléon). This is the circumventory route that the Emperor took on his way to Grenoble after arriving on the mainland from Elba in 1815. In the lower half of Alpes-Maritimes between the plateau and the sea, conducive conditions have given rise to the cultivation of flowers such as roses and carnations – hence the regular flower as well as vegetable market. The region of Grasse provides the principal blooms for extracting essences – rose, jasmin and orange blossom – supplemented by lavender and herbs including thyme and rosemary. It is possible to tour some of the town's perfumeries.

Iles d'Hyères

The Hyères or Golden Isles are three islands lying off the Maures coast strung out in a line east of the **Giens peninsula**. The latter is an unprepossessing land mass which, but for the two parallel sand bars connecting it to the mainland, would itself be another island. In between them is the Salins des Pesquiers, still being worked for salt, and a lake of the same name to its south which is a breeding ground for a variety of water fowl. The village of Giens, sheltering on the northern shore of the body of the peninsula, is a little seaside resort overlooked by the ruins of a château, and on the very southern tip is the Porte de la Tour Fondue, your embarkation point for the nearest, **Ile de Porquerolles**.

This is the largest of the Hyères and it has no real population save for its one village, consisting of a church, some fishermen's cottages and a few small hotels. There's a selection of walks through the lush vegetation, notably the one which crosses to the lighthouse on the south coast (the island is only two miles wide). Going east out of Porquerolles you will come to the pine-skirted beaches of the Grande Plage.

The middle and smallest isle of **Port Cros**, a national park, is hillier but no less attractive, covered in woods and forest. Again, there are defined walks from Port Cros village, the most beaten path being through Solitude Valley, almost continuously in shade. Excursions can be made here from Hyères-Plage, Le Lavandou, Cavalaire-sur-Mer and even St Tropez, though the last is a two-hour sea run. A narrow strait separates it from the third Golden Island, **Levant**. Most of this is occupied by the French navy, with the exception of the village of Héliopolis on its western tip, which is a seasonal nudist colony.

The Loup Valley and Gorge

The River Loup begins a zig-zag journey in the Pre-Alps north of Grasse and meets the sea between Cagnes-sur-Mer and Antibes. Along the way it runs through a beautiful gorge and strings together a few pretty villages. The D2210 will take you from Vence to the gorge at **Tourrette-sur-Loup**. Not only does this comely medieval village offer winding alleys and hidden corners but it also keeps alive its traditional craft of weaving. Examples – not cheap, of course – can be bought along with other hand-produced artefacts from the various potters and sculptors who have established themselves here. The road then winds on along the edge of the hills on its way towards the point where the valley broadens and the gorge begins. At Pont-du-Loup you head north on the D6 following the gorge along its eastern side until it peters out before Bramafan. By turning around at this point into the D3 you can then treat yourself to even more spectacular views as you make your way south down the gorge's other side to the popular hilltop village of **Gourdon**. Once again crafts abound, but it's worth stopping for the sweeping vistas from the church square. The D3 eventually meets the main road to Grasse but if you wish to take in a final detour, at this juncture pick up the road to **Le Bar-sur-Loup** in the flower-growing country that provides this former town with its raw products. Le Bar is yet another picturesque village, its little maze of streets winding round an imposing sixteenth-century castle.

Nice

Queen of the Riviera (to use a well-worn phrase), fifth largest conurbation in France, centre of festivals and flowers and a long favourite winter resort of the English – to many people Nice epitomises the South of France. It also conjures up pictures of boulevards of palms like the Promenade des Anglais with the opulent architecture of its hotels evoking a society and life-style of pre-war years. The most famous, the Negresco, goes back even further. But probably of more interest to the itinerant visitor is the old town which is squashed into the eastern corner of Nice's central area. Terraces cast in the shadow of tall, narrow apartments, some with a balcony on every storey, some decked out with potted flowers or climbing greenery, make their stepped way up to the Château that isn't. This hill, overlooking the town's rooftops and the bay, once did have a fort which was destroyed. Due north from the old town on another rise is Cimiez, the smart residential suburb where Queen Victoria used to stay and where her statue still stands. Much earlier on the Romans, too, made an impression with a population large enough to support important public places such as the baths and amphitheatre – the remains are still visible. In the villa by the latter is the Matisse Museum dedicated to that giant of twentieth-century art who spent some years in Nice.

Going back towards Nice's centre via the Boulevard de Cimiez, you can pay homage to another artist of similar stature, Marc Chagall, whose collection of works is housed in a purpose-built gallery and museum.

Port Grimaud

The acceptable face of marine development. Unlike the many architectural attempts along the French Mediterranean coast to blend sea, sky and concrete in harmonious aesthetics, this example of buildings by water is pretty well successful. The formula seems to be very much a forerunner of the Prince Charles school of thought in returning to traditional values: you could easily believe that here was a revitalised old Provençal harbour, but in fact it was built only in the last twenty years. Opposite the visitors' car park (compulsory, pricey, yet necessary) the seemingly ordinary façade on the landward side conceals a pleasant, wide courtyard planted out with trees and full of shops, restaurants (expensive) and crêperies with less expensive light meals. Bridges lead off to a series of 'islets', along the quays of which sit rows of old-style houses and apartments with roofs attractively finished in terracotta tiling. The basin is filled with all kinds of boat from simple, wooden-decked sailing yachts to the chrome and smoked glass of flashy cabin cruisers. Standing on its own central island is the Church of St Francis of Assisi, looking straight out of the twelfth century. The austere, buttressed, almost windowless design harks back to the style of the fortress church of Stes Maries-de-la-Mer in the Camargue.

St Paul-de-Vence

A magnificently placed medieval village on the edge of a steep, wooded promontory, looking south over the narrow valley below towards the sea, and best approached from La Colle-sur-Loup on the D7. Full of colour and charm, St Paul is a favourite stop for coach parties and other snap-happy tourists in season but fortunately their numbers never seem to diminish its charm. Art and antique establishments occupy several of the sixteenth-century buildings which line the pedestrianised main street, entered through a stone gateway.

Equally superb, but for entirely different reasons, is the other attraction for visitors here. Outside the town, a turn-off on the D7 will take you through the shade of a pine wood to the Maeght Foundation. This is nothing less than a shrine to the pioneers of modern art and a venue for exhibitions of those who followed in their footsteps. The gardens surrounding the main building – architecture becoming sculpture almost, in brick, glass and concrete – form two areas: the front lawn containing large metallic 3D pieces by the likes of Arp and Calder, and the rear terraces composed and decorated by Miró. Linking the two is a paved courtyard, bare save for a group of those mesmerising, emaciated Giacometti figures, frozen in space as well as time. Inside the museum the greats such as Bonnard, Braque and Matisse, to name but three, are represented. Don't be surprised at the minimal display – here is quality not quantity.

St Tropez

There is a little more to St Tropez than Brigitte Bardot, topless beaches (a local contentious issue) and 'celebs', both present and passé. True, Mlle Bardot's longstanding residence here has always helped to maintain its myth of glamour; true, the beaches of the cape are some of the Côte d'Azur's finest: but looking beyond the jams of trippers and trendies – not to mention the jams of traffic on the N98, the main route here that makes Oxford Street seem a short-cut by comparison – the town does have some attractive qualities. Of course, either side of the high season will allow you to be more appreciative of the harbour's typical Mediterranean quayside of warm, buff-coloured, shuttered buildings, seeming to jostle each other for space as much as the visitors to the chic cafés and shops.

Nowadays the majority of moorings are taken up by pleasure craft rather than the fishing boats which were numerous in the past. Behind the Quai Jean-Jaurès you can find small, quieter streets around the church and maybe eventually follow one to the Old Tower on a spit of land between two picturesque coves. Above the town is the Citadel which houses an interesting maritime museum and from its vantage point you have views looking across the Golfe de St Tropez to St Maxime and the Maures Massif.

If you happen to be around at the beginning of May or in the second week of June, you may catch one of the Bravades, Festivals of Defiance. The earlier celebrates the town's namesake who was said to be a Christian centurion martyred by Emperor Nero. The other remembers a seventeenth-century routing of a Spanish fleet. When you have tired of the beaches and the crowds, take yourself out of St Tropez into the hills of the peninsula to find **Ramatuelle** where you can unwind in the atmosphere of a classic *ville ancienne*.

Vence

Vence, rather like its neighbour St Paul, has assets of both historical and artistic interest. It is an attractive and lively little town, even more so when the mid-week market is in full swing. The old town, a self-contained area within Vence's environs, has Roman origins but the surviving architecture dates from the fifteenth century. As it used to be protected by surrounding walls, entry was by way of five gates. The stone arch of Porte Peyra introduces you to a delightful square overlooked by a square tower. Here was the forum of the Roman town and it still retains the flavour of a communal meeting-place, animated by people milling around the simple but eye-catching fountain. This old part of Vence has as its axis a cathedral which incorporates some five hundred years of additional building and decoration. Vence's artistic connection is not in fact in the town proper. Going out on the D2210 to St Jeannet you will find an anonymous-looking white building behind iron railings. Once you examine it more closely, however, you realise this is no ordinary piece of architecture, with blue roof tiles and an open, iron cross topped with a gold sun and moon. This is the Chapelle du Rosaire or, more famously, the Matisse Chapel. Conceived by the artist himself, it was created by way of thanks to the order of Dominican Sisters who had once nursed him through illness. The all-white interior acts as a canvas – not this time for opaque pigment but for the play of vivid primary-coloured patterns of light through small stained glass windows. His hand is elsewhere in the fluid black lines of his stark wall graphics depicting the stations of the cross. The chapel, designed and built between 1947 and 1951, was to be Matisse's last major undertaking.

Tourist offices

Comité Régional du Tourisme
   (Provence/Alpes/Côte d'Azur)
2 rue Henri Barbusse
13241 Marseille
Tel 91.08.62.90

Comité Régional du Tourisme
   Riviera/Côte d'Azur
55 promenade des Anglais
06000 Nice
Tel 93.44.50.59

Agay

Douce Quiétude

3435 Boulevard Jacques Baudino,   tel 94.44.30.00
83700, St Raphaël

High-tech campsite of a regimented appearance; handy for nearby St Raphaël

Douce Quiétude has been allowed to slip into the pages of the guide by virtue of the fact that it's the closest campsite to St Raphaël. On a hill near the town, this site is a flat clearing of ten hectares, surrounded by pine forest. The camping ground is a rather dull, grid arrangement of straight avenues, with marked-out *emplacements* set in back-to-back parallel rows. A light covering of shade is provided by a few cypresses and pines. In the high season, with row upon row of tents, the site appears rather like an army camp. The self-service restaurant has an impressive entrance of tall, glass doors, surrounded by art nouveau-style wooden frames. There's a bar in which to relax

One of the 500 computerised phone lines that provide each emplacement with a direct link to the outside world

with a drink and a variety of camp facilities that range from a swimming-pool to a play-room for the kids. At the time of inspection an unofficial babysitting service was organised by couriers of the mobile home operators. But for the ultimate in futuristic camping, the site (possibly one of the first in France to do so) offers satellite TV at each electrical hook-up point. Businessmen or women might like to use one of the 500 computerised phone-lines that provide each *emplacement* with a direct link to the outside world. What more could you want on holiday?

🌓 Ⓜ 🧍 🏊 🛥 ✕ ♀ 🍴 🐟 🎣 🚻 🔌 📺 🌿 🎵

Directions: Take the D100 out of Agay. After a straight stretch of road, through an open copse, you will pass (just to the right of a right-hand bend) a small, stone Bronze Age monolith, shaped like half a banana. Immediately opposite is a left-hand turn. Further down this road, continue over crossroads (camp sign is here). Camp is on your right, with large camp sign facing road. If approaching from the west, from the direction of the A8 at Puget-sur-Argens, take the N7 to Fréjus. Follow to the first roundabout. Go straight ahead here, on to the D100 (at the back of the town). Pass the stadium on the left then, soon after, go straight across at the crossroads (at Fontaine Hotel). Filter left at the next T-junction on to the Boulevard Jacques Baudino, where the camp is situated **Ground:** Hard **Children:** Organised events **Wheelchair:** Not suitable **Food-cooling:** Ice sold **Sport:** Tennis, volleyball, ping pong, gym **Season:** June to Sept **Reservation:** Advisable peak season **Charge:** 3 people, pitch and car 163 fr

Le Dramont (Les Campéoles)

83700 St Raphaël   tel 94.82.07.68

A good, practical choice for a leisurely stop-over: roomy, quiet and shady, with a nearby beach

Les Campéoles is a national camping chain with 30 sites throughout France. Le Dramont is appropriately described as a high-quality site in their brochure. Not in the holiday camp mould, though: it's more of a select camp for the independent camper and tourer. The lightly wooded environment, recent well-kept development and the beach are the three important factors that make this camp a favourable base. Pitches are spread randomly over a large area, adequately shaded by tall

pine trees and made-up roads lead around the sedate camp. The
two *sanitaires*, of an attractive, modern design, are cool, clean
and immaculately maintained. If you're self-catering there's a
supermarket along the main road, or you might be tempted to
visit one of the restaurants in Boulouris or Agay. Following the
site's left-hand avenue you'll reach a tiny, picturesque marina
with a breakwater of boulders and pines that goes down to the
water's edge. From here, members of the diving centre based in
the camp set out to sea. The beach can be reached by walking to
the centre of the back perimeter fence. As the beach is stony,
you'll need an airbed or a couple of chairs. The shoreline is not
shallow here, so children must be watched. Just off-shore is the
small Ile d'Or, with its old square light-tower that makes an
attractive composition for the odd holiday snap.

Directions: Heading west out of Agay on the N98 towards St Raphaël,
the road takes you into a suburb called Boulouris. As soon as the road
returns to the coastline (after Cap du Dramont), you will see on your
left the site, with tennis courts near the road and a large camp sign
saying 'Les Campéoles' **Ground:** Hard **Children:** Playground
Wheelchair: Suitable **Food-cooling:** Ice sold **Sport:** Tennis,
volleyball, ping pong, mini-golf **Season:** Mid-Mar to mid-Oct
Reservation: Advisable peak season **Charge:** 3 people, pitch and car
135 fr; extra adult 28 fr; electricity 17 fr

Parc-Camping Agay Soleil

83700 St Raphaël   tel 94.82.00.79

*Hang loose on a reasonably-priced beach site that's an
ideal tourer's stop-over*

A carefree atmosphere characterises this small camp,
frequented by a young clientele. You could imagine yourself
riding down the coast on a Harley-Davidson to pull in among
the VW campers driven by earnest clean-limbed Dutch guys,
and put up your 'igloo' tent on one of the few available pitches
reserved for tourers. A walk back up the slope will take you to
the bar/restaurant where you can sip your beer on the terrace
that overlooks the site and the whole of the pretty Agay bay.
Food at this site is definitely not gourmet, being mostly fastfood
or hot snacks. For a busy site, the single *sanitaire* is kept quite

clean and there's the thoughtful touch of a special kiddies' washing cubicle behind 'ladybird' swing-doors. A short stay at this site won't see you out of pocket (although if you want to be near the beach, the tariff is slightly higher). The beach part of the camp is rather narrow and crowded, so you might prefer the wider stretches of ground elsewhere in the camp. After improving your tan and enjoying some windsurfing, you may feel it's time to move on, to St Raphaël perhaps, that is, if the traffic jams allow you to move.

● Ⓢ 𝄃 ≈ 🛁 ✕ ⛾ ☞ ⌂ 🍴 ▣

Directions: Right on the main road (N98), on the eastern side of Agay bay, a big sign and flags indicate the camp entrance **Ground:** Sandy
Children: No special facilities **Wheelchair:** Not suitable
Food-cooling: Ice sold **Sport:** Ping pong **Season:** 1 Mar to 15 Nov
Reservation: Advisable peak season **Charge:** 2 people, pitch and car 68 fr; extra adult 22 fr; electricity 14 to 19 fr

you pull in among the Harley Davidsons

❀ *Vallée du Paradis*

83700 Agay	tel 94.82.01.46

Not Paradise itself, but a good choice at this seaside resort; peace and quiet, with reasonably-priced good food

The birds that sing all night, as if no one has told them to fall silent after dusk, somehow add to the tranquil atmosphere at Vallée du Paradis. It's a small, cultivated site on a quiet road at the back of town. The main body of the camp, an attractively landscaped grassy glade, is under the shade of small trees. This area has open pitches; the marked, hedged *emplacements* (which are a little more private) are at the back of the reception building. The whole site has been thoughtfully designed and is serviced by one modern, well-appointed *sanitaire*, which is tiled throughout. On one side of the camp, the still, calm River Agay flows by and there's access to a spot where you can settle down in a chair to read, or just meditate. Perhaps at the end of the day you'd prefer to contemplate the deepening shadows on the Rastel d'Agay – a jagged rock of a hill, visible from some of the pitches. The joy of Vallée du Paradis is that the delightful, near-perfect bay of the town and the beaches and restaurants are just a short walk down the road. If you don't want to leave the camp, a roadside grill-restaurant serves reasonably-priced food such as fresh trout with almonds, or folded pizzas cooked *au feu du bois*. It's also a favourite haunt for locals, which adds to the atmosphere of *bonhomie*. You might seriously consider becoming a permanent beach-bum in Agay, and Vallée du Paradis does everything to convince you that it's a feasible proposition.

● ⑤ ♫ ⌂ ✕ ♀ 🍴 ⌂

Directions: Take a right-hand turn off the main road (N98) that follows the beach. This is the D100. Follow under a railway bridge and after a couple of bends, two campsites appear on your left. Vallée du Paradis is the second one **Ground:** Hard **Children:** Playground **Wheelchair:** Not suitable **Food-cooling:** Ice sold **Sport:** Ping pong **Season:** 20 Mar to 20 Oct **Reservation:** Advisable peak season **Charge:** 4 people, pitch and car 93 fr

---

In the event of your losing your passport or having it stolen, immediately report this to the police who will issue an official form in lieu of your loss.

Antibes

Le Pylône

Avenue du Pylône, BP32 La Brague, 06601 Antibes	tel 93.74.94.70

All the amenities you could want at this well-maintained all-year site, but its size might be a drawback for some

The four main campsites for Antibes are north of the town centre, just off the busy Nice road, in a commercial suburb parallel to the shoreline. The back road on which they're situated is an uninviting, dusty, suburban street. Le Pylône is a huge site. It is a typical example of a 'holiday village' style of camp, and is packed with statics (many owned by British mobile-home operators). A lot of the on-site couriers are English and so, too, are those who work in the reception; together with the British campers, a 'Little England' is created in Antibes. The site's endless avenues have some shady, hedged pitches and are reasonably quiet if you are away from the centres of activity. This position is not too difficult to achieve as activities are on the periphery of the grounds (poorly signposted – a site plan is essential) and may require a bit of a hike, depending on your pitch location. An attractive pool complex is landscaped with shrubs and boulders and has a grass sunbathing terrace and paved patio. Strict rules are enforced in this area, such as no ball games or alcohol. Another trek will lead to a well-stocked general shop and the Auberge, Le Pylône's restaurant and bar with terrace. Entertainment at this site includes beauty contests, beer drinking contests and discos into the early hours. Nearby, the town's beaches, nightspots and the fair provide other diversions.

Directions: The N7 to Nice runs north from Antibes. Filter left to take the D4 to Biot (just past the railway station opposite). Turn off at a funfair and 'Marineland'. Take the first left turn and, at a T-junction at the end of the road, turn right. Camp entrance is on your left
Ground: Hard **Children:** Playground, organised events
Wheelchair: Not suitable **Food-cooling:** Ice sold **Sport:** Volleyball, ping pong **Season:** All year **Reservation:** Advisable peak season
Charge: Pitch 15 fr; person 30 fr; vehicle 10 fr; pitch with electricity 20 fr

Rossignol

06600 Antibes   tel 93.33.56.98

Small, well-kept, shady site in a good position for a touring stop-over

You may wonder as you drive through the rather tacky-looking suburb of Les Breguières, if this is indeed a place where you would find a reasonable campsite. As a site Le Rossignol may not be grand – strictly for the tourer – but it does offer a quiet stay near the town. As soon as you turn into the forecourt you catch a glimpse of the camp's pleasant, small pool with a shallower extension for the children. To the rear of the reception area is a small bar, with seating outside under vines. There is also a *dépôt de pain*, an ice-cream counter and a take-away service. Prominent fire-points indicate a well-organised camp. The *sanitaire* further along is quite basic, but in good order, with some seated toilets. The pitches are Le Rossignol's chief attraction: cool, reasonably-sized grass *emplacements*, marked by tall hedges step down in terraces. Birdsong takes over from traffic noise as you descend to the grassy rise at the bottom. You may think the tariff a bit pricey for a camp that is essentially a touring base, but it's in a good position for Cannes, the N85 to Grasse and is away from the holiday campsite 'ghetto' at Antibes.

Directions: The N7 (Nice road) runs north from Antibes. On a straight stretch, filter left for Biot on the D4. There will be a funfair on your left and 'Marineland' on your right. Take the D4 over the A8 motorway, then turn first left after this, signposted D504 Sophia-Antipolis. At the T-junction, turn left again. This time the road takes you under the A8. Follow the road round and the camp is set back on your left. (This is the easiest route if you approach from the north. Once established, you could become familiar with southerly approach from town.)
Ground: Hard   **Children:** Playground   **Wheelchair:** Not suitable
Food-cooling: Ice sold   **Sport:** None   **Season:** 31 Mar to Sept
Reservation: Advisable peak season   **Charge:** 3 people, pitch and car 74 fr; extra adult 19 fr; child (under 5) 10.50 fr; electricity 10 to 15 fr

Spring weather in Lower Provence can still be dominated by the Mistral which blows hard most of the winter. This cold, dry wind blows down from the north through the Rhône Valley from the Massif Central.

Villeneuve-Loubet

Le Sourire

La Tour de la Madone, Route de Grasse	tel 93.20.96.11
D2085, 06270 Villeneuve-Loubet	

French-style, high-grade site; a good base for the area, albeit a bit pricey

Le Sourire is a long-established (30 years), four-star site, to the west of Villeneuve-Loubet, on the fringe of Cagnes-sur-Mer. The site is spread out along the valley of the River Mardaric, which crosses the length of the camping grounds. The camp is fairly well maintained, with a variety of trees that include clipped conifers and tall cypresses, yet there is also a 'scrubby' appearance here and there, typical of the French *laissez-faire* attitude to camping, unlike the fussiness that sometimes characterises Dutch-run sites. Quite a few statics are present, but they are a common feature in sites in this region. Neatly arranged pitches are rather small, but some seclusion is offered by the shrubs and trees that mark-out the plots. *Emplacements* at the side of the main road tend to be noisy during the day. Sanitary appointments are not modern, but the décor is passable and there are some seated toilets. The focus of the camp is the small commercial centre, providing produce and camping gas, as well as a first-aid post, a small games-room and a bar/restaurant. Meals can be enjoyed in the open-air on the terrace and sunbathing by the attractive pool alongside. This part of the camp springs to life in the evening, with organised contests, soirées and sometimes live musical entertainment. Although Le Sourire does not offer the superior 'outdoor hotel' facilities that families might expect, it is none the less a comfortable base from which to explore the area.

Directions: Take the D2085 heading west from Villeneuve-Loubet (the route to Grasse). The road begins at a small roundabout and crosses the Loup via a level-bridge. Further on, as you round a bend, you will see a sign warning of the site's proximity on the left. Then shortly after (again, on the left) you will see the camp by the roadside
Ground: Hard   **Children:** Playground, swimming, organised events
Wheelchair: Suitable   **Food-cooling:** Ice sold   **Sport:** Tennis,

volleyball, ping pong, mini-golf, practice-golf **Season:** 1 Apr to 7 Sept
Reservation: Advisable peak season **Charge:** 2 people, pitch and car
85 fr; child (under 5) 14 fr

▄▄▄ Carqueiranne ▄▄▄▄▄▄▄▄

Le Beau Vezé

Route de la Moutonne,   tel 94.57.65.30
83320 Carqueiranne

Small, comfortable site, in a good position for the beaches

Le Beau Vezé lies in a very attractive, dense, terraced wood. A
calm atmosphere immediately welcomes you as you drive into
the entrance at the end of a hard day on the road to find that
little bar terrace waiting by the pool, dark under the canopy of
its small trees. Here, too, at the stone-wall counter, you can
order a *plat cuisiné* or a take-away to transport to your peaceful
little nook. Made-up avenues take you around the hill on
which the camp sits, and tall pines shelter secluded, marked
emplacements in small enclaves bounded by stones. As this is a
small site there's a communal atmosphere in season, with
organised soirées and dances, by courtesy of your patron,
M Gras; the site fits in well with our 'small is beautiful'
philosophy. Le Beau Vezé is midway between Toulon, a huge
town which is the base for the French navy, and Hyères, a place
of palm boulevards and elegant buildings, with a picturesque
old quarter. There are places such as La Fenouillet, a small
summit behind the town with a good panorama, and the Iles
d'Hyères (off the Giens peninsula) that are worth a visit. The
two larger islands, a short boat trip away, have some beautiful
wooded walks.

● Ⓢ ⚡ ⌂ 🏊 ♆ 🍴 ⚓ 🏠 ▣ ⚲ ♫

Directions: The N98 by-passes Hyères town centre to the south and
continues towards Toulon (be prepared for heavy traffic). There will be
a left-hand turn where the railway goes under the road. This is the D76
to La Moutonne. Follow through to a T-junction and turn left towards
the village, passing its centre on the right. The road takes you down to a
wooded path. Just after this, you will find the camp entrance with
signboard on your left **Ground:** Hard to giving
Children: Playground, swimming, organised events **Wheelchair:** Not
suitable **Food-cooling:** Ice sold **Sport:** Tennis, volleyball, ping pong
Season: 1 June to 20 Sept **Reservation:** Advisable peak season
Charge: Pitch 31 fr; person 30 fr

▰▰▰ Castellane ▰▰▰▰▰▰▰▰▰▰▰▰▰▰▰▰▰

Camp des Gorges du Verdon

Chasteuil, 04120 Castellane	tel 92.83.63.64

Small, shaded, well-kept site, in an attractive position

If the likes of a largish family camp is not what you had in mind, Camping des Gorges du Verdon is an attractive option in this isolated area around Castellane; far smaller than its neighbouring site, it's a more informal camp. Plentiful shade is provided by an attractive pine wood and *emplacements* are of a random layout and open appearance, the general 'scrubbiness' of the pitches deriving from the site's natural aspect rather than from neglect. The bright-orange surfaces of the modern, roomy *sanitaire* almost sparkle. Welcoming coloured parasols greet you outside the attractive roadside bar/restaurant decorated with tubs of flowers. Opposite is an equally tempting rectangular pool. Like the other camp at Verdon, the river flows along the back of the grounds, with a stony beach facing the cliffs. The site's small size, coupled with the friendly management and the reasonable tariff, make this camp a good bet for a touring stop.

● ⑤ 🏊 ⛵ 🏊 🛥 ✕ 🍴 👕 🏠 ♿ 🔲 🎿 🎵

Directions: Follow the D952 to Moustiers, along the hairpin bends of the Verdon Gorge. Eventually the roadside bar/restaurant of the site appears on your left **Ground:** Hard **Children:** Playground, organised events **Wheelchair:** Suitable **Food-cooling:** Ice sold
Sport: Volleyball, ping pong **Season:** 1 Apr to 20 Sept
Reservation: Advisable peak season **Charge:** 3 people, pitch and car 74 fr; child (under 4) 9,50 fr; extra adult 15.50 fr

Camp du Verdon

Domaine de la Salaou, 04120 Castellane	tel 92.83.61.29

A comfortable family retreat, and a prime site for exploring this attractive area

Because of its location and facilities, this four-site campsite almost has a monopoly on family holidays in the region and is well established with British package operators. Camp du Verdon occupies a small plain on the bend of the river of the famous Gorges du Verdon. After pulling off the road, you dip down towards the main rustic Provençal stone buildings, which include a circular turret with a tiled roof. A lot of activity is centred around this front part of the site, with the reception, bar, reasonably-priced restaurant and swimming-pools. The pools are set in their own terrace behind the buildings. The smaller of the two is shallower but isn't a kiddies' pool as such. To the left is a more recent area of straight roadways and nursery trees providing little shade; the cooler part of the site is in the centre, where thin foliage provides some shade. The older-style *sanitaire* blocks could do with a bit of smartening up and all three blocks are positioned along one side of the camp, which could mean a long trek through a maze of tents if you're not pitched nearby. The site is on the large side, but a not too arduous walk will take you to the river *plages*. It might be best to take a couple of seats with you as the beaches are stony. The steep, verdant hills of the gorge provide a background to the riverside and the two small lakes (one for fishing) on site. A courteous and helpful German lady oversees the proceedings at this pleasant, attractive camp.

Directions: From Castellane, take the D952 to Moustiers, which branches off the main square of the town. Go under a stone, ivy-covered bridge with a wrought-iron crucifix on top. Continue past a couple of small campsites. After a winding drive along this narrow road, as it bends to the left by a restaurant, you will see the camp spread out on your left **Ground:** Hard **Children:** Playground, organised events **Wheelchair:** Not suitable **Food-cooling:** Ice sold, fridge hire **Sport:** Volleyball, ping pong, mini-golf **Season:** 15 May to 15 Sept **Reservation:** Advisable peak season **Charge:** 3 people, pitch and car 91 fr; pitches with electricity 105 to 115 fr; extra adult 23 fr

The olive, cultivated in abundance throughout Provence, was originally brought to the French Mediterranean by the Greeks around 2,500 years ago. Olive oil (as 'virgin' oil) comes from the first pressing after the harvest and 'fine' oil is that which is derived from adding water to the mashed olives when pressed for a second time. Until the 1800s the oil was used in Marseilles soap when it was replaced by other vegetable oils such as coconut.

▅▅▅ Cavalaire-sur-Mer ▅▅▅▅▅▅

Camping de la Baie

Boulevard Pasteur, 83240   tel 94.64.08.15
Cavalaire-sur-Mer

A relaxed, wooded camp in the heart of town, close to shops, harbour and beaches

Who would have thought that after negotiating the traffic in a hot, packed seaside town you'd end up in an oasis of peace and calm? The group of low, 'sculptured' buildings, with palms and an inviting little bar terrace at La Baie's entrance, have something of a Caribbean flavour. This impression is reinforced by a restaurant that's a riot of colour: murals of palm beaches à la Bounty Bar advertisement, artificial palms supporting bright, soft-toy parrots, bamboo poles, bouquets of flowers – all contributing to a festive atmosphere for diners. The main body of the quiet camping ground is on two levels – the flat area behind the main buildings is suitable for caravans, and beyond, a heavily wooded hill has *emplacements* for tents. The simple architecture of the modern *sanitaires*, the flowers and the variety of terrain gives La Baie its character, which is something lacking in the campsites around Cavalaire. The attractive environment seems to induce relaxation and the camp's central position allows easy access to the town's shopping centre or to the nearby beach.

● Ⓜ ⫝̸ ⪴ ✕ ⚲ ☞ ⚹ ⋔ ⊟ ▣ ♫

Directions: Take the main road leaving the centre of town in the direction of Toulon. At the first crossroads, beyond the centre, you will see a camp direction sign telling you to turn left. Turn left at the next T-junction (another sign here). This is followed by a first right (coming up after a service station on your right). The camp sign on this corner is obscured. On your right, further along, you will see the flags of the site entrance (also on your right) **Ground:** Hard **Children:** Playground, organised events **Wheelchair:** Not suitable **Food-cooling:** Ice sold **Sport:** Volleyball, ping pong **Season:** 15 Mar to 22 Sept **Reservation:** Advisable peak season **Charge:** 3 people, pitch and car 84 fr; extra adult 19.50 fr

The Préfecture of Alpes-Maritimes has decreed that, for reasons of hygiene, the département's campsites must not accept campers' coolpacks for freezing.

Cros de Mouton

83240 Cavalaire-sur-Mer	Out-of-season tel 94.64.05.54 tel 94.64.10.87

A good, relatively cheap site for the tourer: modest fare in tranquil surroundings and handy for town

Not far from the bustle of the town, Cros de Mouton occupies a high hill, covered in oak and pine, and from the terrace of the simple bar you can sit and look over Cavalaire and the sea. Simple is perhaps the key word to describe this camp, as it is definitely not the dynamic, high-life fun type. The attraction here is that you have the best of both worlds: most of the day will probably find you on the busy beach or in the town but a five-minute drive will take you back to the shade and calm of this peaceful, very French site. The character of the site is epitomised by the single-storey reception building that has a little shop: the whole is unpretentious, with attractive shrubbery. The camping ground comprises parallel rows of terraces, with sand-based *emplacements* forming steps down through the trees to the bottom of the site. There are some statics but these are hidden away on the upper levels. The *sanitaire*, while rather old, is quite presentable, with at least one seated toilet. The congenial proprietor arranges soirées, perhaps along the lines of a Mexican evening, and at the friendly little bar you can sit out under the clear night sky, filled with the scent of mimosas, while a pianist tickles the ivories.

Directions: In the centre of Cavalaire, take the right-hand lane to filter off the main road, going south through town (camp direction sign here). Go straight ahead at a mini-roundabout. Follow the road to continue ahead at second mini-roundabout (another camp sign). The road sweeps to the left to take you out of town. Eventually you come across the marked site entrance on your right, off the road and up an incline. A sharp right-turn will take you to reception **Ground:** Hard to giving **Children:** Playground **Wheelchair:** Not suitable **Food-cooling:** Ice sold **Sport:** Ping pong **Season:** 1 Mar to Oct **Reservation:** Advisable peak season **Charge:** Pitch 19.50 fr; person 18 fr; child (under 7) 10 fr

It's normal for your stay on a campsite to be charged from midday on the day of arrival to midday on the day of departure.

La Colle-sur-Loup

Les Pinèdes

Route du Pont de Pierre, 06480 La Colle-sur- Loup

tel 93.32.98.94

Well-maintained, shady, tranquil site, convenient for the coast, too

We came to the conclusion that this is the best-kept site of the Loup valley region. The camp's atmosphere is one of tranquillity which helps you unwind after a day's sightseeing and negotiation of the hairpin bends in the hills beyond. Les Pinèdes has orderly, level, stone-walled terraces ascending a steep hill with most of the *emplacements* laid to gravel (some are grass). Pine and oak trees provide abundant shade for these well-kept, generously-sized pitches. The two strategically placed *sanitaires* are well planned and pleasingly decorated with warm, honey-brown tiling. The main facilities are a short walk down the hill and include a large roadside bar/restaurant, with an outdoor terrace under a canopy of vines. Here you can pick up bread and milk in the mornings and a take-away supper in the evenings. On the higher ground, overlooking the main road, is the swimming-pool, which has a shaped shallow corner providing safe waterplay for children. The usual family fun and games are laid on in summer, which in a small camp such as this gives a communal feel to the festivities. There's not too much to do in the camp outside the high season but it's really a site in which to escape any sort of energetic or lively régime. And if you fancy slipping away for a candle-lit dinner, the Bacchus, a sophisticated restaurant serving *haute cuisine* in a cool grey-and-white stone-vault interior, is just next door. Contemporary paintings and interesting lighting accessories reflect the refined taste of the maître d'.

● ⓢ ⚐ ⇌ ✕ ⚲ 🐀 🍴 ⛁ 🔋 ♫

Directions: Take the D6 leading west from La Colle-sur-Loup, which skirts the town. This road descends from the town around a couple of bends. As you pass these, you will see the roadside bar/restaurant and site entrance on your right **Ground:** Hard **Children:** Playground, organised events **Wheelchair:** Not suitable **Food-cooling:** Ice sold **Sport:** Ping pong **Season:** 18 Feb to 24 Nov **Reservation:** Advisable

peak season **Charge:** Pitch 32 fr; vehicle 9 fr; child (under 5) 8 fr;
extra adult 15 fr; electricity 9 to 15 fr

▬▬ La Croix-Valmer ▬▬▬▬▬▬▬▬
Sélection Camping

83420 La Croix-Valmer-Plage   tel 94.79.61.97

For families and the young-at-heart alike, this medium-sized site offers quiet surroundings by day and plenty of night-time entertainment

A very pleasant site, Sélection Camping comprises banked terraces cut into a hillside lightly shaded by tall pines. These trees, the sandy avenues and level sandbeds of the *emplacements* create a visually attractive setting for this reasonably-sized camp. Overt signs of good organisation in the numerous bins, prominent fire-extinguisher points and clear labelling of paths must be commended. The astute yet approachable Madame runs an efficient business here, providing adequate facilities for her clients. There are numerous modern, clean, washing-cubicles and toilets. Similar good facilities for the handicapped also include special showers. Natural-wood play equipment is to be found in the good playground, not that children will want to hang around the site for too long, as the beaches are a ten-minute walk down the road. On top of the on-site barbecue parties, theme evenings and discos organised in season, the flesh-pots of St Tropez are only a car-ride away, going north. Sélection Camping is also a convenient spot for visiting the pretty beach resorts along the Corniche des Maures of the Côte d'Azur. The buildings at the entrance hide a bijou bar where, in the morning when the camp is quiet, you could enjoy a cup of coffee and a paper on the small, enclosed terrace. It may wake you up a bit after the frolics of the night before!

◐ Ⓜ 𝗑 🗲 ✕ ♀ 👍 🐾 ♺ ⊟ 🗑 ⅋ ♫

Directions: Going south on the D559 outside La Croix-Valmer (to Le Lavandou you will see, on your right, a large roundabout direction sign. By this is a white board with green lettering giving a 400m warning to the site. At the roundabout itself, take the first exit and Sélection is on this road, a little further, on a bend. Entrance is on your right
Ground: Giving **Children:** Playground, organised events, baby

273

facilities **Wheelchair:** Suitable **Food-cooling:** Ice sold
Sport: Volleyball, ping pong **Season:** Easter to 15 Oct
Reservation: Advisable peak season **Charge:** 3 people, pitch and car
108 fr; child (under 7) 15 fr; extra adult 30 fr; electricity 17 fr

▬▬▬ Esparron-de-Verdon ▬▬▬

Le Soleil

04550 Esparron-de-Verdon — tel 92.77.13.78

*Small, secluded and full of charm, this sublime site
overlooks the beautiful waters of the Verdon*

Directions to this campsite may be a little complicated, but the
intrepid tourer will be amply rewarded by what he or she
discovers at the end of the journey. Le Soleil is perched on a
slope where the River Verdon has expanded to form a small
lake. The site goes down to the water's edge where, in the
evening, the sun sets over the silent hills and still water. On the
opposite side of the inlet is Esparron, which, despite all the
tourists, maintains an air of of serene isolation. You can snap its
tcnth-ccntury château or take a lake cruise on the 'hydrobus'
from the creek. At the top of the camp is the main site building,
a modern, white chalet structure with natural stained doors,
windows and shutters. Opposite, good sanitary arrangements
are provided in the main *sanitaire*, which includes some seated
toilet facilities for the handicapped. (Because of the steep
nature of the rest of the site, wheelchair users might be
confined to the top, level terraces near here and the reception.)
From this part of the camp a steep, zig-zagging road descends
the hill, with terraces leading off. The lower you go, the more
secluded the pitches and right at the bottom is the tiny, rocky
plage. Also on-site, the snack-bar serves good *plats cuisinés*, from
grills cooked *au feu du bois* to Provençal specialities, as well as
crêpes and take-aways. If ever there was a campsite that set out
to nourish the spirit and ease the mind, this must be the one.
Here you can experience camping *en plein air* in the wild beauty
of the Verdon, without lacking creature comforts; cordial
management makes you feel like a guest in someone's home.

Children should be discouraged from playing around shower blocks.

Directions: Reach Esparron via Quinson, just off the D13. Entering the village (from the south), take the left turn clearly marked by a sign. This takes you on a winding road that, after bearing left at a T-junction, straightens out through fields of lavender and vine. Twisting once again, you are eventually led towards Esparron. As you round a right-hand bend towards the village, there is a left-hand turn with camp sign clearly marked. Site entrance appears on the right (perhaps difficult if towing). **Ground:** Hard **Children:** Playground
Wheelchair: Suitable **Food-cooling:** Ice sold **Sport:** Ping pong, 'Tennis-Love' self-play machine **Season:** Easter to 30 Sept
Reservation: Advisable peak season **Charge:** Pitch 21 fr; person 18 fr; child (under 4) 10 fr

▬▬ Fréjus ▬▬▬▬▬▬▬▬▬▬▬▬▬

Sites summary All the campsites in the Fréjus area are in the north and west, away from the town. La Baume is a 'caveat' entry, Le Colombier a large family site and Les Pins Parasols a more modest, French-style site. Des Pêcheurs and Moulin des Iscles are, in fact, at Roquebrune-sur-Argens, a village 10 kilometres west of Fréjus (as the crow flies). We decided to designate these as sites for Fréjus as there is a good road connection via the N7. For more of a country drive, which will also lead to the nearby coast, the D7 links Roquebrune with the resort of St Aygulf.

⑦ *La Baume*

Route de Bagnols, 83600 Fréjus   tel 94.40.87.87

Open-air hotel-style camping with plenty of entertainment and luxury pool complex; it may be too crowded and cramped for some

La Baume, with its additional complex, La Palmeraie, is definitely 'big business'. The camping ground is spread out through a light wood between the twin recreation centres, and from the marked *emplacements* near the main building, through to the smaller, random ones further away, pitch space is at a premium. The glossy brochures for both holiday sites are full of photos of the ostentatious pool complexes decked out with palms and waterslides. When your tired of pretending those sumptuous pools are in your Bel-Air back garden, and have had enough tanning for one day, you could always participate in one of a whole range of activities, from yoga to gym sessions and basketball to tennis lessons. A large, cool restaurant with a shady terrace under olive trees overlooks the pools. At night you can be entertained with cabaret acts in the purpose-built open-air theatre or discos and competitions that will keep you from turning in early. On the minus side, we did hear of a camper who visited the site during the low season and was given a pitch next door to what amounted to a building-site (complete with JCB chugging away in the background), this 'site' being the present holiday complex which was nearing completion. Not the sort of treatment that you would expect from the management of a four-star camp. However, if you expect no less than four-star facilities when camping abroad, La Baume has the ingredients that will appeal – there's no denying the luxurious 'open-air hotel' setting it offers, along with all the other trappings of holiday high-life under the sun.

Directions: Head north along the D4 to Bagnols-en-Forêt (off the N7 west of Fréjus). The road takes you past other campsites on your right. After approximately 4 kms, you will eventually see the sign for La Baume on your left **Ground:** Hard **Children:** Swimming, organised events **Wheelchair:** Not suitable **Food-cooling:** Ice sold **Sport:** Tennis, volleyball, ping pong, basketball, archery **Season:** June to Sept **Reservation:** Advisable peak season **Charge:** 2 people, pitch and car 120 fr; pitch with electricity 150 fr; extra adult 27 fr; extra child (under 7) 18.50 fr

Camping-Caravanning des Pêcheurs

83520 Roquebrune-sur-Argens   tel 94.45.71.25

A welcome sanctuary of coolness at this shady site, with some seclusion and good facilities for all the family

Camping-Caravanning des Pêcheurs, outside the village of Roquebrune-sur-Argens, is in the lowland that lies beneath the lone, red sandstone outcrop of Mont Roquebrune, its severe silhouette against the sky suggesting a petrified citadel. It's a popular site with British campers, as a couple of package companies operate here. The camp is one of the few that guarantees extreme shade, as the dense woodland in which it's situated gives a sense of seclusion but not of isolation. Amenities are set at either end of the camp, but being a small site this layout poses no problems. The far side has the swimming-pool in its own clearing, along with a bar and terrace: perfect surroundings for relaxing at the end of an afternoon's motoring perhaps, allowing you to cool off either by taking a dip in the clear water of the pool or by drinking an iced liquid. Near the reception, discreetly tucked away, is a small bar/restaurant with outdoor seating, offering an informal rendezvous for an evening drink. This is a family orientated camp, with plenty of organised activity in season. Extra facilities for children include a baby bath with changing area, in the acceptable sanitary appointments. Mention must be made, of course, of the lake across the road from the camp. This stretch of water in the lee of the mountain doesn't quite conceal its origins as a gravel pit, but nevertheless offers the opportunity of swimming or sunbathing on its beach. It's here that you'll find the camp's tennis court and mini-golf. Civilisation is nearby in the shape of the village, or the D7 to St Aygulf and the N7 to Fréjus.

Directions: Roquebrune-sur-Argens is on the D7 south of the N7 between Le Muy and Fréjus. Before you reach the village, you will go under a railway bridge. Here, you will see a red and white camping sign warning you of the site at 300m. Further along you will see another sign for the camp, on your left. This is the entrance, directly opposite a lake and mountain **Ground:** Hard **Children:** Playground, swimming, organised events **Wheelchair:** Not suitable **Food-cooling:** Ice sold **Sport:** Tennis, volleyball, mini-golf, fishing **Season:** Easter to Sept **Reservation:** Advisable peak season **Charge:** 2 people, pitch and car 88 fr

Le Colombier

Route de Bagnols-en-Forêt, 83600 Fréjus   tel 94.51.56.01

A large site that aims to please all the family; the camp disco, set in woods, sums up its unique blend of styles

The reception you receive at this site, set on a wooded hill, is a warm one in your own language, for the management here speak very good English. One couple we met couldn't commend them enough for the practical help they received after their car was robbed *en route*. An effort is made to make your stay an amicable one and this is no cliché. Attractive, modern *sanitaires* under pantile roofing are kept in good order and have the addition of kiddies' toilets. There are nine *sanitaires*, which gives you some idea of the spread of the grounds, as well as the high-season population. In fact, you'd be wise to hang on to the site plan you're given when you arrive. A maze of avenues, through a very shady natural wood, leads to the scattered *emplacements* – and if you're pitched at the road end of the camp it's a bit of a hike to find the restaurant perched on the hill. This establishment, while not very appealing by day, comes into its own at night, with campers thronging the bar terrace under the open, star-filled sky. From here, not only do you see the lights of Fréjus, but you can feel the muted throb of the music playing in the purpose-built disco directly opposite. In the day-time, the pool at the far end of the camp forms a large rectangle of inviting water under the burning sun. A huge 'umbrella' pine on the terrace edge provides a cool retreat if you tire of sunbathing. Usually, a site in which walking boots might be an asset just to reach the amenities does not fare well with us, but this single drawback is far outweighed by the fact that Le Colombier has such an attractive environment. This, coupled with friendly service, goes a long way towards making you feel satisfied.

● Ⓛ ⛹ 🛶 ⚖ ✕ ♀ 🍴 🐝 ⛺ ⛴ 📻 ♫

Directions: Head north along the D4 (which turns off the N7 west of Fréjus) to Bagnols-en-Forêt. Le Colombier is on your right, distinguished by a tall, singular flagpole with a string of national flags
Ground: Hard **Children:** Playground, swimming, organised events, playroom **Wheelchair:** Tricky **Food-cooling:** Ice sold
Sport: Tennis, volleyball, ping pong **Season:** 15 Mar to Sept
Reservation: Advisable peak season **Charge:** 2 people, pitch and car 85 fr; electricity 20.50 fr

---

Riviera Radio is an all-English commercial station broadcasting on 106.5 Khz. FM and can be picked up between the Italian border and St Tropez. It gives international and home news as well as French national news, world stock market reports, traffic conditions, up-dates on festivals and other events, and plays up-to-the-minute chart music.

Moulin des Iscles

83520 Roquebrune-sur-Argens   tel 94.45.70.74

Enjoy peace and solitude at this tiny, attractive, get-away-from-it-all camp

A setting of complete seclusion and colourful buildings, with roses and climbing plants adorning the owner's beautiful villa, are the outstanding features of Moulin des Iscles. There is a double-staircase outside leading to his first-floor front door. Installed in the large arch, which the steps form against the house wall, are the remnants of machinery: perhaps a water-wheel. To enter the camp you cross a bridge over a wide ditch that might have taken water from the nearby River Argens. Next to the bridge is an enchanting dovecote, with its residents cooing away under pantile roofing. Opposite, across a small courtyard, a simple two-storey L-shaped building with an upstairs veranda completes the scene of an attractive blend of trees, plants, flowers and architecture. Here, on the restaurant patio, you can sit under the red-purple sky at the end of the day and meditate on your surroundings. Tucked away behind the buildings is the well-maintained grass camping ground with open pitches. One small, neat building of a *sanitaire* is all that's needed for a site of this small size (under 100 *emplacements*). M Eloi's leaflet states that in season there is a weekly cinema: pre-war black and white weepies, we bet! Or, rather, we would like to think so, with Moulin des Iscles being shut away from the commercial chaos of the coast, we can temporarily forget the mundane of the present. This camp might be a tourer's closest idea to a camping Nirvana.

Directions: Roquebrune-sur-Argens is a village south of the N7, on the D7 between Le Muy and Fréjus. After leaving the village, watch out for the sign announcing the village limits (the town-name with a red diagonal through it). The road rises here. As it drops on the other side be prepared to take an immediate left-turn. The camp sign is here **Ground:** Hard **Children:** Organised events **Wheelchair:** Not suitable **Food-cooling:** Ice sold **Sport:** Ping pong **Season:** All year **Reservation:** Advisable peak season **Charge:** 3 people, pitch and car 72 fr; extra adult 14 fr; child (under 7) 7 fr; electricity 10 to 15 fr

Les Pins Parasols

Route de Bagnols, 83600 Fréjus · · · · · · · · · · · · · tel 94.40.88.45

A modest, relatively quiet and efficiently-run site in the French style; reasonable amenities are offered for its price

A simpler way of life can be enjoyed at this site, although that's not to say the atmosphere is totally sedate. Most of this lightly-wooded site is quite pleasant, but recent developments have yet to blend in. The bar/restaurant is more of a snack/pizza place with the option of outdoor eating on the terrace or take-away food, if you wish. Reaching the swimming-pool, at the back of the bar, the landscape seems rather bare in appearance and the pools themselves are at first hidden from view by a high, pink-white concrete wall. The main pool is consolation, though, with a separate kiddies' pool to one side, and there's a bit of fun provided by a waterchute. As a backdrop, the terrace rockery planted out with cacti and palms doesn't relieve the monotony of the expanse of sparse, level concrete provided for sunbathing. Perhaps more thought could have gone into the landscaping, but this is a minor point. For those not interested in the high-life and night-life of the likes of Le Colombier, but want to be close to Fréjus and St Raphaël, Les Pins Parasols is as good a place as any to stay.

Directions: As for Le Colombier, continue north on the D4. You will see the large white lettering of the sign on your right, followed by the camp entrance (also on your right) **Ground:** Hard
Children: Playground, swimming, organised events
Wheelchair: Suitable **Food-cooling:** Ice sold **Sport:** Tennis, volleyball, ping pong **Season:** Easter to 1 Sept
Reservation: Advisable peak season **Charge:** 2 people, pitch and car 66 fr; extra adult 22 fr; child (under 7) 14 fr

---

The olive, cultivated in abundance throughout Provence, was originally brought to the French Mediterranean by the Greeks around 2,500 years ago. Olive oil (as 'virgin' oil) comes from the first pressing after the harvest and 'fine' oil is that which is derived from adding water to the mashed olives when pressed for a second time. Until the 1800s the oil was used in Marseilles soap when it was replaced by other vegetable oils such as coconut.

▰▰ Gilette ▰▰▰▰▰▰▰▰

Moulin Nou

Pont Charles Albert, 06830 Gilette   tel 93.08.92.40

Well-kept, but not very shady camp in an isolated, scenic spot; a good base for exploring the area

The camp of Moulin Nou sits isolated in a flat clearing between the road and the River Esteron, beneath hilly ranges. This is a campsite favoured by package operators, so you'll find plenty of fellow compatriots here. Orderly, marked *emplacements* (not that large) lead off the main avenue that cuts through the long strip of the camping ground and eventually leads to the decorative pool area screened by hedges. Nearby is the pleasant small restaurant and bar. Floral arrangements even enhance the *sanitaires*, making an attractive scene to complement the beautiful panorama beyond. Lack of shade might be a drawback for some, but assuming you'll be venturing forth into the hills for most of the day, this may not present too much of a problem. Although a very peaceful site, there are soirées and dances in the summer to put you in a party mood: nothing too wild, though, it wouldn't suit the general atmosphere. The village of Gilette, with its prominent bell-tower, looks across from on high, perched on a rugged green-forested hill, overlooked by the towering peak of the distant Mont Vial. As Moulin Nou is close to the N202, you have access to Nice and the Riviera and if you travel west on the D17 you'll also encounter the beautiful mountain scenery and villages of the valley of the Esteron.

Directions: The N202 is the main Digne to Nice route. Approximately 16 km north of its junction with the A8 outside Nice is the Pont Charles Albert, crossing the Var. Cross this bridge and immediately turn left onto the D2209 (camp direction sign here). Take this winding road along the valley floor and pass a large, red-brown camp direction sign. Soon after, you will go through a tight right-hand bend with a metal barrier by a small industrial plant. Soon after this bend, the site entrance is on your left **Ground:** Hard **Children:** Playground, swimming, organised events **Wheelchair:** Not suitable **Food-cooling:** Ice sold **Sport:** Tennis, volleyball, ping pong **Season:** Easter to Sept **Reservation:** Advisable peak season **Charge:** 4 people, pitch and car 132.40 fr

▬▬ Le Lavandou ▬▬▬▬▬▬▬▬▬

⑦ *Le Camp du Domaine*

La Favière, 83234 Bormes-les-Mimosas   tel 94.71.03.12

Huge beach site occupying a shady hillside; atmosphere may be lacking for some

More often than not, when you see the word 'domaine' in a camp name, you can be pretty sure it's a large site, and this site is no exception. In fact, it's one of the largest in the guide with over 1,000 pitches. The camp occupies an enviable position on a large, shady, pine-covered hill overlooking the bay of Le Lavandou and its marina. The grounds descend to the excellent beach of fine sand and fine views, with *emplacements* lining the site's promenade road. First impressions are quite favourable when you enter from inland: smart tennis courts by a small, modern bar (listing cocktails amongst its liquid offerings) set the tone. When you climb into the woodland via made-up avenues, you may have second thoughts. The extent of the grounds is such that you start to wonder when you will reach the sea (the detailed site map looks more like a battle plan with its numerous pitch numbers and demarcation lines and somehow manages to conceal the scale). The avenues on the summit undeniably give a wonderful view of the bay and, peeping through the foliage of the aleppo pines, the coastal hills beyond. On the other side of the hill is the beach – packed, of course. Le Camp du Domaine is an extremely popular site with Continental visitors. The more exposed pitches tend to be filled with caravans and are laid to grass up to the beach edge. However, the pitches here come equipped with bamboo pergolas to give you a little shade. On the eastern side of the beach is a small commercial centre with a self-service, bazaar, pizzeria, café and *crêperie*. At this point the main thoroughfare leads back to the reception and tennis courts. We have decided to include this campsite as a caveat for three reasons. First the very size of the place rules out a communal atmosphere. Second, and knowing that this is an important matter, there is a complete absence of seated toilets in the *sanitaires*. Third, we have heard of a rather inflexible management attitude.

Nevertheless, the camp's location does have its merits, not the least of which is a good beach nearby. Early booking is essential here (ask for a site plan marking available pitches when you write).

● ⓛ 🧍 🏊 🐟 ✕ 🍷 🍖 ⛲ 🍳 📷 🎣

Directions: Head west out of Le Lavandou on the D559. Take the third exit onto the D298 at the roundabout (camp direction sign here). Stay on this road and eventually you will come across the site on the left, with flags at the entrance **Ground:** Hard to sandy **Children:** Playground, organised events **Wheelchair:** Not suitable **Food-cooling:** Ice sold, fridge hire **Sport:** Tennis, sailboard and pedalo hire **Season:** Apr to Oct **Reservation:** Advisable peak season **Charge:** Pitch 23 fr; person 18.50 fr; child (under 7) 9.50 fr

▰▰▰ Mandelieu La Napoule ▰▰▰

L'Argentière

Boulevard du Bon Puits,   tel 93.49.95.04
06210 Mandelieu La Napoule

An ideal touring stop with a communal atmosphere: secluded yet with good access to the town and beach

L'Argentière is really a watering hole rather than a holiday site, but if you're passing through in the camper-van then it's worth trying on spec. The site is just far enough away from the hurly-burly of Mandelieu town centre to be considered secluded. It is quite small (only 66 *emplacements*), neat, laid to grass, shady and well maintained by a relaxed, informal management. In a matter of days you could explore the town by night, the beach by day (it can be approached via a detour through a nature trail reserve across the road) or go and drool over the amount of floating dollars in the marina of La Napoule's port next door. When you're ready to travel on, stock up at the hypermarket close by.

● ⓢ 🏊 ✕ 🍷 ⛲ 🍳 📷

Directions: Entering on the main A8, leave at the Mandelieu interchange, which puts you down in the heart of town. Join the Avenue des Cannes which is part of the N7. Head west in the direction of Fréjus. After going under the A8, pick up the main fork to the left

(Avenue Maréchal) which goes over a flyover. Go straight ahead at the roundabout at the bottom. Immediately ahead is a little bridge over a stream, where you will see green and white camp direction signs on the left. About 1500 yards further on, L'Argentière's entrance is on your right **Ground:** Hard **Children:** Not suitable **Wheelchair:** Not suitable **Food-cooling:** Ice sold **Sport:** Ping pong **Season:** Easter to Sept **Reservation:** Advisable peak season **Charge:** 2 people, pitch and car 96 fr

▬ Montpezat ▬

Coteau de la Marine

04730 Montagnac- Montpezat   tel 92.77.59.34

An attractive, handy base for a touring family; children will enjoy the pools and atmosphere

This four-star camp is popular with the Continentals and its picturesque aspect, coupled with high-grade amenities, makes it an ideal base from which to explore the wild and wonderful area of the Verdon. The pleasant pool area with a circular kiddies' pool to one side is the camp's focus, along with the main buildings containing a self-service, bar and an attractive little restaurant. From the pitches here the level grounds stretch towards the river through the light shade of pine and oak. The ground surface is very stony, so if you're camping with a tent, be prepared with some strong stakes. Coteau de la Marine overlooks a width of the River Verdon, to the West of the Ste Croix Lake. Good views of the rolling hills exist at the site, either from the restaurant terrace raised above the pools, or, if you're lucky enough, from your own *emplacement* at the back of the camp. Here the translucent, topaz green of the slow river snakes its way through the grey cliffs with their clinging foliage. La Marine, well run by a young family, provides fun and family entertainment, and the usual soirées or sports tournaments can be enjoyed in a relaxed atmosphere. The camp is a bit lacking in shade generally, but this may not affect you unduly if you're out taking in the beautiful scenery in this region.

Directions: The D11 runs on the north side and parallel to the Lac de Ste Croix. To the west of this lake take the D211 on your right (assuming you're coming from the south). Camp direction sign is here.

As you descend into the valley, you will see the camp laid out on your right **Ground:** Hard **Children:** Playground, swimming, organised events **Wheelchair:** Suitable **Food-cooling:** Ice sold **Sport:** Tennis, ping pong, pedalo-hire **Season:** 15 Mar to 15 Nov
Reservation: Advisable peak season **Charge:** 3 people, pitch and car 96 fr; extra adult 17 fr; child (under 7) 11 fr

▬▬ Nans-les-Pins ▬▬▬

Camping International de la Ste Baume

83860 Nans-les-Pins   tel 94.78.92.68

Attractive, secluded spot, offering the tourer a stop-over in a relaxed atmosphere

The grand name of this site is perhaps a little misleading. Far from being a lively holiday camp, the International is a very secluded, attractive site in light woodland and rather a beautiful place to be, if you value a quiet time. The *sanitaires* are modern and there is a grocery store to supplement shopping in the village. *Emplacements*, which are marked out with stones under the light shade of oaks and pines, are generally hard and gravelly. As the camping ground is circular, you don't have far to travel from any one point to the communal hub comprising playground, barbecue, pools and bar which also serves snack-meals. On its terrace, under a striped awning, you can sit and watch others cooling themselves off in the pool or relaxing on the nearby area of stone paving. If you are touring or towing through the delightful countryside on the west side of Var, this site is worth a try. Nans-les-Pins could be described as comatose rather than sleepy, but there's one really cool, picturesque café to sit outside for a snap to show them back home. Or you could wander into St Maximin to the north and pay a visit to the splendid basilica there.

🌣 Ⓢ ⚡ 🛶 🛒 ⛱ 🍴 ⛪ ✋ 🏮 🎣 🔌 ✂

Directions: Nans-les-Pins lies east of Marseille, just south of the N560 on the D80. Approaching the village from the north on this road, you will see the camp entrance on the left, clearly marked **Ground:** Hard **Children:** Playground, swimming **Wheelchair:** Not suitable **Food-cooling:** Ice sold **Sport:** Tennis, volleyball, ping pong, horse-riding **Season:** Apr to Sept **Reservation:** Advisable peak season **Charge:** 2 people, pitch and car 50 fr; electricity 8.50 to 11 fr

Pégomas

St Louis

06550 La Roquette-sur-Siagne	tel 93.42.26.67

The nearest 'family-type' camp to Cannes and Grasse; a good place for a long stay in reasonably secluded surroundings

Very few commercial sites we've seen have such high hedgerows, which so effectively screen neighbouring campers, as here in St Louis: your *emplacement* can become a private little garden. The main camping ground is centred on two parallel avenues. Rows of precisely marked pitches lead off, reasonably protected from the sun by trees that give the illusion of a wood. At the back of the camp, which looks out on to wooded hills, the foliage becomes sparser and the hedges are not so full, making this rear part not as pretty. Pitch size varies, but some are generously proportioned for such a small site. Coupled with the benefit of these above-average *emplacements* are the equally attractive modern *sanitaires*. Their light and airy construction of four open 'corner' sections linked to a central hub, covered by beamed and clay-tile roofing and quarry-tiled throughout, makes them functional pieces of architecture as well as being visually pleasing. Away from the tents, a smart villa-style building houses the reception, shop and a bar under two large, white umbrella-canopies. Its attractive terrace provides the venue for evening entertainment. Across the way is a good pool with a separate one for the kiddies; the adjacent garden is their playground. This is above all a very acceptable, high-grade family site.

Directions: Take the D9 out of Pégomas. Just outside the town, there's a sweeping left-hand bend and the camp is immediately on your left. There are no prominent signs warning you of the site's proximity. If you're coming from the coast (e.g. N7 or N98), heading north up the D9, you again will see no camp signs, so keep a look out for its pink wall on the right as you approach Pégomas town **Ground:** Hard **Children:** Playground, swimming, organised events **Wheelchair:** Not suitable **Food-cooling:** Ice sold **Sport:** Tennis, volleyball, ping pong **Season:** 1 Apr to 1 Oct **Reservation:** Advisable peak season **Charge:** 2 people and tent 100 fr

▬ Port Grimaud ▬

Camping-Caravanning des Mûres

83360 Grimaud   tel 94.56.16.97

Good amenities are on offer at this very French, three-star beach site

The grounds of this very large camp lie to either side of the N98, on the northern side of the Golfe de St Tropez. The broader inland area of the grounds has some reasonably shady spots, notably near the entrance under a group of tall trees. There's no shade on the beach side, although you have the advantage of being right on the shoreline, which allows you to use your own caravan or camper as a beach-hut at this long stretch of good, sandy beach. From the sands, you have unimpeded views looking out over the bay to St Tropez. Pitch space is far tighter here than across the road. Both grounds are linked by a handy pedestrian tunnel under a very busy main road. Site facilities include a restaurant, self-service, *boulangerie*, *boucherie*, bazaar, fresh fruit and vegetable stall, and a launderette. *Sanitaires* are acceptable, with a few combined shower and wash-basin cubicles. Some of you, though, may be disappointed by the dearth of seated toilets: you have to search for them but the few British campers we saw here didn't seem put out.

● ⑫ 🏃 🛖 🏪 ✕ 🍴 🍷 ⛏ 🏠 🛏 📻 ⚒

Directions: On the busy N98 north-east out of Port Grimaud, you will see on a straight run of road a large red and yellow sign on your left, by a cluster of tall trees. This is the camp entrance **Ground:** Some hard; some sandy **Children:** Playground **Wheelchair:** Not suitable **Food-cooling:** Ice sold **Sport:** Volleyball, ping pong, mini-golf **Season:** Easter to Sept **Reservation:** Advisable peak season **Charge:** 2 people, pitch and car 75 fr

---

A good alternative to a rigid plastic container for keeping a water supply at the pitch is a pliable 'sac'. This is a plastic bag of heavy-duty material finished at either end with a wooden rod to help keep its shape and with a stop-cock at the bottom of one side. It can be strung up from the nearest branch and, when travelling, has the advantage of packing flat.

The Préfecture of Alpes-Maritimes has decreed that, for reasons of hygiene, the département*'s campsites must not accept campers' coolpacks for freezing.*

☼ *Domaine des Naïades*

St Pons-les-Mûres, 83310 Cogolin   tel 94.56.30.08

A campsite with discreet style, offering shady pitches, a luxurious pool complex and plenty of entertainment for all the family

It would be difficult not to be impressed by the attractive pool complex that greets you at Domaine des Naïades, a site run under the auspices of the Automobile Club de France. An Olympic-size pool has a separate, circular children's pool alongside and the snake-like, twisting tubes of a giant aquachute. The higher level of the large restaurant terrace allows you take in this vista while enjoying a beer under the cool, dense canopy of mature vine. This must rank as one of the best campsite bar terraces between Antibes and St Tropez (and we've sipped a lot of beer on a lot of terraces!). Domaine des Naïades seems to cater for all tastes. Leaving the main building, an unassuming two-storey building in white (a relief from the surfeit of pink-painted architecture hereabouts), you enter a beautiful wood of pine, cork-oak and mimosas. Random, levelled *emplacements* offer a tranquil natural environment where you can really feel away from it all. Many pitches have bamboo porches or pergolas, perhaps as car ports, erected for extra shade. Not only does this site offer ideal camping conditions, but plenty of entertainment is laid on: *soirées dansantes*, 'gourmet' evenings, video shows, live entertainment, regular competitions and organised children's games.

● Ⓜ 🜨 ⪫ 🜏 ✗ ♀ ☞ ☀ 🜚 ⌂ 🖳 ♫

Directions: On the N98 going east (just outside Port Grimaud), take the second exit at the roundabout. Further along you will pick up the camp direction sign on a left-hand bend. After the bend, the site entrance appears ahead on the left **Ground:** Hard
Children: Playground, organised events **Wheelchair:** Suitable
Food-cooling: Ice sold **Sport:** Pool table **Season:** Mar to 1 Oct
Reservation: Advisable peak season **Charge:** 4 people, pitch and car 137 fr

---

Destination signs appear to point across the road rather than parallel to it and may take a little getting used to. The 'arrow' traffic light for road filters is far more common than in the UK and should be watched for at junctions and turn-offs.

Régusse

Les Lacs du Verdon

83630 Régusse   tel 94.70.17.95

Luxury, open-air hotel-style site, ideal for family camping near the Verdon

The holiday-villa-style buildings near the entrance convey the impression that Les Lacs du Verdon has something a little extra to offer. As it is a member of the Castel et Camping chain, it ought to. Indeed, among the amenities on offer is access to a private yacht club on the impressive Lac de Ste Croix, a short scenic drive away. The site is quite popular with British families and English-speaking staff work at the reception. The grounds are spread through a forest-parkland of conifers, with broad drives leading to shady, good-sized *emplacements* bounded by stones. The camp is quite level and spacious, but not so large that you have to trek any great distance to get around. It straddles a road, with the majority of the pitches on the facilities' side. The 'annexe' comprises a rather different environment of more random pitches in less shady surroundings. Sanitary appointments are of a good standard and some have combined shower and wash-basin cubicles. In spite of its four-star grading, the site doesn't run a full restaurant: a snack-bar provides basic fare and take-aways. There's a decent pool in the shape of a stubby T (the 'tail' acting as a shallow section for children), and plenty of organised activity is laid on to keep all members of the family happy. Discos are regularly run for the teens. But it's really the scenery that you come for in this region and each fresh-scented morning should find you setting out to explore one more facet of the Verdon's spectacular terrain.

Directions: The D30 by-passes Régusse to the north. Leading off it just outside the village is the D9, signposted for St Jean and the camp itself. The road takes you up to a roundabout in the form of a rockery with conifers. Take the first exit (camp sign here). After, take the first left (another sign). A winding road takes you through holiday villas. The camp will appear on the right of this road, behind a wire fence. Turn right at the end of this for the entrance **Ground:** Hard to giving

Children: Playground, organised events **Wheelchair:** Not suitable
Food-cooling: Ice sold **Sport:** Tennis, volleyball, ping pong, mini-golf, sailing, wind-surfing **Season:** 1 May to 15 Sept
Reservation: Advisable peak season **Charge:** 2 people, pitch and car 74 fr; child (2-7) 16 fr; electricity 13 to 19 fr

▬▬ St Aygulf ▬▬

Sites summary The five principal campsites for St Aygulf, a popular and busy seaside resort with a long promenade and beach, are on the D7 going north from the town. Three merited entries in the Guide. There is a luxury holiday camp, l'Etoile d'Argens, with two smaller, quieter sites. Au Paradis des Campeurs is a beach site and Les Lauriers Roses is further inland.

Etoile d'Argens

83370 St Aygulf	tel 94.81.01.41

A large 'outdoor Hilton' of a camp, with a range of facilities and prices

As soon as you drive down the expansive drive at l'Etoile d'Argens, with its flower beds and date palms, fronting a group of sophisticated contemporary buildings, you can see the place has style. Amenities include no fewer than four tennis courts as part of a self-contained open-air sports complex, two pools plus a kiddies' pool and a subterranean discothèque. Opposite the pools across a courtyard terrace is a large, airy restaurant decorated in cool pastel tones. A la carte or table d'hôte menus are available. The camping ground behind these amenities is a long, flat section stretching to the River Argens. A grid system of two 'arterial' avenues with smaller parallel ones leads to the generously-sized, regimented *emplacements*, marked out by small hedges. Individual sanitary blocks housing all appointments (except for the handicapped facilities which are at the main buildings) are positioned at the end by each small avenue. Little touches include wall-mounted dishracks above the sinks and showers tiled in aquamarine blue. Some may consider the site too large (it has 22 rows of avenues) but the whole lies under abundant shade. Pitch numbers 7-85 and 401-433 (not so shady), are the nearest to the main amenities, so it might be worth trying to reserve one of these when booking. When you reach the river at the back of the site, you'll find a reasonably pretty spot with a calm stretch of water for fishing or boating. There's also the novelty of the camp's very own waterborne taxi service down the river to Fréjus-Plage.

● ⓛ 𝍐 ⏚ ⏚ ✕ ♀ 👌 ⚑ ⋔ ⊟ ▣ ⁊ ♫

Directions: The D7 runs north behind the town of St Aygulf. After a straight run of road some way along, you eventually enter a sweeping left-hand bend where there's a traffic island. Turn at the right-hand junction, signposted D8 Fréjus (by a nursery). On the first bend down this road is a camp sign pointing to a right-hand turn to the camp entrance, on your left **Ground:** Hard to giving
Children: Playground, swimming, organised events
Wheelchair: Suitable **Food-cooling:** Ice sold **Sport:** Tennis, volleyball, ping pong, football, boating, fishing, basketball, mini-golf
Season: 1 Apr to Sept **Reservation:** Advisable peak season
Charge: 3 people, pitch and car 133 fr

☀ *Les Lauriers Roses*

Route de Roquebrune, 83600 St Aygulf   tel 94.81.24.46

Prime little spot, efficiently run by caring management

The young André, who speaks perfect English, will welcome you to his small, attractive site and immediately make you feel at home. Regular British campers, who swear by Les Lauriers Roses as the place to stay in these parts, banter and joke with him like old friends. The camp is set on a lightly wooded hillside (mostly oak trees) and from the entrance you can see the gentle rise of terraces, the top of which overlooks Fréjus, St Raphaël and the sea. You'll find secluded pitches, but not abundant shade, as the foliage is not as dense as it first appears. Nevertheless, the very appealing camping ground is peaceful and the atmosphere is that of an intimate club. This ambience can best be experienced at the neat, modest poolside, where the huddle of crisp, modern, Provençal-style buildings coloured with blooms and climbers makes a very relaxed, comfortable corner in which to pass the time. The immaculate washing facilities include showers combined with wash-basins and another *sanitaire* has low pedestal toilets for toddlers. If you feel energetic, a little gym is at your disposal and there are aerobic sessions or water-polo matches. Along with enjoyable evenings in good company and exhilarating days on the coast or in the hills, you've reason enough to book up, but be warned – Les Lauriers Roses is small and very popular so its 100 pitches are usually reserved quite early on.

○ ⓢ ♫ ⌂ ⚓ ♀ ☞ ♨ 𝄫 ⬒ ▣ ℘

Directions: Take the D7 north out of St Aygulf. You will soon pass a small lake on the right. Further on you will see a modern, pinkish rectangular building standing on its own on your left. Immediately after is the yellow and red camp sign, indicating a left-turn to the camp **Ground:** Hard **Children:** Playground, swimming, organised events, babysitting if required, using alarms **Wheelchair:** Suitable **Food-cooling:** Ice sold **Sport:** Volleyball, ping pong, gym **Season:** 7 Apr to 13 Oct **Reservation:** Advisable peak season **Charge:** 2 people, pitch and car 76 fr

Au Paradis des Campeurs

83370 St Aygulf   tel 94.96.93.55

Small, immaculate, family-run site with direct access to a good beach

On the coastal run going south from St Aygulf to Les Issambres is a fine beach called La Gaillarde-Plage. Directly opposite, tucked away behind the road, is Au Paradis des Campeurs. It is run by an Italian, who speaks nearly every other European language except English, and his two sons who do. Au Paradis is a good example of a small camp with an informal yet caring management attitude. The site is kept scrupulously clean, right down to the clearing of rubbish from a pitch straight after a departure. Numerous shrubs and colourful blooms give the small ground a pretty appearance. The camp's layout follows a squared 's' shape, the middle portion being the less shady. Although small trees segregate the pitches, their aspect is more open than secluded. The main *sanitaire* near the front is a large, well-designed building that maintains the high standard of upkeep on this site. A bar, restaurant and well-stocked shop are by the road above the site (the camp's lower level helps reduce traffic noise here). In general the place is quite peaceful. The beach can be reached from your pitch via a path at the back of the camp which goes under the N98 through a short tunnel. Once there you can enjoy a lovely sweeping view across the bay to St Raphaël and the hills beyond.

◐ Ⓢ 🏊 🚤 🛒 ✕ 🍷 ⛵ 🐾 ⛺ 🏕 🗃

Directions: Going out of St Aygulf on the coastal N98 en route to Port Grimaud, you will see a 1 km camp direction sign on the right. Further along, opposite a beach with roadside parking on your left, there is a short stretch of dual carriageway. On the right, opposite this, is a large camp sign in big red letters. Turn right at this point and immediately after, turn right again down a track taking you to the site entrance
Ground: Hard   **Children:** Playground   **Wheelchair:** Not suitable
Food-cooling: Ice sold   **Sport:** Volleyball, ping pong   **Season:** Easter to Sept   **Reservation:** Advisable peak season   **Charge:** 3 people, pitch and car 88.15 fr

▰▰ St Maximin-la-Ste-Baume ▰▰

Camping-Caravanning Provençal

Chemin de Mazaugues, 83470   tel 94.78.16.97
St Maximin-la-Ste-Baume

Well-run, if rather scruffy site, in a good position for town; popular with French campers

Don't be too disappointed with the rather bare-looking entrance with caravans parked in the forecourt and the beginnings of a scrubby wood beyond the reception. Further into the camp the grounds become more landscaped, with the addition of a few willows. Near the centre of the camp, there is a well-kept *sanitaire* with seated toilets. At the back of this is the main swimming-pool overlooked by a raised terrace with bar and pizzeria. It's in this area that all the social goings-on occur, bringing the camp to life with fancy dress competitions and the like. The French family campers, who really go to town on such occasions, create a great party atmosphere. At other times, decorum prevails as the management keeps the running of the place on a tight rein. The site is a curious mix of pleasant areas, such as the children's well-equipped playground in its own little cultivated patch, and the more unkempt reaches at the back of the camping ground. Camping Provençal is worth considering as a base in this area. Its biggest asset is that it's right on the doorstep of St Maximin. From the wide pavement cafés and restaurants in the town square you can watch others go about their business, while taking your time over an inexpensive yet palatable lunch.

● ⑤ 🌊 🏊 ✕ ♀ 🥄 🏠 🛏 🔋 ⚒

Directions: Just outside St Maximin going south on the N560, is a
railway bridge. Take the first left after passing under it, signposted D64
Mazaugues. You will see a big red and white sign to the camp. Continue
straight across at the crossroads with traffic-lights. Further on, take a
fork to the right and the site will be immediately on your right
Ground: Hard **Children:** Playground, swimming, organised events
Wheelchair: Not suitable **Food-cooling:** Ice sold **Sport:** Volleyball,
ping pong **Season:** Easter to Sept **Reservation:** Advisable peak
season **Charge:** Pitch 17 fr; person 15 fr; child (under 7) 10 fr;
electricity 9 to 16 fr

▰▰▰ St Paul-en-Forêt ▰▰▰▰▰▰

☼ *Camping-Caravanning Le Parc*

St Paul-en-Forêt,   tel 94.76.15.35
83440 Fayence-en-Provence

*Tranquil, attractive, forest site, with little in the way of
entertainment*

The loudest sound to greet our ears at this densely wooded site
was the miaow of the resident cat. Three words sum up
everything about Le Parc: serenity, seclusion and shade. The
glare of the sun vanishes as you enter the gently sloping terrain
of a cool pine forest. Pitches spread through the trees are given
breathing space and are roomy enough for caravans. The
grounds are small in terms of camping accommodation, but
large enough to prevent any feeling of claustrophobia. The
single *sanitaire* (with seated toilets) is attractively decorated
with colourful blooms. Its long, low, white building with dark
wooden doors looks appropriate in the forest scene. On the
higher camp ground the main amenities are grouped together
in an area exposed to the sun – the swimming pool, a large
snack-bar and a shop that offers delicatessen fare among its
provisions. From the balcony terrace at the bar you can sit back
and relax while watching others sweat it out on the tennis court
immediately below. Perhaps you'd prefer to relax in docile,
nearby St Paul or its neighbouring village, Bagnols-en-Forêt.
An alternative might be a tour around old Provençal villages,
with castles and crafts, to the north (D563): Fayence,
Tourrettes, Callian, Montauroux. And if this isn't enough,

spend an afternoon in the verdant scenery of Lac St Cassien (D562, east to Grasse) for some fishing or bathing. While the site is not suitable for a family that needs entertaining, those who seek a little sanity and spiritual recharging will be more than satisfied.

● ⑤ 🏄 🛶 🛒 ⬛ 🍖 🎋 ▣ 🔧

Directions: St Paul-en-Forêt lies on the D4 between Fréjus and Fayence. If you are coming from the south, as you enter the village there is a high grey-stone wall of the car park on your right. At the end of this, the D4 turns off right (camp direction sign here). Further along this road you will see ahead of you a large pink house set back in its own grounds and by this another camp direction sign. This is followed immediately by another camp sign on your left, telling you to take a right-hand turn. The camp is on this road, on your left **Ground:** Hard **Children:** Playground, swimming **Wheelchair:** Not suitable **Food-cooling:** Ice sold **Sport:** Tennis, volleyball, ping pong, badminton **Season:** All year **Reservation:** Advisable peak season **Charge:** Pitch 23.50 fr; person 20 fr; child (under 7) 10 fr; electricity 12 fr

Vence

Domaine de la Bergerie

06140 Vence   tel 93.58.09.36

Cool, sedate surroundings, but no pool at this quiet camp

Hidden among the cool shadows and greenery of natural, unspoilt grounds, at first glance Domaine de la Bergerie could be just another desirable, stone-built private villa whose garden and driveway broaden out into a thick conifer forest. The appearance of caravans confirms that this is indeed a campsite. The absence of the conventional focus of amenities surrounded by marked-out *emplacements* makes this camp very unusual indeed. The attraction at this camp is first and foremost its atmosphere of seclusion and silence. You won't find any entertainment here (except perhaps the odd cinema show) and the athletic, young camping clientele are the last sort of people who would relish staying at La Bergerie. It positively encourages the older and more sedate holidaymaker who appreciates a quiet time. On a practical level, there's a small snack-bar with outdoor seating where tasty *plats cuisinés* are served. Washing arrangements consist of two older blocks with showers too small to swing a cat in, and a far more modern, larger block with better facilities that include provision for wheelchair users. The nearby thriving little town of Vence is a good venue for shopping and eating out, or even a visit to the municipal pool if you fancy a dip.

● Ⓜ 〽 ⚑ ✕ ♀ ☞ ⌂ ⊟ ⚲

Directions: In Vence, follow the main road (to the top of town) which filters right (camp direction sign here). After traffic-lights and then the D2210A Tourrette-sur-Loup road takes you under a road-bridge. Just beyond, you cross a small valley via a level bridge. At the roundabout, take the third exit. Continue straight on at the crossroads (camp direction sign here). Drive down this residential road and you will see a green camp sign on the right, immediately followed by a right-hand turn to the site entrance. (Because of the one-way system, going back to Vence from the camp, you will turn right at the above-mentioned crossroads.) **Ground:** Hard **Children:** Not suitable
Wheelchair: Suitable **Food-cooling:** Ice sold **Sport:** Volleyball, ping pong **Season:** Apr to Oct **Reservation:** Advisable peak season
Charge: 3 people, pitch and car 60.50 fr; pitch with electricity 73.50 fr

showers too small to swing a cat in

Dordogne

The Dordogne beloved by the British holidaymaker is not quite that of the administrative *département* of the same name. Rather, it is the broad parcel of land that encompasses the valley of the River Dordogne from Brive and Périgueux in the north, to the banks of the Lot in the south (see the map overleaf), an area more akin to the original Périgord and Quercy regions of old. For many, the essence of this region is captured in scenes of dramatic precipices rising from the meander of a wide, sedate river capped with golden-walled châteaux. In other parts, as you cruise along some leafy by-way, you might for a split second think that you were in Surrey, so comfortably familiar is the greenness of it all.

Abutting the south-eastern border of Dordogne is the Lot – again the name for both river and administrative region. The River Dordogne clips its most northerly tip, carrying with it the heavier concentration of tourist sights, while the Lot lies in the southern half. Between these two twisting waterways (which cartography depicts as a pair of pythons wriggling from west to east) the lie of the land settles into large stretches of contrasting terrain. At its western edge long empty roads, such as the one going south from Domme, traverse hectares of general agriculture towards the more specific crops of tobacco, maize and vine that find benefit in the warmer climes and rich soils of the Lot valley itself. In the centre of the *département* are the Causses, large tracts of wilder country consisting of gorges and plateaux. This hinterland, while having less 'touristy' appeal, does offer high rolling hills and wide horizons.

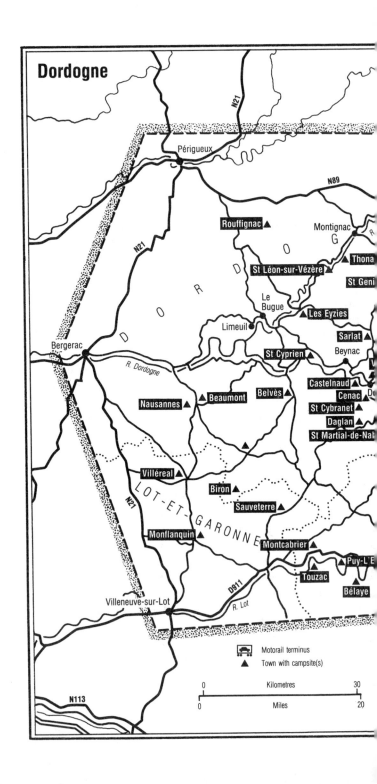

Dordogne

Périgueux

N21

N89

Rouffignac ▲   Montignac
                                    G
St Léon-sur-Vézère ▲   ▲ Thona

O   St Geni

D   Le
         Bugue ▲ Les Eyzies

Limeuil ●   Sarlat ▲

R   Beynac ●

Bergerac   St Cyprien ▲

R. Dordogne   Castelnaud ▲
                                            Cenac ▲
         ▲ Beaumont   Belvès ▲   St Cybranet ▲
Nausannes ▲   Daglan ▲
                                 St Martial-de-Nab

                        ▲

Villéreal ▲
         Biron ▲
         Sauveterre ▲

L O T - E T - G A R O N N E

Monflanquin ▲   Montcabrier ▲
                                    Puy-L'E

N21   ▲
                        Touzac
         D911   Bélaye
Villeneuve-sur-Lot ●   R. Lot

N113

| | Motorail terminus |
| ▲ | Town with campsite(s) |

| 0 | Kilometres | 30 |
| 0 | Miles | 20 |

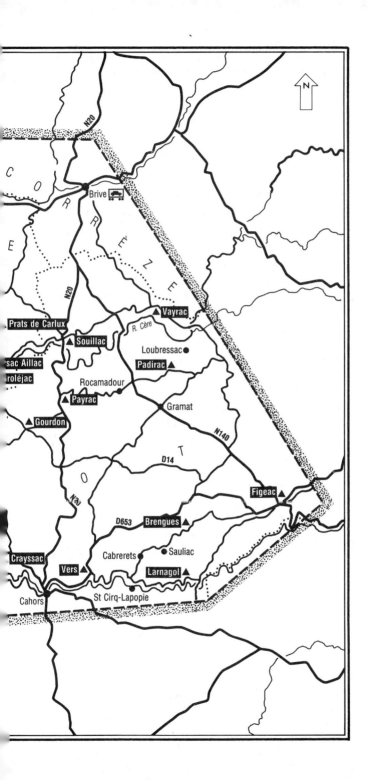

The River Lot effuses a quieter beauty than the Dordogne, with lush green woods reflected in smooth waters and small villages nestling on its banks. Up-river between Cahors and Figeac is a tributary called the Célé, which flows along a limestone gorge rather than zig-zagging lazily through a wider plain. Instead of relishing the water scenery you can find roads that will lead you over higher ground, where you can take in whole vistas of oak-covered plateau cut with limestone scars. This is the land of the ancient province of Quercy, whose name is derived from 'Cadurci', a term describing the Celtic tribes who lived there at the time of the Roman invasion.

The Vézère is a tributary of the Dordogne running south-east from Brive and although on a less grand scale it has its own attractive quality with its heavily wooded banks. But the more important aspect of the valley is that it is the cradle of Western Europe's prehistory. The major factor that contributed to early man's population of the area – other than a favourable climate and a source of good food – was the natural shelter offered by caves and rock hollows. These had long been created by the process of water eroding the limestone strata found there. Nowadays sightseers can explore the more cavernous of these *grottes* to be awed by spectacular netherworld scenery of sculptural stalactites and stalagmites, referred to as 'concretions' in the cave world.

But such geological phenomena must play second fiddle to the experience of witnessing the first tentative image-making of our prehistoric ancestors. Evidence of the existence of Homo Sapiens in the form of Neanderthal Man dates back to the Lower Palaeolithic period around 800,000 years ago, but it was his successor who gave us his unique inheritance – the birth of Art. Cromagnon Man didn't appear until 30,000 years ago. His presence in the Dordogne was discovered in 1868 at Les Eyzies where excavations revealed the remains of four adults and a young child. Cave painting itself came much later on – from twelve to twenty thousand years later – and was most prolific in a cultural period of the Upper Palaeolithic era known as Magdalenian. It was at this time that the development of the lamp, in the form of a hollowed-out stone containing animal fat and a wick, enabled people to illuminate cave interiors. The absence of domestic evidence suggests that such caves were never lived in. Far from being mere decoration, painting deep underground must have had some ritualistic or magical significance. Nearly always, the subject matter is animal, mostly horses, bison, deer or mammoths. Human figures are few and are depicted only as archetypical stick-men or anonymous silhouettes. In fact, the portrayal of Man – or more specifically Woman – is far more frequent in the sensitively carved stone figures of this and earlier periods.

Over and above the summary of caves and grottoes listed at the end of this region's introduction, special mention must be made of **Lascaux**. It was here in the autumn of 1940 that some local boys looking for their dog in fissures in the ground stumbled on probably the most important find of prehistoric art. Completely preserved in their brilliant ochre hues were depictions of whole herds of animals from bulls to bison. The irony of such a discovery was that while the paintings had remained intact for thousands of years, it took only twenty, exposing them to the inquisitive public, to cause their deterioration. The original Lascaux cave is now closed to all but professionals in the field. This does not mean, however, we are deprived of experiencing this unique site. With typical Gallic enterprise, Lascaux II was built nearby, painstakingly modelled to reproduce every crevice and contour of the original. Each position of the drawn animals was plotted on a complicated grid, transferred to the artificial cave and then painted in near-authentic colours. You enter an ante-room containing an explanatory display of both the making of Lascaux II and the visual aspects of the paintings, and then are taken into the semi-darkness of our distant past to return for a moment to our spiritual beginnings.

Although this welter of prehistory is supremely impressive, for many visitors the true taste of the region lies on the plate. If France has educated Europe in culinary aspirations, then here must be one of the seats of learning. Food is important to the *Périgourdin*, not only as a pleasure but also as a prime source of income. Every so often you pass on the road a goose farm where the flat, open ground heaves with dull brown waves of feathered flesh as huge gaggles of birds move as one to a multi-horn accompaniment. Their eventual force-fed demise gives the world *foie gras* – that most refined of French gastronomic delights. Incredibly, the separate family-run concerns collectively produce nearly 2,000 tons of the product every year.

Often associated with *foie gras* as an optional ingredient is that rare, much-prized subterranean fungus, the truffle. But the more accessible *cèpes* – mushrooms with a rich, nutty taste – can still provide the palate with an enjoyable exercise. A local dish of *omelette aux cèpes* becomes more than just a mushroom omelette when the *cèpes* have first been fried with garlic in duck or goose fat. Produce found throughout this region is remarkably diverse, from walnuts to strawberries and prunes, goat's cheese to *confits* and pâtés, rabbit to pork and beef. All can of course be enjoyed with the wines of Bergerac and Cahors. There is even a nut liqueur (*eau de noix*).

The camping menu is equally diverse. Such an area of concentrated tourism has given rise to all types of sites, from mere canoeing bases to open-air hotels. In the *département* of the Dordogne, there seem to be two generic types, especially prominent to the south of the river: new-generation camps and older, more established places. With the former you find not just more modern appointments but young French owners who are committed to high standards and a willingness to please. Some of these camps haven't developed full amenities, such as a restaurant on-site, but are nevertheless being continually improved.

The latter type comprises what could be called the 'hardy perennials' of Dordogne camping. These are usually the larger, longer-running sites more often than not favoured by the big package holiday companies. With a jaundiced eye you might view them as money machines where expenditure on minor improvements is not considered necessary as uncomplaining punters keep coming back year after year anyway. There are of course notable exceptions.

It all comes down to the attitude of management – something which can be judged from the presentation of their literature and booking conditions. Other than a quirky use of English in some brochures ('*We are especially attached to the cleanlines of the modern and functional toilet blocks*'; '*Two enlightened boule areas*'), rules and regulations can give a revealing insight into how a site owner is predisposed to his or her clientele. Although you may read that visiting friends who don't respect the management's request to check out when leaving may induce some '*very unpleasant action*' or that in warm, dry weather '*you should be so kind as to water our young trees (no waste water)*', such officiousness is not really to be taken seriously once one is happily browning away by the pool of the camp in question. It is interesting to note that such an approach to site management is one predominantly associated with Dutch ownership – not uncommon in the Dordogne. It is also worth considering that an 'efficient' camp is not necessarily one blessed with character.

Camping in the country between the two great rivers further south doesn't offer much for those who rely on a good standard of amenities and surroundings as a priority for relaxed holidaymaking. The better sites are those nearer the Lot and the Célé but even some of these don't match the sophistication of the larger Dordogne camps. You are drawn into a simpler, quieter daily existence of pottering around local towns or soaking in the landscape with a bit of walking, rambling or canoeing, rather than 'doing the sights' and poolside tanning.

Beynac and Castelnaud

These twin towns on the River Dordogne present the eye with a splendid marriage of architecture and water. Both are dominated by the fortifications which are a heritage of the Hundred Years War. The more château-like version at Beynac is best seen from the river, while Castelnaud's ruined fort gives commanding views of the valley plain.

Brive

Brive is the northern gateway to Périgord, especially for users of Motorail. Although outward bound you'll probably see no more than the breakfast cafeteria, you may like to take a stroll through its centre if you have time to kill at the other end of the holiday. A short walk from the station in the tackier part of town takes you to the old heart of the city, now a successfully pedestrianised area of small, tidy streets consisting of smart shops and cafés. Here, too, is a Monoprix supermarket useful for that last-minute shopping.

Cabrerets

Not far from the confluence of the Rivers Lot and Célé the village of Cabrerets, with its rows of houses lining the river edge, sits under a low cliff overhang. There is a museum of prehistory inspired by the nearby *grotte* (Pech-Merle) that equals any of the Vézère valley – see the end of this introduction.

Cahors

This is the focal point of the Quercy region, once the ancient capital and now the centre of a thriving wine and tourist economy. There is plenty to see, notably the Pont Valentré, a possible contender for Europe's most beautiful bridge. It was conceived in 1308 as a fortress to control that part of the river and afford the town some security. It spans the River Lot with seven graceful, buttressed Gothic arches and is unique in having three tall, square towers along its length. There is a legend attached to its construction in which the architect, despairing at the slow progress of its building, made a pact with the Devil to bring at once all the necessary materials, in return for his soul. Towards the end of the bridge's completion the architect cheated by asking the Devil to bring him water in a sieve – a task which, for all his powers, Satan admitted impossible to do. In revenge he broke off the top stone of the central tower, known to this day as Devil's Tower. Also worth seeing is the cathedral of St Etienne, which has foundations that date from the sixth century, although the main structure was erected around the beginning of the 1100s. Successive centuries have added their respective decorations but the overall appearance is of Byzantine influence, as with Périgueux cathedral. For a lovely view of the town, get to the hill just south of the river (Mont St Cyr) towards dusk.

Domme

A must on any sightseer's itinerary. It lies set back from the River Dordogne, on a near-perpendicular cliff. From below, you have little impression of what it might hold. Domme is an example of a *bastide* town, many of which are situated between the Dordogne and the Lot. *Bastides* were built in the Middle Ages by both the English and the French during their prolonged battles for this part of France and are essentially fortified towns with grid-based streets. Founded in 1283, the village within its walls is remarkably preserved, enhanced by a profusion of flowers. There is also a profusion of souvenir, craft and local produce shops along the main thoroughfare, but you will eventually reach the square at the top which has one of the finest panoramas of the valley. Here, too, is the covered market (market day is Thursday) which also houses the entrance to an insignificant *grotte*.

Les Eyzies-de-Tayac

The so-called capital of prehistory (see below for numerous geological and prehistorical visits in the vicinity). Lying squat against a rock overhang, this one-road town is packed – but *packed* – in season. Gazing out from the cliff by the National Museum of Prehistory is an Epsteinesque statue representing Cromagnon Man, apparently wishing he could be anywhere else but there. As a diversion from ancient archaeology, try the trade fair which is in effect a high-quality indoor market of local produce. Market day is Tuesday.

Figeac

One of the two most important towns of the region along with Cahors, Figeac is a focus for trade and commerce. The N140 thunders down to it from Brive and the rest of northern France, so it isn't a prepossessing place save for the old quarter, where a few pedestrianised streets are quite attractive. You wouldn't expect to find a museum on Egyptology in south-west rural France but there's one here. It honours one of Figeac's more famous sons, Jean-François Champollion (1790-1983), who was the first person to decipher the mysteries of hieroglyphics.

Gramat

The Parc de Vision (south of Gramat on the D14, south-east of Rocamadour) is a nature reserve (and botanical garden) set up by various bodies to protect the indigenous species of the region, and contains wolf, lynx, boar, badger, bison, deer, wild sheep as well as birds of prey. The Causse de Gramat is a large expanse of limestone plateau that can be summed up as high, wild and beautiful.

Limeuil

If you climb up the steeply inclined streets to the château, you are rewarded by a fine view of the union of the Rivers Vézère and Dordogne, south-west of Les Eyzies.

Loubressac

Just to the north-east of Padirac on the D118, Loubressac is a typical village of Haute Quercy with its stone-tiled houses surrounding a modest fifteenth-century château. From here can be enjoyed panoramic views of the Dordogne, Bave and Cère valleys. The same goes for the Château de Castelnau, a few kilometres to the north, but the building itself is a much grander affair. This great walled, redstone fortress, once housing a garrison of 1,500 men, was originally built in the eleventh century and was then extended during the Hundred Years War.

Montignac

At the northern end of the Vézère valley, Montignac is the stopping-off point for the Lascaux cave (see below). It is a bottle-neck for road-users but nowhere near as bad as Les Eyzies down-river in high season. Small and bustling, it has a useful range of shops and one or two banks, plus the inevitable Palaeolithic souvenir items. It is an interesting place to be during the August Fête as you can watch water-borne jousting tournaments on the river beyond the town bridge.

Périgueux

Périgueux is the historical capital of the Périgord region, dating from Roman times. Its two main attributes are the large market, which seems to spill over with produce from across the Dordogne, and a beautiful multi-domed cathedral – more imposing outside than in. Its appearance suggests a hint of the Orient which stems from the Byzantine style of architecture. Market day is Saturday.

Puy-l'Evêque

From almost any angle Puy l'Evêque is a picture-postcard town, clustered around a small promontory alongside the river bank. England once occupied the town during the Hundred Years War. The old town by the water's edge comprises picturesque pieces of architecture, such as the fifteenth-century bell tower. Here, too, are vineyards associated with the famous wines of Cahors, lying some kilometres up-river. Villages such as **Bélaye** and **Crayssac** (on the D8 and D9 respectively) on winding roads leading up from the valley floor will reward visitors with wide vistas of the landscape.

Rocamadour

This was once Europe's most visited places of pilgrimage during the Middle Ages. It still attracts vast numbers, such are its photogenic attributes. Nearly every café and campsite within a radius of twenty kilometres has a poster of it, and you might be persuaded that you have no need to experience it for yourself. This would be a pity, for if you are prepared for the overcrowded roads and streets, the sheer dramatic presence of this edifice in the surrounding landscape is something that needs witnessing at first hand. Pressed hard against a 500-foot precipitous, bare limestone cliff are the buildings of this medieval fortress town, the most prominent being the twelfth-century church of St Sauveur. Above that and crowning the whole rock is the château looking out across a small, sparse canyon. Within the walls, pierced by five gates, the town has been extensively restored. The incline of the main street takes you to the Via Sancta, a stone stairway of over 200 steps leading up and up to the château and various sanctuaries. One houses the Vierge Noire – the Black Virgin – an austere early Gothic piece of sculpture in wood. For those for whom the many steps are daunting or impossible a lift service is provided. A diversion from history can be found in the rock's permanent ornithological residents – various birds of prey, including eagles and vultures, with daily flying demonstrations in season.

St Cirq-Lapopie

The *'Première Village de France'* sits tightly on top of a rocky edifice overlooking a bend in the River Lot; it is indeed a beautiful village, with quaint old houses and church in narrow streets, and its height gives splendid views. Traditionally it was a centre for woodworkers, and a variety of hand-made crafts from ceramics to leather goods can be bought from local artisans. St Cirq is but a couple of paddlestrokes from where the Célé joins the Lot. Its course descends from Figeac in the north-west through an attractive gorge.

Sarlat

Sarlat-la-Canéda, to give it its full name, lies a dozen or so kilometres north of the river and is by far the largest town of the tourist heartland. This being so, it's a bit of a driver's nightmare but well worth finding a parking space to be able to spend some time in the old quarter. Here you can appreciate the beautifully restored yellow sandstone buildings, with stone-tiled roofs that date from the twelfth to the eighteenth centuries, because the narrow streets are pedestrianised. Many a film director has exploited the ornately carved window surrounds and gables as the perfect Middle Ages backdrop. Street entertainers such as puppeteers are ever-present and between mid-July and mid-August there's an annual open-air drama festival. Market day is Saturday.

Sauliac

At Sauliac on the River Célé, halfway between Cahors and Figeac, is the Musée de Plein Air de Quercy. Established on the lands once belonging to Cuzals Castle, it is in essence an exhibition of the culture and industry of the Quercy people. Many traditional crafts are represented as well as agricultural methods and machinery. In season there are also numerous demonstrations.

Souillac

Souillac is a centre of commerce rather than a tourist spot with the usual attributes of banks, hotels and fastfood establishments (although there are a few decent restaurants). As it straddles the main north-south route of the N20, it perpetually hums with traffic but little side streets tucked behind the main road give the visitor a quieter area to walk around. There is a sprinkling of small, interesting shops as well as a twelfth-century Byzantine-style church. Market day is Friday.

Geological and prehistorical visits

Some of the remarkable variety of geological and prehistorical phenomena of this region are summarised below.

Bara-Bahau (Le Bugue, south-west of Les Eyzies): a mixture of *grotte* and cave art – examples of the oldest discoveries by way of line drawings. Also flint-cut animal engravings.

Cap Blanc (east of Les Eyzies, on the D48): a rock shelter rather than a cave, with a forty-five foot long frieze of deeply etched animals, plus a remarkably sophisticated relief carving of a horse.

Castel-Merle (Sergeac, south-west of Montignac): prehistoric village with Magdalenian sculptures.

Centre d'Art Préhistorique (north of Thonac, south-west of Montignac): a piece of modern architecture set on the hill of Le Thot houses displays and explanations of cave art in relation to different periods. Outside is a small animal park, the residents of which, such as small deer, are meant to be representative of species found in prehistoric times.

Font-de-Gaume (Les Eyzies): ticket reservations ensure entry to this popular cave which, with its beautifully subtle polychrome paintings, is the next best thing to being in the original Lascaux.

Le Gouffre de Padirac (north-east of Rocamadour): another great honeypot of a sight. It is a big hole in the ground: in fact, it is a 32 metres wide and 75 metres deep hole, and could have originated from a collapsed cavern. Lifts are provided for the descent into its bowels but a succession of steps allows you to walk all the way down if you wish. Once down, you are taken by boat along an underground river into numerous subterranean chasms.

La Grotte de Carpe-Diem (north-west of Les Eyzies): a 200-metre long chamber with a profusion of stalactites dripping from the ceilings.

La Grotte aux Cent Mammouths (Between Rouffignac and Les Eyzies off the D32): over a hundred linear drawings of mammoths, bison and so on, lying deep in the hillside. You are taken on an electric train ride into the long narrow chambers. The guide nearly gives you a heart attack by stopping the train and turning the cave lights off! This is to allow him to demonstrate with the aid of a torch the sort of conditions in which Cromagnon Man had to work at his art.

Grotte de Grand Roc (Les Eyzies): set high in the cliffs about the town and river. Interesting and well-illuminated concretions.

Grotte du Pech-Merle (Cabrerets): a vast cavern filled with paintings of mammoths, bison, horses and antelopes.

Gouffre de Proumeyssac (south of Le Bugue): a huge, beautifully lit chasm known as the 'Crystal Cathedral': geology's answer to Gothic architecture. Special arrangements can be made for those confined to a wheelchair.

Lacave (north-west of Rocamadour): an electric train journey deep into the cliffside takes you to a lift that ascends to larger chambers of subterranean lakes stage-lit to display the concretions and reflections there to maximum effect.

Lascaux (Montignac): a simulated experience (see introduction) but worthwhile nevertheless. A reasonable restaurant is situated near the entrance to the original cave.

La Madeleine (north of Les Eyzies): the site of this rock shelter beside the Vézère gave its name to the Magdalenian culture, so important were the finds here. You can see various excavations, dwellings and a permanent exhibition.

National Museum of Prehistory (Les Eyzies): concise collection of artefacts representing Palaeolithic technology as well as many carvings and figure sculptures.

La Roque St Christophe (between Tursac and Le Moustier, north-east of Les Eyzies): a long cliff face consisting of five storeys of what are known as aerial *cluseaux* (from the latin '*clusellus*', an enclosed space). These dwellings, hyped up as being a Troglodite fortress, are not as impressive as they sound but the geological structure of the cliff's fractured horizontal strata is interesting enough.

Tourist offices

Office Départemental du
   Tourisme de la Dordogne
16 rue Wilson
24009 Périgueux
Tel 53.53.44.35

Camping Information Dordogne
24290 Montignac-Lascaux
Tel 53.50.79.80

Comité Départemental du
   Tourisme du Lot
Chambre de Commerce
46001 Cahors
Tel 65.35.07.09

Loisirs-Accueil dans le Lot
Maison de l'Agriculture
430 avenue Jean-Jaurès
46000 Cahors
Tel 65.22.55.30

▰▰▰ Beaumont ▰▰▰▰▰▰▰▰▰▰

Les Remparts

24440 Beaumont-du-Périgord	tel 53.22.40.86

A small, shaded, fairly basic but well-kept site. A good stop-over

This small but well-shaded campsite nestles in a pinewood behind the local municipal recreation ground. There's an attractive bar area with a covered terrace by a neat rectangular pool. Although not much is on offer in the way of food other than snacks, Beaumont, a *bastide* town, is literally round the corner for restaurants and provisions. The site seems well kept and lays on minimal facilities such as an area in which to do ironing. While not a place for a family to linger at any great length, it does make for a good break in a cross-country journey, especially with those cool and shady pines easing the heat of a sightseeing day.

Directions: At the crossroads in Beaumont take the road signposted Villéreal. A few hundred yards down this road on your right is a small municipal sports ground. The camp is behind this **Ground:** Giving
Children: Playground **Wheelchair:** Suitable
Food-cooling: Coolpacks frozen **Sport:** Tennis **Season:** Easter to 15 Oct **Reservation:** Advisable peak season **Charge:** 2 people, pitch, car and caravan 45 fr; electricity 11 fr

▰▰▰ Belvès ▰▰▰▰▰▰▰▰▰▰

Les Hauts de Ratebout

24170 Belvès	tel 53.29.02.10

Tautly run and well-appointed tent town for the gregarious. Parents will relish all the distractions for their offspring

Welcome to the country club of the Dordogne, complete with gravelled courtyard and stone fountain. In this Dutch-run camp, prices and hiring fees are generally on the high side but you do have nearly every facility at your disposal, and the recipe attracts much repeat custom. As much English can be heard as on Brighton beach. There's a gym (keep it clean, please) if you feel like sweating indoors instead of under the high summer sun. Perhaps a better way to burn energy is to hire a camp bike and take in the surrounding countryside. If you get really bored there is even a video room (no noise allowed). An exploration of the immaculately restored farmhouse buildings reveals a daintily laid out restaurant, while British families galore have a splashing good time round the pool that is the camp's centrepiece. In high season plenty of organised activities take place, such as tournaments and soirées, and the weekly disco is, according to one courier, not allowed to play one minute over midnight. The packed terraces offer less in the way of shade than further down the hill, where it is also a lot quieter. If you mind more about a launderette with two dryers than lots of space, this camp is not to be knocked.

🌑 ⓛ 🏃 ⛵ 🏧 ✕ ♀ 🛒 🐛 🍴 ⛁ 📻 ✦ 🗝 🎵

Directions: From Belvès, go south on the D710. Fork left on to the D54, then follow winding track at signpost, leading you up high on a hill (well-signposted) **Ground:** Hard to giving **Children:** Playground, swimming, organised events, playroom **Wheelchair:** Suitable **Food-cooling:** Ice sold **Sport:** Tennis, ping pong, hire-bikes, gym, canoe trips, badminton, pool table **Season:** 1 May to 21 Sept **Reservation:** Advisable peak season **Charge:** Pitch 38 fr; person 25 fr; electricity 40 fr

❀ Le Moulin de la Pique

24170 Belvès   tel 53.29.01.15

Elegant, photogenic and serene site in which to unwind, but plenty to occupy the children too

To the manor born – or so you could pretend, as long as you ignore the tents. Set in the grounds of an imposing nineteenth-century yellow stone clay-tiled villa, this site is on the small side but perfectly formed. A serene atmosphere prevails, even around the pools. The villa itself contains most of the amenities – shop, bar, laundry, squeaky-clean washing facilities and so on, plus a small library and reading room upstairs. An adjacent block in the same architectural style serves as holiday apartments. Behind both, well-shaded *emplacements* encircle a small, picturesque lake, but the newer camping areas are more exposed. The first-floor restaurant is a cool, high-ceilinged room with wooden flooring, modest décor, rattan furniture and a balcony terrace bounded by square pillars at one end: the whole smacks of a gentlemen's club set in some oriental clime.

Directions: Take the D170 going south out of Belvès. You'll see the camp sign along the road. Soon you'll see what looks like a small road off to your left: this is in fact the site entrance (again, signposted) **Ground:** Hard to giving **Children:** Playground, swimming, toddlers' playroom, TV room **Wheelchair:** Suitable **Food-cooling:** Ice sold, coolpacks frozen **Sport:** Ping pong, boating, fishing **Season:** Easter to 1 Oct **Reservation:** Advisable peak season **Charge:** Pitch 27.50 fr; person 20.50 fr; electricity 12 fr

the whole smacks of a gentlemen's club set in some oriental clime.

Les Nauves

Le Bos Rouge, 24170 Belvès	Out-of-season tel 53.29.07.87
	tel 53.29.12.64

Secluded and spacious modern site, perfect for horse-riders and relaxation-seekers

A hard-working young couple run this peaceful site with gusto. They are particular about the chlorine-free pool (salt only); and are careful to preserve a sense of spaciousness. The camp is in the middle of fields and hills belonging to the estate. You can choose between generously sized *emplacements* in either a well-shaded copse area or a larger, more open (therefore sunnier) one. The buildings are modern and suitably appointed, the tidy restaurant unpretentiously decked out in check tablecloths and simple wooden furnishings. Barbecue evenings are occasionally laid on. The site isn't geared up for children other than horse-mad ones, with riding to be enjoyed in the surrounding woodland on gentle steeds from the camp's own stable. And if it is just the two of you, there couldn't be a better place for a very private holiday.

Directions: From Belvès take the D53 towards Monpazier. Look for a left-hand turn with camp's signpost. This should be the turning for Larzac. Take this lane and you'll come across a left fork, where another camp sign directs you to the entrance **Ground:** Hard
Children: Playground **Wheelchair:** Suitable
Food-cooling: Coolpacks frozen **Sport:** Ping pong, horse-riding, canoeing-trips **Season:** 1 June to 30 Sept **Reservation:** Advisable peak season **Charge:** Pitch 26 fr; person 18 fr; electricity 12 fr

■■■■ Biron ■■■■■■■■■■■■■■■■■■■■■■■■■■■■

Étang du Moulinal

24540 Biron	tel 53.40.84.60

How the French like to camp – no fancy frills but aesthetically pleasing. Good value and plenty of organised activities

Imagine . . . the hint of an evening breeze has sprung up once more. You are sitting under a cane canopy relishing a generous three-course meal which will not leave a hole in your pocket. Beyond the terrace, a small, still lake reflects a patchwork of colour from the tents clustered on the bank. Idyllic it sounds, and idyllic it can still be, despite having been discovered by the package scene: informal pitches at a neighbourly distance (but not too tight), restful views, a good family atmosphere generated by mostly French visitors and aesthetically designed shower-blocks hinting at Provençal architecture, with red-tiled roofs and pebblestone floors. As night falls the disco music drifts over the water from the bar. Why turn in early? Let the lights and sounds entice you to dance away under the stars.

● ⊙ Ⓜ ⟟ ⌲ ▭ ▰ ✕ ♀ ☛ ✵ ⋔ ⊟ ⓪ ⟁ ♫

Directions: Find Lacapelle-Biron, a small village lying north of Fumel on the Lot. On the D255 west of this village, you will see a lake. The site is here (well-signposted) **Ground:** Hard **Children:** Playground, organised events, kindergarten **Wheelchair:** Suitable
Food-cooling: Ice sold, coolpacks frozen **Sport:** Tennis, volleyball, ping pong, fishing, aerobics, archery (inclusive in special-rate family 'club' scheme), horse-riding, bike-hire **Season:** 1 April to 30 Sept
Reservation: Advisable peak season **Charge:** Pitch 31 fr; person 22.45 fr

▰▰▰ Brengues ▰▰▰

Le Moulin Vieux

Brengues, 46320 Assier   tel 65.40.00.41

Comfortable modern site in scenic river gorge

No 'moulin vieux', but that's not a major disappointment for this camp is in an extremely pleasant clearing on the banks of the Célé and all but surrounded by the wooded cliffs of the river gorge. The first thing to command your attention is the field of maize right in the middle; otherwise there is plenty of space to run around in. As with many recently built camps hardly any fault is to be found with fittings and fixtures. The site shop is cool, with a well-stocked delicatessen. A tidy, wooden open-air bar overlooks the pool area, or for shadier swimming, there's a mini-*plage* by a shallow waterfall at the back of the camp. It's here, too, that you can get good afternoon shade for your pitch. There's a restaurant literally across the road or it's down to the bar for take-away *frites*. For its size this scenic camp has just about everything in terms of basics that a larger camp can provide and, bearing in mind the dearth of sites with any facilities to speak of in this area, it's a fair bet for a comfortable, relaxed stay.

Directions: Brengues lies on the D41, which comes off the main D13 from Figeac, in the direction of Cahors. The D41 is the second left-hand junction you'll come to, just before the railway goes over the D13
Ground: Hard **Children:** Playground **Wheelchair:** Suitable
Food-cooling: Coolpacks frozen **Sport:** Volleyball, football, mini-golf, badminton, canoeing **Season:** Easter to 15 Oct
Reservation: Advisable peak season **Charge:** Pitch 20 fr; person 18 fr

▬ Carsac-Aillac ▬▬▬▬

Le Rocher de la Cave

Carsac, 24200 Sarlat   Out-of-season tel 53.28.12.57
                                    tel 53.28.14.26

One for the canoeists. For others, a commendable, laid-back short stay on a beautiful stretch of river

For the young and fit, on honeymoon perhaps, this tiny, pretty, reasonably priced site on the Dordogne is a must. Even those for whom the honeymoon is but a faded memory will love the drive up the twisting road just to linger at the open-air bar beneath a huge circular tarpaulin, keeping the day's heat at bay, while gazing at a magnificent cliff with its little caves reflected in the water. The more adventurous can hire a canoe here to journey along its meandering course. At the bar, the 'Boss' – as the owner is referred to by his friendly staff – will chat happily away to you in an *'Allo 'Allo* accent. At the time of our visit the company was cordial, the food nourishing, the loos clean, and the pebble beach free of beer cans – all in all, for what is officially graded as a two-star site, a pleasant surprise. The shop supplies morning basics – milk, bread, butter – and the village of Carsac is nearby.

Directions: From Sarlat take the D104 in the direction of Gourdon. As you enter Carsac, take the right-hand turn before arched bridge. Proceed down the road ignoring camping symbol on first right. Go up steep incline and round bends. Then a right-hand fork will take you past another site to this one **Ground:** Giving **Children:** Playground **Wheelchair:** Suitable **Food-cooling:** Ice sold **Sport:** Volleyball, ping pong, boating, canoeing **Season:** 1 June to 30 Sept **Reservation:** Advisable peak season **Charge:** Pitch 16 fr; person 12.40 fr; child (under 7) 7 fr; electricity 7 fr

▰▰▰ Castelnaud ▰▰▰▰▰▰▰▰▰

Maisonneuve

Castelnaud, 24250 Domme	tel 53.29.51.29

A very pretty basic site, but you'll have to cater for yourselves

Lying in the lee of an imposing wooded cliff, complete with cave on high, the Maisonneuve is one of a few 'new-generation' sites to be found along this stretch of D57: modern, clean buildings, young, courteous French management and the small, babbling Céou in which to float the dinghy. A split site, this, with the reception-cum-bar, small grocery and pool on one side of the lane and the main area with clearly marked *emplacements* on the land opposite, between lane and river. Some shade is to be picked up in the afternoon from tall, mature trees bordering the Céou, but the camp is otherwise quite open.

⊙ ⓢ ⚲ ⌇ ▭ ▮ ⚲ ⚑ ⋔ ⊟

Directions: On the D57 to St Cybranet you'll see a big sign for the camp on your left and a left fork off the main road. Over a little bridge, a bend to the right and you're there. **Ground:** Hard **Children:** Playground, video-games room **Wheelchair:** Suitable **Food-cooling:** None **Sport:** Volleyball, ping pong, billiards **Season:** Easter to 1 Oct **Reservation:** Advisable peak season **Charge:** Pitch 20 fr; person 17 fr; child (under 7) 8.60 fr; electricity 10 fr

Pitching by a river or lake may seem an attractive idea but gnats and mosquitoes feel the same way. An easy remedy is to rub or spray repellent on your limbs at night or, if you prefer, use a slow-burning diffuser for the tent. You may also be thankful that you packed the ant-powder.

▬▬ Cénac ▬▬▬▬▬▬▬

Le Pech de Caumont

Cénac en Périgord, 24250 Domme   tel 53.28.21.63

Penny plain stop-over

Nothing special except the panoramic view of the citadel of
Domme on the next peak. Modern blocks house clean, newish,
basic facilities, but the gravel drives are worn and the trees thin
in growth. There's only a small shop in season so stock up in the
few shops in bustling Cénac at the foot of the hill. You have to
toss up between peace and lack of shade near the buildings, or
shade and the sound of traffic way below at the far end of the
site.

● ⑤ 🏊 🛶 🛝 ✗ ♀ 🎪 🛏 🔲

Directions: Take the D46 towards Cahors from Cénac (Domme). In
the village, just past the road junction, is a small public parking area.
Turn left just by it when you see the camp sign. At the T-junction up
this road turn right and go all the way up the hill. The camp sign and
entrance will appear on your right **Ground:** Hard **Children:** Not
suitable **Wheelchair:** Suitable **Food-cooling:** Ice sold, coolpacks
frozen **Sport:** Volleyball, ping pong, bike-hire, games room
Season: 1 April to 30 Sept **Reservation:** Advisable peak season
Charge: 2 people, car and caravan 52 fr; child (2-7) 8 fr; electricity 10 fr

▬▬ Crayssac ▬▬▬▬▬▬

⑦ *Les Reflets de Quercy*

46150 Catus   tel 65.30.91.48

Attractive, busy site in quiet countryside

Quercy does have a lot going for it – not too far from the Lot
and in an agreeably quiet stretch of the country on an equally
quiet road. The grounds are fairly open, but shade is provided
by the low branches of the trees that are spread over a large part
of the site. *Emplacements* are pretty well packed-in, so in peak
season it's a busy place. Gravel paths (it's a stony place all
round) take you down to the central clearing in which there's a
very attractive pool with a little *crêperie* alongside. On the whole

it is the sort of environment that one would expect at a four-star establishment. Unfortunately there are one or two 'buts'. We've been informed by a British couple that at the tail-end of the high season, facilities are run down if the depletion of number warrants it, but the management are not so quick to think in compatible terms where the tariff is concerned! The other drawback it that the *emplacements* have a base of packed gravel as hard as concrete. When you arrive, you have to borrow 'The Drill' to make the holes that are going to take your tent stakes: not the sort of thing you'd be wanting to do, surely, after a few hours' sweaty drive. So along with the usual symbols accompanying a campsite entry, perhaps there should be a little silhouette of a Black & Decker in future?

Directions: Crayssac is a village lying south of the D911 (west of Cahors). From the D911, take the D23 turn-off for Crayssac. Before the village turn right down a country lane. The site will appear on your right **Ground:** Hard **Children:** Playground **Wheelchair:** Not suitable **Food-cooling:** Ice sold, coolpacks frozen **Sport:** Tennis, volleyball, ping pong, canoeing centre 5 km **Season:** Easter to Oct **Reservation:** Advisable peak season **Charge:** Pitch 60 fr; person 18 fr

Daglan

Le Moulin de Paulhiac

24250 Daglan   tel 53.28.20.88

Spotless, modern site under energetic management

One of the two or three 'new-generation' sites in this area: young management, modern appointments, constant improvements, a fresh atmosphere. Paulhiac has been improving its official star rating annually, and the original mill building should now be in full swing as a simple restaurant offering a few *plats du jour* (take-away possible). It's quite a spread-out site, although *emplacements* are not as generous as some. Shade is definitely at a premium except for one or two prime pitches (e.g. No. 4). By contrast, the bar is cool and airy with large patio-style windows, and the shop has a minimalist feel – cool, neutral tones and clean lines. Paulhiac's standards of cleanliness defy criticism, and for anyone whose constant beef is that the French never provide enough hooks in the washing cubicles, here there are *three* to every *lavabo*. The site backs on to the stream of the Céou with its eddies and waterfalls; parts are quite accessible for paddling or taking a shallow dip as an alternative to the pool.

Directions: From Castelnaud take the D57 going south. The site is along this road on your left (well-marked) **Ground:** Hard **Children:** Playground **Wheelchair:** Suitable **Food-cooling:** Coolpacks frozen **Sport:** Tennis, volleyball, ping pong, rugby **Season:** 1 July to 15 Sept **Reservation:** Advisable peak season **Charge:** Pitch 38 fr; person 18.50 fr; child (under 4) free; electricity 11.50 to 16 fr

Les Eyzies-de-Tayac

Le Vézère Périgord

24620 Tursac-Les Eyzies   tel 53.06.96.31

If you forgive the plumbing, then good for a pleasant short stay – longer if you're not fussy. Friendly and unpretentious

Le Vézère Périgord is the place to go for the Carefree Holiday. Who cares if the grounds aren't landscaped and the pool is nothing more than utilitarian?; or if the shower-blocks aren't exactly up to date?; or if the bar/restaurant hasn't five-star décor? And what a change that little English conversation is to be heard. Within these dense, pine-enclosed terraces you will find friendly service from the young staff and a pervading good-humoured spirit among the campers. Midway up the incline is a low chalet housing the bar and little restaurant, with a take-away (trout, chips and salad?) round the back. A step up from here is a self-contained kiddies' area with play equipment and its own paddling-pool. Beyond is the main block-house, basically a large roof covering the various washing facilities. One camper was observed to volunteer a temporary repair to a faulty tap while cleaning dishes – but with humour, not complaint. And that small episode really sums up Le Vézère Périgord.

Directions: Take the D706 at Les Eyzies (towards Montignac). After several bends, when the road straightens out, you will see a goose farm on your left, before coming to camp entrance with flagpoles on your right **Ground:** Hard **Children:** Playground, swimming **Wheelchair:** Tricky **Food-cooling:** Coolpacks frozen **Sport:** Tennis, ping pong **Season:** Easter to 30 Sept **Reservation:** Advisable peak season **Charge:** Pitch 22.50 fr; person 17.50 fr

▬▬ Figeac ▬▬▬▬▬▬▬▬

⑦ *Municipal Les Rives du Célé*

46100 Figeac   tel 65.34.59.00

Noisy under canvas, but good-sized emplacements *and ample distractions at the nearby Parc des Loisirs*

This well laid-out site at the edge of the town by the Célé has the great advantage of lying behind the *Parc des Loisirs*. It is a very pleasant, green recreation park, having grassy banks by the boating lake, swimming-pool and water-chute, and a bar with restaurant – all with a lido atmosphere. The camp itself – a completely separate concern – consists of an open area of ground laid to grass by the river, in the shadow of a pretty, wooded hill. Good-sized *emplacements* are just about defined by isolated shrubs and nursery trees. The reception runs a *dépôt de pain* in the mornings as well as a snack counter and there are the amenities mentioned above on your doorstep. The *sanitaire* is well looked after and there are no complaints on that score. However, this must qualify for the 'noisiest site in France' award. We mean the N122, a main arterial route to the north-east that runs close by, and the sluice station which we assumed controls the flow of the Célé, on the perimeter of the camp. Imagine, if you will, camping in Hyde Park – the Park Lane side – with a giant toilet flushing every 25 seconds. Behind the closed door of your caravan, tight under the sheets at night, this may not be any hardship.

○ ⑤ ♨ ♀ ⋔ ⊟

Directions: This site is situated 600 m from the centre of Figeac. Take the N140 towards Rodez **Ground:** Giving **Children:** Not suitable **Wheelchair:** Suitable **Food-cooling:** Ice sold **Sport:** Ping pong, trampolines **Season:** 15 May to 15 Sept **Reservation:** Advisable peak

Gourdon

season **Charge:** Pitch 25 fr; person 15 fr; child (under 10) 9 fr; electricity 10 to 12 fr

▬▬ Gourdon ▬▬▬▬▬▬▬▬

Municipal Ecoute s'il Pleut

c/o Mairie de Gourdon	Out-of-season tel 65.41.06.37
46300	tel 65.41.06.19

Brisk efficiency in a densely wooded retreat. Ideal for a self-catering holiday

On the plus side: the camp lies at the edge of Gourdon, a circular medieval town with good restaurants, shops and a market (also a cinema and discothèques, even its own annual music festival), so an evening drink can be enjoyed in town. Drink up early because Ecoute s'il Pleut shuts its gates prompt at 10. That gives an indication both of the peace and quiet at this lovely, heavily wooded spot, and of the superb order kept by an efficient management. On the minus side: the *emplacements*, levelled pitches cut into a slight hill are artificially based with sand and gravel, so strong stakes and a heavy mallet are called for when pitching a tent; and there's nothing on site for refreshment – not even a bar. Although there's no shop either, a bread lady brings fresh baguettes, croissants and *pain chocolat* in her van every morning. After breakfast, you could stroll along the small lake at the bottom of the site, perhaps, or pore over the map and plot the day's outing. All the while, the gentle light of the warming morning sun filters through the young oak and thin conifer to spread a patchwork of brightness across the woodland floor.

Directions: As you leave Gourdon on the D704 to Sarlat, the road descends round some bends. On your left you will see a Municipal camping sign. Take this left fork and further along, a second left-hand fork. The site is a little way down this road **Ground:** Hard
Children: Playground, swimming **Wheelchair:** Not suitable
Food-cooling: Ice sold, coolpacks frozen **Sport:** Tennis, volleyball, ping pong, boating, wind surfing, fishing **Season:** 15 June to 15 Sept
Reservation: Advisable peak season **Charge:** Pitch 17 fr; person 15 fr; child (under 7) 9 fr; electricity 9 fr

323

▰▰ Groléjac ▰▰▰▰▰▰▰▰▰

Les Granges

Groléjac, 24250 Domme   tel 53.28.11.15

Good for children but fairly ordinary otherwise

Once a farm, like many camps in the Périgord, Les Granges has
many of the attributes of a high-grade site, but overall comes
over as slightly characterless. This is a split-level environment,
the upper half consisting of stone buildings arranged around
three sides of a grass quadrangle and two large pools on the
fourth. Sunbathe here all day, nibbling at a lunchtime quiche
from the take-away. The site steps down away from here
towards shadier and mostly reasonably sized *emplacements* at the
bottom of the hill. Surprisingly, there is no camp shop, your
breakfast order of bread and croissants being collected from that
take-away counter, but there's a shop outside the camp on the
main road. Les Granges is a busy place with plenty of activities
to keep children happy, and a games organiser is employed in
the high season.

● Ⓜ 🛉 ⌚ 🐾 ✕ ♀ 🐚 🐞 🏛 ⏃ ▣ ♫

Directions: Take the D704 from Sarlat going south towards Gourdon
into the village of Groléjac. In the village, attached to a Stop sign, you
will see the camp signpost. Turn right here. Immediately after going
under a bridge, turn left **Ground:** Giving **Children:** Playground,
swimming, organised events, activity room **Wheelchair:** Tricky
Food-cooling: Ice sold, coolpacks frozen, fridge hire **Sport:** Tennis,
volleyball, ping pong, mini-golf, canoe hire **Season:** 1 May to 30 Sept
Reservation: Advisable peak season **Charge:** 4 people, pitch and car
115 fr; electricity 14 fr

▰▰ Larnagol ▰▰▰▰▰▰▰▰▰

Le Ruisseau de Treil

Larnagol, 46160 Cajarc   tel 65.31.25.39

*Quiet, rural little site, ideal for exploring the Lot and
its environs*

Larnagol is a beautiful, tiny village perched on a curve of the
River Lot and well worth a detour, if only to stop and stretch

one's legs. Le Ruisseau is equally tiny and is probably yet another example of a farmer turning a small parcel of land to his advantage. On the track leading to the entrance is a drying shed for the local crop – tobacco. Behind the tractor shed you'll see a very attractive enclosure mainly laid to grass with young trees. There is a main building, perhaps a converted barn, a sectioned-off playground in the shade of more established trees and two small swimming-pools. A couple of thoughtful inclusions for very young children include low pedestal toilets and an enamel baby bath with hand-shower attached. Each washing cubical is provided with cleaning equipment too. It's a pity that such thoughtfulness hasn't been carried through to the arrangement of the two swimming-pools. These are sunk into an area of crazy paving, laid down such as to leave a roughly hewn edge of about one and a half foot in height (toddlers may have to be watched around here and on the concrete 'bridge' that leads to the pools). But having said all this, the site as a whole has the advantage of providing a tranquil base from which to explore the immediate vicinity.

Directions: Cajarc lies on the D19 south-west of Figeac. Leave Cajarc on the D19, turn right on the D662 and follow this river road until you come to Larnagol. Just as you enter the village, take the first right (site signposted) and then immediate right-hand track **Ground:** Hard **Children:** Playground **Wheelchair:** Suitable **Food-cooling:** Ice sold, fridge hire **Sport:** Volleyball, ping pong **Season:** 15 April to 15 Oct **Reservation:** Advisable peak season **Charge:** Pitch 25 fr; person 25 fr; child (under 4) 15 fr

■■■ Monflanquin ■■■

Municipal de Coulon

47150 Monflanquin
Out-of-season tel 53.36.41.09
tel 53.36.47.36

Unpretentious bustling site, popular with French families

Coulon is a three-star municipal site, which is to say that while it's not spilling over with luxuries, it's nevertheless a worthy base for a touring family. The loo doors may be old and wooden, not shining melamine, and there may be a distinct absence of potted plants but as long as there's a square of dirt for *pétanque* and a sense of camaraderie, that is enough for your average French camper. The site offers much in the way of distractions for it is right next to local amenities including swimming-pool (none on site), pedalo lake, crazy golf and a Centre des Loisirs, equivalent to an organised playschool where youngsters can be left to get to grips with the rudiments of French. As these activities are not related to the camp you will have to fork out extra but, considering the cheapness of the site, this should not be an undue imposition.

● Ⓜ 𝍅 ⩰ ⛴ ✕ ⚲ ⚘ ⋔ ⇱ ℘

Directions: Take the D676 from town towards Villeréal. Then fork right on the D124. Just after that (to the right) is the camp entrance (signposted). Fork left at the municipal sports area. The camp lies beyond **Ground:** Hard to giving **Children:** Playground **Wheelchair:** Suitable **Food-cooling:** Ice sold **Sport:** Tennis, volleyball, football, crazy golf **Season:** All year **Reservation:** Advisable peak season **Charge:** Pitch 14.30 fr; person 7.20 fr; per vehicle 4.40 fr

▰▰▰ Monpazier ▰▰▰▰▰

Le Moulin de David

Gaugeac, 24540 Monpazier   tel 53.22.65.25

Small, wooded and very active yet laid-back site

Moulin de David – small, informal and attractive with abundant foliage and rough stone buildings – lies off the main road, strung out along the foot of a hill by a small brook. Lush, tall trees at one end disperse to provide a sunny clearing for the pools and the bar. A wide, covered terrace will keep you cool over coffee while you watch the kids having a morning dip. If you stay on site there's a choice of weight-training, gymnastics, trampolining, archery or organised canoeing – it's not really the site for lazing around in. Or you might take off on one of the organised day trips or hire-bikes. Musical soirées, banquets and in the high season quite a few jolly activities for children keep up the pace in the evenings. The place is quite popular with the French and there's a strong GB contingent of regulars happy to return annually.

Children should be discouraged from playing around shower blocks.

● Ⓢ 🏂 🛶 ⚡ ✕ ♀ 🖐 ♒ ⬒ ▣ ⚓ ♫

Directions: Take the D2 from Monpazier towards Villeréal, then a left-hand turn down a track **Ground:** Hard to giving **Children:** Playground, swimming, organised events, baby facilities **Wheelchair:** Suitable **Food-cooling:** Coolpacks frozen **Sport:** Tennis, volleyball, ping pong, canoeing trips **Season:** 28 April to 30 Sept **Reservation:** Advisable peak season **Charge:** Pitch 34 fr; person 24 fr

Municipal Plan d'Eau de Véronne

Marsalès, 24540 Monpazier   Out-of-season tel 53.22.60.38
tel 53.22.62.22

Pretty spot for an undemanding stop-over

An attractive site, with a large lake (pedalos and sail-boarding) and a sandy beach. The *plage* snack bar serves up fast-food only, but on the opposite bank, cooled in the shade of waterside trees, is a neat little bar with outdoor seating, and Monpazier is just a few minutes' drive away. Just the spot to get out the deckchairs.

● Ⓛ 🚶 ⬚ ♀ 🖐 ⚓ ♒ ⚓

Directions: Take the D660 from Monpazier towards Beaumont. You will see a big sign where you branch right on to the D26E. A lake will appear on your left: this is where the site is **Ground:** Giving **Children:** Playground **Wheelchair:** Suitable **Food-cooling:** Ice sold, coolpacks frozen **Sport:** Tennis, volleyball, ping pong, pedalos, boating, horse-riding **Season:** 1 June to 30 Sept **Reservation:** Advisable peak season **Charge:** 2 people, pitch, car and caravan 45 fr; 15 fr for each extra person; electricity 8.50 to 12 fr

Montcabrier

Moulin de Laborde

Montcabrier, 46700 Puy l'Evêque   tel 65.24.62.06

A quiet and restful site with basic facilities

Laborde is no more than a clearing in the middle of the thickly wooded hills of the Thèze valley. You can see the whole site as you arrive: a small, level, exposed plain for camping; a wood to the left where an open barn acts as a cover for table-tennis (horses are kept in the back); at the rear a swimming-pool, then, beyond wrought-iron gates, what's left of a seventeenth-century watermill at the foot of a steep, verdant cliff. Lack of shade may deter those who like to keep their tents cool. The central sanitation block is modern and well appointed. Not a lot goes on at this congenial, Dutch-run site, it's not the kind of place where you would want it to – just riding or walking in the woods. A small stream on the edge of the site is suitable for paddling. Bar victuals are of the pizza and burger variety.

Directions: In Montcabrier take the D58 going out of town. At the crossroads with the D673 turn right. There's a signpost for the camp here. Further along at a bend you'll see another sign on your right, followed by a flagpole and camp entrance on your left **Ground:** Hard **Children:** Playground, organised events **Wheelchair:** Suitable **Food-cooling:** Coolpacks frozen **Sport:** Volleyball, ping pong, horse-riding **Season:** 15 May to 30 Sept **Reservation:** Advisable peak season **Charge:** Pitch 27 fr; person 20 fr; child (under 7) 10 fr

Padirac

Les Chênes

46500 Padirac

Out-of-season tel 65.33.64.69

tel 66.33.65.54

Well-appointed conviviality for all the family in this touristy area

Monsieur Robert Tournie, a real *vieux paysan*, is everyone's archetypal Frenchman, minus the regulation Gitane hanging from the lower lip. He and his family have been developing this site over the past few years to include a swimming-pool, tennis court and all mod-cons in terms of sanitation. The camp lies just off a busy road to the magnet of the Gouffre de Padirac (see the Introduction to this section), so the air hums a bit, but it's quiet at night. It's a good base providing very reasonable shade on spread-out terraces with well-proportioned *emplacements*. Exceptional combined shower/washing cubicles give you in effect your own mini-bathroom with space enough for simultaneous cleaning of children. There's an adequately stocked shop in the main building that also houses the reception and a small eatery. Monsieur Robert – a *bon vivant* – is hot on family competitions and *soirées dansantes* in the high season. He doesn't speak English but patiently puts up with a lot of bad French.

● Ⓜ 🕴 🛶 🏕 ✕ 💺 🍴 🐛 🏠 ♿ 📻 🔑

Directions: Padirac itself sits on the D673. Going north from the town is the D90, which takes you to the famous Gouffre de Padirac. Les Chênes is further on down the road, on a wide sweeping bend (well-signposted). You will see a gravel driveway off the main road with the camp in full view **Ground:** Hard **Children:** Playground, swimming **Wheelchair:** Tricky **Food-cooling:** Coolpacks frozen **Sport:** Volleyball, ping pong **Season:** Easter to 15 Sept **Reservation:** Advisable peak season **Charge:** Pitch 15.50 fr; person 15.50 fr; child (under 8) 8 fr

▰▰▰ Payrac ▰▰▰

Les Pins

46350 Payrac   tel 65.37.96.32

Time and a half for the kids, at least

Les Pins is set on a hill as you come into Payrac. Shady pitches at the top end in the pine wood are very neighbourly. If you want more of a sense of space around you, erect the tent down the hill round an open lawn area. The drawback here is that the road at the bottom happens to be the main N20. However, this problem does not bother the children who have ample exciting distractions to choose from: an upper and lower playground with good climbing equipment, also an upper and lower pool. Alongside one of those play areas, twisting through grassy banks for sunbathing, is the blue snake of an aquachute, available for campers but also popular with the public. Generally the site is reasonably maintained. There is no restaurant as such but standard take-away fare is available or snacks can be eaten at the bar.

● Ⓢ 🕴 🛶 🏕 ✕ 💺 🍴 🐛 🏠 ♿ 📻 ✂ 🎵

Directions: Payrac lies on the N20 south of Souillac. Go through the town, out the other side, and as you climb a hill the camp is situated on a bend, with the entrance on your right **Ground:** Hard to giving

Children: Playground, swimming, organised events **Wheelchair:** Not suitable **Food-cooling:** Coolpacks frozen **Sport:** Tennis, volleyball, ping pong **Season:** 1 April to 30 Sept **Reservation:** Advisable peak season **Charge:** Pitch 38 fr; person 25 fr; child (under 7) 15 fr

▬▬▬ Prats de Carlux ▬▬▬

La Châtaigneraie

24370 Carlux

Out-of-season tel 53.59.03.61
tel 53.31.08.41

Good value for fun-loving families

Cheaper than some of its neighbouring sites it may be, but if your tastes are for a smaller, quieter spot, yet where children are given sufficient entertainment, this site represents a good deal. There's a wooden fort for an imaginative game or two, a BMX track for hire-bikes through the wood across the road, and of course the pool and crazy-golf too. Because it's a newer site than most the sanitation blocks are fresher in appearance and function. The cool, sophisticated bar wouldn't look out of place in a Mediterranean hotel as far as décor is concerned and the ceiling seems to have as many lights as Stringfellows on disco evenings. This is a well-designed camp with a choice of sunny pitches or shadier ones on the slope of a hill beyond. With open surroundings and cheerful, helpful management on call, there's little to disappoint here. Only the lack of a proper restaurant prevents La Châtaigneraie from being a very competitive alternative to some of the more established sites.

● Ⓢ ♨ ⌂ ⚓ ✕ ⚲ ☙ ⚑ ⋔ ⧓ ⊡ ℘ ♫

Directions: Take the D47 from Sarlat to Ste-Nathalène. Turn right at the war memorial and stone cross. Follow the signs **Ground:** Giving **Children:** Playground, organised events **Wheelchair:** Suitable **Food-cooling:** Ice sold, coolpacks frozen **Sport:** Tennis, volleyball, ping pong **Season:** 15 June to 15 Sept **Reservation:** Advisable peak season **Charge:** Pitch 20 fr; person 18 fr

---

A good alternative to a rigid plastic container for keeping a water supply at the pitch is a pliable 'sac'. This is a plastic bag of heavy-duty material finished at either end with a wooden rod to help keep its shape and with a stop-cock at the bottom of one side. It can be strung up from the nearest branch and, when travelling, has the advantage of packing flat.

Puy-L'Evêque

Municipal Camping de la Plage 'Le Méoure'

46700 Puy-L'Evêque, Lot	Out-of-season tel 65.30.81.72
	tel 65.30.81.45

Peaceful, utilitarian site for an en-route break

One couldn't actually describe this as a campsite but we thought it worth an inclusion as a useful stop-over for even just a few hours' visit. Close to the town, and through the vineyards of Château l'Evêque, is a *Village des Vacances* consisting of orderly rows of holiday chalets. Adjacent to this is a very basic camping ground which, considering its two-star grading, has quite generous hedge-bordered *emplacements*. The only facilities are one shower-block with hot and cold running water (toilets are of the 'hole-in-the-floor' order) and a snack-bar where you can sit and have a crêpe with your beer. The main asset is the tiny *plage* on a beautifully serene stretch of the River Lot – a place to get away from behind the driving wheel for a while and relax.

◐ ⓢ ⚲ ▭ ⛾ ⋔ ▣

Directions: 30 km from Cahors. Travel north-west from Cahors on the D911 towards Villeneuve, to Puy-L'Evêque **Ground:** Hard **Children:** Playground **Wheelchair:** Suitable **Food-cooling:** Ice sold, coolpacks frozen **Sport:** Ping pong **Season:** Easter to 30 Sept **Reservation:** Advisable peak season **Charge:** 10 fr person for pitch; electricity 6 fr

Rouffignac

Cantegrel

24580 Rouffignac-St Cernin	tel 53.05.48.30

Peace and quiet prevail at this immaculate, small site, with beautiful views

The air-filled silence that greets you is a good indication of the height of Cantegrel, and the marvellous vista of forest-blanketed hills that stretches out beyond the reception leaves you in no doubt. The main part of this immaculate little camp straddles a ridge between two steep valleys. Small groups of trees offer a certain amount of privacy for *emplacements*, and the tranquillity which pervades the site is in no way spoiled by the more energetic campers who frequent the pool and the tennis courts. The drawback for families is that there isn't much for the children to do: a couple of swings and a roundabout pass as a playground. But there is a games-room in the rustic bar which forms one side of the restaurant courtyard. Regular soirées on the lines of a pizza evening with a singer and occasional dance music in the bar all promise an agreeable ambience in the evening. Well-groomed horses in a nearby field can be hired to explore the surrounding countryside.

● ⑤ 🏄 🛶 🦺 ✕ ♀ ☛ 🎋 ⊟ 🔟 ⚟ ♫

Directions: Go north from Rouffignac on the D31. Site is signposted at a right-hand fork, with small white-painted triangular island in the road. Turn right and follow the road for 500 metres until you see sign for Reception **Ground:** Giving **Children:** Playground, baby facilities **Wheelchair:** Suitable **Food-cooling:** Coolpacks frozen **Sport:** Tennis, ping pong, horse-riding **Season:** 1 April to 15 Oct **Reservation:** Advisable peak season **Charge:** 3 people pitch 78 fr; extra adult 19 fr; child (under 9) 10 fr

▰▰▰ St Cybranet ▰▰▰

Bel Ombrage

St Cybranet, 24250 Domme   tel 53.28.34.14

Efficient site, ideal for self-caterers and water-lovers

This reasonably shady, open site in the middle of woodland bordering the Céou is known to quite a few British tourers. Everything here is clean and orderly in well-maintained modern buildings – all under the supervision of enthusiastic French management. The site covers quite a lot of ground with generous *emplacements*. Most activity centres around the three small pools by the main building complex, which range from shallow to deep. An alternative to these is the tiny river beach on the Céou itself. The almost total absence of on-site food supplies may be a drawback, but how about barbecuing some fresh trout from the fish farm over the road? Within walking distance are a restaurant and a supermarket, and there's a butcher in Castelnaud. You can also buy certain foods in the camp when the bread lady does her morning rounds and you may come across an itinerant wine and cheese merchant.

Directions: Take the D57 going south from Castelnaud. The camp is on your left as you drive towards St Cybranet **Ground:** Hard to giving **Children:** Playground, swimming **Wheelchair:** Suitable **Food-cooling:** Ice sold **Sport:** Tennis, volleyball, ping pong, boating, fishing **Season:** 1 June to 15 Sept **Reservation:** Advisable peak season **Charge:** Pitch 34 fr; person 19 fr; child (under 7) 10 fr; electricity 15 fr

⑦ *Le Céou*

St Cybranet, 24250 Domme   tel 53.28.85.71

Sedate and old-fashioned enclave popular with the British

Le Céou is the complete antithesis of Bel Ombrage above. A mature site, it seems to convey a loss of what perhaps was once a glorious little retreat. Set either side of the road, the camp comprises a level field with a swimming-pool, and opposite, hillside terraces among the trees. The first, less attractive section, has an old-fashioned, tatty *sanitaire*, its heyday glimpsed at by the fussy touch of shower curtains. The main part of Le Céou across the road is quite pretty, with an abundance of shade under low trees lining the steep terraces. It is a sedate place indeed, the smallness of the camping ground lending itself to an air of calm. To be fair, the *sanitaire* here is somewhat better in appearance. There is a little restaurant tucked in by the road end, along with Madame's house. Madame – who is Dutch – prefers a 'select' clientele, we learned. She loves the English, specifically the 'Professional English', to use her terminology. The 'select' nature of her establishment is borne out by some of the notices we observed. One asked those interested to enrol for a game of bridge, another advised that reservations be made for the restaurant. If you do want to shut yourself away from the twentieth-century world of holiday fun and enjoy the company of your fellow countrymen (there are many here thanks to a package operator), then this is obviously the place to come. You can be assured of a fine welcome, especially if you have the right credentials. Do take a book, though. In fact, take six. There is little else to do here. You won't need to pack the cards . . . they definitely have those.

Directions: From St Cybranet take the D57 south to Daglan. The site entrance is on your right along this road. Park in the camp's other site on the opposite side of the road, and walk across to reception **Ground:** Giving **Children:** Playground, swimming **Wheelchair:** Not suitable **Food-cooling:** Coolpacks frozen **Sport:** Ping pong **Season:** May to Sept **Reservation:** Advisable peak season **Charge:** Pitch 30 fr; person 25 fr

St Cyprien

Municipal Le Garrit

St Cyprien, 24220 Dordogne   tel 53.29.20.56

Tidy, no-frills camping and a popular place to bathe make this a good stop-over

A neat and pleasant campsite under amicable management. If you don't mind the basic hole-in-the-ground toilet facilities, the cheap rates will make up for the lack of creature comforts. If you're towing the 'van or taking a bike cross-country, you should be happy enough to cool down with a dip in the grand Dordogne, play a little ping pong in the shade of the games-house and then drift into nearby St Cyprien for a bite to eat in the evening.

Directions: Leave St Cyprien on the D48 south of the town. Follow the road over the automatic rail crossing, right down to the Dordogne river, where the site sits between a road bridge to your left and a rail bridge to your right **Ground:** Giving **Children:** Playground **Wheelchair:** Suitable **Food-cooling:** Ice sold **Sport:** Ping pong **Season:** 1 May to 30 Sept **Reservation:** Advisable peak season **Charge:** Pitch 18 fr; person 13.50 fr; electricity 10 fr

Make a beeline for the Syndicat d'Initiative in your nearest town. This will supply you with all your sightseeing information as well as the latest on exhibitions, festivals, etc. Many Syndicats recruit English-speaking staff.

St Geniès

La Bouquerie

24590 St Geniès   tel 53.28.98.22

Family fun in the open countryside, with bonhomie

In a dip in open fields adjoining woodland, La Bouquerie looks immediately inviting as you approach it from higher ground – the converted old stone farm buildings, neatly arranged tents and tennis court catch the eye. Walking through the camp one does feel a definite sense of *joie de vivre*, possibly due to the extrovert proprietor who exudes good humour. The camp is a British favourite and has been colonised by at least one package company. Of course, being a higher-grade site with a range of facilities to match it's more pricey than some. Try the excellent delicatessen for a variety of cold meats or gateaux made by the camp chef. Swim in the pool or from the lakeside beach. There's plenty of shade to be enjoyed in the open wood, or feel the sun in the more exposed portion of the camp if you prefer. Organised competitions by the site *animateur*; soirées twice a week; barbecues with live bands; and the Saturday disco (not all included outside the high season) make this a good spot for families.

● Ⓜ 🕴 ⛵ 🖥 🏪 ✕ ⛳ 🖖 🏊 🎪 🛗 📷 ⚡ 🔦 🎵

Directions: From Montignac take the D704 south towards Sarlat. After some distance there is a left-hand turn off the main road. Watch out, as you proceed down the narrow road, for a left turn into fields. You will spot the site lower down ahead of you (well-signposted)
Ground: Hard to giving   **Children:** Playground, swimming, organised events, baby facilities   **Wheelchair:** Suitable
Food-cooling: Coolpacks frozen   **Sport:** Tennis, volleyball, ping pong
Season: Easter to 15 Sept   **Reservation:** Advisable peak season
Charge: Pitch 34 fr; person 24 fr; child (under 7) 15 fr; electricity 14 fr

---

Pitching by a river or lake may seem an attractive idea but gnats and mosquitoes feel the same way. An easy remedy is to rub or spray repellent on your limbs at night or, if you prefer, use a slow-burning diffuser for the tent. You may also be thankful that you packed the ant-powder.

▰▰▰ St Léon-sur-Vézère ▰▰▰▰▰▰▰

☼ *Le Paradis*

St Léon-sur-Vézère, 24290 Montignac   tel 53.50.72.64

Top-grade efficiency at this well-landscaped site, popular with all ages

For some, this is what camping is all about. If you want everything laid on and are prepared to shell out for it, this is the place to come. Even so, the sophistication of the place doesn't undermine the relaxed atmosphere in any way. And if the prime consideration is to get the kids off your hands, then here you can make them disappear for the rest of the day. There are no fewer than three pools, a BMX track, a hard-working courier, and enough families of different nationalities to allow them to make their own new friends in the miniature adventure playground. The layout of the camping area comprises gravel avenues landscaped with decorative plants, with 'enclaves' containing reasonably spaced *emplacements*. There is a sensible separation of activity areas: courtyard bar away from pool, away from BMX track, and so on. There is, of course, for a site of this standard, the obligatory fully equipped launderette – but dishwashers? It must be said that Dutch-run Le Paradis is probably one of the best organised sites in the central Dordogne; proof of this must surely be their *Guide du Paradis* booklet, which not only gives you all the necessary camp information but lists an abundance of sightseeing venues together with opening times.

● ① ⚥ ⌂ ⚡ ✕ ♀ ☞ ☘ ⋔ ⊿ ▣ ∥ ℘ ♫

Directions: Take the D706 north-east of Les Eyzies, in the direction of Montignac. The site lies midway between the towns, on the right-hand side of the road (not obviously signposted but watch out for tall, white flagpoles), before you reach St Léon itself **Ground:** Hard to giving **Children:** Playground, swimming, organised events, baby facilities, BMX track (bike hire) **Wheelchair:** Suitable **Food-cooling:** Ice sold, coolpacks frozen **Sport:** Tennis, ping pong, canoeing, mountain bike rides and walks organised **Season:** 15 June to 15 Sept **Reservation:** Advisable peak season **Charge:** Pitch 8.70 fr; person 7.60 fr; child (under 10) 4.60 fr; electricity 7.40 fr

▬ St Martial-de-Nabirat ▬

Le Carbonnier

24250 St Martial-de-Nabirat   tel 53.28.42.53

A worthwhile stop for good, interesting food and countryside views

It's beautifully quiet up here on high ground overlooking wide-open country but the large, airy restaurant at the entrance to this modern site might well be popular with locals as well as campers. The young, formidable Madame Christine Lagard speaks good English and, with Monsieur Lagard, is responsible for the interesting choice of *plats cuisinés* on the menus. Le Carbonnier covers quite a lot of ground. Behind the roadside reception and restaurant is the L-shaped swimming-pool (heated), in an expanse of exposed grassland. A long path leads down to the camping ground itself, on a small, sparsely wooded rise. The sanitation block is modern and clean. This is not yet a mature enough site to have established a full range of amenities or, for that matter, a character, but otherwise it's worth a stop – if only to check out Mme Lagard's cooking.

Directions: Take the main D46 from Cénac (Domme) in the direction of Cahors and follow to the village of St Martial-de-Nabirat. The site is literally at the end of this village, on the left, marked by a couple of tall, white flagpoles **Ground:** Hard to giving **Children:** Playground, organised events **Wheelchair:** Suitable **Food-cooling:** Ice sold **Sport:** Tennis, volleyball, ping pong, billiards **Season:** Easter to 30 Sept **Reservation:** Advisable peak season **Charge:** Pitch 34 fr; person 24 fr; child (under 3) free; (3-7) 15 fr; electricity 12.50 fr

▬ Sarlat ▬

Les Chênes Verts

24370 Calviac-Carlux   tel 53.59.21.07

Welcoming management typifies this tranquil, value-for-money site

Imagine settling down to a good book in 20 acres of gently sloping pasture and wooded hills. That's more or less Les

Chênes Verts in a nutshell. The activities evoke a sedate and cultured tone, with various trips organised to places of geological interest, plus local cuisine evenings when the chef gives an introductory talk on the Périgordian delights to follow. As if that isn't peaceful enough, there's a 'quiet' room for board games just off the main building, a beautiful country house of stone and climbing greenery. Not a lot is organised for children – not even a weekly disco – so entertainment with new-found friends might be cowboys and Indians in the trees? The pleasantly surprising thing is that this site, for all its calm, is so accessible as it sits by (but well back from) the main D704.

Directions: From Sarlat take the D704 heading south towards Gourdon. A few kilometres down, fork left on to the D704A and after a little while, the camp entrance appears on your left, just off the main road **Ground:** Hard to giving **Children:** Playground **Wheelchair:** Suitable **Food-cooling:** Coolpacks frozen **Sport:** Volleyball, ping pong, bike-hire **Season:** 1 May to 30 Sept **Reservation:** Advisable peak season **Charge:** Pitch 29 fr; person 17 fr; child (under 7) 8 fr; electricity 12.50 fr

Les Grottes de Roffy

Ste-Nathalène, 24200 Sarlat   tel 53.59.15.61

Compact, busy camp with comprehensive facilities for all the family

There is a high British profile at this 'Hôtel de Plein Air'. On a hillside, with pleasant views across the valley, its only disadvantage might be that shady pitches are at a premium. Uppermost is a renovated complex of farm buildings housing an interesting-looking delicatessen and a launderette. Sanitation blocks are adequate but given the site's four-star grading there's perhaps room for improvement. Outside the main complex three pools and a Jacuzzi vie for your attention. A well-equipped playground including climbing frames should fully occupy the children, and there's plenty organised for adults, too. Take-aways, *frites* for example, are somewhat pricey and you do have to dig into your pockets for use and hire of the various amenities. Close to the recreational area pitches are tight, so it's best to stipulate a site further down the terraces if you prefer quieter evenings.

● Ⓜ 🧍 🛶 🎣 ✕ ⛾ 👌 🎣 🔲 ✂ 🎵

Directions: The D47 leaves Sarlat from the north-eastern quarter of the town. Follow until it turns right at a crossroads in Croix-d'Alon just outside Sarlat. Before Ste-Nathalène there will be a narrow road up an incline to your right, leading off the D47 (signposted at this point). **Ground:** Hard to giving **Children:** Playground, swimming, organised events **Wheelchair:** Suitable **Food-cooling:** Ice sold **Sport:** Tennis, volleyball, ping pong, BMX bikes to hire **Season:** 1 April to 30 Sept **Reservation:** Advisable peak season **Charge:** Pitch 34.50 fr; person 24 fr; pitch and electricity 44 fr; child (under 7) 18 fr

Maillac

24200 Sarlat   tel 53.59.22.12

Functional, with farmhouse cooking occasionally on offer. Good for a short stop and lots of room for the children

Maillac is a busy utilitarian site very popular with the French. It is not in the mould of a holiday camp – more a convenient base from which to tour the surrounding countryside. The land belongs to a farm whose crops of maize are adjacent and the wife of the farming family who run it provides occasional *plats cuisinés*, certainly a better bet than the normal take-away available on other nights. (Nice *frites* – shame about the steak.) The site is split by a public road, with the amenities on one side and on the other, behind a wall, the 'prairie', a large expanse of completely open grassland with *emplacements* regulated in rows. At its edges, a wood provides less well-defined but much shadier pitches. At the time of our inspection, during the high season, the toilet block by this open area was not that clean. However, we were told by a British regular that this was the exception rather than the rule. The block further into the woods seemed to bear this out.

● Ⓛ 🧍 🛶 🎣 ⛾ 👌 ⛺ 🔲 ✂

Directions: From Sarlat, take the D47 west towards the village of Ste-Nathalène. Take a left turn coming into the village, down a country lane. Turn left at a T-junction, then first right (signposted) **Ground:** Giving **Children:** Playground, swimming

339

Wheelchair: Suitable **Food-cooling:** Ice sold, coolpacks frozen
Sport: Tennis, ping pong, mini-golf **Season:** 15 June to 15 Sept
Reservation: Advisable peak season **Charge:** Pitch 19 fr; person 13 fr;
child (under 3) free; electricity 10 fr

Moulin du Roch

Route des Eyzies, 24200 Sarlat	tel 53.59.20.27

Steep and heavily-wooded seclusion, not cheap

First impressions of the Moulin du Roch, part of the Castel et
Camping chain of sites, are mixed. One of the first sights you'll
encounter is a pretty, babbling brook beneath an overhanging
tree by the stone-built reception and bijou bar/restaurant. Next
to this are the showers, take-away kitchen and shop. The shop,
however, is rather a makeshift affair – more like a covered
market stall with not even a delicatessen counter. Beyond this,
parallel to the road, is an open grassy area containing pool and
play activities. On its periphery are the 'ground-floor' pitches
and, rising behind, terrace upon terrace of enclosed
emplacements leading further up a steep, heavily wooded hill.
This is where Roch scores – not only do you find excellent
shade but privacy and seclusion. While the jollities of daily site-
life carry on far below, you can sit by your tent in absolute
silence with that doorstop of a bestseller. There is a second
sanitation block midway on these heights. The only snag is that
it's a long haul back with the take-away, so train up those thigh
muscles. Moulin du Roch demands an extra premium for its
attributes (ice is expensive) but many do pay and are
unquestionably satisfied.

Directions: Take the D704 going north from Sarlat, towards
Périgueux. Just outside town take a left fork, signposted D6 Les Eyzies.
This later becomes the D47. Continue to follow. A big green and white
sign on the right-hand side of the road points to site entrance opposite
(between two low stone pillars). Don't drive too fast otherwise you will
miss it **Ground:** Hard to giving **Children:** Playground, swimming
Wheelchair: Tricky **Food-cooling:** Ice sold **Sport:** Tennis,
volleyball, bike-hire, fishing **Season:** 1 May to 30 Sept
Reservation: Advisable peak season **Charge:** 3 people, pitch 100 fr;
extra adult 25 fr; child (under 3) free

La Palombière

Ste-Nathalène, 24200 Sarlat | tel 53.59.42.34

Good value and spacious, with fun for all the family

Monsieur Dubost's relaxed style of management sets the tone of this charming, rambling site which spreads itself over a small vale and hill. The modestly landscaped farm buildings are out of sight of the *emplacements* which are scattered in the distant woodland. An airy restaurant and bar with terrace sit high on a ridge overlooking the swimming-pool (with separate kiddies' pool attached). Because of its spacious nature, there is definitely less of a 'holiday camp' atmosphere yet you can still enjoy the advantages of plenty of family entertainment: a weekly barbecue with cabaret, a weekly disco and the Funny Club, which runs organised events for children. La Palombière is good value, compared to the similar price of the big 'holiday camp' sites in the region.

● Ⓜ 〰 ⌇ ⌁ ✕ ♀ ☞ ★ ⋔ ⊿ ▣ ⤳ ♫

Directions: Take the D47 from the east side of Sarlat, towards Ste-Nathalène. Before hamlet is a right-hand fork, with a large sign up an incline **Ground:** Hard to giving **Children:** Playground, swimming, organised events **Wheelchair:** Tricky **Food-cooling:** Coolpacks frozen **Sport:** Tennis, volleyball, ping pong, mini-golf, archery **Season:** 15 April to 17 Sept; restaurant 15 May to 25 Sept **Reservation:** Advisable peak season **Charge:** Pitch 38 fr; person 26.50 fr; child (under 7) 18 fr

Les Périères

24203 Sarlat | tel 53.59.05.84

Rather sedate, old-fashioned high-grade site

Orderliness is the word that sums up this high-grade but rather colourless site. At its centre are the pools and tennis court, and circling this a horseshoe-shaped tarmac drive, the incline of which may be a bit steep for some. On its edges are the upper camping terraces. The clipped grass verges remind one of a town park, and if you fancy holidaying in the style of a Bournemouth pleasure garden on a hill then this is the place to stay: it's the sort of place for a quiet read on the bar veranda (there's a small library here). The *crêperie* near the pool is a worthwhile addition to the comprehensive eating facilities, but the big plus here is the proximity of the bustling medieval town of Sarlat – the focal point of Périgord.

Directions: Take the D47 from Sarlat. As you climb the hill outside the town, you will come across the entrance on your right
Ground: Giving **Children:** Playground, swimming
Wheelchair: Tricky **Food-cooling:** Coolpacks frozen **Sport:** Tennis, volleyball, ping pong, billiards **Season:** Easter to 30 Sept
Reservation: Advisable peak season **Charge:** 3 people, electricity 114 fr; 3 people, no electricity 100.20 fr

Le Val d'Ussel

Proissans, 24200 Sarlat   tel 53.59.28.73

Isolated rustic charm – and all that that entails!

A camping oasis deep in wooded valleys, occupying a sun-drenched clearing in a sheltered, wooded dale, Le Val d'Ussel has a glassy blue-green lake, a watering-hole of a bar which would not be out of keeping in a Bacardi commercial, a small collection of old stone buildings and is characterised by a general mood of splendid isolation. Perhaps the site is too quiet for a family with troops to entertain, although there are the accepted games tournaments and the odd travelling circus has been known to visit. The long, narrow cut in the trees which constitutes the main drive is primarily the caravan park; tents are pitched further into the site and through the bordering woodland. The shower-blocks (perfumed!) are a circular affair under an independently supported roof – rather like cubicle merry-go-rounds. Solar panels heat the water and the temperatures are inclined to be unreliable: so-called hot water was found to be tepid in the late afternoon. If all you really want to do is sip your *vin du pays* outside your tent, gazing up at a thousand stars in a velvet-black sky after a long hot day, then there probably isn't a better place to do it.

Directions: From Sarlat take the D704 towards Brive for approximately 7 kms. Look for signs for the commune of Proissans
Ground: Hard to giving **Children:** Playground, swimming

Wheelchair: Suitable **Food-cooling:** None **Sport:** Tennis, ping pong, mini-golf **Season:** 1 May to 30 Sept **Reservation:** Advisable peak season **Charge:** Pitch 34 fr; person 26 fr; child (under 7) 16 fr; 2 adults, 2 children 120 fr; electricity 17 fr

▄▄▄ Sauveterre ▄▄▄▄▄▄▄▄▄▄▄

☼ *Moulin du Périé*

Sauveterre-la-Lémance, 47500 Fumel   tel 53.40.67.26

Efficient and welcoming family site in lovely setting

Secluded but not too far from civilisation in the shape of the nearby village of Sauveterre, Moulin du Périé is a typically efficient Dutch-run site exemplified by tidy flower beds and ultra-modern shower-blocks. Don't be misled by the relaxed style of management: madame keeps everything, including the grass, spotless, but doesn't seem to mind if the kids get a bit boisterous. Ancient and modern share an idyllic little site, ancient represented by rustic buildings with hanging vines and dusty clay tiles, the oldest being a redundant 200-year-old watermill, and modern in the form of up-to-the-minute sanitation facilities. Périé is a welcoming, family site where children are made to feel comfortable. They have the privilege (parents are forbidden entry) of the Children's House which is a stone hut with a split-level loft. The camp's own spring supplies a natural pool and alongside are two purpose-built pools, one shallow and one deep. A small courtyard is the ideal venue for the weekly banquet-style communal supper. Although well suited for the youngsters, teenagers might possibly get a little restless here.

🌙 ⓢ ♨ 🚣 🏋 ✕ ♀ 🍴 🐟 ⛺ 🔔 ▱ 🔲 ✂

Directions: Sauveterre is on the D710 north of Fumel. Turn off this main road, at the traffic lights and level crossing, into the village. Just at the other end is a left-hand turn for Loubejac (the C201). You won't see any signs for this site until the one at the entrance on your right
Ground: Hard to giving **Children:** Playground
Wheelchair: Suitable **Food-cooling:** Coolpacks frozen
Sport: Volleyball, ping pong, archery, trampoline **Season:** 1 April to 30 Sept **Reservation:** Advisable peak season **Charge:** Pitch 29 fr; person 24 fr; child (under 7) 12 fr; car 7 fr (free if parked in carpark); electricity 14.50 fr

Souillac

Le Domaine de la Paille Basse

46200 Souillac	tel 65.37.85.48

Bustling 'designer' site with wooded, rustic charm

Many British campers are attracted by the highest accolade awarded by the *Michelin Camping Guide*. In a private estate of 220 acres of woods, hills and valleys, the site is established in a renovated village – the main buildings are full of rustic character and surrounded by plants in tubs. Leaving your car, surrounded by Mercedes estates and various four-wheel-drive vehicles, you'll find Madame at reception is, surprisingly, blonde and English. One of the highest points around Souillac, it is approached through thick forest and getting to the heart of the estate involves a long drive through the trees. Only about 15 per cent of the grounds are actually used for camping so tents are not as spread out as you might expect. The main pool with a terrace overlooking the valley can be busy. The second

.... *you may need to be pretty sharp to secure a pool-side lounger*

pool is only a tenth of the size of the other. A new *crêperie* has been built near the pool, selling ice-creams and soft drinks. In the height of the season you may need to be pretty sharp to secure a pool-side sun-lounger. It's also essential to book for the restaurant. This and the adjoining bar, with its stone vaulting and people sitting about in their cable-knits, give an incongruous après-ski feeling and it may be cool up here at night. On our visit food did not quite live up to expectations; it's also worth noting that the restaurant shuts at 9.30pm prompt. Other amenities include a launderette, a TV room in a fourteenth-century farmhouse, and a shop. Night-lifer teens will love it here for the bar atmosphere, the young, good-looking poseurs for staff, and of course the games machines and twice-weekly discothèque. Barbecue evenings are also arranged.

Directions: Approaching Souillac from the north on the N20, turn right at the crossroads with traffic lights. Follow the road around a tight, right-hand bend and leave the town via the D15. You will start to see camp signs leading to a right-hand fork and the site **Ground:** Stony
Children: Playground, swimming, organised events
Wheelchair: Tricky **Food-cooling:** None **Sport:** Tennis, ping pong
Season: 11 May to 15 Sept **Reservation:** Advisable peak season
Charge: Pitch 42 fr; person 26 fr; child (under 7) 15 fr; electricity 16 fr

Thonac

Le Castillanderie

24290 Montignac tel 53.50.76.79

Remote peace and an open aspect in this British-run site

Run by a Brit by the name of Alan Jones, the site is off the beaten track, in a clearing encircled by verdant hills and is much frequented by British campers. La Castillanderie is a useful short-stay site because of its backwater calm and proximity to Vézère with its prehistoric associations (see the introduction to this section). Facilities are scrupulously maintained. The place could do with a swimming-pool, although there is a small lake for unsupervised bathing, as well as a tennis court, table-tennis and some perfunctory climbing ropes. The site as a whole is fairly exposed to sun and nursery trees have been planted out, which should offer better shade in a few seasons' time. Eats are basic but Thonac seems to have more restaurants than houses.

○ ⑤ 𝒩 ⊟ ⵊ 𝆖 ⋔ ▣ 𝒫

Directions: Look for the site sign at the crossroads in Thonac. Continue up the road, then turn right into a single-lane track, also signposted. Follow the long, winding drive through woodland until you reach the site **Ground:** Hard to giving **Children:** Playground
Wheelchair: Suitable **Food-cooling:** Coolpacks frozen
Sport: Volleyball, ping pong, swimming allowed in the small lake
Season: 1 April to 31 Oct **Reservation:** Advisable peak season
Charge: Pitch 16 fr; person 16 fr; child (2-8) 8 fr; electricity 10 fr

▬▬ Touzac ▬▬▬▬▬▬▬▬▬▬

Le Ch'Timi

46700 Puy l'Evêque   tel 65.36.52.36

Small and friendly British enclave

A small site on a moderately busy road near the village of Touzac, Le Ch'Timi (pronounced 'shteamy') is owned and run by a hard-working British couple. According to the visiting clientele it may appear as a distant outpost of the Empire or a jolly pub somewhere in the Yorkshire Ridings. The camp may seem a bit worn compared to some, but its cheery, homely atmosphere more than compensates. On the road side of the camp the *emplacements* are reasonably sized and have the most shade. Daytime fast-food snacks are offered and basic cooked meals three times a week in the evenings. There's a little shop and regular visits by a mobile butcher and fishmonger. Most activity centres on the L-shaped swimming-pool and in the peak season there's a weekly kiddies' picnic afternoon, with a disco for them later on in the evening. For the adults, minibus trips are laid on to local vineyards for tours of the winemaking process and a sample of wares. The end of the day sees everyone back in the bar for convivial supping up. At the extreme eastern end of the camp is a steep path with steps cut into the ground, descending to the Lot. Here is to be found an independently run canoe station, also with a bar and the added surprise of a small illuminated cave decked out with tables and chairs. At the end of a night's revelries the thought of the stiff climb back could be a sobering one, to say the least.

⦿ Ⓢ ⚚ ⛵ 🏩 ⚱ ✊ 🐾 ⛲ ♨ ▣

Directions: Take the D911 Fumel to Cahors road and cross the narrow suspension bridge to Touzac. At this point you will see the first camping sign. Continue straight through the town and out the other side. Eventually you will come round a bend to see a sunflower field. The site entrance (with flags) is on your left **Ground:** Hard
Children: Playground, organised events **Wheelchair:** Suitable
Food-cooling: Ice sold **Sport:** Tennis, volleyball, ping pong, pool table, badminton, bike-hire **Season:** 12 May to 30 Sept
Reservation: Advisable peak season **Charge:** Pitch 23 fr; person 15 fr; electricity 8.50 fr

▬▬ Vayrac ▬▬▬▬▬▬▬▬

Les Granges

46110 Vayrac   tel 65.32.46.58

Reasonable rates and open spaces are the attractions of this well-situated site

Les Granges is situated on the flat river plain, with the River Dordogne running at the back of the camp. The site has an open aspect, with a lot of ground shaded by mature growth, and there is a railway line in the vicinity. It's a fact that the closer you get to Brive, lying north from here, the less you can escape trains, as that town boasts one of the busiest stations in France. So don't think you're tucked away from civilisation on this site. Having said that, Les Granges offers a reasonable and not unattractive environment. It is generous with its space, dispensing with the canvas claustrophobia that one can experience elsewhere. Although the large, airy bar/restaurant (snack meals only) is new, the appointments could perhaps do with a little updating, but this shouldn't be taken as a reason for driving on. For a comparatively moderate fee, it has most of the standard amenities required for a budget holiday. Vayrac is close by for shopping or eating out and there's some very pleasant scenery to drive through on a day out visiting the *grottes* or châteaux.

⦿ Ⓜ ⚚ ⛵ ▭ 🏩 ✗ ⚱ ✊ 🐾

If arriving at an unfamiliar site on spec, you should be allowed the privilege of inspecting its suitability before you commit yourself to booking in.

Directions: Vayrac lies on the D703 east of the main N20 going south from Brive. Approaching on the D703 west of Vayrac, turn right at main road traffic lights when entering town. Continue over level-crossing until T-junction. Turn right (camp sign here). Further on there is a left-hand fork, again with camp sign. Take this road and you are there **Ground:** Hard **Children:** Playground, swimming
Wheelchair: Suitable **Food-cooling:** Coolpacks frozen
Sport: Volleyball, ping pong, mini-golf **Season:** 15 May to 15 Sept
Reservation: Advisable peak season **Charge:** Pitch 20 fr; person 17 fr; child (under 10) half-price; electricity 10 fr

▰ Vers ▰

La Chêneraie

Vers, 46090 Cahors   tel 65.31.40.29

Compact site, a good base from which to visit the Cahors area

Clustered on a rise behind and to one side of the main road, this small site contains only 24 *emplacements*. It comes complete with a small, tidy shower-block and a spacious contemporary bar and restaurant, outside which are the inviting pools, pleasantly screened with greenery and bordered by a sun terrace with tables and parasols. The camp population is largely French and sometimes parties arrive to stay in the holiday bungalows. Their lively soirées with home-made cabaret can be quite fun. This neat little spot is a handy springboard for taking in the local area, either through La Chêneraie's organised canoe trips or horse rides, or by your own steam to Cahors or the Lot's pretty villages.

● ⓢ ⚲ ⌓ ✕ ♀ ⋔ ⊿ ▣ ⚲ ♫

Directions: Take the D653 east of Cahors, towards Figeac. After a while you will suddenly see the large camp sign, situated to the left of a level-crossing. Take a left-hand turn leading to the site. If approaching in the opposite direction (via Vers), it's the second level-crossing you will meet **Ground:** Hard **Children:** Playground, swimming
Wheelchair: Suitable **Food-cooling:** Coolpacks frozen
Sport: Tennis, volleyball, ping pong **Season:** 15 April to 15 Sept
Reservation: Advisable peak season **Charge:** 2 people, pitch and car 56 fr; extra adult 14 fr; electricity 10 fr

Villeréal

☼ *Les Ormes*

47210 St-Etienne-de-Villeréal   tel 53.36.60.26

Sophisticated facilities and entertainment for all ages

The emphasis at Les Ormes is firmly on entertainment whilst steering away from the 'holiday camp' atmosphere. At the entrance, which is the highest point, the entire site is spread out in front of you in an open vale. To the left it leads into the woods; in the middle ground is the adventure playground with assault course equipment, tennis courts and swimming-pool and at the extreme right the lakeside *plage*. A converted barn with a beamed interior houses the restaurant, and the reception and bar with covered terrace are similarly housed in converted farm buildings. There's a choice of pitches ranging from sunny to deeply shaded. The philosophy of the Dutch management seems to be 'keep the children happy and the adults will be happy' and a special effort is made for all, with facilities all the way from a special baby bath and toddler toilets, to a 'clubroom' for teenagers to get away from parents in the evenings. There's also a games and TV room, a library with English reading matter, and the unique distraction of a miniature children's farm. Barbecues and soirées form the evening entertainment. Les Ormes is probably one of the best sites both for environment and facilities in the immediate area. The only drawbacks are the long climb from your tent to the buildings complex and a restricted choice for the avid sightseer in the surrounding location. The site is roughly 15 miles from either the Dordogne or the Lot and even further from some of the sights mentioned at the beginning of this section. However, it is central to a group of Bastide towns – Beaumont, Castillone, Monpazier and of course Villeréal. The Château de Biron, more a fortress, is also not far away and worth a visit.

Directions: Take the D676 south of Villeréal, then turn left for St-Etienne – a small hamlet. Go along the country lane, then take right-hand turn into site (signposted) **Ground:** Hard to giving
Children: Playground, swimming, organised events, baby facilities
Wheelchair: Suitable **Food-cooling:** Coolpacks frozen

Sport: Tennis, volleyball, ping pong **Season:** 1 April to 30 Sept
Reservation: Advisable peak season **Charge:** Person 19.50 fr; pitch
26 to 30 fr; child (under 7) half-price; electricity 12 fr

▬▬ Vitrac ▬▬▬▬▬▬▬▬▬

❀ *Soleil Plage*

Vitrac, 24200 Sarlat   tel 53.28.33.33

Charming, friendly riverside haunt

Soleil Plage is a happy, relaxed, informal, bustling site opposite
one of the most picturesque stretches of river. At 10.30 in the
morning a PA system springs into life with an upbeat little tune
to introduce a 'Bonjours Campers'-type of message announcing
the events for the day. But this is only a minute or two and as
the music signs off, you're left to do your own thing. The site is
peculiarly divided into sections and one portion is even reached
by a 300-yard walk across another property. Not too helpful for
carting back the take-aways maybe. The only improvement in
facilities could perhaps be a more modern shower-block – not
that this is any criticism of standards of hygiene – the only
separate washing cubicles are for women. One feels that here is
a community enjoying a well-earned rest. Subdued
conversation drifts over hedges marking out generous
emplacements and in the early evening barbecue smells fill the
air. Good, but reasonably priced local cuisine is on offer at the
colourful veranda restaurant where a holiday night out mood
prevails. You can't go too wrong with a take-away either – a
boeuf bourguignonne back at the tent if you wish! One of the
main attractions of this site is the sand and pebble beaches
overlooked by the magnificent precipice of the cliff towering
above it. The smaller beach immediately across the road seems
to be more the family one for kids, whereas the larger one
further along is suited to the serious business of getting a tan.

● Ⓜ 🚶 ⛵ ▭ 🪣 🍴 ⚲ 🍴 🦌 🏛 ♻ ▣ 🎣

Directions: Take the D46 south from Sarlat towards Vitrac. Arriving at
Vitrac, the road swings round a tight right-hand bend. Take an
immediate left-hand turn. Follow this road (under a cliff overhang)
until you see a signboard at the junction with a right-hand hairpin.
Turn down this to a T-junction. Turn right. At the river, ignore the first
campsite, and continue a few hundred yards along riverside road to

site **Ground:** Giving **Children:** Playground, swimming, organised events **Wheelchair:** Suitable **Food-cooling:** Ice sold **Sport:** Tennis, ping pong, canoeing, mini-golf **Season:** 1 April to 30 Sept; restaurant 20 May to 20 Sept **Reservation:** Advisable peak season
Charge: Pitch 36 fr; person 24 fr; child (under 7) 13 fr; electricity 12.50 fr

For the naturist

We found two camps for this section which provide totally different environments. One may be familiar to some of you, the other could be quite a discovery. *La Tuque* has long been established and it is a firm favourite with British regulars. Robert and Christine Berard-Astic have developed a self-contained little park of open grass and light woodland, high up in the Quercy countryside. We're not sure but Eden could have appeared like this. On offer are a bar, delicatessen, sauna, tennis, volleyball, children's playground and paddling-pool. The centre of the site is dominated by the main pool. Entertainments are family orientated and a whole programme of activities is laid on from June through to August. Beautifully serene.

Le Couderc presents another kind of tranquillity. It is a cross between Camping à la Ferme and being the personal guests of the Family Postel. It is indeed a farm, totally secluded in rolling, open country a little south of the Dordogne. Comprising four meadows ('no insecticides or fertiliser for the last 20 years'), the site is a fairly exposed one. Running through the middle is a crystal-clear stream which provides the camp's drinking water and replenishes the natural pool for swimming. Again, the management is very much concerned to please children as well as adults, with organised activities such as a day trip out in the country on hay wagons with picnic and river visit. The centrepiece of Couderc must be the wonderful barn with its large fireplace. The whole community can dine together at the end of the day.

La Tuque: Bélaye, 46140 Luzech Tel 65.21.34.34
Le Couderc: Naussannes, 24440 Beaumont-du-Périgord Tel 53.22.40.40

Checklists

These are designed to help you pack. See Organising your holiday on page 19 for more details.

Documents

Passport
E111
Personal holiday insurance
Euro / traveller's cheques
Credit / cheque card(s)*
Ferry / Motorail tickets
Campsite correspondence

International Camping Carnet
Driving Licence
Vehicle registration document
Certificate of insurance
Green Card
Breakdown insurance
MOT

* Make sure you take with you contact numbers for your bank and credit card company for reporting any loss straight away.

The car

Service

The following checklist is by no means exhaustive and only serves as a reminder for the essentials. Ask advice at your garage when booking the car in for its pre-holiday check.

Battery	Cooling system	Fan belt	Tyres
Brakes	Exhaust	Fluid levels	Wiper blades

Spares etc.

Bulbs
Fire extinguisher
First aid kit (see below)
GB sticker
List of French dealers of your
make of car

Manual
Tool kit
Tow rope
Tyre pressure gauge
Warning triangle

You can buy on a 'sale or return' basis a spares kit from your dealer or motoring organisation.

Camping equipment

The basic list below can obviously be added to or subtracted from according to your personal needs:

For the tent

Airbeds / camping beds
Air-pump
Camping lamps
Chairs
Cooker
Mallet

Portable barbecue
Sleeping bags
Spare guy ropes
Stakes
Table

Kitchenware

Beakers
Binbags
Cloths
Corkscrew
Eating utensils
Foil
Food boxes
Hanging larder
Kettle
Kitchen roll
Plastic food containers
Plastic mugs

Plastic plates
Plastic bowls
Scourer
Tea towels
Teapot
Tin opener
Vegetable knife
Vegetable peeler
Washing-up bowl
Washing-up liquid
Wooden spoons

Personal

Adaptor for plugs
Deodorant
Flannel
Hairdryer

Mirror
Razor / shaver
Shower gel
Soap

Sun lotion
Toothbrush
Toothpaste
Towel

First aid kit

Antiseptic cream
Bandage and tape
Calamine cream
Cotton wool

Insect bite cream
Insect repellent
Pack of plasters
Paracetamol

Small scissors
Sterile gauze
Thermometer
Tweezers

Miscellaneous

Brush and pan
Camera film
Clothes pegs
Cord for clothes line
Hangers
Detergent (liquid soap)

Matches / lighter
Scissors / penknife
Sewing kit
String
Toilet paper (starter kit)
Torch

Sightseeing index

This index covers all the towns and villages, as well as geological and prehistorical sights, that are mentioned in the Guide's regional introductions. Campsites are not indexed but are shown on the maps and appear within each region by alphabetical order of the nearest town.

Sightseeing index

Report form

Please tell us about your stay at any campsite in the South of France or the Dordogne, whether or not it appears in this Guide. Use a plain sheet of paper if you would prefer, and send brochures or other material if you would like.

Name of campsite: _____

Address: _____

_____

I visited this campsite on: _____

My report is:

Name and address: _____

_____

Signed: _____

Report form

Please tell us about your stay at any campsite in the South of France or the Dordogne, whether or not it appears in this Guide. Use a plain sheet of paper if you would prefer, and send brochures or other material if you would like.

Name of campsite: _____

Address: _____

_____

I visited this campsite on: _____

My report is:

Name and address: _____

_____

Signed: _____

Report form

Please tell us about your stay at any campsite in the South of France or the Dordogne, whether or not it appears in this Guide. Use a plain sheet of paper if you would prefer, and send brochures or other material if you would like.

Name of campsite: _____

Address: _____

_____

I visited this campsite on: _____

My report is:

Name and address: _____

_____

Signed: _____

Report form

Please tell us about your stay at any campsite in the South of France or the Dordogne, whether or not it appears in this Guide. Use a plain sheet of paper if you would prefer, and send brochures or other material if you would like.

Name of campsite: _____

Address: _____

_____

I visited this campsite on: _____

My report is:

Name and address: _____

_____

Signed: _____

Report form

Please tell us about your stay at any campsite in the South of France or the Dordogne, whether or not it appears in this Guide. Use a plain sheet of paper if you would prefer, and send brochures or other material if you would like.

Name of campsite: _____

Address: _____

_____

I visited this campsite on: _____

My report is:

Name and address: _____

_____

Signed: _____

Report form

Please tell us about your stay at any campsite in the South of France or the Dordogne, whether or not it appears in this Guide. Use a plain sheet of paper if you would prefer, and send brochures or other material if you would like.

Name of campsite: _____

Address: _____

_____

I visited this campsite on: _____

My report is:

Name and address: _____

_____

Signed: _____